Cultural Anthropology

A PROBLEM-BASED APPROACH

Cultural Anthropology

A PROBLEM-BASED APPROACH

THIRD EDITION

RICHARD H. ROBBINS

State University of New York at Plattsburgh

THOMSON
———✳———™
WADSWORTH

Australia • Canada • Mexico • Singapore • Spain
United Kingdom • United States

Edited by John Beasley
Picture research by Cheryl Kucharzak
Production supervision by Kim Vander Steen
Cover and interior design by Lucy Lesiak Design
Composition by Point West, Inc.
Printed and bound by McNaughton & Gunn

Cover image: Stone/Gerald Del Vecchio

ISBN: 0-87581-443-3
Library of Congress Catalog Card No. 00 136657

Wadsworth/Thomson Learning
10 Davis Drive
Belmont CA 94002-3098
USA

For information about our products, contact us:
Thomson Learning Academic Resource Center
1-800-423-0563
http://www.wadsworth.com

For permission to use material from this text, contact us by
Web: http://www.thomsonrights.com
Fax: 1-800-730-2215
Phone: 1-800-730-2214

Printed in the United States of America
10 9 8 7 6 5 4 3

Photo/illustration credits
3: Richard H. Robbins; **5:** Reuters/Corbis-Bettmann; **8:** Christopher Arnesen/Tony Stone
Images; **9:** Museo de América/Gabinete de Bibliofilia; **22:** *Animals Animals*/Charles
Tyler/Oxford Scientific Films; **25:** UPI/Corbis-Bettmann; **40:** M. Shotak/Anthro-Photo;
47: Robert Cruikshank drawing; **51:** Corbis-Bettmann; **60:** Neg. no. 2A 3642. Courtesy
Department of Library Services, American Museum of Natural History; **63:** From Die
Feurland by Martin Gusinde, 1937. Museo Histórico Nacional de Chile, Santiago;
63: James L. Stanfield/National Geographic Image Collection; **77:** Richard H. Robbins;
87: Reuters/Supri/Archive Photos; **93:** Ted Grudowski/Danita Delimont & Assoc.;
104: Courtesy American Cancer Society; **105:** *Animals Animals*/Zig Leszczynski;
108: Neg. no. 86-2842. Smithsonian Institution; **110:** Illustrations from the Rider-Waite
Tarot Deck®, known also as the Rider Tarot and the Waite Tarot, reproduced by permission
of U.S. Games Systems, Inc., Stamford, CT 06902 USA. Copyright © 1971 by U.S. Games
Systems, Inc. Further reproduction prohibited. The Rider-Waite Tarot Deck® is a registered
trademark of U.S. Game Systems, Inc.; **115:** Kobal Collection; **117:** © Abbas/Magnum Photos;
121: Corbis-Bettmann; **125:** Greg Johnston/Danita Delimont & Assoc.; **125:** Stuart
Westmorland/Danita Delimont & Assoc.; **130:** Neg. no. 1659-A-1. Smithsonian Institution;
132: Archive Photos; **151:** National Geographic Society Image Collection; **154:** Peter
Essick/*Aurora*; **157:** UPI/Corbis-Bettmann; **173:** Kobal Collection; **180:** Mike Greenlar/The
Image Works; **184:** I. De Vore/Anthro-Photo; **189:** Martha Cooper/Viesti Associates, Inc.;
202: © Eugene Richards/Magnum Photos; **205:** Corbis Bettmann; **209:** From Nott and Glidden,
Indigenous Races of the Earth, 1868, taken from *The Mismeasure of Man*, by Stephen Jay Gould.;
220: Martha Cooper/Viesti Associates, Inc.; **226:** © Kryn Taconis/Magnum Photos; **242:** Wide
World Photos; **251:** Spencer Grant/PhotoEdit; **254:** From *Unforgettable Fire, Pictures Drawn by
Atomic Bomb Survivors*, Japan Broadcast Publishing Co., Ltd. © 1977; **261:** Reuters/Corbis-Bettemann.

CONTENTS

Anthropologists enjoy a unique perspective on education. For us, learning and teaching form part of a cultural process affected by a host of social, cultural, individual, and situational factors. For the anthropologist, a classroom constitutes but one of many learning environments and, like other environments, influences the kind of learning that occurs within its boundaries. For us, classrooms have their own unique cultures, some of which may be more or less conducive to the kinds of learning to which teachers and students aspire.

I designed *Cultural Anthropology: A Problem-Based Approach* to help instructors and students in introductory courses in cultural anthropology to foster a classroom culture that, regardless of class size and instructional technique, actively involves students in the learning process, promotes critical thinking, and impresses on students that they, along with other peoples and cultures of the world, are cultural animals worthy of anthropological study.

How can the use of this book contribute to active learning? I think in at least three ways. First, the material is organized by problems and questions, rather than topics. Each of the first eight chapters of the book focuses on a specific problem of anthropological—as well as general—concern:

- How can people begin to understand beliefs and behaviors that are different from their own?
- How do we explain the transformation of human societies over the past 10,000 or so years from small-scale, nomadic bands of hunters and gatherers, to large-scale, urban-industrial states?
- How do we explain the emergence of the modern nation–state?
- Why do people believe different things, and why are they so certain that their view of the world is correct, and that others are wrong?
- What does a person have to know to understand the dynamics of family life in other societies?
- How do people determine who they are, and how do they communicate who they think they are to others? Why are modern societies characterized by social, political, and economic inequalities?
- How do societies give meaning to and justify collective violence?

While these problems may have no definitive solutions, they drive much intellectual inquiry. From each are derived specific questions, each of which is amenable to study and research and from which it is possible to come to a more or less definitive conclusion. These include:

- Is modern medicine more effective than traditional curing techniques?
- How do people come to accept social hierarchies as natural?
- What are the characteristics of peaceful societies?

Chapter 9 presents some applications of anthropology to solving problems reflecting cultural diversity.

The selection of specific problems and questions for the text was a difficult one. It is impossible in an introductory-level textbook in cultural anthropology to present all problems and questions of relevance to cultural anthropologists. However, I have tried to select problems and questions central to anthropological concerns, and that allow discussion of anthropological subjects and works typically covered in introductory courses in cultural anthropology. The Topic-Questions Correspondence Chart, which links topics to questions considered in the text, can be used in guiding discussion.

TOPIC-QUESTIONS CORRESPONDENCE CHART

The following chart indicates the chapters or questions in which topics treated in the typical cultural anthropology textbook are addressed.

TOPIC	*CORRESPONDING QUESTIONS OR CHAPTERS*
Applied Anthropology	Chapter 9
Art	Question 4.2
Caste	Question 6.1
Colonialism	Question 2.3; Question 2.5
Corporations	Question 3.3; Question 3.4
Cultural Evolution	Question 2.1
Cultural Relativism	Question 1.2
Culture Change	Chapter 2; Chapter 9
Culture Concept	Chapter 1
Ecology	Question 1.5; Question 2.3
Economic Anthropology	Chapter 2; Chapter 3; Question 7.1; Question 7.2
Education	Question 3.3; Question 4.2; Question 6.3; Chapter 9
Family Organization	Chapter 5
Feud	Question 8.1; Question 8.3
Fieldwork	Question 1.3
Food Production	Question 2.2; Question 2.3
Gender Roles	Chapter 5; Question 6.2; Question 6.3; Question 7.3
Gift Giving	Question 5.3; Question 6.4; Question 6.5
Globalization	Question 2.2; Question 2.3; Question 2.5
Hunters and Gatherers	Question 2.1; Question 2.5; Question 8.2
Identity	Chapter 6

TOPIC	CORRESPONDING QUESTIONS OR CHAPTERS
Industrialization	Question 2.2; Question 2.3
Kinship	Chapter 5; Question 6.2; Question 7.4
Language and Culture	Question 1.4; Question 4.1; Question 4.3; Question 6.3; Question 7.4; Question 8.2
Marriage Rules	Chapter 5
Medical Anthropology	Question 2.4
Nation–State	Chapter 3
Peasants	Question 2.1; Question 2.3; Question 2.5; Chapter 5
Political Organization and Control	Chapter 3; Question 7.5; Question 8.2; Question 8.3; Question 8.4; Question 8.5
Religion	Question 1.1; Question 1.2; Question 3.3; Chapter 4; Question 6.4
Revolution	Question 7.2; Question 8.4
Ritual	Question 1.4; Question 1.5; Question 2.4; Question 4.2; Question 4.3; Question 6.2; Question 6.3; Question 6.4; Question 6.5
Sexuality	Question 1.5; Question 4.2; Question 4.4; Question 6.2; Question 6.3
Sexual Stratification	Question 5.1; Question 5.2; Question 5.3
Social Stratification	Chapter 7
Status and Rank	Question 2.1; Question 2.2; Question 2.3; Chapter 7; Chapter 9
Subsistence Techniques	Question 2.1; Question 2.2
Symbolism	Question 1.1; Question 1.4; Question 1.5; Question 4.1; Question 4.2; Question 4.3; Question 6.3; Question 6.4
Systems of Exchange	Question 6.5
Urbanism	Question 7.4
War and Feud	Chapter 8

In providing the material to explore answers to the questions posed in the textbook I have tried to present a balanced approach and to invite readers to form their own informed responses, and I have tried to select studies and writings that represent both those classical studies typically found in introductory-level courses as well as newer or less well-known works that bear on contemporary concerns.

A second way that *Cultural Anthropology: A Problem-Based Approach* will contribute to active learning is through exercises, case studies, and simulations—some of which are included in the textbook, while others are included in the instructor's manual, *A Handbook for Active Learning*, available with the text. These are designed to help students realize some of the implications of the problems or questions for their own lives, as well as for others. They may be used by students and instructors in various ways. They can serve as discussion questions, writing exercises, or as topics of group inquiry or cooperative learning. I have used them as topics of group work in classes as large as 75 students, and I believe they can be used effectively in even larger classes. If used as group inquiry topics, the exercises are designed to take no more than 15 to 20 minutes for group work. As writing exercises they can be used to prime classroom discussion; students can prepare brief responses prior to class, and these responses can be used as a starting point for discussion. My own experience is that the use of these exercises conveys to students the positive value, the enjoyment, and the necessity of intellectual exchange. The exercises also allow students to bring to the class and contribute their own informed responses to the questions discussed in the textbook. The instructor's manual also includes suggestions on using the exercises, as well as information on what to expect in the way of student responses. It includes a guide to articles in introductory readers, and film and video material to accompany each question raised in the book, along with suggestions on how the films or videos can be used to stimulate discussion.

The third feature that will contribute to active learning stems from my conviction that people learning about the cultures of others cannot fully appreciate them without first understanding something of their own cultural perspectives. That is, to appreciate the fact that people construct their worlds, students must appreciate the fact that they, as cultural animals, do the same. For that reason, the textbook contains numerous comparisons of world cultures with American cultures, and many of the exercises in the textbook and instructor's manual invite students to apply what they have learned to the analysis of their own behaviors and beliefs.

To assist students and instructors there is a dedicated Web site for the book at:

http://faculty.plattsburgh.edu/richard.robbins/ca/

The Web site includes study resources for students, articles, additional links to other sites, and resources for instructors.

Finally, I have included in the book links to Web sites related to the topics and questions we discuss. There are also some excellent Web sites that maintain links to anthropology sites. These include:

Anthropology Resources on the Internet
http://home.worldnet.fr/~clist/Anthro/index.html

Lisa Mitten's Home Page
http://www.pitt.edu/~lmitten

Department of Anthropology at the University of California, Santa Barbara
http://www.anth.ucsb.edu/links/pages/

Anthro.Net
http://www.anthro.net/

Implicit in the textbook and the manual materials is the conviction that the culture of the classroom should foster cooperation. However, cooperation does not preclude conflict and critique. In fact, it assumes it. I would be grateful for comments from instructors and students about the book, the questions, and the general approach, as well as for suggestions for additional exercises, videos or films, or other materials that would enhance the use of *Cultural Anthropology: A Problem-Based Approach*. I also would be happy to distribute those suggestions to others who are using the book. I can be contacted at the Department of Anthropology, SUNY at Plattsburgh, Plattsburgh, NY 12901, or through electronic mail at richard.robbins@plattsburgh.edu.

Richard H. Robbins

ACKNOWLEDGMENTS

A book such as this is truly a collaborative effort. Among the many whose contributions have made this book possible are the late James Clifton, Leo Weigman, Dan Spinella, Gloria Reardon, Janet Tilden, Rachel Dowty, Ali Pomponio, Jon McGee, Pat Hoffmann, Elvin Hatch, Rosemary Gianno, James Armstrong, Mark Cohen, Philip Devita, Tracy Hopkins, Jeffrey Hopkins, Pat Higgins, Tom Moran, Joyce Waite, Deborah Light, Tina Charland, Christine L. Fry, Susan Abbott-Jamieson, Charles O. Ellenbaum, Stanley M. Newman, Myrdene Anderson, Thomas Hakansson, Cheryl Kucharzak, Kim Vander Steen, and John Beasley. Ted Peacock and Dick Welna have continually offered their support, and I am most grateful for that. The students in my introductory anthropology course who have used and commented on the text contributed significantly to its development. Responsible also are the researchers whose studies of human behavior and belief provided the substance for the text, and the peoples of cultures around the world whose cooperation has helped enrich our understanding of them, ourselves, and our common humanity. Finally, I wish to acknowledge the patience and help of my family—Amy, Rebecca, Michael, and Rachel—and my parents, Al and Yetta, to whom the book is dedicated.

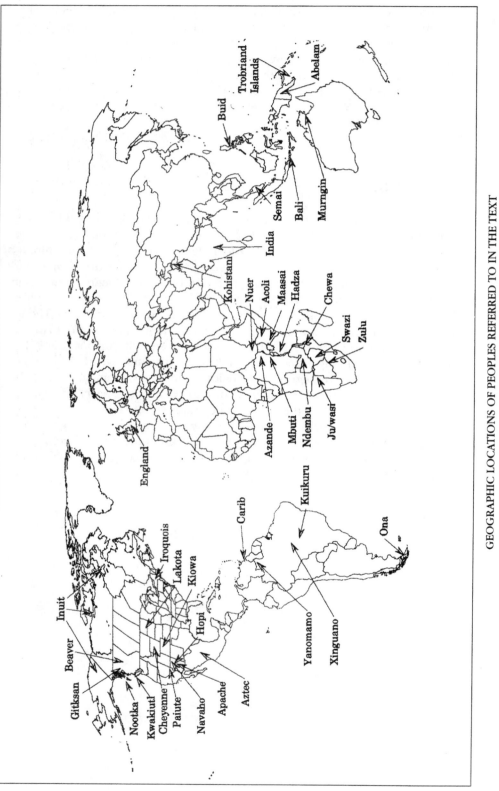

GEOGRAPHIC LOCATIONS OF PEOPLES REFERRED TO IN THE TEXT

C H A P T E R 1

CULTURE AND MEANING

PROBLEM 1: HOW CAN PEOPLE BEGIN TO UNDERSTAND BE-
LIEFS AND BEHAVIORS THAT ARE DIFFERENT FROM THEIR OWN?

[W]e have come to think of our social and cultural world as a series of sign systems, comparable to languages. What we live among and relate to are not physical objects and events; they are objects and events with meaning; not just complicated wooden constructions but chairs and tables; not just physical gestures but acts of courtesy or hostility. If we are able to understand our social and cultural world, we must think not of independent objects but of symbolic structures, systems of relations which by enabling objects and actions to have meaning, create a human universe.

Jonathan Culler

INTRODUCTION: *The World Behind Everyday Appearances*

In **cultural anthropology**, as in every science, we strive to look beyond the world of everyday experiences to discover the patterns and meanings that lie behind that world. Take, for example, the typical classroom combination chair and desk.

In our taken-for-granted, everyday world this piece of furniture is a utilitarian object: something to sit on, or write on, or even put our feet on. But for the cultural anthropologist the classroom chair and desk tells some interesting tales and poses some interesting questions. For example, why do we have chairs at all? Many societies don't; people sit or squat on the ground or the floor or sit on stools or benches. Historically, the chair likely first appeared in Europe or the Near East but wasn't even common in Europe until the eighteenth century. And why does the classroom chair take the form it does? Why don't we sit on stools? One feature of the chair that anthropologists might explore as they try to decipher the meaning of the classroom chair and desk is the erect position into which it forces the body—compelling it, in effect, to "pay attention." We might take a clue from French philosopher Michel Foucault; he refers to the shaping of the human body as a "political anatomy," a way that people's bodies are controlled by others to operate with the necessary speed and efficiency. Political anatomy produces, Foucault says, "docile bodies."

An anthropologist might suggest that the combination classroom chair and desk is part of the political anatomy of educational settings, part of the system of relations that gives meaning to the classroom; that is, this piece of furniture forms the body into a shape that prepares it (or forces it) to attend to a teacher and not to others in the same room. Moreover, it is appropriate to its unique setting in the classroom, as are other objects of furniture. Imagine, for example, replacing classroom chairs with swiveling bar stools, whose main purpose is to promote bodily mobility and conversation with others.

Once alert to the idea that the classroom chair might serve as an instrument of control, we might notice other ways in which classroom design serves as a mode of discipline. The distribution of people in space, with each person in a particular "spot" in neat, ordered rows, serves to discipline people to "pay attention" to the classroom center and not to others around them. We might also notice the distinctive ordering of time and the use of clocks, bells, and whistles

Cultural anthropologists find patterns of meaning even in objects as simple as a classroom chair.

to control the movement and activities of people in school settings. One can even take our analysis a step further and examine the discipline of the school setting sequentially, from kindergarten through high school; contrast, for example, the wide-open space of the kindergarten classroom with its unrestricted, movable chairs and tables and teacher's desk set off to the side, with the enclosed, partitioned space of a second- or third-grade classroom with its neatly arranged desks facing the centered desk of the teacher. This demonstrates the evolution of classroom discipline.

Students, of course, do not always obey the subtle commands that direct their bodies to do certain things at certain times. One only has to examine the strange bodily contortions of students as they resist the form into which the classroom chair would force them. We try, occasionally, also to resist the isolation imposed by the arrangement of classroom furniture, or the timetables set by clocks, bells, and whistles.

The way that specific societies order behavior through the arrangement of space and time is but one small area examined by cultural anthropology, but it can serve as an example of how, from an anthropological perspective, we cannot take anything about even our own beliefs and behavior for granted, let alone the behavior and beliefs of those whose backgrounds and histories differ from our own.

This book is about how cultural anthropology can help us see beyond our taken-for-granted world. We will examine how cultural anthropology helps us to understand others, and, in the process, to better understand ourselves. We will also examine how knowledge of others and ourselves can be applied to areas such as health care, communication, education, economic development, business, law, and international relations.

Since any area of inquiry always begins with certain basic issues or questions, this book is organized around eight general problems that arise from the human condition—problems such as how to understand people with different beliefs and behaviors, reasons why ways of life change, how people justify violence, whether there is any solution to problems of social inequality, and so on. These are problems that concern everyone, not just cultural anthropologists, and none has a definitive answer. The best we can really do is reach a greater understanding of why the problem exists and what we might do about it. There are some specific questions, however, that we can ask concerning these problems, for which anthropologists have sought answers. These are the questions on which we will focus. At various points you will be asked to supply your own answers to questions and, perhaps, to discuss your solutions to these questions with others. Understanding others requires you to recognize that your behaviors and beliefs, as well as those of people in other societies, are socially patterned and constructed. For that reason, you will find many comparisons between American life and life in other societies.

In considering the principal problem of how we can begin to understand beliefs and behaviors that are different from our own, in this first chapter we will explore five questions. The first and most basic is why human beings differ in their beliefs and behaviors; that is, what is it about human nature that produces such a variety of ways of believing and behaving? The second question involves values. More often than not, people react to different ways of life with shock, scorn, or disapproval. Are such reactions warranted, and, if they aren't, how do we judge the beliefs and behaviors of others? The third question is critical to anthropological inquiry. Is it possible to set aside the meanings that we ascribe to experience and see the world through the eyes of others? Fourth, assuming that it is possible to come to some understanding of how others see the world, how can the meanings that others find in experience be interpreted and described? The final question concerns what learning about other people can tell us about ourselves.

QUESTIONS

1.1   Why do human beings differ in their beliefs and behaviors?
1.2   How do people judge the beliefs and behaviors of others?
1.3   Is it possible to see the world through the eyes of others?
1.4   How can the meanings that others find in experience be interpreted and described?
1.5   What can learning about other peoples tell Americans about themselves?

QUESTION 1.1:   Why Do Human Beings Differ in Their Beliefs and Behaviors?

From an anthropological perspective, members of a society view the world in a similar way because they share the same **culture**; people differ in how they view the world because their cultures differ. A good place to start to understand

Grief is suppressed in some cultures and openly displayed in others. Here, bereaved relatives weep over the body of a 40-year-old kinsman slain in clashes between police and armed civilians in Moldova in 1990.

the concept of culture is with the fact that members of all human societies experience specific life events such as birth, death, and the quest for food, water, and shelter. All societies have what are for them appropriate rules for courtship, ideas about child rearing, procedures for exchanging goods, methods of food production, techniques for building shelters, and so on. But from society to society, the meanings people give to such events differ.

Attitudes toward death provide one example. For some people, death marks the passage of a person from one world to another. For others, death is an ending, the final event of a life span, while still others consider death a part of a never-ending cycle of birth, death, and rebirth. The Kwakiutl of British Columbia, for example, believe that when a person dies the soul leaves the body and enters the body of a salmon. When a salmon is caught and eaten, a soul is released and is free to enter the body of another person.

Some societies fear the dead; others revere them. In traditional China, each household contained a shrine to the family ancestors. Before any major family decision, the head of the household addressed the shrine to ask the ancestors' advice, thus making the dead part of the world of the living. In southern Italy, however, funeral customs were designed to discourage the dead from returning. Relatives placed useful objects such as matches and small change near the body to placate the soul of the deceased and ensure that it did not return to disturb the living.

Members of some societies accept death as a natural and inevitable occurrence, while others always attribute death to the malevolent act of some person, often through sorcery. In these societies every death elicits suspicion and a demand for vengeance. Members of other societies require great demonstrations of grief and mourning for a deceased. Some, such as the Dani of New Guinea, require a close female relative of a recently deceased person to sacrifice a part of a finger. In southern Europe, widows were required to shave their heads, while in traditional India, widows were cremated at their husbands' funerals. In the United States, survivors of the deceased are expected to restrain their grief almost as if it were a contagious disease. To Americans, the sight of southern Italian women pulling their hair and being restrained from flinging themselves into an open grave is as bewildering as their own restraint of grief would be to southern Italians.

Or take the area of food. No society accepts all items in their edible universe as "good to eat." Only a relatively few items are so designated. Insects such as grubs, beetles, and ants are acceptable fare in some societies, while people in others regard eating insects with horror. Americans generally do not define insects as food (although federal regulations do allow a certain percentage of insect matter to be included in processed food). Most Americans like and are encouraged to drink milk, although some people in China consider milk undrinkable, while the Chinese practice of raising dogs for meat is repulsive to most Americans. American children who have raised pet guinea pigs would have a hard time accepting the Peruvian practice of raising guinea pigs for food. Many American tastes in food originate in biblical definitions of what is considered edible and inedible. Thus, of edible land animals, the book of Leviticus says that they must chew their cud and have split hoofs, consequently eliminating not only pig, but camel and rock badger as well. Of animals of the water, edible things must have scales and fins, removing from a biblical diet such things as clams, lobster, and sea urchins. And of animals of the air, only things that have wings and fly are legitimate dining fare, eliminating penguin, ostrich, and cassowary. Thus, human beings create and define for themselves what they may eat and what they may not eat, independent of what is or is not truly edible.

Of all the some two million species of living organisms that inhabit the Earth, only humans dwell largely in worlds that they themselves create by giving meanings to things. This creation is what anthropologists mean by the term *culture*. Human beings are cultural animals; they ascribe meanings of their own creation to objects, persons, behaviors, emotions, and events and proceed to act as though those meanings are real. All facets of their lives—death, birth, courtship, mating, and food acquisition and consumption—are suffused with meaning.

Clifford Geertz suggests that human beings are compelled to impose meaning on their experiences because, without these meanings to help them comprehend experience and impose an order on the universe, the world would seem a jumble, "a chaos of pointless acts and exploding emotions." Geertz says that human beings are "incomplete or unfinished animals who complete themselves through culture—not culture in general, but specific forms of it: Balinese, Italian, Ilongot, Chinese, Kwakiutl, American, and so on." When people share the meanings they give to experiences, they share and participate in the same culture.

Differences in culture arise in part from the fact that different groups of human beings, for various reasons, create, share, and participate in different realities, assigning different meanings, as previously stated, to death, birth, marriage, and food. Objects, persons, behaviors, emotions, and events in a human world have the meanings ascribed to them by those who share, use, or experience them. The clothes people wear, the way they wear them, the food they eat (or refuse to eat), even their gender, are defined through the meanings these people give them.

EXERCISE 1.1

Food is a cultural creation; that is, human beings define what is and what is not food. Consider, for example, the items listed below, all of which serve as food among one group of people or another. Which of these would you eat, and which would you not eat? If there are any you would not eat, explain why.

	Yes	No
eel		
kangaroo tail		
dog		
guinea pig		
raw squid		
sea urchin (sea slugs)		
ants		
monkey brains		
grubs		
opossum		
rattlesnake		
iguana		
horse		
dolphin		
pickled pig's feet		
haggis (stuffed sheep or calf intestines)		
cow brains		
blood sausage		
raw steak		
rotten meat		
armadillo		

One of the problems that cultural anthropologists address is understanding why different groups of human beings have different cultures. Why does one group assign one set of meanings to what they experience, while another group assign it another set of distinct meanings? Many of the questions to be addressed in later chapters concern how these differences can be explained. We may be able to overcome our initial shock or bewilderment upon confronting different cultures if we understand something of why cultural differences exist. But how should we react if the meanings that others ascribe to experience differ from our own? It is difficult enough to look beyond everyday appearances at our own beliefs and behaviors, but it is far more difficult when we confront beliefs and behaviors of others that we initially consider wrong, horrible, or bizarre.

RESOURCE 1.1

Web Resources on the Culture Concept

You can find a good summary of Clifford Geertz's treatment of the culture concept at: **http://www.wsu.edu:8001/vcwsu/commons/topics/culture/culture-definitions/geertz-text.html**

The University of Manitoba also maintains a site dealing with the culture concept and its history at: **http://www.umanitoba.ca/faculties/arts/anthropology/courses/122/module1/concept.html**

QUESTION 1.2: How Do People Judge the Beliefs and Behaviors of Others?

Richard Scaglion is fond of telling the story of his friend, a member of the Abelam tribe of Papua New Guinea, who was looking through an issue of *Sports Illustrated* magazine. The friend, dressed in full ceremonial regalia with a feather through his nose, was laughing uncontrollably at a woman shown in a liquor advertisement. When he managed to stop laughing long enough to explain what he thought was so funny, he said, "This white woman has made holes in her ears and stuck things in them." When Scaglion pointed out that his friend had an ornament in his nose, the reply was, "That's different. That's for

The ceremonial attire worn by this Hove villager in Papua New Guinea, conveys beauty and meaning to the members of his tribe, while modern American fashions might seem odd.

To protect their world from potential destruction, Aztecs in the 1500s offered blood to the gods through rituals of human sacrifice and self-mutilation.

beauty and has ceremonial significance. But I didn't know that white people mutilated themselves."

Scaglion's friend confronted a problem that many do when they confront behavior or beliefs that seem to differ from their own, and his response was not unusual. He was both shocked and mystified at the strange behavior. And this poses a dilemma; since there are so many versions of what the world is like, how do we go about trying to understand each of them without making positive or negative judgments? *Which version is correct?* Are there any we can reject or condemn? Can we say, as so many have, that one culture is superior to another?

In the catalog of human behaviors and beliefs, it is not difficult to find practices or ideas that may seem bizarre or shocking, even to trained anthropologists. Cultural anthropologists have described the beliefs of the Ilongots of the Philippines, who must kill an enemy to obtain a head they can throw away in order to diminish the grief and rage they feel at the death of a kinsman or kinswoman. They have studied the historical records of the Aztecs of Mexico who, when contacted by Cortes in 1519, believed that the universe underwent periodic destruction, and the only way to ward off disaster was to pluck the hearts from live sacrificial victims to offer to the gods. They have reported on the circumcision practices of the people in the Nile Valley of the Sudan where, in order to ensure a young girl's chastity and virginity, her genitalia are mutilated to close the vaginal opening so completely that additional surgery is often required to allow intercourse and childbirth later in life. They have also studied modern states that routinely engage in or sanction torture, terror, and genocide. The question is, how should we react to practices and beliefs such as these?

The Ethnocentric Fallacy and the Relativist Fallacy

If we do condemn or reject the beliefs or behaviors of others, we may be committing the **ethnocentric fallacy**, the idea that our beliefs and behaviors are right and true, while those of other peoples are wrong or misguided. Cultural anthropologists have long fought against **ethnocentrism**. They try to show that what often appears on the surface to be an odd belief or a bizarre bit of behavior is functional and logical in the context of a particular culture. They find the ethnocentric fallacy *intellectually* intolerable; if people everywhere think that they are right and others must be wrong, they can only reach an intellectual and social dead end. Furthermore, if we assume that we have all the right answers, our study of other cultures becomes simply the study of other people's mistakes.

EXERCISE 1.2A

After the class has been divided into groups of four to six, *individually* write down whether you "agree" or "disagree" with each statement that follows. Then, going over each statement in order, check to see if anyone in your group disagrees with each statement being considered. If even one person disagrees, the group should change the wording so that the statement is acceptable to *all* the members of the group. You may not simply "agree to disagree." Choose one member to record the revised statements.

STATEMENTS:

1. The fact that the United States was able to place people on the moon proves its technological superiority.
2. Foreigners coming to live here should give up their foreign ways and adapt to the new country as quickly as possible.
3. Many of the world's populations do not take enough initiative to develop themselves; therefore they remain "underdeveloped."
4. Minority members of any population should be expected to conform to the customs and values of the majority.

Because of the intellectual implications of ethnocentrism, cultural anthropologists emphatically reject this position. But the alternative to ethnocentrism, **relativism**, is equally problematical. Relativism, simply stated, holds that no behavior or belief can be judged to be odd or wrong simply because it is different from our own. Instead, we must try to understand a culture in its own terms and to understand behaviors or beliefs for the purpose, function, or meaning they have to people in the societies in which we find them. In other words, relativism holds that a specific belief or behavior can only be understood in relation to the culture—the system of meanings—in which it is embedded.

For example, according to Renato Rosaldo, the ceremonies and rituals accompanying a successful headhunting expedition psychologically help the Ilongot manage their grief over the death of a kinsperson. Rose Oldfield-Hayes explains that, even to the women of the northern Sudan, the genital mutilations of young girls makes perfect sense. Since family honor is determined in part by the sexual modesty of female family members, the operation, by preventing intercourse, protects the honor of the family, protects girls from sexual assault, and protects the honor and reputation of the girl herself. Moreover, says Oldfield-Hayes, the practice serves as a means of population control.

However, relativism poses a *moral* predicament. We may concede that it is permissible to rip hearts out of living human beings, provided you believe this is necessary in order to save the world, or that it is permissible to subject young girls to painful mutilation to protect family reputations or control population growth. But this quickly leads us into the **relativistic fallacy**, the idea that it is impossible to make moral judgments about the beliefs and behaviors of others. This, of course, seems morally intolerable because it implies that there is no belief or behavior that can be condemned as wrong. So we are left with two untenable positions: the ethnocentric alternative, which is intellectually unsatisfactory, and the relativist alternative, which is morally unsatisfactory. How do we solve this problem?

Virginity Testing in Turkey and Fighting Poverty in Brazil

To illustrate further the dilemma of relativism, and the difficulty of appreciating the cultures of others without making moral judgments, a couple of years ago an American-based human-rights group issued a report condemning the practice of virginity testing in Turkey. Traditionally, young women in Turkey, as in some other cultures, are expected to avoid sexual relations prior to marriage, although the same rule does not apply to men. The bride's virginity is revealed by displaying, the morning after the wedding, the sheet that was spread on the couple's wedding bed with the telltale hymenal blood stain. The human-rights report condemns the traditional testing as well as the reported practice of forcing tests on hospital patients, students, and applicants for government jobs. Here's the question: Is the human rights group being ethnocentric in judging Turkish customs by American cultural norms, or is it correctly identifying abuses of women that must be corrected? And does it help if we further understand the so-called logic behind the belief?

Anthropologist Carol Delaney, in her book on Turkish village society, *The Seed and the Soil*, describes how virginity testing is related to the way that Turkish villagers conceptualize and explain the reproductive process. They see producing children as analogous to the planting and growing of crops; the man provides the "seed" with his semen, and the woman serves as the "soil" in which the seed germinates and grows. As a metaphor for reproduction, the idea of the seed and the soil provides villagers with a way of thinking about and understanding reproduction. However, the metaphor of seed and soil has at least one very important implication; since seeds do not have a limited life span, as we know semen to have, villagers believe that, once planted, the seed (semen) may grow at any time. Consequently, if a woman has had sexual relations with a man other than her husband at any time prior to her marriage, the paternity of the child will be in doubt. Since descent in traditional Turkish villages is closely tied to many things, including property rights, uncertainty about the identity of the true father can have major implications. Thus, in the context of Turkish beliefs about procreation, virginity testing may be said to make sense. Furthermore, Turkish beliefs about conception are not that far removed from our own, since our language draws from the same agricultural metaphors to explain reproduction as does the language of Turkish villagers. We talk about women being "fertile" or "barren," and semen "fertilizing" "eggs." "Sowing one's oats" as an expression of sexual activity is still heard in parts of the United States and Canada. Furthermore, these views are reinforced by religious proscription, legitimized in the Koran and the Old Testament. Thus, before we either condemn or accept the Turkish villagers for their treatment of women, we need to examine what their beliefs tell us about our own. Ours may be equally problematical.

Objectivity and Morality

The conflict between ethnocentrism and relativism is not just a theoretical one for anthropologists. In the choice of research subject, the anthropologist may face the dilemma of maintaining a "moral distance" from the objects of her or his study and remaining "objective," or becoming actively involved in criticizing behavior or beliefs they encounter (e.g., genital mutilation).

The contradiction between "objective" anthropology and a politically committed anthropology became apparent to Nancy Scheper-Hughes when she returned as an anthropologist to a shantytown in Brazil where, previously, she had worked as a community organizer. The women with whom she worked became angry, asking why, when as a community organizer she had helped them organize to fight for clean water, decent wages, and protection from police brutality, was she now, as an anthropologist, so passive, so indifferent to the destruction around her? She tried to explain that as an anthropologist her work was different, that she was there now to observe, document, and write about their lives as truthfully as she could. The women refused to accept that and insisted that, if they were to work with her, she had to also work with them to fight for better lives. "What," they asked, "is anthropology to us?"

As a consequence of her experience, Scheper-Hughes (1995:416) argues for a politically committed, morally engaged, and ethically grounded anthropology. "Those of us who make our living observing and recording the misery of the world," she says, "have a particular obligation to reflect critically on the impact of the harsh images of human suffering that we foist upon the public."

Scheper-Hughes proposes a more womanly anthropology, one that is concerned with how people treat one another. Moral relativism, she says, is no longer appropriate to the world in which we live, and anthropology, if it is to be worth anything at all, must be, as she puts it, "critically grounded." Anthropologists cannot ignore the massacres and disappearances of vulnerable people that often occur in communities in which anthropologists work. Anthropologists must, she insists, serve as witnesses and reporters of human rights abuses and the suffering of the poor and the oppressed.

But even serving as a witness for the poor and oppressed can lead to still other moral dilemmas for the anthropologist when the people with whom the anthropologist works engage in behavior that may appear morally questionable.

Scheper-Hughes confronted this question when she discovered and reported that impoverished women in the Brazilian shantytowns would sometimes allow their starving infants to die, in the belief that they were doomed anyway. When Phillipe Bourgois studied the world of crack dealers on the Upper East Side of New York City, he worried about the negative images he would convey if he reported the personal violence, sexual abuse, addiction, and alienation he witnessed. He recalled the advice of anthropologist Laura Nader, who advised others not to study the poor and powerless, because whatever is said will be used against them.

Human-rights activists, particularly, are skeptical about the idea of cultural relativity. If, they say, we must tolerate the beliefs and practices of other cultures because to do otherwise would be ethnocentric, how can we ever criticize what seem to be violations of basic human rights, such the right to bodily integrity, or the right to be free from torture, arbitrary imprisonment, slavery, or genocide? Cultural relativism, say human-rights advocates, makes arguments about human rights meaningless by legitimizing almost any behavior.

Take the case of the practice in some areas of India of *sati*, the burning of a widow on her husband's funeral pyre. In 1987, Roon Kanwar, an 18-year-old girl, was burned alive on her husband's pyre. Women's rights groups protested, but relatives claimed that it is an ancient Indian custom and accused protestors of being Western imperialists, imposing their own cultural standards on them. While the practice is outlawed, prosecutors rarely enforce the law because of the difficulty of obtaining evidence. Does it matter if Roon Kanwar committed sati voluntarily? What would happen if she objected? Does it matter that it is only women who are burned? Is sati a practice to deny a widow the inheritance of her husband's family's land?

Elizabeth Zechenter, who makes the argument for the establishment of some universal principles for human rights, says that cultural relativists are right to claim that the endorsement or rejection of certain foreign customs risks imposing one's own cultural prejudices on others. But the idea that we can make no judgments without being ethnocentric is illusory:

> One simply cannot avoid making judgements when faced with oppression and brutality masquerading under the guise of cultural tradition. Such a non-judgmental tolerance of brutality is actually an ultimate form of ethnocentrism, if not an outright ethical surrender. (1997:336)

There is obviously no easy answer to the question of when or if it is proper to judge the beliefs and practices of others to be right or wrong, or when to actively work to change behaviors or beliefs that we find objectionable. Ideally, our attempts to understand what at first seems puzzling in some culture, and our arrival at some solution to that puzzle, should result in questioning what it was about us that made the behavior or belief seem puzzling in the first place. In addition, we need to understand that, if each culture orders the world in a certain way for its members, it also blocks off or masks other ways of viewing things. We need to appreciate that there are perspectives different from our own, and our ethnocentric biases may blind us to those alternatives. In other words, while culture provides us with certain meanings to give to objects, persons, behaviors, emotions, and events, it also shields us from alternative meanings. What our culture hides from us may be more important than what it reveals.

EXERCISE 1.2B

You have been doing anthropological research in the United States with a religious group that believe they must live the life described in the Bible, particularly as described in the Book of Acts. They live communally, sharing all property; they believe that women should be subservient to their husbands; and they enforce rules against drinking alcoholic beverages, smoking, and so forth. The group have lately come under attack by individuals in the local community as being a "dangerous cult." You know that, while their beliefs and practices differ from the larger society around them, that they are not dangerous, and, in fact, lead lives of harmony. They have asked you to speak in their defense. Can you do this without sacrificing your objectivity?

QUESTION 1.3: *Is It Possible to See the World Through the Eyes of Others?*

This question lies at the heart of the anthropological enterprise. The anthropologist must be able to look beyond everyday appearance to decipher the often hidden meanings of beliefs, objects, and behaviors, while, at the same time set aside her or his preconceptions of what is normal or proper. The anthropologist must also learn one culture and then relate what she or he learns to members of another culture, to translate the meanings of one world into the meanings of another.

Anthropologists, as do other social scientists, use surveys, written documents, historical accounts, and questionnaires as part of their research toolbox. But the unique feature of cultural anthropology is the application of the **ethnographic method**, the immersion of the investigator in the lives of the people she or he is trying to understand and, through that experience, the attainment of some level of understanding of the meanings those people ascribe to their existence. This immersion process utilizes the techniques of anthropological fieldwork, which requires **participant observation**, the active participation of the observer in the lives of his or her subjects.

The ethnographic method is only part of the anthropological enterprise. The anthropologist also seeks to explain why people view the world as they do and to contribute to the understanding of human behavior in general. But fieldwork is the beginning of the enterprise. Fieldwork involves the meeting of at least two cultures: that of the researcher and that of the culture and people the researcher is trying to understand. Anthropological researchers must set aside their own views of things and attempt to see the world in a new way. In many respects they must assume the demeanor and status of children who must be taught, by their elders, the proper view of the world. And like children making their way in a world they do not fully comprehend, anthropologists often find themselves in awkward, embarrassing, or dangerous situations and must be prepared to learn from these moments.

The Embarrassed Anthropologist

Awkwardness and embarrassment are a part of fieldwork, as well as a part of the process through which the fieldworker learns about another culture. Richard Scaglion spent over a year with the Abelam of Papua New Guinea. Shortly after he arrived in the field, he observed and photographed an Abelam pig hunt in which the men set out nets and waited while the women and children made lots of noise to drive the pigs into the nets. Soon after, he was invited by the Abelam to participate in a pig hunt, and he took this as a sign of acceptance, that the people "liked him." He started to go with the men, but they told him they wanted him to go with the women and children to beat the bush, explaining "We've never seen anyone who makes as much noise in the jungle as you." Later, wanting to redeem himself, Scaglion offered to help an Abelam who was planting crops with a digging stick. A crowd gathered to watch as Scaglion used a shovel to try to dig a demonstration hole. After he had struggled for several minutes to get the shovel into the hard-packed soil, someone handed him a digging stick, and he was amazed at how easy it was to use. Later he found out that several Abelam had shovels but rarely used them because they didn't work.

After months of answering Scaglion's questions about their view of the natural world, such as the moon, sun, and stars, some Abelam asked him about his views of the universe. Feeling on safe ground, he gave the usual grade school lecture about the shape of the earth, its daily rotation and travels around the sun. Using a coconut, he showed them the relative positions on the earth of New Guinea, Australia, Europe, and the United States. Everyone listened intently, and Scaglion thought it went well until about a week later, when he overheard some elders wondering how it was that Americans walked upside down!

Beginning again, Scaglion used the coconut to explain how, as the earth rotates, sometimes the United States would be upright and New Guinea would be on the bottom. The Abelam rejected this because they could see that they were *not* upside down, and no one, not even some of the old people in the community, remembered ever having walked upside down. Scaglion began to draw on the physics he had in college, and as he tried to explain Newton's law of gravity (or "grabity," as his friends pronounced it), he suddenly realized that he didn't understand "grabity" either. It was something he had accepted since third grade, a concept that even physicists simply take for granted as a convenient theoretical concept.

EXERCISE 1.3

Think of some awkward or embarrassing situation created by something you did or didn't do, said or didn't say. What was inappropriate about your behavior, and why did it lead to misunderstanding or embarrassment? What did you learn from the experience about the meaning of your or others' behavior?

Confronting Witchcraft in Mexico

Awkward or embarrassing moments in the field may help anthropologists to understand a culture, or even to question their own view of the world. But the possibility of seeing the world through the eyes of others remains a subject of contention among them. Obviously, to communicate with anyone, even members of their own society, people must share some of the meanings they ascribe to objects, persons, behaviors, emotions, and events. But what happens when views of the world are completely different?

When Michael Kearney traveled to the town of Santa Catarina Ixtepeji in the valley of Oaxaca, Mexico, he intended to study the relationship between the people's view of the world and their social arrangements and environment. He began his work secure in his knowledge of the scientific and materialist view of the world in which he was reared, but he was often fascinated by the differences between his view and that of the people of Santa Catarina Ixtepeji. Theirs was a world controlled by mystic notions of "fate," the will of God, and malevolent witches and other harmful and sometimes lethal spiritual forces. He became familiar with the Ixtepejanos' view of the world, never doubting that it was "unscientific" but justified, perhaps, by a life in which suffering, disease, and death were common.

Kearney's faith in his own view of the world was momentarily shattered by an incident that began innocently enough. Walking to an appointment, he came upon an obviously distressed woman, Doña Delfina. She was known as a witch, and Kearney had been trying unsuccessfully to interview her. When they met she explained that her sister-in-law had a "very bad disease in her arms," and she wanted him to help. Kearney accompanied Doña Delfina to her house, where he found that the sister-in-law's arms were ulcerated with deep, oozing lesions that looked to him like infected burns. They rejected his offer to take the sick woman to a doctor for medical treatment, so Kearney said he had some ointment that might help, and they eagerly agreed that he should use it. He got the ointment, which contained an anesthetic, and daubed it on the woman's sores. Much to the amazement of Doña Delfina, her sister-in-law immediately felt better. By that afternoon, her arms had greatly improved, the next morning scabs had formed, and the day after she had completely recovered.

Kearney was credited with a "miraculous cure." But the same day, an Ixtepejanos friend asked Kearney what he had done and he proudly explained. The friend replied, "Why did you do that? It was not a good thing to do." The sick woman, he said, had been the victim of black magic; another woman, Gregoria, was trying to take Delfina's brother away from his wife and was using black magic to make Delfina's sister-in-law sick. Delfina was using *her* magic to keep her brother in the household, but Gregoria was winning. Now, the friend explained to Kearney, he had intervened, tipping the balance of power back to Delfina but creating a powerful enemy in Gregoria. "Maybe you should leave town for a while until Gregoria calms down," Kearney's friend suggested. But Kearney did not take seriously the danger and may never have done so were it not for two incidents that occurred soon afterward.

A young doctor in town asked Kearney, who had medical training, to assist in an autopsy of a man who had died in a fall off a truck. It was a particularly long and gory autopsy, accomplished only with rusty carpenter's tools in a dimly lit room; images of the scene and the cadaver disturbed Kearney's sleep over the next few days. One night, about a week later, as the wind beat cornstalks against his house, Kearney felt an itching on his arm. Rolling up his sleeve, he discovered several angry welts that seemed to be growing as he watched them. Immediately he thought of the chancrous arms of Delfina's sister-in-law, realizing at the same time that Gregoria's house was only 50 yards from his and she could be trying to kill him. "She got me!" he thought. The image of the cadaver on the table jumped into his mind, followed by a wish that he had gotten out of town while there was still time. As Kearney put it, he was witnessing the disintegration of his scientific, materialist view of the world and grappling with forces with which he was unprepared to deal.

Kearney is not sure how long his initial terror lasted—seconds, perhaps minutes. As he struggled against it, he realized that he was suspended between two worlds, that of the Ixtepejanos and his own. He was questioning a world of meanings that he had, until then, taken for granted. Kearney is not sure how long he was able to truly believe that the world was as the Ixtepejanos saw it, but as he retrieved his own view of the world, the Ixtepejanos' world view, filled with witchcraft and magic, ceased to be only intellectually interesting. It acquired a reality and a sense of legitimacy for him that it did not have before he experienced the real fear that he had been bewitched. Kearney came to realize through his experience that systems of belief are eminently reasonable when viewed from within, or, as we will see in a later chapter, when we participate in the lives of people who hold those beliefs.

The Endangered Anthropologist

The risk of injury, disease, or hostile reactions has always been a feature of anthropological fieldwork. But as anthropologists increasingly work in areas where human rights violations are common, these risks are intensified. When, in their work, anthropologists such as Nancy Scheper-Hughes threaten the control, authority, or prerogatives of powerful groups, they often expose themselves to violent retaliation. Working with crack dealers in New York City, Phillipe Bourgois feared violent retaliation when he embarrassed a gang leader by accidentally calling to the attention of others that the leader could not read.

At least four anthropologists have been murdered as a consequence of their fieldwork: In 1982 South African anthropologist and antiapartheid activist Ruth First was killed by a mail bomb in her office at Maputo University in Mozambique. In 1984 Melanesian anthropologist Arnold Ap was tortured and killed by the Indonesian army, his body dumped by helicopter into the sea. In 1989 South African anthropologist David Webster was shot and killed by members of a pro-apartheid death squad. And in 1990 Guatemalan anthropologist Myrna Mack was stabbed to death by a soldier, ostensibly for her work with Mayan refugees and their experiences in the government's counterinsurgency war of the early 1980s in which hundreds of thousands of people were killed. In addition, at least two anthropologists, Ricardo Falla and George Aditjondro, are in exile and under threat of assassination because of their work. These real dangers faced by anthropologists may serve to provide insights into how the people with whom they are working experience the threat of violence.

In 1989 and 1990 Nancy Green was doing fieldwork in the Guatemalan community of Xe'caj. As with many similar communities, Xe'caj was only beginning to recover from some 35 years of violence. Beginning with a military coup orchestrated largely by the United States CIA against a democratically elected government in 1954, Guatemala experienced regular violence as the militarized state tried to suppress attempts to overthrow the military regime. Hundreds of thousands of Guatemalans were killed, mostly by the government, in an attempt to suppress the revolt. The late 1970s and early 1980s were particularly brutal as the government embarked on a campaign to destroy peasant villages and relocate people to government-controlled towns. In addition, paramilitary groups, largely supplied and supported by the regular military, embarked on campaigns of terror and torture in an attempt to control the largely peasant population.

The people of Xe'caj lived in a state of constant surveillance from the military encampment located above the town. Many of the residents had husbands, fathers, or sons taken away by the military. There were rumors of death lists. They had difficulty sleeping and reported nightmares of recurring death and violence. Soon, said Green, "I, too, started to experience nighttime hysteria, dreams of death, disappearances, and torture."

Green interviewed women who were widowed by the conflict. Without prompting, the women recounted in vivid detail their stories of horror, the deaths and disappearances of husbands, fathers, sons, and brothers as if they had happened last week or month rather than six to eight years before.

Then one day, when Green arrived to continue the interviews, the women were anxious and agitated. When she asked what had happened, they told her that the military commissioner was looking for her and that people were saying that she was helping the widows and talking against other people in the community. When Green told the women that she was going to go see the commissioner, they pleaded with her not to go, explaining that they knew of people who had gone to the military garrison and never returned. Green decided to visit the garrison alone, a visit that would provide a vivid experience of the kinds of fears confronted by the villagers. As she approached the garrison, she says (1995:116):

> I saw several soldiers sitting in a small guardhouse with a machine gun perched on a three-foot stanchion pointed downward and directly at me. The plight of Joseph K. in Kafka's *Trial* flashed through my mind, he accused of a crime for which he must defend himself but about which he could get no information. I didn't do anything wrong, I must not look guilty, I repeated to myself like a mantra. I must calm myself, as my stomach churned, my nerves frayed. I arrived breathless and terrified. Immediately I knew I was guilty because I was against the system of violence and terror that surrounded me.

Fortunately the commandant said he knew nothing about why she was being harassed, and assured her that she could continue with her work, and everything went smoothly from there; but Green gained a fuller understanding of the experiences of people who must live under the constant threat of violence.

The experiences of these three anthropologists—Green, Kearney, and Scaglion—highlight certain features of the ethnographic method. They especially illustrate the attempt of anthropologists to appreciate the views of others while at the same time questioning their own views of the world. They also illustrate what makes the ethnographic method unique; by participating in the lives of others and in their cultural practices, the anthropologist can take himself or herself as a subject of investigation. If he or she succeeds in seeing the world as others do, if even for a brief moment, then understanding and describing that world becomes far easier. It also helps the anthropologist understand how others can believe what they do. Tanya M. Luhrmann learned this when she studied contemporary witchcraft in England, and, after reading materials surrounding the practice of contemporary witchcraft, and attending ceremonies, she found herself interpreting events in the world in much the same way as the people she was working with. But we will return to her experiences in a later chapter.

Claude Levi-Strauss, one of the leading anthropologists of the twentieth century, says that fieldwork, and the attempts of anthropologists to immerse themselves in the world of others, makes them "marginal" men or women. They are never completely native because they cannot totally shed their own cultural perceptions, but they are never the same again after having glimpsed alternative visions of the world. Anthropologists are, as Roger Keesing put it, outsiders who know something of what it is to be insiders.

RESOURCE 1.3

Ethics in Fieldwork

Doing anthropological research (or any research for that matter) always has the potential to put the subjects of the research at risk. Participant observation poses special problems. The researcher may say or do the wrong thing, embarrass community members or others who have helped her or him, or put people at risk in other ways. Anthropologists do not always include accounts of their mistakes in their writings. In some cases, particularly when the researcher represents himself or herself as someone he or she is not, serious ethical concerns arise. The question of ethics in research gained special attention late in 2000 with a claim by investigative journalist Patrick Tierney in his book *Darkness in El Dorado: How Scientists and Journalists Devastated the Amazon* (W. W. Norton, 2001) that researchers, including anthropologists, were responsible for the deaths of hundreds of Yanomamo, and the devastation of their culture. Some of Tierney's claims have been questioned, but his account raises once again the responsibilities for researchers to, at a minimum, do no harm to the people with whom they work. The American Anthropological Association has available a "Code Of Ethics" that outlines some of the moral responsibilities of researchers at: **http://www.ameranthassn.org/committees/ethics/ethcode.htm**

You can also explore some specific issues related to the moral responsibility of researchers in the *Handbook on Ethical Issues in Anthropology* at: **http://www.ameranthassn.org/committees/ethics/toc.htm**

Or, if you want to find out more about doing anthropological fieldwork, you can explore Laura Tamakoshi's site at: **http://www.truman.edu/academics/ss/faculty/tamakoshil/index.html**

You can follow the reports on the Yanomamo at: **http://home1.gte.net/ericjw1/yanomamo.html**

QUESTION 1.4: How Can the Meanings That Others Find in Experience Be Interpreted and Described?

In one Sherlock Holmes detective story, Dr. Watson, Holmes's assistant, decides to teach the great detective a lesson in humility. He hands Holmes a pocket watch owned by Watson's late brother and challenges Holmes to infer from the watch the character of its owner. Holmes's interpretation: "[Your brother] was a man of untidy habits—very untidy and careless. He was left with good prospects, but he threw away his chances and finally, taking to drink, he died."

Watson, astounded at the accuracy of Holmes's description of his late brother, asks if it was guesswork. "I never guess," replies Holmes:

> I began by stating that your brother was careless. When you observe the lower part of the watch case, you notice that it is not only dented in two places, but it is cut and marked all over from the habit of keeping other hard objects, such as coins or keys, in the same pocket. Surely it is no great feat to assume that a man who treats [an expensive] watch so cavalierly must be a careless man. Neither is it a very far-fetched inference that a man who inherits one article of such value is pretty well provided for in other respects.

"But what about his drinking habits?" asks Watson. Holmes responds:

> Look at the innerplate which contains the keyhole [where the watch is wound]. Look at the thousands of scratches all around the hole—marks where the key has slipped. What sober man's key could have scored those grooves? But you will never see a drunkard's watch without them. He winds it at night, and he leaves these traces of his unsteady hand. Where is the mystery in all this?

Had Sherlock Holmes been an anthropologist, he might have been tempted also to draw some inferences about the society in which the watch was manufactured, particularly about the conceptions of time then current. In some societies time is task-oriented, not clock-oriented; for example, time might be measured by how long it takes to cook rice, as in Madagascar. In other societies, time patterns depend on natural events such as the rising of the sun or the ebb and flow of tides. British anthropologist E. E. Evans-Pritchard, in his classic account of the life of the Nuer of the Sudan, noted that:

> The Nuer have no expression equivalent to "time" in our language, and they cannot, therefore, as we can, speak of time as though it were something actual, which passes, can be wasted, can be saved, and so forth. I don't think they ever experience the same feeling of fighting against time because their points of reference are mainly the activities themselves, which are generally of a leisurely character. Events follow a logical order, but they are not controlled by an abstract system, there being no autonomous points of reference to which activities have to conform with precision. Nuer are fortunate.

An anthropologist might also infer that clocks are instruments of discipline; they tell us when to get up, when to go to bed, when to eat, when to start work, when to stop work. Our work patterns themselves are defined by clocks, and our wages may depend on the constant repetition over time of a particular task. Historian E. P. Thompson notes that, until the institution of modern notions of time and the need to measure it with clocks, work patterns were characterized by alternating bouts of intense labor and idleness, at least whenever people were in control of their own working lives. He even suggests that this pattern persists today, but only among a few self-employed professionals such as artists, writers, and small farmers, and, he further advises, college students.

Watson's brother's watch was a product of Western society, part of its culture. Holmes "read" the watch as if it were a collection of symbols or words, a **cultural text** that revealed the character of its owner. He could just as easily have viewed it as a text inscribed with the symbols that revealed the ideas about time and work that characterized the civilization that produced it.

One way to think about culture is as a text of significant symbols: words, gestures, drawings, natural objects—anything, in fact, that carries meaning. To understand another culture we must be able, as Holmes was with a pocket watch, to decipher the meaning of the symbols that comprise a cultural text. We must be able to interpret the meaning embedded in the language, objects, gestures, and activities that are shared by members of a society. Fortunately, the ability to decipher a cultural text is part of being human; in our everyday lives we both read and maintain the text that makes up our own culture. We have learned the meanings behind the symbols that frame our lives, and we share those meanings with others. Our task in understanding another culture is to take the abilities that have enabled us to dwell in our own culture and use them to understand the cultures of others.

Deciphering the Balinese Cockfight

To illustrate how an anthropologist might decipher a cultural text, imagine yourself coming upon a cockfight on the island of Bali. You see a ring in which two roosters with sharpened metal spurs attached to their legs are set at each other until one kills the other. Surrounding the fighting cocks are men shouting encouragement to their favorites, each having placed a wager that his favorite will kill its opponent.

What do you make of this? Your first reaction might be shock or disgust at the spectacle of the crowd urging the cocks to bloody combat. After a while you might begin to find similarities to events that are meaningful to you, such as some American sport. But what if, like Sherlock Holmes (or like Clifford Geertz, from whom this example is taken), you want to understand the meaning of what is happening and what that meaning tells you about how Balinese view their world? If you assume that the cockfight is a feature of Balinese culture—a Balinese text filled with symbols that carry meaning about what it is to be Balinese—how might you proceed to read this text?

You might begin by determining the language the Balinese use to talk about the cockfight. You would no doubt discover that the double entendre of cock as both a synonym for rooster and a euphemism for penis is the same for the Balinese as it is for Americans. The double entendre even produces, says Geertz, the same jokes, puns, and obscenities in Bali as it does in the United States. You would discover that *sabung*, the Balinese word for cock, has numerous other meanings and is used metaphorically to mean hero, warrior, champion, political candidate, bachelor, dandy, lady-killer, or tough guy. Court trials, wars, political contests, inheritance disputes, and street arguments are compared with cockfights. Even the island of Bali is thought of as being cock-shaped. You would also

In Balinese society, cockfighting is a major sporting event that is closely tied to cultural interpretations of manhood, competition, and status.

find that men give their fowls inordinate attention, spending most of their time grooming them and even feeding them a special diet. As one of Geertz's Balinese informants put it, "We're all cock crazy."

Having discovered the importance of cockfights to the Balinese and the connection they make between cocks and men, you next examine the cockfight itself. You learn that cockfights are public events held in arenas of about 50 square feet, from late afternoon until after sundown. Handlers, expert in the task, attach sharp spurs to the cocks' legs; for a cock thought to be superior to an opponent, the spurs are adjusted in a slightly disadvantageous position. The cocks are released in the center of the ring and fly at each other, fighting until one kills the other. The owner of the winning cock takes the carcass of the loser home to eat, and the losing owner is sometimes driven in despair to wreck family shrines. You discover that the Balinese contrast heaven and hell by comparing them to the mood of a man whose cock has just won and the mood of a man whose cock has just lost.

You find out that while the Balinese place odds on cockfights, there are strict social conventions that dictate the wagering. For example, a man will never bet against a cock that is owned by someone of his family group or village or a friend's family group or village, but he will place large bets against a cock owned by an enemy or the friend of an enemy. Rarely is a cockfight without social significance (e.g., between two outsiders), and rarely do cocks owned by members of the same family or village fight each other. Moreover, the owners of the cocks, especially in important matches, are usually among the leaders of their communities. You might learn that cockfights come close to encouraging an open expression of aggression between village and kin-group rivals, but not quite, because the cockfight is, as the Balinese put it, "only a cockfight."

Given the social rules for betting and the ways odds are set, you might reason, as Geertz did, that the Balinese rarely make a profit betting on cockfights. Geertz says, in fact, that most bettors just want to break even. Consequently, the meaning of the cockfight for a Balinese has little to do with economics. The question is the meaning of the cockfight for the Balinese. What is the cockfight really about, if it is not about money?

Geertz concludes that the Balinese cockfight is above all about status, about the ranking of people vis-á-vis one another. The Balinese cockfight is a text filled with meaning about status, as the Balinese see it. Cocks represent men, or, more specifically, their owners; the fate of the cock in the ring is linked, if only temporarily, to the social fate of its owner. Each cock has a following consisting of the owner, the owner's family, and members of the owner's village, and these followers "risk" their status by betting on the cockfight. Furthermore, Geertz maintains that to the degree that a match is between near equals, personal enemies, or high-status individuals, the more the match is about status. And the more the match is about status, the closer the identification of cock and man, the finer the cocks, and the more exactly they will be matched. The match will inspire greater emotion and absorption, and the gambling will be more about status and less about economic gain.

For Geertz, the cockfight is like any art form; it takes a highly abstract and difficult concept—status—and depicts it in a way that makes it comprehensible to the participants. The cockfight is meaningful to the Balinese because it tells them something real about their own lives, but in a way that does not directly affect their lives. They see the struggle for status that is part of everyday life vividly portrayed, even though, in the cockfight itself, no one really gains or loses status in any permanent sense.

A few words of caution are necessary concerning what we might learn about the Balinese from this particular cultural text. First, it would probably be a mistake to assume that the people either gain status by being on the winning side or lose it by being on the side of the loser. The status outcomes of the cockfight do not translate into real life any more than the victory of your favorite sports team increases your status. Instead, says Geertz, the cockfight illustrates what status is about for the Balinese. The cockfight is a story the Balinese tell themselves about themselves. It would also be a mistake to assume that the character of the Balinese could be read directly from the cockfight; that is, a conclusion that the cockfight is indicative of an aggressive, competitive, violent national character would quickly be dispelled. The Balinese are shy about competition and avoid open conflict. The slaughter in the cockfight represents things not as they are literally, but as they could be. Finally, the cockfight reveals only a segment of the Balinese character, as Watson's brother's watch revealed only a segment of its owner's character. The culture of a people, like the possessions of a person, is an ensemble of texts—collections of symbols and meanings—that must be viewed together to provide a full understanding.

QUESTION 1.5: What Can Learning About Other Peoples Tell Americans About Themselves?

Anthropologists do not limit themselves to the study of cultures that are different from their own. Rather, they often apply concepts and techniques that are useful in understanding and interpreting other cultures in order to understand and interpret their own. One of the objectives of studying other cultures is to help us recognize the meanings we impose on our experiences. When Renato Rosaldo asked the Ilongots why they cut off human heads, they replied that rage, born of grief, drives them to kill others; by severing the heads of their victims, they are able to throw away the anger born of bereavement. Rosaldo found it difficult to accept the ideas that the death of a kinsperson could cause anger or rage and that such rage in itself could drive a person to kill another. He questioned the Ilongots further but could obtain no other reason for their head-hunting; he devised other theories to explain it, but none were satisfactory. Only his own experience of grief and anger at the accidental death of his wife, Michelle, while both were doing fieldwork among the Ilongots helped him realize how grief can generate rage and how grief drove the Ilongots to hunt the heads of their enemies. At the same time that he began to understand the Ilongots, he began to understand his own grief and reaction to death.

A Balinese Anthropologist Studies Football

Whether we approach other cultures as anthropologists, as travelers, or as professionals who need to communicate with people of other cultures, the confrontation with other ways of believing and behaving should cause us to reflect on our way of viewing the world. To illustrate, try to step outside yourself and objectify an experience whose meaning you take for granted. Pretend you are a Balinese anthropologist who suddenly comes upon a spectacle as important in its way to Americans as the cockfight is to the Balinese: a football game.

As a Balinese, your first reaction to this American text might be one of horror and revulsion to see men violently attacking one other while thousands cheer them on to even more violent conflict. As you settle in, however, you would soon find some obvious similarities between the football game and the cockfight you are familiar with at home. Both are spectator sports in which the spectators sort themselves into supporters of one side or the other. In fact, in football, the sorting is even more carefully arranged, since supporters of one team are seated on one side of the arena and fans of the other team are seated opposite them.

Your next step (as in interpreting the cockfight) would be to examine the language Americans use to refer to the football game. You discover that they use similar expressions in talking about football and war: *defensive line, blitz, bomb.* Coaches talk about getting "revenge" for defeats, as generals might talk about getting revenge on the battlefields. You conclude that Americans seem to feel the same way about football as they do about war.

One of the words Americans use to refer to players is *jock*, a term also applied to an athletic supporter worn only by men. Since you see only men attacking one another, you might assume that the gender meanings of cockfights and football games are also similar. *Cocks* stand for men; football players are men. Moreover, football players dress to emphasize their maleness: large shoulders, narrow hips, big heads, pronounced genitals. You might test your interpretation with an American spectator who would argue that football gear is simply protective but, if pressed, would have to admit that it is used offensively as much as

Football, a highly popular American spectator sport, conveys cultural messages about how to achieve success in the business world.

defensively. Furthermore, you see young women participating in the spectacle as cheerleaders, dressed to highlight their femininity in the same way the players dress to accent their masculinity. This contrast between male and female in American society leads you to conclude that football is also a story about the meanings that Americans ascribe to gender differences.

You soon discover that winning and losing football games is as important to Americans as winning and losing cockfights is to Balinese. Winners engage in frenzied celebrations called *victory parties*, and losers are often despondent in defeat. As anthropologists know, this is not always the case in other societies. When the Gahuku-Gama of the Highlands of New Guinea started playing soccer, they always played until a committee of elders decided that the score was tied, and then the match was considered completed. So you speculate that football is also about the meanings that Americans give to the idea of success. You learn that success in America (like status in Bali) is a highly abstract idea; because it is abstract, its meaning is embedded in activities whose meanings are shared by members of the society. You need to find answers to certain questions about the meaning of success in American society: How is success defined? How is it obtained? Why doesn't everyone who follows all the rules for gaining success attain it?

Through your fieldwork, you find that Americans believe that "all men are created equal," and every person has (or at least should have) an equal opportunity to succeed. People compete for success, and they ought to compete on an equal footing, on a "level playing field," as some put it. Success, Americans believe, comes from hard work, sacrifice, and self-denial. But you wonder how Americans know that hard work, sacrifice, and denial bring success. Aren't there instances where they do not? How do Americans explain why women and minorities succeed less often than white males do? And why do some people achieve more success than others? You conclude that it is, in fact, impossible to prove directly in real life the correctness of this American success model, which maintains that hard work and sacrifice lead to success. Faith in the value of work and self-denial must be generated in other ways. As a Balinese anthropologist studying the American custom of football, you conclude, then, that in addition to its meanings relative to war and gender, the meaning of American football also lies in its demonstration of the American success model as it is supposed to work.

Anthropologists have found that football, like the Balinese cockfight, is carefully controlled by fixed rules so there is only one outcome: Almost always there is a winner and a loser. As a text that carries meaning about success, *who* wins is unimportant; it is only important that *someone* wins. ("A tie," it has been said, "is like kissing your sister.") But more than that, football tells Americans what it takes to win or lose. Success in football not only takes hard work and sacrifice but, as one American anthropologist, William Arens, points out, it requires teamwork, specialization, mechanization, and submission to a dominant authority—the coach. Two other American anthropologists, Susan P. Montague and Robert Morais, note that the football team looks very much like one of the most important settings in which Americans seek success—business corporations. Both football teams and corporations are compartmentalized, hierarchical, and highly sophisticated in the coordinated application of a differentiated, specialized technology, and they both try to turn out a winning product in a competitive market. Football coaches sometimes are hired to deliver inspirational lectures to corporate groups on "winning"; they may draw analogies between football and corporate life or portray the sport as a means of preparing for life in the business world.

Anthropologists therefore can conclude (as did Montague and Morais) that football provides for Americans, as the cockfight does for the Balinese, a small-scale rendering of a concept (status in the case of the Balinese, success in the American case) that is too complex to be directly comprehended. Football is compelling because it is a vivid demonstration of the validity of the value of success, as well as imparting a dramatic set of instructions on how to attain it. Consequently, the audience for a football game is led to believe that if the rules that govern the world of football are equated with the business world, then the principles that govern success on the football field must also apply in the world of work. That is, if hard work, dedication, submission to authority, and teamwork lead to success in a game, they will lead to success in real life. The rules by which success is won in football can also be applied to win success in the real world.

Of course, football is also a game that people enjoy. Analyzing it should not reduce our enjoyment of it but rather should heighten our fascination with it. By looking at football from the same perspective from which Geertz viewed the cockfight, we should gain an understanding of why the meaning carried by the game is important. While understanding the cockfight heightens our appreciation of the football game, it also helps us to see similarities between Americans and Balinese. If you were shocked by the cockfight, seeing the similarities to football should lessen that shock, while at the same time making football seem just a bit more exotic.

An Anthropological Look at a "Happy Meal"

Nothing is too mundane to provide some insights into the culture of which it is a part. Take the "Happy Meal" advertised by one of the many fast-food establishments in the United States. It consists of a hamburger, French fries, a cola drink, and a plastic toy, generally a "Barbie" doll or a "Hot Wheels" car. What can we learn about the culture of the United States by looking beyond the "taken-for-granted" quality of this meal? Among other things we can get some idea of American demographic and ecological patterns, agricultural and industrial history, and gender roles.

Why, for example, is meat the center of the meal? Most cultures have diets centered on some complex carbohydrate—rice, wheat, manioc, yams, taro—or something made from these—bread, pasta, tortillas, and so on. It is the spice, vegetables, meat, or fish that, when added to these foods, gives cuisine its distinctive taste. But meat and fish are generally at the edge, not the center, of the meal. Why is beef the main ingredient, rather than some other meat, such as pork, which was, for the first half of the twentieth century, the most popular meat in the U.S.?

Anthropologists Marvin Harris and Eric Ross note that one advantage of beef has been its suitability for the outdoor grill, which became more popular as people moved from cities into suburbs. Suburban cooks soon discovered that pork patties crumbled and fell through the grill, whereas beef patties held together better. In addition, to reduce the risk of trichinosis, pork had to be cooked until it was gray, which makes it very tough.

Beef farmers, as well as the farmers who grew the corn fed to beef to achieve a desirable fat content, benefited from the definition of a hamburger set by the United States Department of Agriculture:

> "Hamburger" shall consist of chopped fresh and/or frozen beef with or without the addition of beef fat as such and/or seasonings, shall not contain more than 30 percent fat, and shall not contain added water, phosphates, binders, or extenders. Beef cheek (trimmed beef cheeks) may be used in the preparation of hamburgers only in accordance with the conditions prescribed in paragraph (a) of this section. (quoted in Harris 1987:125)

As Marvin Harris noted, we can eat ground pork and ground beef, but we can't combine them and still call it a hamburger. Even when lean, grass-fed beef is used for hamburger and fat must be added as a binder, the fat must come from beef scraps, not from vegetables or a different animal. This definition of the hamburger protects both the beef industry and the corn farmer, whose income is linked to cattle production. Moreover, it helps the fast-food industry, because the definition of hamburger permits the use of inexpensive scraps of fat from slaughtered beef to make up to 30 percent of its content. Thus an international beef patty was created that overcame what Harris called the "pig's natural superiority as a converter of grain to flesh."

The cola drink that accompanies our hamburger is the second part of the fat and sugar-centered diet that has come to characterize our culture. People in the United States consume, on the average, about 60 pounds of sugar a year. Why so much? Sugar, as anthropologist Sidney Mintz suggests, has no nutritional properties, but it provides a quick and inexpensive energy boost for hardworking laborers with little time for a more nutritious meal. Sugar also serves as an excellent compliment to the fat in hamburgers, because it has what nutritionists call "go-away" qualities that remove the fat coating and the beef aftertaste from the mouth.

We can also learn from the Happy Meal that the fat and sugar diet is highly environmentally destructive. Beef-raising is among the most environmentally inefficient and destructive form of food-raising. For example, half the water consumed in the United States is used to grow grain to feed cattle, and the amount of water used to produce ten pounds of steak equals the household consumption of a family for an entire year. Fifteen times more water is needed to produce a pound of beef protein than an equivalent amount of plant protein.

Cattle-raising plays a major role in the destruction of tropical forests in Brazil, Guatemala, Costa Rica, and Honduras, where forests have been leveled to create pasture for cattle. Since most of the forest is cleared by burning, the creation of cattle pasture also creates carbon dioxide and, according to some environmentalists, contributes significantly to global warming.

Sugar is no less destructive a crop. Sugar production alters the environment in a number of ways. Forests must be cleared to plant sugar; wood or fossil fuel must be burned in the evaporation process; waste water is produced in extracting sucrose from the sugarcane; and more fuel is burned in the refining process. Not only has contemporary sugar production in Hawaii destroyed forests, but waste products from processing have severely damaged marine environments. "Big sugar," as the sugar industry is called in Florida, is largely responsible for the pollution, degradation, and virtual destruction of the Everglades.

Thus one of "texts" anthropologists can read from a Happy Meal relates to the extent to which consumption patterns associated with our culture create waste and environmental damage. Because of these consumption patterns, the average child born in the United States will, in the course of his or her lifetime do twice the environmental damage of a Swedish child, 3 times that of an Italian child, 13 times that of a Brazilian child, 35 times that of an Indian child, and 280 times that of a Chadian or Haitian child.

And what of Barbie dolls and Hot Wheels? Clearly there is a message about the definition of gender roles, as dolls are expected to be chosen by girls, and cars by boys. But one who looks closely enough can deduce even more about our culture from this meal.

EXERCISE 1.5

We've examined some of the lessons we can learn about our culture from the Happy Meal. But there are obviously others. See what you might deduce about the following dimensions of life in the United States from the Happy Meal.

What can you say about gender roles in the United States?

What can you deduce about race relations?

What can you say about the physical attributes of people favored in the United States?

RESOURCE 1.5

Resources on American Culture

Horace Miner's article on the Nacirema of North America (a people located roughly between Canada and Mexico) remains a classic reading for introductory anthropology students. You can find out more about the Nacirema, along with Miner's article, at: **http://www.beadsland.com/nacirema/**

CONCLUSIONS

This chapter has considered five questions, each having to do with the problem of how to understand ways of life that are different from our own. Why do human beings differ in what they believe and how they behave? One answer is that human beings, unlike other animals (or, at least, to a greater extent than other animals), create their own worlds and ascribe meanings to objects, persons, behaviors, emotions, and events, meanings that together constitute a culture. As Clifford Geertz suggests, human beings are compelled to create meanings if only to create some sense of order in their lives.

The judgments we make about the beliefs and behaviors of other people create a dilemma. If, on the one hand, we assume the meanings that others give to their experiences are wrong, silly, or absurd simply because they are different from ours, we are committing the ethnocentric fallacy. Ethnocentrism is intellectually awkward because it allows individuals to believe that their views are correct, and the views of others are wrong. This would make any kind of intercultural understanding virtually impossible. If, on the other hand, we conclude that the beliefs and behaviors of others can be judged only in the context of their cultures, we are confronted with the relativistic fallacy, which implies that any belief or behavior is acceptable, provided it makes sense to the people of the society in which it occurs. This places us in a moral dilemma because we must then accept virtually any belief or behavior.

Whether it is possible to set aside the meanings we ascribe to experience and see the world through the eyes of others is another question. Anthropologists conclude that the understandings of other cultures that they reach can be, at best, limited. Furthermore, in many ways, the ethnographic method transforms the fieldworker into a "marginal" person, an outsider who knows only something of what it is to be an insider.

One way we describe and interpret the meanings other people find in their experiences is to consider a culture as a text inscribed with symbols whose meaning can be deciphered. We can examine virtually any cultural activity this way and find in it a portion of the overall view of the world of a people.

Finally, if we approach our own culture in the same way we approach other cultures, we should gain a better understanding of the meanings we give objects, persons, and events. If we objectify our own beliefs and behavior in the same way we objectify the beliefs and behaviors of others, our own culture should become more exotic, while the cultures of others become less strange, shocking, or bizarre.

REFERENCES AND SUGGESTED READINGS

INTRODUCTION: THE WORLD BEHIND EVERYDAY APPEARANCES The epigraph comes from Jonathan Culler's article, "In Pursuit of Signs," in *Daedalus*, vol. 106 (1977), pp. 95–112. The discussion of the meaning of the classroom chair derives from some of the ideas of Michel Foucault in *Discipline and Punishment: The Birth of the Prison* (Vintage Press, 1979). An excellent anthropological study of American education is Norris Brock Johnson's *Westhaven: Classroom Culture and Society in a Rural Elementary School* (University of North Carolina Press, 1985).

WHY DO HUMAN BEINGS DIFFER IN THEIR BELIEFS AND BEHAVIORS? The descriptions of concepts of death come from Stanley Walens's account of Kwakiutl ritual and belief, *Feasting with Cannibals: An Essay on Kwakiutl Cosmology* (Princeton University Press, 1981); Daniel David Cowell's article, "Funerals, Family, and Forefathers: A View of Italian-American Funeral Practices," *Omega*, vol. 16 (1985–86), pp. 69–85; and Renato Rosaldo, *Culture and Truth: The Remaking of Social Analysis* (Beacon Press, 1989). A comprehensive review of beliefs about death can be found in "Death: A Cross-Cultural Perspective," by Phyllis Palgi and Henry Abramovitch in the *Annual Review of Anthropology*, vol. 13 (1984), pp. 385–417. Clifford Geertz's treatment of the concept of culture is from his essay, "The Impact of Culture on the Concept of Man," in *The Interpretation of Cultures* (Basic Books, 1973).

HOW DO PEOPLE JUDGE THE BELIEFS AND BEHAVIORS OF OTHERS? Richard Scaglion's tale of his experiences among the Abelam is told in his article "Ethnocentrism and the Abelam," in *The Humbled Anthropologist: Tales from the Pacific*, edited by Philip Devita (Wadsworth Publishing, 1990), pp. 29–34. The example of headhunting among the Ilongot comes from Rosaldo's *Culture and Truth*, cited above. A description of Aztec ritual sacrifice is found in Marvin Harris's *Cannibals and Kings: The Origins of Culture* (Vintage Books, 1977). The account of female circumcision comes from Rose Oldfield-Hayes's article, "Female Genital Mutilation, Fertility Control, Women's Roles, and the Patrilineage in Modern Sudan: A Functional Analysis," *American Ethnologist*, vol. 2 (1975), pp. 617–633. The debate between Nancy Scheper-Hughes and Roy D'Andrade about whether or not anthropology should be more morally committed appeared in *Current Anthropology*, Volume 36 (1995). Nancy Scheper-Hughes's dilemma concerning the treatment of infants in the shantytowns of Brazil is described in *Death Without Weeping: The Violence of Everyday Life in Brazil* (University of California Press, 1992). You can read about the experiences of Phillipe Bourgois in *In Search of Respect: Selling Crack in El Barrio* (Cambridge University Press, 1995). An excellent critique of cultural relativism is Elizabeth Zechenter's article, "In the Name of Culture: Cultural Relativism and the Abuse of the Individual" in a special issue of the *Journal of Anthropological Research*—Universal Human Rights Versus Cultural Relativity—volume 53 (1997) pages 319–348.

IS IT POSSIBLE TO SEE THE WORLD THROUGH THE EYES OF OTHERS? Michael Kearney describes his brush with witchcraft in "A Very Bad Disease of the Arms," in *The Naked Anthropologist* (Wadsworth Publishing Company, 1991), pp. 47–57. Nancy Green's account of her fieldwork in Guatemala comes from her article "Living in a State of Fear", in *Fieldwork Under Fire: Contemporary Studies of Violence and Survival*, edited by Carolyn Nordstrom and Antonius C. G. Robben (University of California Press, 1995). Claude Levi-Strauss's observations about the role of the anthropologists are from *Triste Tropiques* (Atheneum Publishers, 1974). Roger Keesing's observations come from his article "Not a Real Fish" in *The Naked Anthropologist*, pp. 73–78. Three classic accounts of fieldwork experiences are Richard Lee's paper, "Eating Christmas in the Kalahari," first published in *Natural History Magazine*, December 1969; Jean L. Briggs's account of her fieldwork among the Eskimo in *Never in Anger* (Harvard University Press, 1970); and Laura Bohannan's account of her experience translating *Hamlet* to the Tiv, "Shakespeare in the Bush," originally published in *Natural History Magazine*, August/September, 1966.

HOW CAN THE MEANINGS THAT OTHERS FIND IN EXPERIENCE BE INTERPRETED AND DESCRIBED? The use of Sir Arthur Conan Doyle's Sherlock Holmes story, "The Sign of the Four" from *The Complete Sherlock Holmes*, vol. 1 (Doubleday, 1930), to illustrate the deciphering of a cultural text was inspired by its use by Manfred F. R. Kets de Vries and Danny Miller in "Interpreting Organizational Texts," in *Journal of Management Studies*, vol. 24 (1987), pp. 233–247. The description of the Nuer conception of time comes from E. E. Evans-Pritchard's book *The Nuer: A Description of the Modes of Livelihood and Political Institutions of a Nilotic People* (Clarendon Press, 1940), p. 103. The discussion about time and discipline appears in E. P. Thompson's article, "Time, Work-Discipline and Industrial Capitalism," in *Past and Present*, vol. 38, pp. 56–97. The approach to culture as a text is best formulated by Clifford Geertz in his 1973 book, *The Interpretation of Cultures*. Geertz's analysis of the Balinese cockfight, "Deep Play: Notes on the Balinese Cockfight," first appeared in *Daedalus*, vol. 101 (1972), pp. 1–37.

WHAT CAN LEARNING ABOUT OTHER PEOPLES TELL AMERICANS ABOUT THEMSELVES? Renato Rosaldo speaks candidly about his struggle to come to grips with his wife's death in *Culture and Truth*, cited above, which also explores the issues of how we learn of other cultures, and what we can expect to understand about them. The analysis of the meaning of American football comes from William Arens's article "Professional Football: An American Symbol and Ritual," and the article by Susan P. Montague and Robert Morais, "Football Games and Rock Concerts: The Ritual Enactment of American Success Models," both in *The American Dimension: Cultural Myths and Social Realities*, edited by William Arens and Susan P. Montague (Alfred Publishing, 1976). A more recent view of the importance of football to American communities in the Southwest can be found in Douglas E. Foley's *Learning Capitalist Culture: Deep in the Heart of Tejas* (University of Pennsylvania Press, 1990). The account of how the Gahuku-Gama of the New Guinea Highlands adapted soccer to their own needs is found in Kenneth E. Read's *The High Valley*, originally published in 1965 by Columbia University Press and reprinted in 1980, pp. 150–152. A look at the role of meat in the American diet is provided in *Food and Evolution: Toward a Theory of Human Food Habits* (Temple University Press, 1987) by Marvin Harris and Eric Ross. An anthropological analysis of the history of sugar is provided by Sidney W. Mintz, in *Sweetness and Power: The Place of Sugar in World History* (Viking Press, 1985). For another treatment of the creation of the American diet see *Global Problems and the Culture of Capitalism* (Allyn & Bacon, 1999) by Richard H. Robbins. An excellent, although somewhat dated, review of anthropological studies of American culture can be found in George and Louise Spindler, "Anthropologists View American Culture," in *Annual Review of Anthropology*, vol. 12 (1983), pp. 49-78.

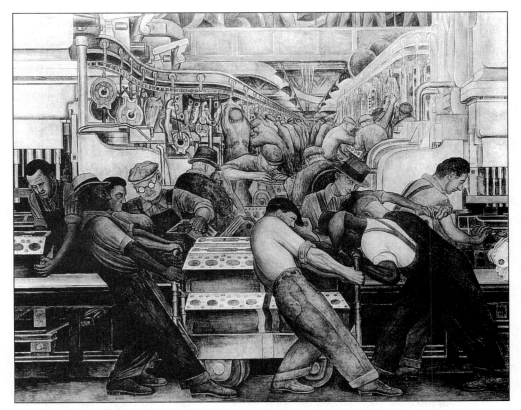

Diego M. Rivera, "Detroit Industry, North Wall" (detail), 1932–1933, fresco. Photograph © 1996 The Detroit Institute of Arts, Gift of Edsel B. Ford.

C H A P T E R 2

THE MEANING OF PROGRESS

PROBLEM 2: HOW DO WE EXPLAIN THE TRANSFORMATION OF HUMAN SOCIETIES OVER THE PAST 10,000 YEARS FROM SMALL-SCALE, NOMADIC BANDS OF HUNTERS AND GATHERERS TO LARGE-SCALE, URBAN-INDUSTRIAL STATES?

list of all parts of dev. of societies

> My position is, that if we have anything to learn from the Noble Savage, it is what
> to avoid. His virtues are a fable; his happiness is a delusion; his nobility nonsense.
> Charles Dickens, upon viewing an exhibit of life among the Bushmen of
> southern Africa in 1847 (Schrire 1984:4)

all imp. stuff bracketed.   substant. underlined.

INTRODUCTION: *The Death of a Way of Life*

We live in an era in which we will witness (if we have not already) the extinction of a way of life that is more than 100,000 years old. We know that, 10,000 years ago, virtually all human beings lived in small-scale, nomadic groups of 30 to 100 people, gathering wild vegetable foods and hunting large and small game as they had for thousands of years. Today virtually no human beings anywhere in the world live by hunting and gathering, although every society in existence is descended from such people. Hunters and gatherers are the common ancestors of us all.

We have also witnessed the creation of a world that is radically divided into wealthy nations and poor nations. While some enjoy a standard of living that gives them abundant food, comfortable shelters, and a plethora of consumer goods, up to three billion people worldwide suffer from hunger and poverty, live in urban and rural slums, and lack even the basics of health care.

paper divided into 5 q's -

The gradual extinction of a type of society that had flourished for at least 100,000 years, and the creation of a world ill-divided into the wealthy and the poor, poses both a riddle and a moral predicament. The riddle is why, approximately 10,000 years ago, after thousands of years of living as hunters and gatherers, some of these societies began to abandon their way of life. Why did they begin to domesticate plants and animals and exchange their nomadic existence for **sedentary** dwelling in villages and towns? And how, over the next 10,000 years, did these villages and towns come to be divided into rich and poor nations? The moral predicament involves our perceptions of the few remaining small-scale, tribal societies that exist in the world today, along with the millions of others who go hungry each day. Do we assume, as many have and still do, that human beings chose to abandon a nomadic, hunting-and-gathering life because they discovered better ways of living? Do we assume that the few existing small-scale tribal societies are remnants of an inferior way of life, and that, given the opportunity, their members also will choose to adopt modern farming, wage labor, or urban life? Do we assume that we can explain the division of wealth in the world by saying that some nations have progressed while others have not? Or is the concept of **progress**—the idea that human history is the story of a steady advance from a life dependent on the whims of nature to a life of control and domination over natural forces—a fabrication of contemporary societies based on ethnocentric notions of technological superiority?

A thumbnail sketch of what we know about the course of cultural history and evolution will be useful before we examine this problem. Combining what we have learned about human history from the work of archaeologists and historians with information provided by cultural anthropologists who have worked

[handwritten: actual 'places' are satellites]

among hunting-gathering and tribal societies creates a relatively clear picture of **culture change.** As stated previously, until approximately 10,000 years ago Earth's inhabitants were scattered in small-scale, nomadic bands of 30 to 100 people who lived by gathering wild plants and hunting small and large game. Since the search for food required mobility, it was probably not unusual for these bands to move every few days. With groups that were small and mobile, simple economic, social, and political arrangements sufficed; there were no formal leaders and little occupational specialization. If there was a specialist, it was likely to be a person who was believed to have special spiritual powers that could be used to cure illness or (if used malevolently) to cause illness or death. Kinship served as the main organizing principle of these societies, and social differences among people were based largely on age and gender. Since there was little occupational specialization and little difference in individual wealth or possessions, relations among persons likely were of an egalitarian nature.

At some point in history, some hunters and gatherers began to plant crops and domesticate wild animals. These groups became sedentary, living in permanent or semipermanent settlements of 200 to 2,000 people. They practiced **slash-and-burn,** or **swidden,** agriculture; forests were cleared by burning the trees and brush, and crops were planted among the ashes of the cleared ground. This land would be cultivated from one to three years, and then another plot of land would be burned and planted. Since larger, more sedentary groups required more formal leadership, certain members assumed the roles of chief or elder, with the authority to make decisions or resolve disputes. Simple occupational roles developed. Villages consisted of extended family groups, and people organized themselves into clans: groups of 200 to 500 people who claimed descent from a common ancestor. As a result of the development of leadership roles, members of some groups were ranked in importance. Later in history, perhaps because of a need for defense against other groups, settlements combined under common leaders to form states consisting of many thousands of persons. The development of agriculture intensified, and slash-and-burn techniques were replaced by plow or **irrigation agriculture.** Leaders organized labor for the purpose of constructing public works—roads, defensive fortifications, or religious structures, such as the pyramids in Mexico or the churches of medieval Europe. Competition between groups over available resources contributed to the development of standing armies; hereditary leaders emerged; and settlements grew into cities. As technological complexity increased, people began to develop specific skills and to specialize in occupational tasks (e.g., herder, baker, butcher, warrior, or potter), and occupational specialization led to increased trade and the evolution of a class of merchants. Some 300 years ago some of these ranked, state societies began to develop into large-scale, industrialized states that now are found all over the world and of which the United States is one. Table 2.1 provides a summary of this brief sketch of human social and cultural history.

One simple explanation for the transformation of societies from nomadic bands to industrial states is that human inventions created better ways of doing things; in other words, human culture progressed. In the past 30 years, however, anthropologists have begun to question the idea that the life of hunters and gatherers was harsh and difficult. They propose instead that in many ways this way of life was superior to that of groups maintained by sedentary agriculture.

(handwritten annotation at top: "(1) ← ———— people ————→ (300)")

TABLE 2.1   SUMMARY OF THE DEVELOPMENT OF SOCIETIES FROM GATHERERS AND HUNTERS TO AGRICULTURAL STATES

	Hunters and Gatherers	*Horticulturalists*	*State Societies*
Population Density	Approximately 1 person per square mile.	Approximately 10 to 15 people per square mile.	Approximately 300 people per square mile.
Subsistence	Hunting, gathering, and fishing.	Slash-and-burn agriculture with mixed livestock herding.	Plow or irrigation agriculture.
Work, Labor, and Production	Very high yield relative to labor expended.	High yield relative to labor expended.	High labor needs relative to yield. High degree of occupational specialization.
Political Organization	Informal political organization. Few, if any, formal leaders. Conflict controlled by limiting group size, mobility, and flexibility of group membership. Little intergroup conflict.	More formalized political organization, often with well-established leaders or chiefs. Increased population density and wealth result in increased potential for conflict. Intergroup warfare, motivated by desire for wealth, prestige, or women, is common.	Highly developed state organization, with a clear hierarchy of authority. Often a two-class society with rulers (landowners) and peasants. Authority of the elite backed by organized use of force (police or army). Warfare for purpose of conquest is common. Well-established mechanisms for resolving conflict (e.g., courts) exist side by side with informal mechanisms.
Social Organization	Small family groups, whose major purpose is economic cooperation. Few status distinctions other than those of sex and age. Marriage for economic partnership and inter-family alliance.	Emphasis on extended family groups. Descent important for the distribution of wealth and property. Status distinctions based on wealth are common, but status mobility is usually possible.	Emphasis on nuclear family. Family is strongly patriarchal, with women holding low status. Strong bonds of intergenerational dependence are built on inheritance needs. Social distinctions between people are emphasized, sometimes based on occupations. Little or no status mobility.

Some have proposed further that slash-and-burn agriculture was more efficient and less wasteful than modern methods of food production. If that is true, what other explanations are there for why groups abandoned hunting and gathering for sedentary agriculture and later developed industrialized societies? Moreover, if life in small-scale, tribal societies is not inferior to modern life, why are people in societies without advanced agriculture and industry starving and dying of disease? And why are small-scale, tribal societies disappearing?

QUESTIONS

2.1 Why did hunter-gatherer societies switch to sedentary agriculture?

2.2 Why are some societies more industrially advanced than others?

2.3 Why don't poor countries modernize and develop in the same way as wealthier countries?

2.4 How do modern standards of health and medical treatment compare with those of traditional societies?

2.5 Why are simpler societies disappearing?

QUESTION 2.1:   Why Did Hunter-Gatherer Societies Switch to Sedentary Agriculture?

The simplest explanation of why hunters and gatherers chose at some point to settle down and domesticate plants and animals is that sedentary agriculture was an easier, less dangerous, and more productive way to get food. People who discovered they could plant and harvest crops and domesticate animals rather than having to search for their food began to do so. They had progressed.

The idea that change occurs because of a desire to progress is well entrenched in Western society, and, beginning in the nineteenth century, anthropologists contributed significantly to this view. Lewis Henry Morgan, a Rochester, New York, attorney who took great interest in the historical evolution of culture, offered his own idea of how humankind had progressed. Morgan first became fascinated with the Iroquois of New York, and later sent out questionnaires to travelers and missionaries all over the world asking them about the family organization and kinship terminology of cultures they visited. In his book *Ancient Society,* first published in 1877, Morgan postulated a theory of human development in which human societies evolved through three stages that he labeled savagery, barbarism, and civilization. He further divided savagery and barbarism into early, middle, and late stages. Some societies, notably our own, had evolved completely to civilization; others had yet to complete their transformation and remained in the stages of savagery or barbarism. The passage of societies from one stage to the next, Morgan reasoned, required some major technological invention. Thus, the advance from early to middle savagery was marked by the invention of fire; from middle to late savagery by the invention of the bow and arrow; from late savagery through late barbarism by the invention of pottery, agriculture, and animal domestication, and so on, until certain societies had progressed to civilization. Other writers (including many anthropologists) have elaborated on the scheme developed by Morgan, assuming, as Morgan did, that humankind was progressing and would continue to do so.

For example, in the mid-twentieth century Leslie White formulated what was one of the more influential evolutionary schemes to explain the historical development of culture. Like Morgan, White saw technology as the driving force of cultural evolution. From White's perspective, human beings seek to harness energy through technology and to transform that energy into things that are required for survival, such as food, clothing, and shelter. By means of technology, energy is put to work, and the amount of food, clothing, or other goods produced by the expenditure of energy will be proportional to the efficiency of the technology available. Because hunters and gatherers had only their own muscle power to work with, the amount of energy produced by their work was limited. As technological advances, such as the plow, the water wheel, and the windmill, enabled people to grow more crops and domesticate animals, they became able to transform more and more energy to their use. Later, when new forms of energy in the form of coal, oil, and gas were harnessed by means of steam engines and internal combustion engines, the amount of energy human beings could harness again leaped forward.

Cultural development, from White's perspective, varies directly with the efficiency of the tools employed. More efficient technology allows human societies to transform more energy to fulfill their needs, and these societies then can produce more food and support larger populations. At some point the increased efficiency in food production allowed a few people to produce enough food for everyone, freeing others to develop other skills and thereby promoting occupational specialization. Specialization then produced widespread trade and led to the development of commerce. The increase in population, along with the increase in contact between groups, required the development of the state to coordinate group activities and organize armies to protect the growing wealth of its members from other groups.

EXERCISE 2.1A

Make a list of what you think are the advantages and disadvantages of civilization, and the advantages and disadvantages of life 10,000 years ago.

White's view of technology as the driving force in cultural evolution was highly influential in the development of anthropological theory in the twentieth century. But more relevant to us, his theories represent the coalescence of a point of view that is prevalent among many people today: the opinion that technology is the true measure of progress, and the more energy human societies can harness through the development of new power sources, the more social, economic, and political problems they will solve.

The benefits of technological progress remain a popular explanation for the transformation of societies, and many people view the application of technology as the solution to continuing world problems. Nevertheless, the progress theory of cultural transformation began to be seriously questioned by anthropologists during the twentieth century. These questions were raised in part by studies of hunting-and-gathering societies, previously alluded to, that suggested that life as a nomadic hunter and gatherer was not nearly as harsh and dangerous as had been supposed. In fact, some anthropologists suggested that hunting and gathering represented something of a lost paradise.

One of the first suppositions about life in hunting-and-gathering societies to be challenged had to do with the roles of males and females. Contrary to common belief, studies found that the gathering activities of women produced by far the greater share of food in these societies; men hunted, but, except in areas such as the Arctic and subarctic regions, meat and fish constituted only about one-quarter of the diet. A second supposition—that hunters and gatherers often went hungry—proved to be unfounded. Apparently they had plenty of food. And contrary to opinion, they did not have to work very hard to get it.

Life Among Hunter-Gatherers: The Hadza and the Ju/wasi

When they were studied by James Woodburn in the 1960s, the Hadza were a small group of nomadic hunters and gatherers in Tanzania, eastern Africa. Woodburn described their territory as dry, rocky savanna, characterized by one traveler as "barren land" and "desert." Hunters and gatherers are often depicted as living on the verge of starvation, but Woodburn found the Hadza area rich in food and resources. Wild game such as elephant, giraffe, zebra, and gazelle was plentiful. Plant foods—roots, berries, and fruit—were also abundant for those who knew where to look and constituted about 80 percent of the Hadza diet. The Hadza spent about two hours a day obtaining food.

Hadza women were responsible for almost all the plant food gathered, while hunting was exclusively a male activity. The men hunted with bow and poisoned arrows, and, when Woodburn lived among them, used no guns, spears, or traps. While the Hadza considered only meat as proper food and may have said they were hungry when there was no meat, there was, in fact, plenty of food available. For a Hadza to go hungry, said Woodburn, was almost inconceivable. Plant food was so plentiful that the Hadza made no attempt to preserve it. Physicians who examined Hadza children in the 1960s found them in good health by tropical standards, and Woodburn says that, from a nutritional point of view, the Hadza were better off than their agricultural neighbors.

The Ju/wasi* peoples of the Kalahari Desert, in Namibia in southwest Africa, are another hunting-and-gathering society that has contributed extensively to what anthropologists have learned about small-scale societies. Lorna Marshall, assisted by her children Elizabeth and John, began research among the Ju/wasi in the 1950s. Their work, along with later studies by Richard Lee and others, has provided us with a good description of Ju/wasi hunting-and-gathering activities. There is some controversy in anthropology over whether the Ju/wasi have always been hunters and gatherers, but that was the way they lived when they were visited by the Marshalls and Lee through the 1960s.

---

*The terms that societies use to refer to themselves are often different than those assigned by others. Unfortunately the latter sometimes become more widely accepted than the former. The Ju/wasi, for example, were referred to as Bushmen by Europeans, and later as !Kung by anthropologists.

Readily available plant foods, such as the nutrient-rich mongongo nut, were the mainstay of the Ju/wasi diet. Here, Ju/wasi women return to camp after foraging for mongongo nuts to feed their families.

Ju/wasi groups lived around water holes, from which they would wander as far as six miles in search of plant and animal foods. Their groups numbered from 30 to 40 people during the rainy season when water holes were full and plentiful and increased to 100 to 200 during the dry season when only the larger holes retained water. Lee found that the food quest was constant among the Ju/wasi, as it was among the Hadza. They did little food processing, so they had to get food supplies every third or fourth day. Vegetable foods constituted 60 to 80 percent of the diet, and women gathered most of it, producing two to three times as much food as men.

Lee reports that the Ju/wasi never exhausted their food supply. The major food source was the mongongo nut, which is far more nourishing than our own breakfast cereals and contains five times the calories and ten times the protein of cooked cereals. Mongongo nuts provided more than 50 percent of the Ju/wasi caloric intake; there are 1,260 calories and 56 grams of protein in 300 nuts. Ju/wasi territory contained more than 80 other species of edible plants, most of which they didn't even use, though they did eat about 20 species of roots, melons, gums, bulbs, and dried fruits. In addition, meat was provided by an occasional giraffe, antelope, or other large game, and the more usual porcupine, hare, or other small game. Their meat intake was between 175 and 200 pounds per person per year, an amount comparable to the meat consumption in developed countries.

In other words, Lee found that the environment of the Ju/wasi provided ample readily accessible food. Their diet consisted of some 2,300 calories a day, with a proper balance of protein, vitamins, and minerals. If the Ju/wasi diet was deficient, it was in carbohydrates, since there was no equivalent to our white bread, pasta, rice, or sugar.

The Ju/wasi did not spend much time getting food. Lee conducted a careful study of Ju/wasi work habits. During the first week in which he recorded the amount of time spent getting food, he found that individuals averaged 2.3 days at this work, with a typical working day of six hours. Overall, the average time spent getting food was 2.4 days, or less than 20 hours of work per week. The most active person Lee observed worked at getting food an average of 32 hours a week. Other time was spent doing housework or mending tools.

Lee concludes that, contrary to the stereotype that hunters and gatherers must struggle with limited technology to obtain the food they need for survival, they do not have to work very hard to make a living. He says that the idea that hunting-and-gathering societies struggle for existence is an ethnocentric notion that assumes that our own technologically oriented society represents the pinnacle of development. But, if Lee and others are correct about the ease of survival of hunters and gatherers, and if their life is not harsh and dangerous, why did those hunters and gatherers of 10,000 years ago abandon hunting and gathering, begin to domesticate crops and animals, and settle in permanent villages and towns?

The Transition to Agriculture

There is a perspective on cultural evolution that views the change from hunting and gathering to modern, industrial society less as development or progress and more as a necessary evil. This perspective emphasizes the influences of population growth and **population density,** the number of people living in a given area. To understand this point of view, we need to examine the transition from hunting-and-gathering to agriculture, also exploring the reasons for the eventual change from relatively simple slash-and-burn agriculture to more complex labor-intensive irrigation agriculture. Comparing modern agricultural techniques and less complex methods used in the production of potatoes also illustrates the point.

Anthropologist Mark Cohen set out to explain why individuals or groups abandoned hunting and gathering for agriculture, and why so many did so in a relatively short period of time. First he examined the reported food-gathering strategies of hunting-and-gathering societies. Hunters and gatherers settle in a given area to collect food, and, as food resources decline in one spot, they enlarge the area within which they travel in search of them. Imagine this area as a series of concentric circles; as the outer circles are approached from the center, the group may decide to move to another area where food is more plentiful in order to reduce the distance members travel. Cohen suggests that when population density in a given geographical area reached a point where different groups began to bump into each other, or when groups found they had to travel farther and farther to get enough food to feed a growing population, they began to cultivate their own crops. Cohen points out that anthropological and archaeological evidence suggests they knew how to do this all along, but chose instead to gather crops until the labor involved in traveling to new food sources surpassed the labor involved in growing their own crops. In other words, the historical transition from hunting and gathering to simple agriculture was a necessary consequence of the growth of population density, rather than a consequence of a discovery or invention that was adopted because it made life better. In a limited way, of course, this transition from gathering to cultivating did make life easier; when people began to harvest crops in a limited area, and remained in villages, groups no longer needed to travel as much. However, Cohen and others argue that agriculture didn't make life better at all; in fact, it made life worse (we'll explore that claim a little later in this chapter).

EXERCISE 2.1B

Here is the situation: The year is approximately 10,000 B.C. You are a group of elders of a hunting-and-gathering group similar to the Ju/wasi. Your band includes some 80 people. For as long as you can remember, you have lived by gathering nuts, roots, fruit, and other foodstuff, and by hunting wild game. Your territory has always been adequate to supply the necessary food for members of the group, but recently people have noticed that they have had to travel greater distances to collect food or to find game. Moreover, the territory that you consider your own now overlaps with that of other hunting and gathering groups.

As do most hunting and gathering peoples, you know how to plant crops and harvest them, and you have come to the realization that there is sufficient wild wheat, yams, maize, or other vegetable foodstuff to support your group as long as you cultivate it (plant it, save seeds for replanting, etc.), harvest it when it is ripe, store it, and settle down next to the stored food.

A group of younger members of the band, tired of traveling greater distances in search of food and fearful of conflict with neighboring bands whose territory overlaps yours, advocate settling down and taking advantage of wild crops.

The Problem: Should you take the advice of the younger members of the group, begin to harvest and store wild foods, and settle down in relatively permanent villages?

If you say yes, you need to give reasons why this is necessary in order to convince others in the group who are against the move. You must tell them what the consequences of not settling down would be.

If you say no, you need to be able to defend your decision to the younger members of the group, and explain to them the consequences of settling down. You also need to tell them the conditions under which you would take their advice.

In most parts of the world, when societies abandoned gathering and hunting, they likely began to utilize slash-and-burn agricultural techniques. Slash-and-burn or swidden agriculture can be practiced by relatively small, kinship-based groups. As a form of growing crops, it is highly efficient and productive. The Kuikuru, who inhabit the tropical rain forest of central Brazil, annually produce about two million calories per acre of land farmed, or enough to feed two people for a year. Moreover, the Kuikuru work only about two hours a day.

However, swidden agriculture requires large tracts of available land because after a plot is farmed for a couple of years, it must lie fallow for 20 to 30 years to allow the brush and trees to grow back so it can be used again. If the population and the amount of land needed to feed it both increase, plots must be used more

TABLE 2.2   DAYS OF LABOR PER ACRE PER HARVEST BY TYPE OF
             AGRICULTURE

Type of Agriculture	Days of Labor per Acre
Advanced swidden	18–25
Plow cultivation	20
Hoe cultivation	58
Irrigation agriculture	90–178

Source: Data from Eric R. Wolf, *Peasants* (Englewood Cliffs, NJ: Prentice-Hall, 1966).

frequently, perhaps every five or ten years. But when land is cultivated more frequently, the yield per acre declines. Thus, swidden agriculture is efficient only as
long as the population and the amount of land available remain constant.

Farmland may become scarce not only because of increasing population,
but also because of environmental changes or the encroachment of other groups.
Then new agricultural techniques must be developed to increase the yield on the
available land. The digging stick may be replaced with the plow, or irrigation
systems may be devised, and each of these developments requires a great deal of
labor. In other words, the more food the group needs to produce, the more complex the technology needed to produce it; and the more complex the technology, the greater the amount of work involved.

Relationships among land, labor, population, and methods of agriculture are
suggested in Tables 2.2 and 2.3. Table 2.2 indicates that the amount of labor required to produce a harvest increases with the complexity of agricultural techniques. For example, it requires up to ten times more labor to produce a harvest
with irrigation agriculture than it does to produce one with swidden agriculture.

Then why abandon swidden agriculture? Because there is not enough land
to support the population. Table 2.3 lists the amount of land needed to feed 100
families using different agricultural methods. For example, as little as 90 acres of
land are required to feed 100 families if irrigation agriculture is used, while 3,000
acres are needed if swidden agriculture is used. If a group has enough land, it
might as well keep its farming methods simple, changing them only if population
increases or the supply of land decreases.

TABLE 2.3   LAND NEEDED TO FEED 100 FAMILIES USING DIFFERENT
             AGRICULTURAL METHODS

Agricultural Method	Number of Acres Needed to Feed 100 Families
Swidden agriculture	3,000*
Swidden with garden plots	1,600*
Irrigation agriculture	90–200

*Includes unworked land that must be allowed to lie fallow to regain fertility.

Source: Data from Eric R. Wolf, *Peasants* (Englewood Cliffs, NJ: Prentice-Hall, 1966).

Robert L.
Carneiro

The history of humankind, however, has in fact been marked by an increase in population and an increase in the ratio of people to land. Robert L. Carneiro (1978) outlines the consequences of population density for cultural development.

The increase in the number of people relative to the available land creates two problems. First, if there are more people than there is available land to feed them, conflict may arise between people vying for the available resources. Second, if a growing population decides to intensify methods of growing crops, there is a need for greater societal organization. Irrigation agriculture, for example, requires the digging of ditches, the building of pumps to bring water to the fields and to drain water from them, and the coordination of one and sometimes two harvests a year. Thus, whether a society deals with an increasing ratio between land and people by intensifying efforts to produce more food, or it addresses the problem by denying some people access to the necessary resources, the groundwork is laid for the emergence of a stratified society and the need for a state organization.

The views of anthropologists such as Cohen and Carneiro suggest that the historical change of societies from gathering and hunting to gradually more labor-intensive methods of agriculture was not a matter of choice. Slash-and-burn agriculture wasn't easier than gathering and hunting, and plow and irrigation agriculture wasn't more efficient than slash-and-burn agriculture. Instead, the changes in food production techniques represented necessities brought about by population increase or an increase in population density, and they created the need for more formal, more elaborate political and social institutions, both to organize labor and to maintain order among more and more people.

If we conclude (and not all anthropologists do) that the transition from hunting and gathering to complex agriculture—along with the associated transformations in social, political, and economic institutions—does not represent progress, isn't it safe to say, at the very least, that Western society, particularly within the United States, has agricultural techniques that are vastly superior to those of small-scale, tribal societies? Those who claim that modern food-producing techniques are far more efficient than any other point out that in American society only 1 calorie of human energy is needed to produce 210 calories for human consumption, while hunter-gatherers produce less than 10 calories of food for every calorie they use collecting the food. But others argue that these figures are deceptive. At the same time we vastly decreased the amount of human labor required to produce food, they say, we vastly increased the amount of nonhuman energy required for food production. From that perspective, we expend 1 calorie of nonhuman energy in the form of nonrenewable fossil fuels (e.g., oil and coal) for every 8 calories we produce.

Producing Potato Calories

To make this point about energy, John H. Bodley compares the production of sweet potatoes in New Guinea with potato production in the United States. In New Guinea, people cultivate sweet potatoes by slash-and-burn agriculture; plots of land are burned, cleared, and planted with digging sticks. When the crops are ready, sweet potatoes are cooked in pits and eaten. In one New Guinea community, sweet potatoes account for 21 percent of the diet of 204 people.

Some of the sweet potatoes are fed to pigs, thus producing protein and accounting for an even larger proportion of the diet. The people use only 10 percent of the arable land, and there is no danger of resource depletion. With their agricultural techniques, the New Guinea farmers can produce about five million calories per acre.

American potato farms produce more than twice as many calories per acre as New Guinea farmers—about 12 million calories an acre. However, as Bodley points out, in addition to the human energy that goes into American farming, vast amounts of nonhuman energy are expended. Chemicals must be applied to maintain soil conditions and to control insects and fungus. For example, in 1996, potato farmers applied 154 million pounds of nitrogen fertilizer (195 pounds per acre), 134 million pounds of phosphate (173 pounds per acre), and 99 million pounds of potash (139 pounds per acre) to their crops. In addition, they applied almost 44 million pounds (55 pounds per acre) of herbicides, insecticides, fungicides, and other chemicals. Thus, while the American system produced more potatoes, the actual energy costs per calorie were lower in New Guinea. Moreover, all kinds of hidden costs from consequences such as soil erosion, pollution, and health problems from toxic chemicals were incurred in the United States.

Americans must also deal with distribution costs, which are minimal in traditional cultures, where most households consume what they produce. In modern industrial societies where 95 percent of the population is concentrated in or around urban centers, the energy expended in distributing the food now exceeds the energy expended in producing it. Taking the food-producing process as a whole—the manufacture and distribution of farm machinery, trucks, and fertilizer; irrigation projects; food processing; packaging; transportation; manufacturing of trucks; industrial and domestic food preparation; and refrigeration—Americans expend 8 to 12 calories of energy to produce a single calorie of food!

Bodley suggests that the reason Americans expend so much energy to produce food is to make money. He maintains that Western agricultural techniques are wasteful and inefficient. To illustrate his point, consider the potato chip. About half of the potatoes grown in the United States are sold as raw potatoes; the rest are processed into products such as instant mashed potatoes and potato chips. On the average, each American consumes 4.6 pounds of potato chips per year. All potatoes undergo significant processing after being harvested. They are mechanically washed, chemically sprayed to inhibit sprouting, colored and waxed to increase consumer appeal, and transported and stored under controlled conditions. Potatoes that are sold for potato chips must also be chemically sprayed weeks prior to planting to kill the stems; otherwise, the starch buildup would produce unappealing (but otherwise nutritious) dark potato chips. These potatoes also are chemically treated to prevent darkening after they are peeled and sliced; oils, salts, and preservatives are added in the cooking; and, finally, the end product is packaged in special containers and shipped. Additional marketing costs and energy are expended by manufacturers to convince consumers to buy the chips.

Thus, the human and nonhuman energy required to convert a potato into potato chips is far greater than the energy expended in New Guinea to produce a more nutritious sweet potato! Moreover, we do not fully appreciate the health risks implicit in our practice of adding some 2,500 substances to our foods to color them, flavor them, or preserve them.

QUESTION 2.2: Why Are Some Societies More Industrially Advanced Than Others?

Even if we agree that hunters and gatherers don't have it that bad, and that simpler forms of agriculture are more energy-efficient than modern techniques for growing crops and delivering food, we still have not explained the vast divisions in the modern world between rich nations and poor nations. If progress is not the reason, why then do most people of the industrial world enjoy a superior standard of living to those in the so-called nonindustrial world or underdeveloped countries of the world? Why, in 2000, did more than a billion people live in absolute poverty, earning the equivalent of less than one dollar a day, while the world's 225 richest people have nearly as much money as the poorest 50 percent of the world's people combined. The three richest people have assets exceeding the combined gross domestic products of the poorest 48 countries (United Nations 2000).

Trying to answer these questions requires an excursion into world economic history of the past 300 years; but rather than try to pack three centuries of history into the next few pages, let's see what we can learn from the story of the expansion of one industry, in one country, during one phase of its development—the textile industry in England in the last half of the eighteenth and the first half of the nineteenth century.

Prior to the beginnings of the **industrial revolution** in Europe, the world was significantly different in its distribution of wealth. China was arguably the richest country in the world during the sixteenth and seventeenth centuries, as gold and silver taken from the mines of South America by the Spanish and Portuguese was funneled into China to pay for Chinese silks, spices, teas, and luxury goods; India was developing a thriving cotton textile industry as Indian calicoes flooded into Europe. Wealthy states were developed in Western Africa, and Islamic traders thrived from Africa into Southeast Asia. Seventeenth-century England was a largely rural and agricultural country; even by 1700 only 13 percent of the population lived in towns of 5,000 or more people. England, however, had long enjoyed a thriving trade in textile goods, most notably raw wool and inexpensive wool textiles.

Early in its development, textile production was largely a handicraft industry, and most steps in the production of wool cloth, from cutting and degreasing the wool, to dying and spinning the thread, to weaving the cloth, were in the hands of rural families or small cooperatives. The finished cloth or wool product might be sold at a local market or fair, or more often to urban-based merchants or traders for resale at fairs or shipment overseas.

But, while the trade in home-produced textiles was profitable for all, traders and merchants discovered they needed to better control the type, quantity, and quality of cloth produced by spinners and weavers. The merchants' first solution to this problem was the **"putting out" system,** in which merchants supplied weavers with materials and required them to produce cloth of the desired type. Some merchants supplied only the wool, cotton, or linen, while others supplied everything, including the looms. The merchants delivered the supplies and tools and picked up the finished products, generally paying the producers for each piece produced. Putting out had numerous advantages for textile merchants;

This cartoon is one of a series by Robert Cruikshank decrying the exploitation of child labor by British industrialists. Prior to 1833, there were no restrictions on ages or hours worked by children in factory jobs.

it gave them more control over the production process, it provided a source of cheap labor as it brought women and children into the production process, and, if demand for their products slackened, the merchant could easily control how much was produced by limiting the materials they put out.

Increasingly, however, beginning in the eighteenth century, English merchants found it expedient to transform the "putting out" system into a **factory system** by bringing the spinners, weavers, and others together in one location to produce the cloth. Factories were neither new nor unique to England. Factories employing more than 15,000 workers existed in France in 1685. Furthermore, merchants were not particularly anxious to invest in factories. Profits from manufacture were not nearly as great as profits from trade, especially long-distance exchange. Moreover, removing people from the home-based family to urban-based factories required new mechanisms of discipline and control, a fact that explains why early factories were modeled on penal workhouses and prisons. Finally, the entrepreneur, who previously could halt putting out when demand slackened, now had to keep his factories busy to pay for his investment in buildings and technology and, consequently, had to create demands for his products.

The only things that made manufacturing investments attractive were various kinds of government subsidies or laws (e.g., vagrancy laws that required people to have jobs) that ensured the flow of cheap labor. Textile manufacturers were able to draw on workers who had been forced off their land by enclosure legislation that pushed peasant farmers off common land at the behest of landowners wishing to grow crops for sale to the increasing population of England. Since there were no minimum wage laws or laws restricting the use of child labor, factory owners could also make even more use of the cheap labor of women and children; thus, by 1834, children under 13 represented 13 percent of the British cotton industry, and by 1838, only 23 percent of textile factory workers in England were adult men. In addition, government also played a major role in creating and defending overseas markets, as well as sources of raw materials such as cotton.

The growth of the textile industry had numerous effects. For example, it fueled the growth of the cities; by 1800 a quarter of the English population lived in towns of 5,000 or more, and Manchester, a center of textile manufacture, grew from 24,000 inhabitants in 1773 to more than 250,000 by 1851. Moreover, the factories spurred the development of the technology. Mechanization of the textile industry began in earnest with Kay's flying shuttle in 1733, which doubled the weavers' output. But since spinners could not keep up with the need for thread for the new looms, bottlenecks developed. To meet this need, James Hargreaves introduced in 1765 the spinning jenny. In 1769 Arkwright invented the water frame, and then in 1779 Crompton developed a mule that combined features of water frame and jenny. Finally, in 1790, steam power was added to the production process. These inventions produced a staggering increase in textile production. A hand spinner in India of the eighteenth century took more then 50,000 hours to process 100 pounds of cotton into thread; in England, Crompton's mule reduced that to 2,000 hours, while power-assisted mules of around 1795 reduced this time still further to 300 hours. By 1825 it took only 135 hours to process 100 pounds of cotton.

The growth of the textile industry obviously produced great wealth and employed millions of workers. In economic terms, it transformed England into the wealthiest country in the world. And textiles were not, of course, the only industry that expanded; trade and manufacture of iron, as well as the agricultural production of food commodities, further increased the wealth of the growing British Empire. But the increase in technology and production created two problems: Where was the market for all these textile products to be found, and where were the raw materials—notably the cotton—to come from?

Some historians point to the large domestic market available to English textile producers in the wake of the growth of the English population from six million in 1700 to nine million in 1800. Moreover, English textile manufacturers were able to sell much of their product to markets in Europe and the growing markets of the Americas. But there was still competition for these markets. England was not the only textile producer; Holland, France, and Spain were busy competing (and often fighting each other) for overseas markets as well as sources of raw materials. This competition, along with the growing military superiority of Western Europe, often had dire consequences for once-prosperous industries in other parts of the world. The story of textiles in India is instructive.

The British in India

Mughal India of the seventeenth century was an empire created by Turks from Turkestan who made their chief, Babur, the first Mughal Emperor in 1527. India was a major trading country, and centuries-old trade networks linked India to the rest of Europe, the Islamic world, and China. In 1690, the British East India Company was granted a monopoly in East Asian trade by the British government. A relative latecomer to trade in India, it established a trade center in Bengal, in the city of Calcutta. The British East India Company soon had some 150 posts trading in India for fine silks, cotton, sugar, rice, saltpeter, indigo, and opium.

In the 1750s the British provoked the rulers of Bengal into war, defeating them conclusively in 1757. As an aftermath to their victory in Bengal, the English plundered the state treasury for some five million pounds and gained control of 10,000 Bengali weavers. By 1765, the British East India Company became the civil administration of Bengal. It promptly increased the tax burden on peasants and artisans, leading to major famines in 1770 and 1783. From its base in Bengal, moreover, the Company gradually began to extend its control over much of the Indian subcontinent.

Prior to the British military takeover, India produced cloth that was cheaper and better than English textiles; in fact, Indian cotton and calicoes—named after the city of Calicut—were the craze of Europe. To meet this challenge, the British government prohibited the British East India Company from importing calicoes into England. To take advantage of the import restriction, English factories began to produce copies of popular Indian textiles for sale both in England and abroad. In addition, India was required to admit English manufacturers free of tariffs. These actions effectively destroyed what had been a thriving Indian textile industry.

But India was still a major producer of raw cotton, although it was not a variety favored by English or American manufacturers; instead it was produced for export to China, although it was primarily opium that led the trade into China.

The British, and Western European nations in general, had a problem with trade into China; Chinese products, notably tea, were in high demand, but there was little produced in England, or the rest of Europe for that matter, that the Chinese wanted or needed. There was a market in China for opium, however, and by 1773 the British East India Company had a monopoly over opium sales. Opium was illegal in China, but the Chinese state seemed incapable of cutting off supplies, and smuggling opium into China was hugely profitable for British, as well as American and French, merchants. When the Chinese government tried to enforce the laws against opium sales in 1839 by seizing opium held by British merchants in warehouses in Canton, the British government successfully intervened militarily and effectively forced the Chinese government to stop enforcing opium laws. An analogy today might be the government of Colombia sending troops to the United States to force acceptance of Colombian cocaine shipments. Moreover, the British demanded and received additional trading rights into China, further opening a market, not only for opium, but for textiles as well.

The British-led opium trade from India to China had three results. First, it reversed the flow of money between China and the rest of the world; during the first decade of the nineteenth century, China still took in a surplus of 26 million silver dollars; by the third decade 34 million dollars left China to pay for opium. Second, it is estimated that by the end of the nineteenth century one out of every ten Chinese was addicted to opium. Finally, the amount of cotton exports from England to India and China had increased from 6 percent of total British exports in 1815, to 22 percent in 1840, 31 percent in 1850, and more than 50 percent after 1873.

Cotton, Slavery, and the Cherokee Removal

Cotton and the growth of the textile industry in England figure not only into the story of the economic decline and British colonization of India and China, but also into the story of slavery and the removal of thousands of Native Americans from their homeland. The British were able to sell raw Indian cotton to China, but Indian cotton was not acceptable to European and American markets. Indian cotton produced a shorter fiber, while cotton produced elsewhere, notably in Egypt and the American South, produced a longer, more desirable fiber. But cotton production in the Americas was labor intensive and, to be profitable, required slave labor.

Slavery was not created by the need for cotton. As an institution it extends well back into antiquity. It was not uncommon for nations at war to utilize captives as slaves. But the slave trade grew from the fifteenth to nineteenth century in response to the economic expansion and demands of European trade, including Spanish demand for labor in the silver mines; Spanish, Portuguese, British, and French demands for cane cutters and millers for the sugar plantations of Brazil and the Caribbean; and American demands for workers on the cotton plantations of Georgia, Alabama, Louisiana, Texas, and Mississippi. From 1451 to 1600 some 275,000 slaves were sent from Africa to America and Europe. During the seventeenth century some 1,341,000 slaves were sent, while from 1701 to 1810 some six million people were forcibly exported from Africa. Another two million were sold out of Africa between 1810 and 1870, many destined for Cuba.

The production of cotton with slave labor might be said to have fueled the industrial revolution in the United States. While England imported raw cotton from its possessions in the West Indies and from Turkey, by 1807 half was coming from the United States. In fact, between 1815 and 1860 raw cotton constituted half the value of domestic exports from the United States!

Part of the reason for the growth of the American cotton industry was Eli Whitney's cotton gin, an invention that easily separated the seeds from the raw cotton fiber. It allowed a person to clean 50 pounds of cotton in the time it had previously taken to clean one pound. As a consequence, American cotton production increased enormously, from 3,000 bales in 1790 to 178,000 bales in 1810, 732,000 in 1830, and 4,500,000 in 1860. But to be competitive, American cotton production required cheap labor, and slave labor cost half the price of wage labor. Each plantation required at least 50 to 200 slaves, depending on the quality of the soil.

The British demand for American cotton was obviously not the cause of slavery, but it ensured its continuance in the United States into the second half of the nineteenth century. Between 1790 and 1860 some 835,000 slaves were moved from Maryland, Virginia, and the Carolinas to Alabama, Louisiana, Mississippi, and Texas in one of the greatest forced migrations of all time. But it was not the only forced migration instigated by the world demand and profitability of cotton. The cotton industry was also the impetus behind the forced removal in the 1830s of 125,000 Native Americans from their homes in Georgia, Alabama, and Mississippi to the Oklahoma territory.

The story of the forced removal of the Cherokee is most instructive in supplying an answer to why some people of the world enjoy higher levels of wealth than others. The Cherokees had always been considered one of the

Reliance on slave labor in the United States was closely tied to the rise of the British textile industry. Here, a slave family picks cotton on a plantation near Savannah, Georgia, during the early 1860s.

more so-called advanced Native American groups, being counted by early American settlers as one of the "civilized tribes" of North America. They were horticulturists, living in large, autonomous villages, and, in the aftermath of the American Revolution, occupying large tracts of fertile land from North Carolina into Georgia. In order to persuade southeastern states to give up claims to territory in the west, Thomas Jefferson instituted what became known as the Georgia Compact of 1802. The compact called for Georgia and the Carolinas to give up claims to western territories in exchange for land held by southeastern tribes, such as the Cherokee. But the tribes fought the removal, embarking on a modernization plan; within decades, the Cherokee had constructed plantations, held slaves, and had their own newspaper, schools, and alphabet. They were also among the soldiers under Andrew Jackson that defeated the British in the War of 1812.

The Cherokee lobbied Congress extensively to repeal the Georgia Compact, but to no avail. Andrew Jackson, who had made Indian removal one of the cornerstones of his presidential campaign in 1828, signed the final order, and the army was sent in to forcibly move the population as land speculators flooded onto what had been prosperous Cherokee farms and plantations. Thousands of additional acres of formerly Indian land was taken over or converted to cotton production by white farmers using black slaves. Thus, much of the future wealth of the young American Republic was created by white farmers using Native American land and African labor to produce cotton for the English and American textile industries.

In sum, the growth of the textile industry in England produced great wealth for some people, but, in the process, destroyed textile manufacturing in India, led to the colonization of India and China, extended slavery in the United States while it drained Africa of productive labor, and enhanced the wealth of the United States while leading to the forced removal of indigenous people from their lands. The mass production of textiles in England and elsewhere in Europe also destroyed textile manufacture by artisans in areas of the world where British textiles were sold; since women were often the main textile producers in many societies, we might also speculate that the textile trade may have led to decline of the status of women in these societies.

We must also consider that England was not the only producer of textiles or the only country seeking to open and control overseas markets; France, Germany, Holland, and, later, the United States also had thriving textile industries. We must remember, too, that textiles represent only one of many industries of Western Europe that required raw materials and new markets. The new demands for sugar, cocoa, palm oil, tobacco, and coffee also led to the conversion of millions of acres of land around the world from subsistence farms to cash crops, further turning self-sufficient peasant farmers into dependent wage-laborers or unemployed poor. And finally, we must remember that we have examined only a brief period of time. In fact, the heyday of European colonial expansion did not occur until the last quarter of the nineteenth century and the first decades of the twentieth. Looking at the bigger picture, we begin to understand why the problems of the so-called nonindustrial nations are due less to their own shortcomings than to the exploitative activities of others, and why a peasant farmer in India in 1400 was significantly better off economically than his Indian counterpart of 1960.

QUESTION 2.3: *Why Don't Poor Countries Modernize and Develop in the Same Way as Wealthier Countries?*

The industrial revolution radically transformed the lives of people in Western Europe and the United States as the vast majority of the population went from being farmers to laborers. In most cases this was not a matter of choice; people began to sell their labor, not because wage labor offered a better life, but because they no longer possessed land on which to secure a livelihood. Moreover, the availability of jobs was subject to the whims of the market and the rise and fall in the demand for products. As long as there was a demand for products, jobs were secure; when demand slackened, people were thrown out of work. Consequently, the development of industry in the nineteenth century was marked by periodic downturns in economic growth and the occurrence of depressions such as those of 1840 and 1873.

Overall, however, the rate of economic growth and technological advancement was astounding, resulting in a dramatic improvement in the standard of living of most people in Western countries. At the same time, many in the industrialized world did not enjoy increased wealth, and people in the Third World often saw their standard of living decline as their countries fell under the influence of European powers.

Regardless, as countries began to gain independence from their colonial dominators, they wished to emulate the lifestyle and standard of living of the industrial powers; the way to do this, they reasoned, was to imitate the colonizer and industrialize. Hence the push for what became known as **"economic development."**

The idea of economic development is based on three key assumptions: (1) economic growth and development is the solution to national as well as global problems; (2) global economic integration will contribute to solving global ecological and social problems; and (3) foreign assistance to undeveloped countries will make things better. Thus, countries that wished to develop sought foreign loans and investments to create an industrial infrastructure: dams for hydroelectric power, coal-fired generators, and nuclear power plants; loans to create a transportation system; ports, roads, and railways; and loans to train and educate workers. The loans would allow undeveloped countries to produce things that developed countries didn't produce themselves—cash crops such as cotton, sugar, palm oil, tobacco, coffee, and cocoa, and natural resources such as oil, metal ores, and lumber. This theory of economic development was not new to the second half of the twentieth century; what was different was the degree of apparent support offered by the wealthy nations of the world themselves. One major Western institution that was to promote economic development was the **World Bank.**

EXERCISE 2.3

It is 1960. You have been hired as a consultant by the World Bank to evaluate a loan application that seeks to help Brazil industrialize. The country is predominantly agricultural, some 70 percent of the population living in rural areas. Most farms consist of subsistence plots worked by small family groups producing crops such as tomatoes, sweet potatoes, and corn. Per capita income is very low, equivalent to about $200 a year in today's currency. Sugar is a major export crop grown largely in the arid northeast region of the country. Virtually all settlement is along the Atlantic coast, while the vast tropical forests of the Amazon are mainly undeveloped, inhabited largely by indigenous peoples and itinerant rubber tappers.

The country is run by a democratically elected legislature whose members are seeking to make Brazil a modern economic and industrial power. Their loan application proposes the following:

1. The building of hydroelectric projects (dams and irrigation facilities) to supply power to attract industry and modernize agriculture.
2. Building of roads into the Amazon to encourage settlement and population redistribution.
3. Funds to resettle people into areas in which roads will be built.
4. Funds to develop new crops for export and expand sugar production.

Your task is to evaluate each proposal, consider the impact it will have on the people of Brazil, and recommend whether or not to fund the proposal. If a proposal is unacceptable, you may propose conditions under which it would be acceptable.

The World Bank was born in 1944 in Bretton Woods, New Hampshire, at a meeting of the representatives of the major industrial nations allied against the Germans, Japanese, and Italians. Their task was to plan for the economic reconstruction of countries devastated by World War II and develop a postwar plan for worldwide economic and monetary stability. Out of that meeting came the plan for the **International Monetary Fund (IMF)** and the International Bank for Reconstruction and Development (the World Bank). Funds for the bank were to be donated by member nations, largely in the form of loan guarantees. The bank would lend money to governments for specific projects—highways, dams, power plants, factories, and the like—and the governments would agree to pay back the loans over a set period of time. The charter also specified that loans must be made without any regard for political or noneconomic factors, and that the bank must not interfere in the political affairs of any member or debtor nation.

The World Bank began operating in 1946, with the initial loans going to European countries to rebuild their economies after World War II. But soon the World Bank was making huge loans to countries such as Brazil, India, and Indonesia—loans that were supposed to transform their economies, bring wealth, and alleviate poverty. Moreover, once the World Bank approved loans, other banks would often follow. But, in spite of the growth of foreign loans to undeveloped countries, many argue that they not only increased poverty, but also led to rampant environmental devastation. How, in spite of apparently good intentions, could this happen?

The Case of Brazil

Brazil has been one of the major recipients of World Bank loans. In the 1960s the government of Brazil made a conscious decision to industrialize. Using money borrowed from the World Bank and other Western lending institutions, along with funds from private investors, Brazil built dams, roads, factories, and industries, and modernized agriculture, becoming a world leader in the export of crops such as soybeans. The economy surged ahead, and Brazil became a model of modern industrialization; factories created jobs, and people flocked to the cities for employment as Brazil's cities began to rival any in the West.

But there was a downside: To pay back its debt to the banks, Brazil needed to earn foreign income. Consequently, landowners were encouraged to expand the production of crops that could be sold for money, especially crops that could be sold in the United States and Europe. Since the West already produced more than enough food (American farmers were being paid by the government not to grow food crops), Brazilian farmers turned to crops with other uses, such as soybeans, sisal, sugar, cocoa, and coffee. To grow more of these products required modern farming techniques and lots of land. Small farmers, forced off their land, had to find farm employment growing cash crops, or migrate to the cities in search of jobs that, for the most part, did not exist. Moreover, the pay of those who found jobs on the large farms was insufficient to purchase the food that they had previously grown themselves on their small plots. Brazil did increase production of some food crops, notably beef, but because poor Brazilians could not pay as much for beef as relatively wealthy Americans and Europeans could, most Brazilian beef was exported.

To make matters worse, in the mid-1980s Brazil and other debtor countries discovered that they could not keep up their payments to the World Bank and other Western financial institutions, and threatened to default on their loans. To help these countries avoid default, the World Bank allowed them to renegotiate their loans. Countries allowed to renegotiate, however, had to agree to change their economies by introducing cost-cutting measures such as reducing government spending on public education, welfare, housing, and health. These cutbacks resulted in still greater hardships for the poorest members of the populations.

Thus, in the wake of its program for economic development, Brazil has increased its total wealth, and some people have become very rich, but it is estimated that more than 40 percent of Brazil's population is living in poverty. And Brazil is not unique; most of Central and South America, Africa, and Southeast Asia followed the same formula for development, and most of these countries also experienced increased poverty and hunger for a majority of their people.

Added to the economic problems, economic development also brought environmental destruction. Between 1981 and 1983, the World Bank began delivering payments on a loan for Brazil to construct a road through the Amazon rain forest and to build new settlements. The economic goal of the Polonoroeste project was to open vast tracts of Amazon rain forest for settlement by displaced peasants, transforming the forest into a cash-producer. As a consequence, nearly half a million settlers flooded into the area between 1981 and 1986. The government, however, was not prepared for that level of migration, and the new migrants were forced to burn forests in order to grow food for survival. But the poor soil of the rain forests would not support agriculture for more than a couple of years, and people ultimately were left with worthless land. The only activity that proved worthwhile was cattle ranching, and that required the burning of still more of the rain forest. The area of Rondnia went from 1.7 percent deforestation in 1978 to 16.1 in 1991. Furthermore, life-threatening diseases developed, rates of malaria approached 100 percent, and infant mortality rates of 25 to 50 percent were not uncommon. Indian land was pillaged, and epidemics ravaged the population. The pesticide DDT (banned in the United States) was used in an attempt to eradicate the mosquitoes that spread the malaria, and rural violence broke out between ranchers and rubber tappers.

Whether the price of progress through industrialization must be increased poverty, hunger, and environmental devastation is, for many, an open question. Many argue that the process of economic and industrial development takes time, and that countries such as Brazil and India are now beginning to see a marked improvement in their economic situation. Some point to the cases of the so-called newly industrialized countries, such as Korea and Taiwan, as examples of what can be done. Yet the non-Western countries that have succeeded in emulating the West (and Japan is foremost among these) were never colonized by the West, as were the poor countries of Africa and South America.

In sum, then, are the people of the world better off now than they were before the industrial revolution? Obviously the answer depends on who you are. If you are fortunate enough to be a laborer, merchant/businessperson, or professional in one of the wealthy countries of the world, you are likely to be materially better off than your counterpart of five centuries ago, provided the price you pay in health risks because of a damaged environment does not offset your material gains. If you are a laborer or small farmer in one of the poor countries of the world, it is difficult to see how you would be better off than your peasant counterpart of centuries past, and if you are among the landless, unemployed, or underemployed of the world, one of the billion without enough food, one is hard-pressed to see how your life could be an improvement over the lives of people in centuries past.

RESOURCE 2.3

Social and Cultural Change

You can find a good Web site for information on social and cultural change—theory, data, syllabi, and additional links—at:

Social Change
http://redrival.net/evaluation/socialchange

For information on how countries got into debt and what can be done about it, you can check these sites. The first two are at the IMF and The World Bank, agencies that many blame for the debt. The third site, Third World Network, portrays a different view of the debt:

Debt Initiative for the Heavily Indebted Poor Countries—IMF
http://www.imf.org/external/np/hipc/hipc.htm

Debt Relief Web Site
http://www.worldbank.org/hipc/index.html

Third World Network
www.twnside.org.sg

You can also find some readings on the subject at the author's Web site at:
http://faculty.plattsburgh.edu/richard.robbins/CA/CA_2.htm

QUESTION 2.4: *How Do Modern Standards of Health and Medical Treatment Compare with Those of Traditional Societies?*

To answer this question we need to examine two things: First we have to ask whether or not we have progressed in our ability to treat disease, and, second, we have to ask whether or not we have fully understood the traditional medical techniques that modern medicine has sought to replace.

Illness and Inequality

One of the supposed triumphs of modern society is the treatment and cure of disease. Life expectancy has more than doubled in the twentieth century; in 1900, the world life expectancy was approximately 30 years. In 2000 it was 63 years. Antibiotics save millions each year from death while modern diagnostic methods and equipment allow medical practitioners to more easily identify the onset of disease. Yet the progress that often we take for granted is not available to all. In fact, the single most important determinant of a country's ability to protect its citizens from disease is the degree of economic equality. Worldwide 32 percent of all deaths are caused by infectious disease; but in the poorer countries of the world infectious disease is responsible for 42 percent of all deaths, compared to 1.2 percent in industrial countries. Another 40 percent of all deaths are caused by environmental factors, particularly organic and chemical pollutants. These pollutants are far more deadly in poorer countries where, for example, 1.2 billion people lack clean, safe water and where industrial wastes are dumped untreated into rivers and lakes. Thus your chances of coming into contact with a deadly pollutant are determined by your income. This is true even in the United States where three out of four off-site commercial hazardous landfills in southern states were located primarily in African American communities, although African Americans represent only 20 percent of the population. The industrialized countries already ship 20 million tons of waste annually to the poor countries of the world.

We can perhaps better judge the extent to which we have "progressed" in the degree to which we are protected from infectious disease by examining what it takes for us to die of an infectious disease. At least four things have to happen: first we have to come into contact with some **pathogen** or **vector**—such as a mosquito, tick, flea, or snail—that carries it. Second, the pathogen must be virulent, that is it must be able to kill us. Third, if we come into contact with a deadly pathogen, it must evade our body's immune system. Finally, the pathogen must be able to circumvent whatever measures our society has developed to prevent it from doing harm. As we will see, our chances of dying are affected at every step by social and cultural patterns, particularly by the degree of economic and social inequality.

First, what actions of human beings increase their likelihood of coming into contact with an infectious pathogen? One of the features of cultural history is that cultural complexity has served to increase our exposure to infectious agents. Large, permanent settlements attract and sustain vermin such as rats and fleas, that serve as hosts to microorganisms and ensure their survival and spread. Permanent settlements also result in the buildup of human wastes. Sedentary agriculture requires altering the landscape in ways that can increase the incidence of disease. Schistosomiasis, for example, is a disease caused by worms or snails that thrive in the irrigation ditches constructed to support agriculture. The domestication of animals such as dogs, cats, cattle, and pigs—another characteristic of advanced societies—increases contact between people and disease-causing microorganisms. The requirements of large populations for the storage and processing of food also increases the likelihood of the survival and spread of disease-causing agents. In the modern world, the poorer you are, the more likely you are to be exposed to infectious pathogens.

In addition to coming into contact with an infectious pathogen, the pathogen must be deadly. But this also can depend on your social and cultural situation and your income. In fact, human actions can make a pathogen more or less harmful. Generally it is not to the advantage of pathogens—viruses, bacteria, parasites— to kill their hosts; it is better for the pathogen to allow its host to live and supply its nutrients. However, if the pathogen does not need its host in order to survive, it can evolve into a more deadly form. This is the case with waterborne infections. For example, diarrheal diseases tend to be more virulent if they are spread by water systems and do not require person-to-person contact. The reason is that disease pathogens that spread by contaminated water can survive regardless of how sick their host becomes, while by reproducing extensively in their host it is more likely that these pathogens can contaminate water supplies through the washing of sheets or clothing or through bodily wastes. Thus you are far more likely to contact a more deadly disease if you do not have access to clean and treated water.

Of course even if you come into contact with a deadly pathogen, your immune system is designed to prevent it from killing you. However, the ability of your immune system to function is clearly a function of your diet, and diet is largely determined by income level. In this respect, we have not progressed. In 1950, 20 percent (500 million people) of the world's population was malnourished; today some 50 percent (3 billion) of the people in the world are malnourished. Insufficient food is one of the main factors that increase the likelihood of immune system failure.

Finally, even if our immune system fails to repel an infectious pathogen, societies do develop methods to cure whatever illness afflicted them. And there is little doubt that the discovery of methods to cure infectious disease marks one of the great success stories of modern culture. Unfortunately, citizens' access to these cures is determined largely by the degree of economic inequality in their country, and not by their country's absolute wealth. For example, the United States, the wealthiest country in the world, ranks 25th in the world (well behind all the other rich countries, and even behind a few poor ones) in life expectancy. Not coincidentally, the United States has the largest income gap of any industrialized country; Japan, with the lowest income gap between rich and poor, has the highest life expectancy, in spite of having triple the cigarette usage of the United States.

RESOURCE 2.4

Global Health

Inequality is one of the biggest killers in the world. It denies health care to billions, largely because they do not have the means to pay for it. You can get some idea of the relationship between disease and level of economic development at the World Health Organization Web site at: **http://www.who.int/whr/1998/fig6e.jpg**

Some of the most up-to-date material on the global HIV/AIDS epidemic can be found at UNAIDS: The Joint United Nations Programme on HIV/AIDS. The United Nations provides some information on infant mortality around the world at: **http://unsd.ics.trieste.it/pmappl/unesco/sld022.htm**

You can find links to many sites on global health and the HIV/AIDS epidemic at the author's Web site at: Resources on Disease and Health, **http://faculty.plattsburgh.edu/richard.robbins/legacy/CA/CA_2.htm**

There is also a collection of readings at: Readings on Health and Disease, **http://faculty.plattsburgh.edu/richard.robbins/legacy/disease_readings.htm**

The relationship between wealth and access to cures is most evident with HIV/AIDS. Some 40 million people in the world are presently infected with HIV, with more than three-quarters living in African countries. Medicines exist to prevent HIV from developing into full-blown AIDS, but they are prohibitively expensive and completely out of reach of victims living in poor countries whose health care systems have been decimated by World Bank and IMF policies.

In sum, while we have indeed made dramatic progress in understanding the curing of infectious disease, we have made no progress—and in fact, have regressed and continue to regress—in our ability to provide access to these cures. At the same time, we have increased global exposure to environmental pollutants and infectious pathogens.

The Meaning of Illness

Even if we conclude that modern societies are more susceptible to contagious disease, have they not at least improved the techniques for curing illness? To answer this question, it is important to realize that the meanings given to illness by members of different societies vary as much as the meanings they give to other aspects of their lives. In American society, illness is most often viewed as an intrusion by microorganisms—germs, bacteria, or viruses. Our curing techniques emphasize the destruction or elimination of these agents. Death can occur, we believe, when we have failed to eliminate them. In many other societies, the interpretation of illness is different. Illness may be attributed to witchcraft, sorcery, soul loss, or spirit possession. Belief in witchcraft or sorcery involves a claim that a witch or sorcerer can use mystical or magical power to inflict illness on another person. Belief in soul loss assumes that illness results from the soul leaving the body. Spirit intrusion or possession is based on the idea that a foreign spirit enters the patient and causes illness. These explanations are not mutually exclusive; the soul, for example, may flee the body as the result of witchcraft or sorcery.

Americans sometimes have difficulty appreciating the meanings others place on events, and the meaning of illness is no exception. We fail to recognize that belief in illness or death by witchcraft, sorcery, soul loss, or spirit possession involves an additional belief that illness has social as well as supernatural causes. Members of societies that believe in spiritual or magical causes for illness do not believe that the witch or sorcerer strikes at random, that the soul leaves the body without cause, or that the spirit possesses just anyone. They believe that there also must be a social reason for the witch to act or the soul to flee. Witchcraft involves relationships between people; the witch voluntarily or involuntarily afflicts someone who has offended him or her, or who has breached a rule of conduct. Likewise, in cases of soul loss or spirit possession, the soul leaves the body of a person who is having difficulty with others, or the spirit possesses a person who has created social problems or who has not honored social obligations.

The Chewa of Malawi in southeast Africa claim that illness and death are caused by sorcery. Max Marwick points out that sorcery-induced illness or death does not strike randomly; it occurs when there is a conflict over judicial rights and claims or when someone fails to observe some social norm. Whereas we react to illness or death by seeking the disease or accident responsible, the

In a healing ceremony designed to restore the patient to his proper place in the world, a traditional Navajo doctor paints an image of the universe with colored sand on an earthen floor.

Chewa ask what wrong has the victim committed, with whom has the victim quarreled, or who is jealous of the victim. The Chewa recognize explicitly the connection between sorcery and social tension; they say that people who have quarreled are likely to practice sorcery against each other.

A Chewa who becomes ill consults a diviner to discover the cause of the illness. During the consultation, the patient and the diviner discuss the social roots of the illness. The diviner needs to know about the patient's relationships with kin, and, if ancestral spirits may be responsible, the genealogy of the patient. Thus, Chewa medical theory, while couched in the idiom of sorcery, is a social theory of illness, not simply a supernatural one. Someone gets ill because of a breach in social relations, not solely because of some magical act.

There is a disease syndrome in Latin America called *susto*. There are other terms for it—*pasmo, espanto, perdida de la somba*—but all are based on the belief that the soul has detached itself from the body. Symptoms of susto include restlessness, listlessness, loss of appetite, disinterest in dress or bodily appearance, loss of strength, and introversion. The onset of the illness is said to follow a fright brought on by a sudden encounter or accident, and the cure begins with a diagnostic session between the patient and a healer. After deciding what brought on the disorder, the healer coaxes the soul back into the body. The patient is then sweated, massaged, and rubbed with some object to remove the illness.

Anthropologist Arthur Rubel, who analyzed specific cases of susto, found that all the cases share two characteristics: Susto occurs only when the patient perceives some situation as stressful, and the stress results from difficulties in social relations with specific persons. In one case of susto, a father was afflicted when he discovered he could no longer provide for his family, and in another a mother was stricken when she was not able to take proper care of her child. A wife lost her soul as a result of not honoring her obligations to her husband, while a young boy lost his after he refused to act in a way thought to be appropriate by his peers. In every case, according to Rubel, susto resulted when a person did not or could not fulfill an expected social obligation. In other words, susto, like witchcraft or sorcery, is a statement about social tensions, not simply a description of a magical event.

These traditional theories of illness—soul loss, spirit possession, sorcery, and witchcraft—all have one thing in common. They are all expressions of an **interpersonal theory of disease.** Simply stated, in the interpersonal theory of disease it is assumed that illness is caused not by microorganisms but by tensions or conflicts in social relations. So-called "natural" explanations for illness fail to take into account that witches, spirits, and souls are mediating concepts; they are theoretical entities that, like germs, provide a link between a social cause—tension and conflict—and a physical result—illness or death.

If giving meaning to an instance of illness involves the attribution of illness to social causes, then it follows that the cure must also be, at least in part, social. Therefore, a curer attempts not only to remove a spell, return the soul to the body, or remove a spiritual object that is causing the symptoms of illness, but to repair the social problem that initiated the episode of illness. To illustrate, Victor Turner provides a look at one society, the Ndembu, an agricultural society in northwestern Zambia.

The Ndembu believe that a persistent or severe illness is caused either by the punitive action of some ancestral ghost or the secret malevolence of a sorcerer or witch. The ghosts punish people when they forget to make a ritual offering to their ancestors, or because, as the Ndembu put it, "kin are not living well together." Explicit in Ndembu interpretations of illness is the idea that illness results either from personal failure to fulfill social obligations or from social conflict.

To effect a cure, the Ndembu patient consults a native doctor. The doctor first inquires about the patient's social relations: Has he or she quarreled with anyone? What is the state of the patient's marital relations? Is anyone jealous of the patient? The doctor asks those whom the patient has quarreled with or insulted to participate in the ceremony, a dramatic affair with chanting and drumming, sometimes lasting for hours. People who have complaints about the patient's social behavior may come forward, and the patient may report grudges against neighbors. At the climax, the doctor may dramatically extract from the patient's body some object that could have been causing the illness. In one case that Turner followed closely, the doctor did indeed succeed in patching up a patient's social relations, along with his physical complaints.

The Ndembu recognize, at least implicitly, that social strain and stress may produce physical illness, and one way to treat illness is to treat the sources of social strain. Western medical practice has been slow to recognize the impact of stress on physical health, but there is significant evidence that certain life events can significantly increase the likelihood of becoming ill. Events such as the death of a spouse, the loss of a job, relocation to a new home, even holidays such as Christmas, can increase the chances of illness. These are the same kinds of events that can trigger the need for ceremonial cures in traditional societies. Thus, rather than viewing the healing practices of traditional societies as somehow inferior, it makes far more sense to recognize that they focus on real causes of illness—social stress—that their curing techniques are well equipped to address.

Furthermore, traditional cures not only can be beneficial, they are also affordable. One of the consequences of medical advances is our increasing dependence on expensive technology. Consequently, while significant advances have been made in medicine, the cost to the patient of many such advances has made them unavailable to all but a small percentage of the world's population. Indeed, they are unavailable to many Americans. But in traditional societies, when healing arts are lost or discouraged by Western-educated government officials who consider them backward, members are left with virtually no medical treatment.

EXERCISE 2.4

In an issue of Parade Magazine, the "Ask Marilyn" column features a letter from a man who recommends that we stop trying to contact alien worlds. "It is very likely," he writes, "that any civilization we find will be far more advanced than our own. History has shown that whenever a more advanced civilization comes into contact with a less advanced one, it leads to the destruction of the latter, even if the intent of the former is not hostile." In her response, Ms. Vos Savant says: "In my opinion we should continue the search…While it may be true that less advanced civilizations are absorbed into advanced ones, we usually call this progress, not destruction. Few of us would wish to return to our ancestor's way of living, unless we've romanticized them beyond reality."

Continue the exchange with Ms. Vos Savant. What might you say to her in response?

Question 2.5: Why Are Simpler Societies Disappearing?

Modern societies have not been kind to traditional groups that have retained or tried to retain a way of life that is thousands of years old. Societies such as the Ju/wasi, the Inuit of Alaska and the Canadian Arctic (the proper term for the people we call Eskimos), and the people of the New Guinea highlands have not fared well when contacted by more complex civilizations. Living in small, scattered groups with little need for complex political structures or technology, they were no match for the well-armed, organized, acquisitive people and governments who coveted their land or labor. Even hunting-and-gathering peoples in isolated, seemingly inhospitable locations have proven susceptible to cultural extermination or genocide.

The Ona, for example, inhabited the island of Tierra del Fuego just off the southern tip of South America, whose climate was described by an early settler as 65 days of unpleasant weather and 300 days of rain and storms. After their

Through disease, starvation, and outright killing, European settlers completely
exterminated the Ona tribe of Tierra del Fuego, just off the southern tip of South
America. The last full-blooded Ona died in 1973.

first encounters with Europeans in the 1870s and 1880s, the Ona were exposed
to deadly European diseases to which they had no resistance, such as syphilis,
measles, and tuberculosis; were systematically hunted and killed by European
sheepherders and miners; and were captured by Argentine soldiers and sent to
mission stations or kept by the soldiers as servants. Those that survived on the
island were pushed farther inland, and the animals on which they depended
for food were systematically depleted by European hunters. Having little food on
which to survive, they began to raid sheep ranches and were shot by hunters or
ranchers who were paid a bounty for every Ona killed. At the turn of the century, Europeans built lumber camps in the last forests in which the Ona could
live without being in permanent contact with Europeans. Finally, in 1973, 100
years after the first European settlement was built on Tierra del Fuego, the last
full-blooded Ona died.

  The extermination of the Ona was not an isolated event. Native groups have
been systematically eliminated by representatives of modern societies all over the
world. The Spanish, for example, totally exterminated the natives of the Florida
peninsula. The indigenous peoples of the American plains, who lived by gathering and hunting as late as the 1860s, were first decimated by disease and then systematically driven from their land by miners and ranchers. Today, Native American
populations that were isolated on reservations by government decree face unemployment rates approaching 90 percent and an infant mortality rate that is five
times the national average. In areas of Brazil that are now being entered by Europeans, members of the native population, many of whom still live by gathering
and hunting or small-scale agriculture, are being hunted and killed much as the
Ona were some 100 years ago.

EXERCISE 2.5

It is the year 1967. You are members of a task force of the Botswana government that has been asked to evaluate the living conditions of the Ju/wasi. Another group of government officials, distressed over the primitive ways of the Ju/wasi, had recommended that they should begin to enjoy the benefits of civilization. Specifically, the group recommended that the government should settle the Ju/wasi in permanent villages, dig wells to ensure a steady water supply, distribute domesticated animals to ensure a ready food supply, and introduce modern health services. The group had also recommended that jobs be found for the Ju/wasi.

You have toured the area and spoken to some of the Ju/wasi. Your specific job is to evaluate the recommendations of the previous government task force and then make your own recommendations to the government on how the lives of the Ju/wasi could be improved. You may agree or disagree with the previous panel, but you must give reasons for your recommendations.

Globalization and Cultural Diversity

The passing of traditional cultures has, in recent years, accelerated, largely because of what is termed "globalization," the expansion into virtually all areas of the world of a culture that assumes that trade is the source of all well-being. For example, in their efforts to pay off debts accumulated over the past three decades, countries have been forced to encourage the export of goods and commodities to gain cash to repay these debts. One of the consequences is to reduce support for small-scale agriculturists or peasant farmers. For example, when Mexico entered into the North American Free Trade Agreement (NAFTA) with the United States and Canada, it precipitated a revolt in the State of Chiapas by peasant farmers (the Zapatistas) whose livelihood would be destroyed by the agreement. The agreement forced Mexico to allow large-scale corn farmers in the United States to sell their product in Mexico at a price lower than that of the peasants. Small-scale Mexican farmers may have been able to compete, but their situation was worsened more by the Mexican government's repeal of a portion of their constitution that allowed peasant farmers access to land on which to grow their crops. Part of the problem was that more land was needed by large-scale cattle ranchers to produce beef to sell to U.S. consumers. As anthropologist James D. Nations pointed out, the peasant farmer was faced with a choice of moving to a city to sell popsicles from a pushcart, working for a cattleman punching cows, or rebelling against a situation that seems to have him trapped.

Often the same economic forces that are undermining the foundations of traditional cultures are also promoting environmental destruction. A case in point is that of the Guaraní of Paraguay. There are about 15,000 Guaraní. For centuries their lives centered on the rain forest where they lived by gathering tree crops, growing food crops, raising animals, hunting, and fishing. The first European governor of the area described them in 1541 as "the richest people of all the land and province both for agriculture and stock raising." They quickly entered into trade with Europeans, mostly by gathering and selling a caffeine-bearing plant called *yerba mate.* These trade arrangements did not greatly affect Guaraní life, since they would gather and sell yerba mate only when they needed some Western trade item, such as a metal pot. Consequently Guaraní culture was able to sustain itself and thrive. Just as importantly, the Guaraní sustained the rain forest by adapting their system of forest exploitation to the ecosystem rather then trying to change it. Then in the 1970s, due largely to international trade arrangements, both the Guaraní and the rain forest began to decline.

In the 1970s, Paraguay, as most developing countries, enjoyed an economic boom fueled largely by loans from the World Bank and other international lending agencies. The boom was also fueled by increasing agricultural production in crops such as soy, wheat, and cotton, and cattle raising. This "economic miracle" was accomplished by bringing new areas of land under cultivation; this involved cutting down the forests, selling the timber, and converting the rain forest into farm land or pasture. The rate of rain forest destruction was enormous. From 1970 to 1976 Paraguayan rain forests were reduced from 6.8 to 4.2 million hectares. Half the rain forest had been cut by 1984, and an additional 5 percent a year is disappearing. At this rate the entire Paraguayan rain forest will be gone by the year 2020.

RESOURCE 2.5

Resources on Indigenous Peoples

One accepted definition of indigenous peoples is that adopted by the UN Working Group on Indigenous Populations proposed by Jose Martinez Cobo, and posted here at the Grand Council of the Crees (Eeyou Istchee) Web site at: **http://gcc.ca/Political-Issues/International/who_are_indigenous.htm**

You can find the identity of indigenous nations that exist near you at Nations of the Indigenous One World at: **http://itsa.ucsf.edu/~cuateme/nations.html** or, if you are in Canada, at Windows on Native Lands: **http://indy4.fdl.cc.mn.us/~isk/maps/mapmenu.html**

At their Web site Human Rights of Indigenous Peoples, **http://www.earlham.edu/~pols/17Fall97/indigenous/index.html** Stephen Renard, Jaime Simmermaker, and Amy Stein provide an excellent discussion of the issues involved in the human and political rights of indigenous peoples.

One of the most prominent groups involved in protecting indigenous rights is Cultural Survival **http://www.cs.org**. Founded in 1972 by anthropologist David Maybury-Lewis, Cultural Survival has sponsored research, forums, and publications dedicated to helping indigenous peoples protect themselves and their resources. You can also find links to other sites at the above or at: The Cultural Anthropology Web site at **http://faculty.plattsburgh.edu/richard.robbins/CA/CA_1.htm** or Third World Network, **http://www.twnside.org.sg/**

The culture of the Guaraní is one other casualty of "economic development." Not only was their livelihood destroyed, but new roads built into the rain forest brought with them thousands of new settlers eager to stake out a claim to some portion of the forest, clear it of trees, and grow cash crops. Unfortunately rain forest soil quickly loses its nutrients once its protective forest canopy is cut. Furthermore, all the animals and plants that Guaraní depended on for subsistence are also destroyed. The result has been the displacement of the Guaraní into squatter settlements in the towns and cities, or along the roads built into the rain forests. The wages that they can make working for farmers or in other odd jobs are inadequate to support families, illness and disease have increased, and suicide rates in the past 10 years have more than tripled.

The dilemma of peasant farmers and peoples such as the Guaraní is shared by thousands of other societies and groups around the world. Equally involved in the dilemma are the so-called civilized societies that are responsible for driving small-scale societies to the edge of extinction or forcing them to enter civilization through its dark side of poverty, disease, and forced labor. What image is cast on the civilized world by the shadows of those extinct or near extinct cultures? More important, if we conclude that progress and the change from simple hunter and gatherer societies to modern industrial states is not all positive, we may be short-changing ourselves. By the systematic destruction of the remnants of small-scale societies, we may be eliminating societies whose systems of meaning hold solutions to compelling current world problems, such as environmental destruction, intergroup and intragroup conflict, poverty, and sickness.

CONCLUSIONS

We began this chapter by noting that in a period of 10,000 years human societies have abandoned a way of life that had survived for some 100,000 years. How do we explain why societies of hunters and gatherers changed into societies of sedentary agriculturists? The need to progress and develop better ways of living might explain the change. However, studies of hunter-gatherer societies reveal that they live quite comfortably and with a minimum amount of effort. If we reject the idea of progress, how do we explain the transformation of human societies over the past 10,000 years? An increase in population or population density may have fueled the transition of societies from hunting and gathering to swidden agriculture, and then to plow or irrigation agriculture. But while the transition to more labor-intensive forms of agriculture may have been the result of population pressure, modern agricultural technology may be simply better and more efficient. John Bodley's analysis of the energy expenditures of modern agriculture suggests that it is difficult to conclude that it is in fact simply better.

When we try to understand the gap between the wealthy and poor nations of the world, we find that we must consider the history of the economic expansion of Europe, and the military, political, and social exploitation of the countries of Asia, Africa, and the Americas. We find that hunger is not so much due to a lack of modern agriculture as it is a consequence of poverty and attempts to industrialize. The need to repay bank loans secured for industrialization has led countries such as Brazil to encourage the development of large farms primarily growing cash crops for export. People are dispossessed of their land and left without enough money to buy food.

But modern societies may have an advantage in health care and methods of medical treatment. Aren't Western standards higher than those of less modern societies? In fact, researchers have concluded that infectious disease is more common in modern societies and that human behaviors associated with industrialization, modernization, and the unequal distribution of wealth often promote the spread and incidence of contagious disease. Moreover, traditional theories of illness and curing ceremonies can be effective in the diagnosis and treatment of illness or disease.

Then why, in spite of all they have to offer, are simpler societies disappearing? The answer is that most are disappearing not because of the choice of their members, but rather because of the actions of so-called civilized countries. The idea of progress may simply be a convenient rationale for one society to impose its economic and political will on others.

REFERENCES AND SUGGESTED READINGS

INTRODUCTION: THE DEATH OF A WAY OF LIFE   The epigraph comes from Carmel Schrire's article, "Wild Surmises on Savage Thoughts," in *Past and Present in Hunter Gatherer Studies,* edited by Carmel Schrire (Academic Press, 1984). A general up-to-date discussion of the issues of cultural evolution and a comprehensive bibliography are provided in William H. Durham's article "Advances in Evolutionary Culture Theory," in *Annual Review of Anthropology,* vol. 19 (1990), pp. 187–210. A classic account of cultural history is Alfred L. Kroeber's *Anthropology* (Harcourt, Brace, 1948). A more recent comprehensive work is Eric R. Wolf, *Europe and the People Without History* (University of California Press, 1982).

WHY DID HUNTER-GATHERER SOCIETIES SWITCH TO SEDENTARY AGRICULTURE?   An excellent account of the history of anthropological theory is John J. Honigmann's *The Development of Anthropological Ideas* (Dorsey Press, 1976). Lewis Henry Morgan's book, *Ancient Society,* was originally published in 1877, and reissued by the Belknap Press in 1964. Leslie White's theories of cultural evolution are summarized in *The Science of Culture* (Farrar, Straus and Giroux, 1949) and elaborated in *The Evolution of Culture* (McGraw-Hill, 1959). The description of the Hadza comes from James Woodburn, "An Introduction to Hadza Ecology," in *Man the Hunter,* edited by Richard Lee and Irven DeVore (Aldine Publishing Company, 1968). Elizabeth Thomas's most noted work among the Ju/wasi is found in her book, *The Harmless People* (Alfred A. Knopf, 1959). Lorna Marshall's work is represented in *The !Kung of Nyae Nyae* (Harvard University Press, 1976). John Marshall is best known for his films about the Ju/wasi, including *The Hunters, Bushmen of the Kalahari* and *Ni: Story of a !Kung Woman.* The description of the Ju/wasi by Richard Lee is found in *The Dobe !Kung* (Holt, Rinehart and Winston, 1984). For some dissenting views on the lives of gatherers and hunters, see Carmel Schrire's article, "Wild Surmises on Savage Thoughts," in *Past and Present in Hunter Gatherer Studies,* edited by Carmel Schrire (Academic Press, 1984). See also Edwin N. Wilmsen and James R. Denbow, "Paradigmatic History of San-speaking Peoples and Current Attempts at Revision," *Current Anthropology,* vol. 31 (1990), pp. 489–512. A comprehensive review of the literature on hunter-gatherers is available in Fred R. Myers, "Critical Trends in the Study of Hunters-Gatherers," in *Annual Review of Anthropology,* vol. 17 (1988), pp. 261–282.

Mark Cohen's *The Food Crisis in Prehistory* (Yale University Press, 1977) contains one of the best explanations of the reasons for the adoption of agriculture. Another view is provided by David Rindos in *The Origins of Agriculture* (Academic Press, 1984). Marvin Harris provides an account, also, in *Cannibals and Kings* (Vintage Books, 1977). The analysis of slash-and-burn (swidden) agriculture comes from Robert L. Carneiro, "Slash-and-Burn Cultivation Among the Kuikuru and Its Implications for Cultural Development in the Amazon Basin," in *The Evolution of Horticultural Systems in Native South America: Causes and Consequences, Anthropologica Supplement 2* (1979), edited by J. Wilbert. Information in the tables on land, labor, and agriculture was adapted from Eric Wolf, *Peasants* (Prentice-Hall, 1966). The material on modern potato farming and the potato chip comes from John Bodley, *Anthropology and Contemporary Problems,* Second Edition (Mayfield Publishing, 1985). *The Statistical Abstract of the United States* (1990) provided the information on how many potato chips Americans consume.

WHY ARE SOME SOCIETIES MORE INDUSTRIALLY ADVANCED THAN OTHERS? A brilliant anthropological account of the industrial revolution and its impact on the non-Western world is contained in Eric Wolf's *Europe and the People Without History* (University of California Press, 1982), but the historical material available is vast. Good general sources include the third volume of Immanuel Wallerstein's three-volume account of the expansion of the capitalist world-system, *The Modern World-System III: The Second Era of Great Expansion of the Capitalist World-Economy, 1730–1840s* (Academic Press, 1989), the second volume of Fernand Braudel's three-volume work, *Civilization and Capitalism 15th-18th Century: Vol. II, The Wheels of Commerce* (Harper & Row Publishers, 1982), and Michel Beaud's *A History of Capitalism, 1500–1980* (Monthly Review Press, 1983). John Bodley also supplies an excellent account in Chapter 11 of his textbook, *Cultural Anthropology: Tribes, States, and the Global System* (Mayfield Publishing Company, 1994). A comprehensive answer to this question can be found in *Global Problems and the Culture of Capitalism* (Allyn & Bacon, 1999) by Richard H. Robbins. A comparison of the life of Indian peasants in the fifteenth century and the 1960s can be found in Ashok V. Desai's article, "Population and Standards of Living in Akbar's Time," in the *Indian Economic and Social History Review,* vol. 9 (1972), pp. 42–62.

WHY DON'T POOR COUNTRIES MODERNIZE AND DEVELOP IN THE SAME WAY AS WEALTHIER COUNTRIES? Excellent accounts of the history of the Bretton Woods institutions (IMF and World Bank) and the impact of World Bank policy on developing nations can be found in *Mortgaging the Earth: The World Bank, Environmental Impoverishment, and the Crisis of Development* by Bruce Rich (Beacon Press, 1994) and in *Faith and Credit: The World Bank's Secular Empire* by Susan George and Fabrizo Sabelli (Westview Press, 1994). Additional information on the impacts of the introduction of cash crops and industrialization can be found in Frances Moore Lappé and Joseph Collins, *Food First: Beyond the Myth of Scarcity* (Random House, 1977). See also Parker Shipton's review, "African Famines and Food Security," in *Annual Review of Anthropology,* vol. 19 (1990), pp. 353–395. An excellent overview of the problem of, and reasons for, world hunger can be found in *Hunger and Public Action* by Jean Drèze and Amartya Sen (Cambridge University Press, 1991). An attempt to explain why the Third World has failed to develop (although without considering its colonial past) can be found in Paul Kennedy's *Preparing for the Twenty-First Century* (Random House, 1993). See also *Global Problems and the Culture of Capitalism* (Allyn & Bacon, 1999) by Richard H. Robbins.

HOW DO MODERN STANDARDS OF HEALTH AND MEDICAL TREATMENT COMPARE WITH THOSE OF TRADITIONAL SOCIETIES? The discussion of infectious disease is based largely on Mark Cohen's *Health and the Rise of Civilization* (Yale University Press, 1989) and the chapter on disease in *Global Problems and the Culture of Capitalism* (Allyn & Bacon, 1999) by Richard H. Robbins. Additional material can be found in Ann McElroy and Patricia Townsend, *Medical Anthropology* (Duxbury Press, 1979), and Marcia C. Inhorn and Peter J. Brown, "The Anthropology of Infectious Disease," in *Annual Review of Anthropology,* vol. 19 (1990), pp. 89–117. Information on traditional curing techniques can be found in Peter Worsley's article, "Non-Western Medical Systems," and Allan Young's article, "The Anthropology of Illness and Sickness," both in *Annual Review of Anthropology,* vol. 11 (1982), pp. 315–348 and 257–285. The account of Chewa beliefs about illness and curing comes from *Sorcery in Its Social Setting* by Max Marwick (University of Manchester Press, 1965). The analysis of susto is found in Arthur Rubel, "The Epidemiology of a Folk Illness: Susto in Hispanic America," in *Ethnology,* vol. 3 (1964), pp. 268–283. Victor Turner provides a brilliant analysis of Ndembu cures in *The Forest of Symbols: Aspects of Ndembu Ritual* (Cornell University Press, 1967). A review of the role of stress in illness can be found in an article by James S. House, Karl R. Landis, and Debra Umberson, "Social Relationships and Health," *Science,* vol. 241 (1988), pp. 540–545.

WHY ARE SIMPLER SOCIETIES DISAPPEARING? The account of the Ona comes from Jason W. Clay's article, "Yahgan and Ona—The Road to Extinction," *Cultural Survival Quarterly,* vol. 8 (1984), pp. 5–8. Material on the plight of peasant farmers in Chiapas can be found in Volume 18 of *Cultural Survival Quarterly* (1994). Cultural Survival, Inc., is an organization whose purpose is to assist tribal societies to resist extinction and exploitation. Information about the services, products, and publications of Cultural Survival can be obtained by writing to 53-A Church Street, Cambridge, MA 02138. The material on the Guaraní comes from Richard Reed's book, *Forest Dwellers, Forest Protectors: Indigenous Models for International Development* (Allyn & Bacon, 1997). For a full discussion of the plight of indigenous peoples see John Bodley's book, *The Victims of Progress* (Mayfield, 1999), and *Indigenous Peoples, Ethnic Groups, and the State* by David Maybury-Lewis (Allyn & Bacon, 1997).

Hicks, Edward. Declaration of Independence. Private collection. Art Resource, NY.

C H A P T E R   3

THE CONSTRUCTION OF THE NATION–STATE

PROBLEM 3: HOW DO WE EXPLAIN EMERGENCE OF THE MODERN NATION–STATE AND THE METHODS THROUGH WHICH PERSONS COME TO BELIEVE THAT THEY OWE THEIR ALLEGIANCE TO THEIR COUNTRY?

We seek to create a homogeneous nation. Can anyone reasonably object to that? Is not this the elementary right of every government to decide the composition of the nation? It is just the same prerogative as the head of a family exercises as to who will live in his house.

Australian Minister of Immigration

INTRODUCTION: *Everyone Needs a Country to Which to Belong*

We consider ourselves Canadians, Italians, Germans, South Africans, Japanese, or whichever nation-state recognizes us as citizens. Most of us have been taught that our country has a glorious tradition, replete with founding heroes and sacred documents, monuments, and buildings. The flag of our nation, whichever it is, symbolizes for most of us our allegiance to this tradition. Yet, in fact, few of the some 200 countries or nation-states in the world have been in existence for more than 40 or 50 years, and only a few go back in their present form to the nineteenth century. States, of course, have existed for thousands of years. But nation-states of the sort that now dominate our political landscape, are modern phenomena. How has the nation-state come to have so much importance in our lives? What determines why we "belong" to one country and not another? Why are people willing to die or to kill for their countries? Why are countries so willing, as we shall see, to kill so many of their own citizens?

Killing and dying are important in understanding the role of the nation-state because the use of deadly force is one of the characteristics anthropologists use to define states. "Stateness," as Elman Service put it, can be identified simply by locating "the power of force in addition to the power of authority." A killing by someone other than representatives of the state, as Morton Fried points out, will result in retribution by state police, militia, or military. Carole Nagengast defines the state as a form of social contract in which the public ostensibly has consented to assign to the state a monopoly on force to constrain and coerce people. Nation-states kill. R.J. Rummel estimates that nation-states, in the twentieth century, killed close to 200 million of *their own* citizens: 61 million Russians from 1917 to 1987; 20 million Germans from 1933 to 1945; 35 million Chinese killed by the Chinese Communist government from 1923 to 1949 and 10 million killed by the Chinese nationalists; almost 2 million Turks from 1909 to 1918; and almost 1.5 million Mexicans from 1900 to 1920.

The power to build loyalty and the deaths that result either directly or indirectly from the existence of the nation-state raise a number of important questions. For example, why did human beings organize into large-scale state organizations? Why did the modern nation-state come into existence, and what functions does it perform? How is the nation-state constructed, and how does it bind together an often diverse citizenry? And how can the nation-state survive in an increasingly globalized world? These are the questions we'll explore in this chapter.

QUESTIONS ─────────────────────────────────

3.1 Why did human beings organize into large-scale state organizations?
3.2 Why did the nation–state come to exist and what functions does it perform?
3.3 How is the state constructed and maintained and how does it succeed in binding together often disparate and conflicting groups?
3.4 How is the state to survive in an increasingly globalized world?

QUESTION 3.1: *Why Did Human Beings Organize into Large-Scale State Organizations?*

States, in any form, have not always existed. Some societies do very well without anything approaching state organization. These societies, called "tribes without rulers," represented the only form of political organization in the world until seven to eight thousand years ago. Relatively simple government in these societies involved a chief or village leader with limited power. In gathering-and-hunting societies most decisions were probably made by consensus. Village or clan chiefs may have had more authority than others, but even they led more by example than by any force. The ability to control people was generally diffused among many individuals or groups.

Larger groups might sometimes form for specific activities such as collective hunts, raids on other groups, or to settle feuds. For example, anthropologists recognize what is called a **segmentary social system** that permits people in stateless societies to form into large groups for certain activities. While a segmentary system may vary from society to society in particulars, the household generally is the basic social unit (see Figure 3.1). Household groups are responsible for most everyday activities such as gathering or growing food. The households can combine into larger groups tied together by relations of kinship. These kin groups may function together for ritual occasions or for economic activities (e.g., a group hunt) that requires a larger number of persons. These family units, in turn, may form into villages, while combinations of villages represent still larger groups (e.g., tribes, chiefdoms) whose members recognize, for certain activities (e.g., war, peacemaking, etc.), a common bond. Within each level groups (household groups, kin groups, villages, tribes) are generally political equals. If not, the system is considered to be stratified and is called a **chiefdom.** However, there were generally no permanent privileged classes or elites in a segmentary social system.

Stratified states in which ruling elites claimed the power to demand tribute or taxes likely developed in the flood plains between the Tigris and Euphrates four to five thousand years ago in what is now Iraq. Why, after thousands of years of living in small groups or towns of 50 to 2,000 persons, did people begin to gather in state-sized political units? Why, after hundreds of thousands of years, did ruling elites with control of armed force emerge to dominate the human landscape?

One theory is that population growth and the need for more elaborate means of food production resulted in the emergence of a class of specialists who gained their authority by directing activities. For example, irrigation agriculture requires the building of dikes, canals, and reservoirs to control water flow. These activities

FIGURE 3.1   SEGMENTARY SOCIAL SYSTEM

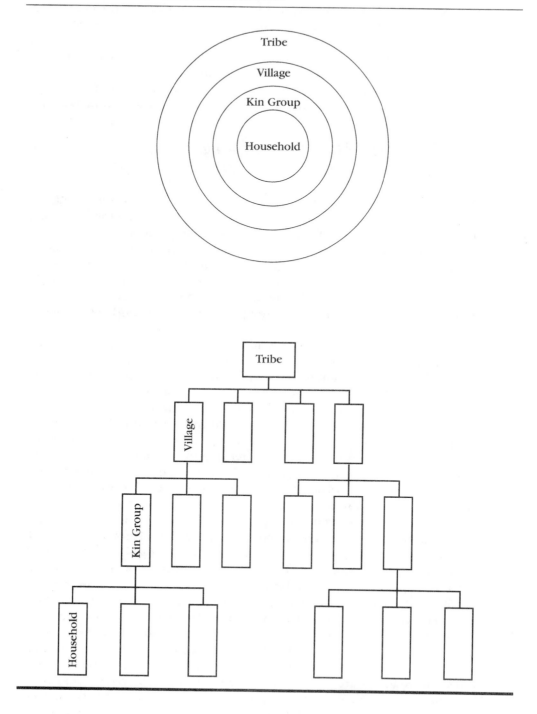

in turn require specialists to plan and direct them. These planners then became an administrative elite that ruled over despotic, centralized states.

Many other frameworks see conflict and the use of force as the central reason for the creation of the state. Karl Marx and Friedrich Engels suggested that early societies were communistic, with resources shared equally among members and little or no notion of private property. In these societies, there was no need for force to protect privilege since resources were shared by all. Technological development, however, encouraged the production of surplus goods that could be taken and used by some persons to elevate their control or power. Asserting control permitted this elite to form a merchant or business class. To maintain their wealth and authority, they created structures of force.

Anthropologist Morton Fried suggests that differential access to wealth and resources creates social stratification. This leads to internal conflict that will require a ruling group to impose their authority and privilege by force. Others propose that external conflict is the motivation for state development. When groups unite under strong central authority, they could, the reasoning goes, easily conquer smaller, less centralized groups and take captives, land, or property. Consequently, if smaller groups were to protect themselves from predator states they, too, had to organize in larger groups, the result being the emergence of competing states, the more powerful ones conquering the weaker ones and enlarging their boundaries. Thus Robert Carneiro suggested that war served to transform isolated, politically autonomous villages into chiefdoms of united villages, thus forming states. At first, war pits village against village, resulting in chiefdoms; then it pits chiefdom against chiefdom, resulting in states; and then it pits state against state, creating yet larger political units.

Elman R. Service suggests that a ruling elite will emerge out of the natural inequalities found in all societies, that some individuals will distinguish themselves and their special qualities, especially during times of need. This will lead people to appreciate the advantages of having someone in control. Thus states and hierarchy emerge as people recognize the advantages of societal integration that formal leadership and bureaucracy can bring.

Of course, none of these theories about the emergence of the state is mutually exclusive; various factors likely played a role in state development. Regardless, large-scale states such as those of ancient Greece, the Roman Empire, or the Chinese dynasties emerged to dominate their historical periods. But these states were likely very different from the modern nation–states to which we belong. There is a difference between a state, as they developed thousands of years ago, and the nation–state as it exists today. A state is a political entity with clearly identifiable components. Citizens of the United States can identify federal buildings (e.g., the Congressional Office Building, the White House, federal courthouse), and name federal bureaucracies (e.g., Congress, the Internal Revenue Service, The Department of Agriculture). They could list the things that state requires them to do—pay taxes, register for social security, obtain citizenship, vote. However to what would they point if asked to give examples of the American nation? They might identify the flag, and say that their nation demands patriotism, but what else? The nation is a far more abstract idea than the idea of the state. A nation is, as Benedict Anderson put it, is "an imagined political community." But why did a new form of political entity develop, and what function did it perform?

QUESTION 3.2: Why Did the Nation–State Come to Exist and What Functions Does It Perform?

Nation-states perform many of the same functions as earlier states; they maintain order, maintain armies, collect tribute and/or taxes, and so on. The major difference between earlier states and the modern nation–state is the extent to which the modern state influences and controls trade. Historically, the increasing importance of trade gave governing elites a greater interest in creating conditions to accumulate profit from trade. Of course, ruling elites have always been interested in the economic life of their subjects. Early states functioned to protect the privileges of the elites by regulating the production of goods and resources, offering protection from other elites, and extracting surplus wealth in the form of tribute and taxes from a largely peasant population. The state also supplied coins and paper money, established standards for weights and measures, protected the movement of merchants and goods, purchased goods, and created and maintained marketplaces where merchants could sell their products.

It was in thirteenth- and fourteenth-century China and, later, sixteenth- and seventeenth-century Europe and Japan that states began to actively promote and regulate trade. By the eighteenth century, rulers were beginning to view trade as the ultimate source of well-being. Consequently states regulated money and passed laws to protect their manufacturers and merchants by imposing taxes and tariffs on goods coming from other states. Military force was used to open markets in other areas, and trading monopolies were granted to groups within their borders. Trading companies such as the East India Company, the Hudson's Bay Company, and the Virginia Company were each granted a charter by state authorities giving them exclusive rights to trade in specific areas. These were the forerunners of today's transnational corporations. States were also responsible for creating and maintaining the infrastructure that made trade possible. States created and maintained ports, built roads and canals, and, later, subsidized railroad construction. States also became major customers. In brief, the nation-state began to develop as a new partnership formed between ruling elites and the merchant class. As Eric Wolf (1982:109) put it:

> The state bought arms and ships. Goods won by force of arms paid for the hiring of mercenaries, for the manufacture of guns and cannon, and for the construction of more ships. The armed merchants foraging overseas needed the state to shield them against competitors and to provide the officialdom capable of holding and consolidating the newly won areas. At the same time the state needed the merchants to lend money to the Crown or to the captains of expeditions; to collect, ship, and sell the goods obtained abroad; and—increasingly—to acquire and export the goods needed in the far-flung outposts of the realm.

Thus the state became the building block of an emerging global economic network. States were guardians of the "national economy," functioning largely to advance the economic life of their citizens. In fact, it would not be inaccurate to say that it is the modern nation-state that creates the conditions that make business profitable, while at the same time ensuring that citizens can afford the things that they want to buy. However, as we shall see, this is possible only if manufacturers do not have to pay the full production cost of what they make and sell, and only if consumers don't have to pay the real cost of things. One only has

One function of the nation-state is to ensure that businesses and corporations profit and that commodities are affordable to consumers. Thus, laws and regulations are written (or not written) that permit corporations to externalize costs so that rarely, if ever, do consumers pay the real price of things. Even a package of Twinkies, which might sell for $1.00, would likely cost far more if externalized costs were included in the purchase price.

to examine the real cost of even the most basic commodities to appreciate the role of the nation-state in making their production and purchase possible. Take, for example, the cost of a Twinkie.

The Nation-State and the Cost of a Twinkie

Twinkies are described by their producers, The Hostess Corporation (a subsidiary of the Interstate Baking Company), as "golden sponge cake filled with creamy filling." More exactly, the Twinkie consists of some 26 ingredients, the main ones being sugar, enriched bleached wheat flour, water, eggs, corn syrup, high fructose corn syrup, partially hydrogenated vegetable shortening, and dextrose.

In the United States and in Canada a package of two Twinkies sells for approximately $1.00. But that is only the store price. To arrive at the real price we would need to examine the hidden costs of each ingredient; in other words we need to calculate the additional monetary and nonmonetary expenses that go to produce and distribute each ingredient in a Twinkie—expenses that, for some reason, are not reflected in the store price. In fact, without the intervention of the nation-state, the real cost of a Twinkie would probably be $10 or higher. The cost is not $10 because of the different ways that the nation-state functions to keep cost accessible and sales profitable.

To illustrate, let us examine just one ingredient that comprises a Twinkie— cane sugar. Environmentally, for example, sugar is not a benign crop. Its production is responsible for damage to coral reefs in Hawaii, water pollution in Buenos Aries, and damage to river estuaries in Brazil and to waterways in the Philippines. Florida's sugarcane industry, situated just south of one of North America's largest freshwater lakes—Lake Okeechobee—dumps phosphorus-laden agricultural run-off that destroys native species and results in the growth of non-native species. As a result, almost $8 billion will be spent over the next two years to fix the Everglades. While some of that cost will be paid by the sugar producers, most of it will be passed on to taxpayers.

Sugar production is also heavily subsidized by the U.S. government, which, through import quotas, limits the amount of sugar that can be imported from other countries. While this raises (rather than lowers) the cost of sugar to the consumer, it also makes sugar production more profitable and results, for example, in the conversion of over 500,000 acres of Everglades wetlands to sugarcane production.

The nation–state also manipulates the price of things by regulating the price of labor. For example, the price of sugar is minimized by paying sugar workers less than a living wage. Thus, while the United States has a "minimum wage," this wage does not apply to agricultural workers, many of whom are migrants from other countries permitted to enter the country, temporarily, only for the purpose of work.

Then there are the hidden health costs. For example, 17 percent of the calories consumed by North Americans are from sugar and other sweeteners. Among other things, that means that our basic nutrition must come from the other 83 percent. While there are no specific data on the direct contribution of sugar to excess weight and obesity (fat is obviously another major culprit), 54 percent of Americans are overweight. One estimate of the direct and indirect cost of obesity in the United States puts the cost at $118 billion annually, or 12 percent of the nation's health care costs. The amount spent on diet drugs and weight loss programs would add another $33 billion. People, of course, are not forced to consume fat and sugar. However food policies and the use of government and tax incentives serve to promote such consumption, particularly among the young.

Indirect subsidies for sugar include government funding of the infrastructure for sugar production and processing. This includes, among other things, the roads, the power system, water and sanitation systems, waste disposal, and so on. The entire water management infrastructure that supports the Florida sugarcane industry, for example, was built with federal tax dollars. Finally, the tax policies of the nation–state are continually adjusted to ensure the maintenance of corporate profits and low prices. Thus in the 1950s the tax bill of corporations in the United States accounted for 39 percent of all federal tax income; in the 1990s the corporate tax bill had been cut to 19 percent.

These are only some of the hidden costs of one ingredient in a Twinkie. To arrive at a real cost we would need to examine each of the other ingredients and then add the hidden costs of processing, packaging, delivery, and waste disposal. The energy and pollution costs of distribution, alone, would be considerable. In Europe and North America a typical food item travels 1,000 miles before it reaches our meal plates. The typical head of lettuce from your local supermarket has traveled an average of 1,200 miles from where it was grown. The shipment of foods, while sometimes necessary, is further encouraged by energy subsidies that allow North Americans to enjoy some of the lowest fuel prices in the world.

Economists estimate that if tax subsidies, government program subsidies, and environmental damage were calculated and other externalities of vehicle use were discontinued, the price of gasoline would be as high as $16.40 a gallon. Instead, gasoline costs less than bottled water.

Then, of course, the nation-state must maintain a standing army—ostensibly to protect us from foreign invaders, but more realistically to guarantee the maintenance of foreign governments with policies friendly to businesses and multinational corporations.

In brief, then, the nation-state creates tax laws, financial policies, environmental regulations, labor laws, and the like, which help corporations and consumers to avoid paying the real cost of production and consumption. These costs are therefore passed on to future generations or people in other countries in the form of low wages, polluted environments, health risks, and the like. Yet, this is, of course, what citizens want. Corporations look to the nation-state to further their interests; to ensure this, corporations spend billions of dollars each year to elect officeholders friendly and sympathetic to their interests. Consumers look to the nation-state to keep the price of things (e.g., Twinkies and gasoline) within their reach. And workers expect the nation-state to enact policies to enhance job and wage growth. None of this could be possible without nation-states to enact and enforce rules and regulations that allow citizens to pass on the real cost of things in the form of environmental damage, health risks, and poverty to people in other countries, as well as to marginalized people in our own countries or to future generations.

EXERCISE 3.2

Each morning, most students begin their day by brushing their teeth, washing their face, and using the toilet facilities. Then perhaps they have a glass of orange juice and maybe a cup of coffee. But what are the hidden costs of these activities? That is, what sort of environmental, health, and economic costs are involved in these activities that we don't pay for directly?

Activity or Product	Hidden Cost
Brushing teeth	
Flushing the toilet	
Orange juice	
Coffee	

QUESTION 3.3: How Is the State Constructed and Maintained and How Does It Succeed in Binding Together Often Disparate and Conflicting Groups?

The maintenance of the national economy is, then, one of the major functions of the modern nation-state. But there remains a problem. To regulate the economic life of its citizens, the state apparatus must promote the economic integration

TABLE 3.1 ETHNIC, RELIGIOUS, AND LINGUISTIC MAKEUP OF SELECTED
NATION–STATES*

Country	Ethnic Diversity	Religious Diversity	Linguistic Diversity
Australia	Caucasian 92%, Asian 7%, aboriginal and other 1%	Anglican 26.1%, Roman Catholic 26%, other Christian 24.3%, non-Christian 11%	English, native languages
Belgium	Fleming 58%, Walloon 31%, mixed or other 11%	Roman Catholic 75%, Protestant or other 25%	Dutch 58%, French 32%, German 10%, legally bilingual
Brazil	White (includes Portuguese, German, Italian, Spanish, Polish) 55%, mixed white and black 38%, black 6%, other (includes Japanese, Arab, Amerindian) 1%	Roman Catholic (nominal) 80%	Portuguese (official), Spanish, English, French
Canada	British Isles origin 28%, French origin 23%, other European 15%, Amerindian 2%, other, mostly Asian, African, Arab 6%, mixed background 26%	Roman Catholic 42%, Protestant 40%, other 18%	English 59.3% (official), French 23.2% (official), other 17.5%
China	Han Chinese 91.9%, Zhuang, Uygur, Hui, Yi, Tibetan, Miao, Manchu, Mongol, Buyi, Korean, and other nationalities 8.1%	Daoist (Taoist), Buddhist, Muslim 2%–3%, Christian 1% (est.) *Note:* officially atheist	Standard Chinese or Mandarin (Putonghua, based on the Beijing dialect), Yue (Cantonese), Wu (Shanghaiese), Minbei (Fuzhou), Minnan (Hokkien-Taiwanese), Xiang, Gan, Hakka dialects, minority languages (see Ethnic diversity entry)
Germany	German 91.5%, Turkish 2.4%, other 6.1% (made up largely of Serbo-Croatian, Italian, Russian, Greek, Polish, Spanish)	Protestant 38%, Roman Catholic 34%, Muslim 1.7%, unaffiliated or other 26.3%	German
Democratic Republic of the Congo	Over 200 African ethnic groups of which the majority are Bantu; the four largest tribes— Mongo, Luba, Kongo (all Bantu), and the Mangbetu-Azande (Hamitic)—make up about 45% of the population	Roman Catholic 50%, Protestant 20%, Kimbanguist 10%, Muslim 10%, other syncretic sects and indigenous beliefs 10%	French (official), Lingala (a lingua franca trade language), Kingwana (a dialect of Kiswahili or Swahili), Kikongo, Tshiluba

TABLE 3.1   ETHNIC, RELIGIOUS, AND LINGUISTIC MAKEUP OF SELECTED
NATION–STATES (CONTINUED)

Country	Ethnic Diversity	Religious Diversity	Linguistic Diversity
Indonesia	Javanese 45%, Sundanese 14%, Madurese 7.5%, coastal Malays 7.5%, other 26%	Muslim 88%, Protestant 5%, Roman Catholic 3%, Hindu 2%, Buddhist 1%, other 1%	Bahasa Indonesia (official, modified form of Malay), English, Dutch, local dialects, the most widely spoken of which is Javanese
India	Indo-Aryan 72%, Dravidian 25%, Mongoloid and other 3%	Hindu 80%, Muslim 14%, Christian 2.4%, Sikh 2%, Buddhist 0.7%, Jains 0.5%, other 0.4%	English, Hindi the national language and primary tongue of 30% of the people, Bengali (official), Telugu (official), Marathi (official), Tamil (official), Urdu (official), Gujarati (official), Malayalam (official), Kannada (official), Oriya (official), Punjabi (official), Assamese (official), Kashmiri (official), Sindhi (official), Sanskrit (official), Hindustani***
Iran	Persian 51%, Azeri 24%, Gilaki and Mazandarani 8%, Kurd 7%, Arab 3%, Lur 2%, Baloch 2%, Turkmen 2%, other 1%	Shi'a Muslim 89%, Sunni Muslim 10%, Zoroastrian, Jewish, Christian, and Baha'i 1%	Persian and Persian dialects 58%, Turkic and Turkic dialects 26%, Kurdish 9%, Luri 2%, Balochi 1%, Arabic 1%, Turkish 1%, other 2%
Mexico	Mestizo (Amerindian-Spanish) 60%, Amerindian or predominantly Amerindian 30%, white 9%, other 1%	Nominally Roman Catholic 89%, Protestant 6%, other 5%	Spanish, various Mayan, Nahuatl, and other regional indigenous languages
Nigeria	Nigeria, Africa's most populous country, is composed of more than 250 ethnic groups; the following are the most populous and politically influential: Hausa and Fulani 29%, Yoruba 21%, Igbo (Ibo) 18%, Ijaw 10%, Kanuri 4%, Ibibio 3.5%, Tiv 2.5%	Muslim 50%, Christian 40%, indigenous beliefs 10%	English (official), Hausa, Yoruba, Igbo (Ibo), Fulani
South Africa	Black 75.2%, white 13.6%, Colored 8.6%, Indian 2.6%	Christian 68% (includes most whites and Coloreds, about 60% of blacks and about 40% of Indians), Muslim 2%, Hindu 1.5% (60% of Indians), indigenous beliefs and animist 28.5%	11 official languages, including Afrikaans, English, Ndebele, Pedi, Sotho, Swazi, Tsonga, Tswana, Venda, Xhosa, Zulu

continued

TABLE 3.1   ETHNIC, RELIGIOUS, AND LINGUISTIC MAKEUP OF SELECTED
NATION–STATES (CONTINUED)

Country	Ethnic Diversity	Religious Diversity	Linguistic Diversity
Turkey	Turkish 80%, Kurdish 20%	Muslim 99.8% (mostly Sunni), other 0.2% (Christian and Jews)	Turkish (official), Kurdish, Arabic, Armenian, Greek
United Kingdom	English 81.5%, Scottish 9.6%, Irish 2.4%, Welsh 1.9%, Ulster 1.8%, West Indian, Indian, Pakistani, and other 2.8%	Anglican 27 million, Roman Catholic 9 million, Muslim 1 million, Presbyterian 800,000, Methodist 760,000, Sikh 400,000, Hindu 350,000, Jewish 300,000 (1991 est.)	English, Welsh (about 26% of the population of Wales), Scottish form of Gaelic (about 60,000 in Scotland)
United States	White 83.5%, black 12.4%, Asian 3.3%, Amerindian 0.8%, Hispanic 11.7%**	Protestant 56%, Roman Catholic 28%, Jewish 2%, other 4%, none 10%	English, Spanish (spoken by a sizable minority)

*Data compiled from the The CIA World Factbook 2000, **http://www.odci.gov/cia/publications/factbook/**

**The U.S. figures total more than 100% because the U.S. Census Bureau considers Hispanic to mean a person of Latin American descent (especially of Cuban, Mexican, or Puerto Rican origin) living in the U.S. who may be of any race or ethnic group (white, black, Asian, etc.). Hence it is not included as a category in the ethnic breakdown. It is added here, however, because it mirrors the linguistic diversity of the United States.

***There are an additional 24 languages in India each spoken by a million or more persons; there are also numerous other languages and dialects that are for the most part mutually unintelligible.

of all those people within its borders, and it must be recognized by its citizens as the legitimate source of authority. It must also regulate the rules through which some people are considered citizens and others are not.

To accomplish these ends the state must create a nation, groups of people who share or who think they share a common culture, language, and heritage, and who willingly identify themselves as members of the nation. Given the fact that virtually all nation-states in the world are composed of peoples with different cultures, languages, and heritages, creating a nation is no easy task. Table 3.1 provides some sense of the ethnic, religious, and linguistic diversity of major nation-states. Somehow these diverse entities must come to see themselves as sharing a common culture, tradition, and heritage to enable state leaders to claim to represent "the people," whoever they might be. Furthermore, if people can be convinced to identify themselves as members of a common political entity, they could more easily accept integration into a national economy, accept the same wages, use the same currency, and demand the same goods. But how does one go about constructing a national identity?

To construct a nation, at least three things need to be done. The first is the creation of the Other, those persons or groups who, by being somehow excluded from or pushed to the margins of the nation-state, accent those persons or groups who are more legitimate members. The Others might be citizens of rival countries who are thought to embody characteristics that are mocked or feared

by members of the nation–state. Thus, for centuries the British could pride themselves on not being Irish or French, while the French could take pride in not
being English. Colonial empires established by the Germans, French, Dutch, and
British would substantiate each country's claim that God or providence had chosen them to rule over "inferior" peoples. In the United States, we maintain our
sense of "nationhood" by drawing boundaries and making Others of migrants
who enter the country, legally or illegally, to work.

The Other may be a category of persons constructed out of largely arbitrary
criteria including physical characteristics, religion, or language. In the United
States, for example, there are movements to establish English as the "official language" of the nation–state, thus effectively implying that non-English speakers
don't quite belong. Others would deny full membership in the nation–state to
those of non-Christian religion, or to people of darker skin colors. By doing this,
people heighten the sense of exclusivity, and, by creating boundaries, more clearly define for themselves their membership in the nation–state.

Race and the Nation–State

Anthropologists have had a curious role in the history of the concept of **race**. In
the nineteenth century, anthropologists participated in trying to construct a
scientific theory of race that legitimized preexisting forms of prejudice and
discrimination (a subject we'll examine in Chapter 7). Then, in the first half of the
twentieth century, anthropologists such as Franz Boas and Ruth Benedict discredited the concept of race to such an extent that over the past twenty years anthropologists have come to virtually reject the idea of race altogether, seeing it
largely as a socially constructed, "folk" concept. In fact, there is virtually no agreement on what race is, only some general agreement on what it is not. Yet it is hard
to dismiss the concept of race when it keeps popping up in pseudoscientific
literature that purports to find "innate" racial differences between groups in one
respect or another, or on official state documents such as census forms, birth or
marriage certificates, or police reports. What does this fascination with racial
classifications have to do with the nation–state?

Political scientists, anthropologists, and political philosophers have generally assumed that membership in the state is voluntary and contractual. In exchange for protection against enemies and the enforcement of rules of behavior,
the idea goes, citizens agree to cede to the state the power to use force. Yet the
premise that citizens make voluntary contracts with the state is not entirely true.
Rather, people are born into the nation–state much as they are born into their
families; they assume the citizenship of one or both of their parents. In fact the
nation–state, by its own rules, decides who is a citizen and who is not. To be a
United States citizen, for example, one must (1) be born in the sovereign territory
of the United States; (2) have a mother who is a United States citizen, or (3) have
a father who is a United States citizen *and* is married to your mother. Or one can
marry a citizen in a ceremony deemed consistent with United States marriage
laws (one wife or husband of opposite gender).* These rules illustrate how the
state defines not only the birth conditions through which a person is deemed a
citizen, but also the rules and nature of what constitutes a legal marriage.

---

*The State of Vermont, the only state that currently recognizes gay marriages, is an exception.

In the same way that the nation–state creates membership rules, it also creates the rules by which people are considered one type of person or another. In the case of race, the nation–state again uses notions of birth and kinship, tempered by geography. Jacqueline Stevens proposes a concept of race implying that degrees of citizenship in the United States are conferred on people based on the degree of closeness to their origins in Europe. For example, what ultimately makes someone black in the United States is understanding that at some point she or he had ancestors in Africa, and what likewise makes someone white is that we understand he or she had ancestors in Europe. Thus, if we recognize that race is by and large a construction of the nation–state to divide citizens by familial origins, a definition of race emerges that sees it as:

> a subpopulation of human beings with observed or imagined physical characteristics understood to correspond with a geographical territory of origins. (Stevens 1999:191–192)

Yet, clearly, the way race is defined is seriously skewed. In the United States individual states determine a person's race by requiring his or her parents' racial identity on birth certificates. Federal forms in the United States require the recording of the race of both parents. Standard forms limit the possibilities. They include: "Other Asian or Pacific Islander," "White," "Black," "Indian (includes Aleut and Eskimo)," "Chinese," "Japanese," "Hawaiian (includes part Hawaiian)," "other non-white," "Filipino." Why are there so many designations for Asians, but no categories "other Black" or "other African?"

For the purpose of entitlement programs and affirmative action policies, the federal government offers the following definition of "Black":

> Black, not of Hispanic origin: A person having origins in any of the black racial groups of Africa.

But what does it mean to have "origins in"? And why "black racial groups?" What about someone who is a descendent of a white South African? The federal government defines an Asian or Pacific Islander as someone "having origins in any of the original peoples of…." But what does "original peoples" mean? Why is it that an Egyptian is classified as "White," when he or she is a member of the Nubian nation and is black?

The point here is that nation–states carefully define the place in the nation–state occupied by various groups, and, through their definitions, clearly privilege one group over another and some individuals over others. Until 1967, the United States had miscegenation laws prohibiting marriage between blacks and whites. Because of these laws, black children of white fathers could not inherit their fathers' wealth. With miscegenation laws and inheritance laws favoring whites on the books into the 1970s, it is no wonder that wealth is distributed the way it is in the United States.

RESOURCE 3.3A

Statement on Race

You can find the American Anthropological Association's statement on race at: **http://www.aaanet.org/stmts/racepp.htm**

Education and the Nation–State

The creation and cultivation of hated or feared Others through such means as war, religion, racial classifications, and empire building—and the marginalization of peoples based on their alleged geographic origins—is not in itself enough to build identity, loyalty, and devotion to the nation-state. Constructing a nation-state also requires the creation of an infrastructure to integrate all members of the state into a common bureaucracy. The nation-state needs to impose some sort of common language on its citizens. It needs to facilitate travel from one area of the state to another; it must build a national media to disseminate information from the state; it must create an infrastructure for the collection of taxes and revenues, and a judicial system through which it maintains authority; it must require military training, and, perhaps most importantly, build a national educational system to train and socialize children to be "good citizens."

Ernest Gellner suggested that the control of education is today even more important than the control of armed force. To perform this role as regulator of the national economy, nation-states must build education systems that enable people to exchange communications with others in a common standardized language. They must be taught to deal with meanings, rather than things such as shovels or plows, and they must learn the complex process through which a button or control activates a machine. In a complex, industrial society, people can't be taught in the family; they must be instructed by specialists operating within a national education system. Most importantly, students must be trained to identify themselves as members of a nation-state, as well as to learn the identity of Others. They must be taught loyalty to their nation-state, and be instructed in patriotism.

For example, in his book, *Learning Capitalist Culture,* a description of a Texas high school, Douglas E. Foley notes how educational process in a Texas town recreates for each generation the attitudes and social structure characteristic of this nation-state. These youth, he says, "learn a materialistic culture that is intensely competitive, individualistic, and unegalitarian." Through team sports and classroom rituals, students learn communication styles that allow them to manipulate their images as well as adult authorities. And they learn the gender and ethnic roles that replicate in their society the divisions on which economic rewards are based.

EXERCISE 3.3

CREATING CITIZENS OF THE NATION–STATE

Students are experts on the role of education in the formation of the nation-state. They are expert because they are the ones most directly involved in the process of creating state citizens, or "patriots." Turn yourself momentarily into anthropological fieldworkers examining the role of education in creating the nation-state. What are some of the activities and the programs that contribute to your identifying with your nation-state?

Violence and the Nation–State

But while the symbolic barriers of excluded Others, infrastructure, and education are essential for nation-building, the use or threat of armed force remains a key instrument in creating and maintaining the nation–state. Killing is the ultimate tool of nation–states. In fact, some anthropologists, among them Pierre van den Berghe, Leo Kuper, and Carole Nagengast, view the nation–state as a genocidal or ethnocidal institution, conspiring to kill or remove those citizens who fail or refuse to conform to the dictates of the imposed national culture, or to destroy their cultures. "Ethnic cleansing" is not a phenomenon of the late twentieth century. For example, the United States, through policies of either aggressive extermination or benign neglect, attempted to kill all indigenous peoples, and assimilate those who remained. Between 1975 and 1979 the government of Cambodia, the Khmer Rouge, systematically murdered some two million of its seven million citizens; in 1994 the Rwandan state slaughtered some 800,000 of its citizens. Carole Nagengast (1994:119-120) wrote:

> The numbers of people worldwide subjected to the violence of their own states are staggering. More than a quarter of a million Kurds and Turks in Turkey have been beaten or tortured by the military, police, and prison guards since 1980; tens of thousands of indigenous people in Peru and Guatemala, street children in Brazil and Guatemala, Palestinians in Kuwait, Kurds in Iraq, and Muslim women and girls in Bosnia have been similarly treated. Mutilated bodies turn up somewhere everyday. Some 6000 people in dozens of countries were legally shot, hung, electrocuted, gassed, or stoned to death by their respective states between 1985 and 1992 for political misdeeds: criticism of the state, membership in banned political parties or groups, or for adherence to the "wrong" religion; for moral deeds: adultery, prostitution, homosexuality, sodomy, or alcohol or drug use; for economic offenses: burglary, embezzling, and corruption; and for violent crimes: rape, assault, and murder.

Pierre van den Berghe claims that what is euphemistically called nation-building is nothing but a blueprint for **ethnocide** at best, **genocide** at worst. Social scientists, says van den Berghe, tend to ignore the genocidal character of the nation-state because of the widespread assumption that nation–states are necessary for maintaining peace and economic stability. Instead, he says, nation–states are, in effect, Mafias or gangs who, through the use or the threat of violence, extract booty for themselves or their elites from rival "gangs" and extract "protection money" from their own citizens.

Other anthropologists share van den Berghe's view of the nation-state as an instrument of force and violence. Carole Nagengast examined not only state killing, but also the use of torture, rape, and homosexual assault to draw the boundaries of the nation-state. State-sponsored violence, she says, serves not only to inflict pain, but also to create what she calls "punishable categories of people," whose existence creates and maintains an Other. These punishable individuals represent an ambiguous underclass believed capable of undermining the accepted order of society. Arrest and torture, she says, stigmatize people and mark them as individuals no one would want to be. Arrest and torture is a way to symbolically mark, discipline, and stigmatize categories of people whose existence or demands threaten the idea, power, and legitimacy of the nation-state. Since torture and violence are committed only against "terrorists," "communists," or "separatists," it becomes legitimate. "We only beat bad people," said a Turkish

The brutalization of East Timor by the Indonesian military and by Indonesian-supported militia from 1975 to 1999 is but one example of how nation–states use force to control its citizens. Here, East Timorese youth are staging a drama portraying the killings of some 271 unarmed protesters by Indonesian troops at the Santa Cruz cemetery on November 12, 1991.

prison official in 1984. "They are no good, they are worthless bums, they are subversives who think that communism will relieve them of the necessity of working." He described with apparent pride the order that he had given that "all prisoners should be struck with a truncheon below the waist on the rude parts, and warned not to come to prison again." "My aim," he said, "is to ensure discipline. That's not torture, for it is only the lazy, the idle, the vagabonds, the communists, the murderers who come to prison" (cited Nagengast 1994:121).

One of the most recent instances of state violence against its own citizens occurred on the island of Timor off the east coast of Indonesia. East Timor had been colonized by the Dutch and the Portuguese, and was granted its independence by the Portuguese in 1975. Five days after a state visit by then Vice President Gerald Ford and Secretary of State Henry Kissinger, the state of Indonesia invaded East Timor. Over the course of the next two decades Indonesians, particularly members and friends of the ruling family, invested millions of dollars in various enterprises. And, as many other countries have done, Indonesia embarked on a campaign of violence and terror in its attempt to integrate the East Timorese into the Indonesian nation–state.

Indonesian anthropologist George Aditjondro, who faced an indefinite jail term for criticizing Indonesian leaders, described the campaign of terror, violence, and torture embarked on by Indonesia against its most recent citizens. It included, among other things, a "pacification war" that lasted from 1975–1979, and continued repression that lasted even after a 1999 United Nations–sponsored referendum in which 80 percent of the population voted for independence from Indonesia. Torture, says Aditjondro, was a standard method of subjugation. Techniques included physical beatings, the use of cigarette butts to burn holes in the skin, electric shock, crushing victims' hands and feet with chair or table legs, poking victims' mouths with bamboo sticks, inflicting pain on the genitals, including raping female victims, and immersing victims in metal tanks filled with water charged with electricity. Also common was the pulling out of fingernails and toenails, cutting the flesh with razors, and cutting penises, tongues, and ears. Torture was used for five reasons according to Aditjondro. First, to obtain information from victims. Second, to crush the fighting spirit of freedom fighters. Third, to weaken the political power of the Catholic Church by obtaining "confessions" of church complicity in pro-independence politics or in sacrilegious or criminal acts. Fourth, to protect the business interests of Indonesians in East Timor, and, finally, to minimize critical press reports from East Timorese newspapers. Some of these offenses were carried out by East Timorese collaborating with the Indonesia military and dressed as ninjas to beat and torture other East Timorese.

But torture was not the only technique of state terror used by Indonesia. There was, for example, physical terror, including mass killings of guerillas— along with women and children—that took place during the first decade of the Indonesian occupation. Some 200,000 people, approximately one-third of the population, were killed or died of deprivations brought about by the terror. Prisoners were thrown to their death from helicopters; people were killed by napalm bombings used also to destroy crops, and thousands died from resulting famines. Many people died in overcrowded prison barracks, some of which were covered with black canvas to turn them into human ovens.

Then there was a campaign to "depurify," as Aditjondro calls it, the bodies of Indonesian women through rape and forced fertility control. Rape was often committed against wives or daughters of men suspected of being involved with the resistance. In other cases rape was committed against women who failed to produce identity cards or who refused to accompany or submit to the sexual demands of soldiers. Other women were forced to spy on resistance forces while serving as sex slaves of Indonesian troops. In other cases, East Indonesian women were forced into brothels for use by Indonesian troops. Rape, says Aditjondro, is also a way of destroying the East Timorese resistance by biologically depurifying their ethnic constituency.

Another means of biologically depurifying the population was through forced contraception. Family planning programs were used as ways of disciplining the population, of symbolically representing state control over human bodies. Thus high school girls were injected with Depo-Provera, a birth control drug, without being told of its function.

There was also symbolic violence that included the building of pro-Indonesian monuments, forcing citizens to participate in Indonesian political rituals, flag raisings, parades, and parties, and subjecting people to arrest, interrogation, and physical torture if they resisted. Language itself was modified with new linguistic expressions for torture and execution becoming common. *Jalan-jalan ke Jakarta* ("Taking a trip to Jakarta") and *Berangkat studi lanjut ke Jawa* ("Going for further study in Java") are euphemisms that meant a person was going to be executed. *Mani laut* ("taking a bath in the sea") referred to the practice of weighting the bodies of people with rocks and dumping them from a helicopter into the sea. *De-Santa Cruz-kan* ("Santa Cruz-ified") is an expression used by mothers to threaten their children with the sinister connotation of a notorious massacre of Indonesian high school students in 1991 who were protesting Indonesian occupation. Finally, some 200,000 people were taken from East Timor and relocated to other parts of Indonesia.

East Timor finally regained its independence from Indonesia in 1999 after a UN-sponsored referendum in which some 80 percent of the population voted for independence. However, before withdrawing from East Timor in September of 1999, Indonesian military and military-trained and military-supported militia laid waste to virtually the entire country, killing thousands of people and driving some 200,000 people out of East Timor and into Indonesia, where many remain under the control of fleeing militia members.

The tactics used by Indonesia to subdue people who resisted integration into the Indonesian nation–state are not unique. In fact, virtually all of these tactics have been used by most, if not all, nation–states at one time or another in their histories. You can get some idea of how nation–states today sponsor violence against citizens by going to the Internet, where information is readily available from organizations such as Amnesty International, Human Rights Watch, and the United States Department of State (see Resource 3.3B).

RESOURCE 3.3B

Web Sites That Report and Detail State Violence

You can find up-to-date information on state violence and human rights at the following Web sites:

Amnesty International: 2000 Annual Report [.pdf]
http://www.web.amnesty.org/web/ar2000web.nsf/

Country Reports on Human Rights Practices for 1999 [Excel]
http://www.state.gov/www/global/human_rights/99hrp_index.html

Concise Guide to Human Rights on the Internet
http://www.derechos.org/human-rights/manual.htm

Human Rights Watch World Report 2000
http://www.hrw.org/wr2k/

Internet Resources on Genocide and Mass Killings
http://www.ess.uwe.ac.uk/genocide.htm

Shielded from Justice: Police Brutality and Accountability in the United States of America—HRW
www.hrw.org/reports98/police/index.htm

QUESTION 3.4: How Is the State to Survive in an Increasingly Globalized World?

Nation-states are presently the political building blocks of the modern world. Citizens derive whatever political rights and privileges they enjoy from their nation-state. Each person is educated, is given or denied permission to travel, compelled to serve in its military, and is bound by the laws of his or her respective state. Yet some people claim that the nation-state is a thing of the past, that in an increasingly globalized world, national boundaries are no longer relevant. Millions of people migrate from their home countries in search of jobs, further blurring national boundaries. Approximately 2 percent of the world's population—120 million people—currently live and work in countries of which they are not citizens. The development of new, transnational institutions, such as transnational corporations, and transnational treaty organizations, such as the World Trade Organization (WTO), are rapidly replacing, some say, the nation-state. Is the nation-state a thing of the past?

The major candidate for the replacement of the nation-state is the transnational corporation. Currently 48 of the richest 100 institutional entities in the world are transnational corporations (see Table 3.2A). One of the reasons for the emergence of the nation-state was to integrate national economies. However, the expansion of the modern global economy requires global, not just state, integration; and the transnational corporation not only has a vested interest in expanding across national boundaries, but also has had the power and financial resources to accomplish that end. One consequence of this development is that corporate interests, as opposed to human interests, dominate the policy agendas of nation-states and the international agencies that they create, support, and control.

A good example of how international agencies can begin to supercede the control of the rules and regulations of the nation-state for corporate interests is the World Trade Organization (WTO). The WTO was established in 1995, by international treaty, with the stated goal of reducing barriers to trade among some 140 member nations. By reducing these barriers, and by ensuring the free flow of goods and services across national boundaries, the proponents of the WTO argue that citizens of all countries will benefit, and they list various benefits to free trade (see Table 3.2B).

However, in spite of these noteworthy goals, the WTO has been the focus of mass public protest. These protests culminated in November of 1999 in Seattle, Washington, when thousands of protesters representing hundreds of labor, environmental, and human rights groups organized to mount what was the biggest demonstration in the United States since the 1968 Democratic National Convention in Chicago. What are these protests to the WTO all about, why should you know about the organization, and what has it to do with anthropology?

The protest involves the question of what constitutes "free trade" and how an unelected body, meeting in secret with no provisions for appeal, can force countries to dismantle environmental, health, labor, and social legislation when it is deemed to be an "unfair restriction on trade."

In brief, when a member country, generally acting for a domestic corporation, feels that the laws and/or regulations of another country or countries

TABLE 3.2A   The Top 100 Global Financial Entities—1999/2000

Rank	Country/ Corporation	GNP/Revenue $US in millions	Rank	Country/ Corporation	GNP/Revenue $US in millions
1	UNITED STATES	8510.675	51	ISRAEL	91.3171
2	JAPAN	3782.946	52	COLOMBIA	90.4063
3	GERMANY	2141.678	53	INDONESIA	88.5515
4	FRANCE	1435.203	54	AXA	87.6450
5	UNITED KINGDOM	1387.440	55	Intl. Business Machines	87.5480
6	ITALY	1169.266	56	SINGAPORE	84.3786
7	CHINA	960.7851	57	BP Amoco	83.5660
8	BRAZIL	776.8286	58	Citigroup	82.0050
9	CANADA	598.8625	59	EGYPT	81.5282
10	SPAIN	554.8851	60	Volkswagen	80.0720
11	MEXICO	424.5240	61	Nippon Life Insurance	78.5150
12	INDIA	420.3054	62	IRELAND	78.3242
13	NETHERLANDS	378.1987	63	Siemens	75.3370
14	AUSTRALIA	363.9098	64	CHILE	74.3185
15	ARGENTINA	339.8068	65	Allianz	74.1780
16	KOREA	310.1118	66	Hitachi	71.8580
17	RUSSIA	283.8242	67	MALAYSIA	67.4845
18	SWITZERLAND	262.6460	68	Matsushita Electric Industrial	65.5550
19	TAIWAN	258.8676	69	Nissho Iwai	65.3930
20	BELGIUM	251.3653	70	PHILIPPINES	64.5262
21	SWEDEN	226.8869	71	PAKISTAN	64.1293
22	AUSTRIA	212.4617	72	PERU	64.0548
23	TURKEY	196.9821	73	U.S. Postal Service	62.7260
24	MYANMAR	189.7544	74	ING Group	62.4920
25	General Motors	176.5880	75	AT&T	62.3910
26	DENMARK	174.1033	76	Philip Morris	61.7510
27	Wal-Mart Stores	166.8090	77	Sony	60.0520
28	HONG KONG	166.4958	78	LIBYA	59.5000
29	Exxon Mobil	163.8810	79	Deutsche Bank	58.5850
30	Ford Motor	162.5580	80	Boeing	57.9930
31	Daimler-Chrysler	159.9860	81	Dai-ichi Mutual Life Insurance	55.1040
32	POLAND	148.9580	82	Honda Motor	54.7730
33	NORWAY	145.8926	83	Assicurazioni Generali	53.7230
34	SAUDI ARABIA	125.8401	84	Nissan Motor	53.6790
35	FINLAND	125.4124	85	CZECH REPUBLIC	53.2500
36	GREECE	120.7235	86	NEW ZEALAND	52.7135
37	Mitsui	118.5550	87	E. ON	52.2270
38	IRAN	118.5098	88	Toshiba	51.6340
39	Mitsubishi	117.7760	89	Bank of America Corp.	51.3920
40	THAILAND	117.0386	90	Fiat	51.3310
41	SOUTH AFRICA	116.3242	91	Nestlé	49.6940
42	Toyota Motor	115.6710	92	SBC Communications	49.4890
43	General Electric	111.6300	93	Credit Suisse	49.3620
44	Itochu	109.0690	94	Hewlett-Packard	48.2530
45	PORTUGAL	107.7889	95	HUNGARY	47.8293
46	Royal Dutch/Shell Group	105.3660	96	UNITED ARAB EMIRATES	47.2339
47	Sumitomo	95.7010	97	Fujitsu	47.1950
48	VENEZUELA	95.0164	98	Metro	46.6630
49	Nippon T & T	93.5910	99	ALGERIA	46.6016
50	Marubeni	91.8070	100	Sumitomo Life Insurance	46.4450

Country GNP data from the World Economic Outlook 1999 Database (IMF) at: **http://www.imf.org/ external/pubs/ft/weo/2000/02/data/index.htm**; Corporate income data from Forbes' Global 500 at: **http://www.fortune.com/fortune/global500/**

TABLE 3.2B   PROPOSED BENEFITS OF THE WORLD TRADE ORGANIZATION*

1. The system helps promote peace.
2. Disputes between nations are handled constructively.
3. Free trade rules make life easier for all.
4. Freer trade cuts the costs of living.
5. Free trade provides more choice of products and qualities.
6. Free trade raises incomes.
7. Free trade stimulates economic growth.
8. The basic principles of free trade make life more efficient.
9. Governments are shielded from lobbying.
10. The system encourages good government.

*See http://www.wto.org/english/thewto_e/whatis_e/10ben_e/10b00_e.htm

constitute an unfair restriction of trade, it can ask the WTO to investigate. If a panel, appointed by member countries, agrees with the claim, it can allow the country to impose trade taxes and tariffs on goods imported from the offending countries or country. For example, most European countries impose a tariff on bananas imported from Central America, but not from some Caribbean countries, such as Jamaica. This policy favors Caribbean countries, since it makes Central American bananas more costly to European consumers. The rationale for the tariffs dates back to when Caribbean counties were colonial outposts of Great Britain and France.

Regardless of the reasons for the preferences, the United States appealed to the WTO, claiming it constituted an unfair trade barrier to bananas coming from Central America. The United States acted largely because Central American banana plantations were owned primarily by United States corporations, some of whom contributed considerable amounts of money to the election campaigns of members of both the Republican and Democratic parties. The WTO ruled that the tariffs imposed by European countries on Central American bananas did, in fact, constitute an unfair restriction on trade. The WTO does not have the power to force countries to change their trade rules; however it can permit offended countries (the United States in this case) to impose tariffs on selected goods of offending countries. Thus the WTO permitted the United States to impose import tariffs on such things as British cashmere and French cheeses, thus increasing their cost to U.S. consumers, and likely reducing the profits of British wool producers and French farmers.

Some rulings of the WTO are deeply disturbing to health, labor, and environmental advocates since the WTO can apply pressure to countries to change health, labor, or environmental laws if its dispute panel rules that these laws constitute an unfair restriction on trade. For example, if a country banned a product from another country because of a fear of health risks, the country in which the product was manufactured or produced could charge the banning country with creating an unfair barrier to trade. The country passing the law would then have to prove to the WTO panel that the ban was "scientifically based." If it could not, then trade sanctions and penalties could be applied to the banning country. A prominent case involves the European ban on hormone-treated beef produced in

"Free Trade" is often simply a way for corporations to pressure nation–states to relax labor, social, and environmental laws. These citizen-activists are protesting actions by the World Trade Organization (WTO) that try to force countries to repeal environmental and labor regulations that the WTO claim represent "an unfair restriction on trade."

the United States and Canada. Injecting hormones into beef cattle is legal in both the United States and Canada; however, there is some research that suggests that treated beef may be harmful. Europeans are particularly sensitive to health threats in meat because of (1) the emergence of mad cow disease (Creutzfeldt-Jakob disease) in Great Britain that is spread by eating meat from animals that have consumed infected feed, (2) the subsequent ban on British beef by European countries, and (3) fears about cancer-causing dioxins in meat and egg products in Belgium.

The United States, at the request of ranchers and beef processors, brought the case to the WTO, claiming that the ban on beef was an "unfair restraint of trade" and that there was no clear scientific evidence of health risks. The WTO ruled in favor of the U.S. corporations, thus forcing European consumers to accept American hormone-treated beef or accept restrictive tariffs on selected European products sold in the United States. So far, Europe has refused to overturn the ban, and the United States has been permitted to impose tariffs on selected European imports, including truffles from Italy. A similar case involves the European ban on genetically engineered produce from the United States, which Europeans also fear may introduce health risks. The U.S. government claims that this also is an unfair restraint of trade (some 40–60 percent of U.S. soy and corn is genetically modified), and that there is no clear scientific evidence that there are risks, and so on.

These disputes threaten the so-called "precautionary principle," which says that if a product or process poses risks to health or the environment, scientific certainty is not necessary to prohibit or control the product or process. Thus Europeans reason that while there is no absolute scientific proof that hormone-treated beef and genetically modified produce are harmful to health, there is enough research to raise real health concerns. However the WTO rejects the precautionary principle; it argues that there must be proof that something is harmful before a country can ban it. Thus, in the case of hormone-treated beef and genetically engineered produce, Europeans must accept their import or allow the United States and Canada to impose penalties on European products, thereby putting political pressure on European governments to lift the bans.

In another case, U.S. environmental laws have run afoul of WTO regulations. The United States sought to protect endangered sea turtles. Legislation was passed prohibiting U.S. importation of shrimp from countries that do not require their fishing boats to use special turtle-excluder devices to prevent turtles from getting ensnared in shrimp nets. The restriction prompted numerous nations to comply by requiring such devices, but other countries—India, Malaysia, and Pakistan—chose to launch a WTO challenge. In 1998, the WTO panel ruled that the law was indeed an "unfair" restriction on trade.

Thus, some critics claim, "free trade" has less to do with trade and helping citizens of WTO member countries than it does with allowing global corporations to force nation–states to alter or remove environmental, health, and social regulations that interfere with their business. Critics claim that international agencies are being controlled and manipulated, for the most part by corporate powers that will determine not only what we buy, but also the conditions under which our goods are produced and how they are distributed.

The power of corporations to influence health, environmental, and social laws through international agencies is just one example of their increasing power and influence. Corporations are also able to work through other agencies and institutions to determine or influence government policy. Among these are private forums, such as the Council on Foreign Relations, the Bilderberg (named for the Hotel de Bilderberg of Oosterbeek, Holland), and the Trilateral Commission, that bring together people from government, business, the media, and academia to discuss public policy beneficial to corporate interests. For example, recommendations made in the late 1930s by the Council on Foreign Relations and its journal, *Foreign Affairs,* prompted the United States to eventually organize the Bretton Woods conference that led ultimately to the formation of the World Bank, the IMF, and the Global Agreement on Trade and Tariffs that evolved into the WTO. The Trilateral Commission consists of 325 people and has included heads of all the major corporations, many who hold influential government posts, as well as American presidents (Carter, Bush, Clinton). Meeting largely in secret, these groups provide forums for corporations to influence and control the policies of nation–states and multilateral organizations of which they are members.

Corporations also promote their interests through lobbying groups and public relations efforts targeted to political leaders and the public. Protected by the free speech provision of the First Amendment, corporations are able to organize massive public relations campaigns to further their interests.

RESOURCE 3.4 ─────────────────────────────

Resources on Globalization Protests

The recent and ongoing protests against multinational agencies such as the WTO, the IMF, and the World Bank are directed against what many people see as undemocratic procedures that transfer power from citizens to corporations and international financial agencies. You can find out more about these protests at the following Web sites:

Citizen's Global Trade Watch Web site
http://www.citizen.org/pctrade/tradehome.html

Corporatism and Globalization
http://www.life.ca/subject/corporate.html

Corporate Watch
http://www.corpwatch.org

You can get the other side of the picture at:

International Monetary Fund
www.imf.org/

World Trade Organization (WTO)
www.wto.org/

Corporations, like nation-states, have even been able to organize armed force to support their interests. In labor conflicts going back to the nineteenth century, corporations have built their own armies and police forces to control employees, and today have been known to work closely with armies in developing countries, even supplying arms and equipment in some cases. In other cases, countries, fearful of not being able to attract or maintain corporate investment, engage in military campaigns against their own citizens who protest the turnover of national resources to transnational corporations. Anthropologists have only recently turned their interest to the implications of these changes for people and cultures throughout the world.

CONCLUSIONS

In this chapter we have examined the reasons why human beings organize themselves politically into large state organizations, and how the use of force is central to any definition of the state.

We then explored the emergence of a new type of organization, the nation-state. Nation-states perform many of the same functions as earlier states, but with a greater emphasis on the control and growth of trade. We proposed that the modern nation-state creates the conditions that make business profitable, while at the same time ensuring that citizens can afford the things that they want to buy. The nation-state performs this function by allowing manufacturers, consumers, and laborers to pass on a great amount of the real cost of things to future generations, to people in other countries, or to marginalized members of their own society.

We then explored how nation–states succeed in binding together often disparate and conflicting groups into one "people." There must be the creation of some "Other." The Other consists of persons or groups excluded from the nation–state, who in turn create boundaries between those persons or groups who are legitimate members and those who are not. The criteria for creating Others can include physical characteristics, religion, or language.

Constructing a nation–state also requires an infrastructure that serves to integrate all members of the state into a common bureaucracy. Chief among these is an education system in which participants learn what it means to be members of their nation–state. Force, violence, and terror have also been instruments of maintaining discipline among the membership.

Finally, we examined the future of the nation–state and the roles of corporations and multilateral institutions, such as the World Trade Organization (WTO), in creating and maintaining the rules and conditions that order our lives.

REFERENCES AND SUGGESTED READINGS

INTRODUCTION: EVERYONE NEEDS A COUNTRY TO WHICH TO BELONG   The opening quote appears on page 6 in Jacqueline Stevens's book, *Reproducing the State* (Princeton University Press, 1999). Classic anthropological analyses of state formation and organization can be found in *Origins of the State and Civilization: The Process of Cultural Evolution* by Elman R. Service (W.W. Norton, 1975) and Morton H. Fried's book *The Evolution of Political Society: An Essay in Political Anthropology* (Random House, 1967). Carole Nagengast provides an excellent review of the literature on state violence in "Violence, Terror, and the Crisis of the State" in the *Annual Review of Anthropology,* vol. 23 (1994), pp. 109–136. A good history of state killing is provided by R. J. Rummel in *Death by Government* (Transaction Press, 1994).

WHY DID HUMAN BEINGS ORGANIZE INTO LARGE-SCALE STATE ORGANIZATIONS?   In addition to the Service and Fried books mentioned above, an excellent review of anthropological literature on the state can be found in *Political Anthropology: An Introduction,* Second Edition, by Ted Lewellen (Bergin & Garvey, 1993). The concept of nation–states as "imagined communities" comes from Benedict R. Anderson, *Imagined Communities: Reflections on the Origin & Spread of Nationalism* (Verso, 1991).

WHY DID THE NATION–STATE COME TO EXIST AND WHAT FUNCTIONS DOES IT PERFORM?   A classic anthropological treatment of the origin and function of the nation–state can be found in Eric Wolf's book, *Europe and People Without History* (University of California Press, 1992). Other classic treatments of the function of the nation–state include Fernand Braudel's *Civilization and Capitalism 15th–18th Century: Vol. II, The Wheels of Commerce* (Translated by Siân Reynolds. Harper & Row, [1979] 1982) and Immanuel Wallerstein's *The Modern World-System III: The Second Era of Great Expansion of the Capitalist World-Economy, 1730–1840s* (Academic Press, 1989).

HOW IS THE STATE CONSTRUCTED AND MAINTAINED AND HOW DOES IT SUCCEED IN BINDING TOGETHER OFTEN DISPARATE AND CONFLICTING GROUPS? There is a comprehensive description of the construction of the nation–state in *Global Problems and the Culture of Capitalism* (Allyn & Bacon, 1999) by Richard H. Robbins. Jacqueline Stevens describes the ways that nation–states define their membership in *Reproducing the State* (Princeton University Press, 1999). The role of education in maintaining the nation–state is discussed by Ernest Gellner in *Nations and Nationalism* (Cornell University Press, 1983) and in *Learning Capitalist Culture* (University of Pennsylvania Press, 1990) by Douglas E. Foley. Pierre van de Berghe's description of the nation–state as "genocidal" is found in "The Modern State: Nation-Builder or Nation-Killer?" in *International Journal of Group Tensions,* vol. 22 (1992), pp. 191–208. The discussion of torture and violence comes from Carole Nagengast's article mentioned above. George Aditjondro describes the violence in East Timor in "Ninjas, Nanggalas, Monuments, and Mossad Manuals" found in *Death Squad: The Anthropology of State Terror* (University of Pennsylvania Press, 2000) edited by Jeffery A. Sluka.

HOW IS THE STATE TO SURVIVE IN AN INCREASINGLY GLOBALIZED WORLD? The future of the nation–state is discussed in *Global Problems and the Culture of Capitalism* (see above). A classic treatment of the power and influence of multinational corporations can be found in David Korten, *When Corporations Rule the World* (Kumarian Press, 1995). An excellent discussion of the role of multilateral institutions on nation–states can be found in *Vanishing Borders: Protecting the Planet in the Age of Globalization* by Hilary French (W. W. Norton, 2000).

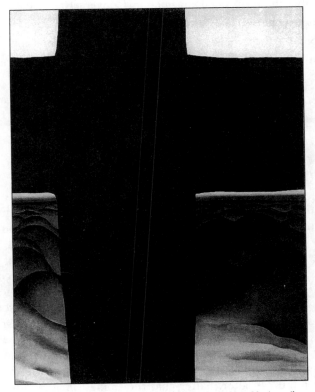

Georgia O'Keeffe, American, 1887–1986, Black Cross, New Mexico, oil on canvas, 1929, 99 × 77.2 cm, Art Institute Purchase Fund, 1943.95. Photograph © 1997, The Art Institute of Chicago, All Rights Reserved.

C H A P T E R   4

THE SOCIAL AND CULTURAL CONSTRUCTION OF REALITY

PROBLEM 4: WHY DO PEOPLE BELIEVE DIFFERENT THINGS, AND WHY ARE THEY SO CERTAIN THAT THEIR VIEW OF THE WORLD IS CORRECT AND OTHER VIEWS ARE WRONG?

There is an obvious rightness about our own world view. It seems, in some way, to mirror reality so straightforwardly that it must be a consequence of direct apprehension rather than effort and imagination. Conversely, alternative beliefs possess an obvious wrongness. The more natural our own perspective becomes, the more puzzling become the strange propositions of ancestors, aliens and eccentrics. How did such mistaken ideas come to be held? However have they remained uncorrected for so long?

Barry Barnes

INTRODUCTION: *The Central Question*

How is it that people can believe in a God whose existence cannot be proven? How can they believe in the existence of ancestor spirits, or witches, or devils, or believe in the power of magic to call forth spirits of the dead? Yet, of course, people do believe these things, and even take these beliefs for granted. Most Americans, for example, believe in the existence of God, and according to most surveys, a vast majority believe in the existence of Satan and the possibility of demonic possession. Many Americans daily consult their horoscope, believing that the position of the stars at their birth somehow affects their destiny. Some Americans believe in witchcraft; there are some 80,000 members of Wicca in America, people who are inspired by witches, wizards, druids, and kabbalists of largely European lore to practice what they consider to be magic, and who claim that mind can alter matter, that the trained imagination can affect the material world.

How to deal with the problem of belief has long been a concern of anthropologists. When confronted with, say, a belief in witches, the temptation is to take for granted that the belief is mistaken. In that case the task of the anthropologist is to explain how it is that people can believe in things that are wrong. Early anthropological efforts at understanding religion took this approach. Edward Tylor, considered by some to be the founder of modern anthropology, wrote in 1871 that religion and a belief in the supernatural developed through people's attempt to explain basic phenomena, such as death and dreaming. What is the difference, Tylor imagined early human beings thinking, between a live person and a dead one, between a sleeping person and someone who is awake? They must have reasoned, Tylor said, that there was something, some kind of essence, that left the body in death, or that traveled to distant places in sleep's dreams. From this reasoning came, Tylor said, a belief in the idea of a soul that animated the body, but that fled the body in death and sleep. That is why, Tylor said, that the word for "breath" and the word for "soul" are the same or similar in so many societies. And it was not unreasonable, said Tylor, for these early philosophers to imagine that other animals and things were also animated by souls.

Once a belief in souls was arrived at, it was a small step to reason that there were places that departed souls resided, and a smaller step to believe that souls became gods. And it was logical, then, for human beings to appeal to these departed spirits for help in controlling life's uncertainties. For Tylor, then, beliefs in gods and spirits developed through the attempts of human beings to explain certain events, to understand why things happened as they did. The answers, he assumed, were of course wrong; but they were founded in the human need to explain and interpret experience.

French sociologist Émile Durkheim also asked, in his classic work *The Elementary Forms of the Religious Life* (1961 [1912]), what suggests to the human mind the existence of God? Durkheim speculated, as did Tylor, that the secret must lie in the beliefs of early human beings. Thinking that the lives of early human beings would best be studied by looking at societies that were relatively underdeveloped, Durkheim undertook to read about the religious beliefs of the indigenous people of Australia, particularly their beliefs about **totemism.** The totem, said Durkheim, was some element of nature—an animal, an insect, a plant, or some celestial phenomenon—that served as a symbol for a group or clan. The totem was worshipped, was considered sacred and holy by the members of the group. It also served as a flag, a concrete representation of the group. If members of the group worshipped the totem, and if the totem was a symbol of the group, was it unreasonable to suppose, said Durkheim, that it was the group—the clan itself—that was being worshipped?

But what would suggest to people the power of the totem, its sacredness? The answer, said Durkheim, lay in the constraints that people feel are imposed on them by the group and by society, and in the special power that people feel when groups come together in celebration and **ritual.** And if in small-scale societies people worship the group through their symbolic representations, as clans worship themselves through their totems, is it not reasonable to suppose that in large-scale societies people worship society through their god or gods? That God is society?

RESOURCE 4.0

Resources on Religion

There are many resources on the Web for the study of religion. Some of the best general resources are:

Adherents.Com
http://www.adherents.com/

BeliefNet
http://www.beliefnet.com/

Comparative Religion—A Directory of Internet Resources for the Academic Study of Religion
http://www.academicinfo.net/religindex.html

Finding God in Cyberspace: A Guide to Religious Studies Resources on the Internet
http://www.fontbonne.edu/libserv/fgic/intro.htm

The Religious Movements Homepage
http://cti.itc.virginia.edu/~jkh8x/soc257/home.html

Virtual Religion Index
http://religion.rutgers.edu/vri/index.html

There were many other attempts to explain what it was that suggested to human beings the idea of God. Sigmund Freud, for example, speculated that people projected on an imagined God the power of the father, that in worshipping God, people were worshipping the father; Bronislaw Malinowski claimed that people turn to gods and spirits to influence life events that they feel helpless to control. But all of these early writers approached the question of God in particular, and religion in general, with the assumption that the beliefs were essentially in error. Nevertheless, they felt that religious beliefs served some purpose: that the beliefs and rituals may have increased group cohesion, or served to provide supernatural sanctions for the violation of group norms.

Recent anthropological attempts to understand belief have built on these early efforts, but the general thrust has been to try to understand how it is that people are persuaded that their view of the world is correct. Some researchers have even extended their studies to include so-called scientific beliefs, reasoning that the processes that result in people taking the existence of God for granted must apply as well to the taking for granted of a naturally ordered universe of atoms, molecules, genes, electrical and magnetic forces, social imperatives, and the like.

To answer the question of how it is that people can so easily believe that their view of the world is correct, we need to examine a number of concepts. Since language is one of the mediums we use to make our knowledge concrete and to communicate with others, it plays a major role in giving us a sense of the universe and ourselves. **Symbolic actions**—the rituals, myths, arts, literature, and music that we enjoy or participate in—all play a role, as we shall see, in organizing and making concrete a particular view of the world. Also, we need to explore how people learn to view the world as they do, and how they defend their beliefs against skeptics. Certainly the fact that others agree or disagree with us about the nature of the world will influence what we believe is true or not true, and also determine how we react to experiences that challenge a particular view of the world. What we believe must also be, in some way, a product of our social, economic, and political life. Finally, we need to ask why people sometimes radically change what they believe.

QUESTIONS

4.1 How does language affect the meanings people assign to experience?

4.2 How does symbolic action reinforce a particular view of the world?

4.3 How do people come to believe what they do, and how do they continue to hold to their beliefs even if they seem contradictory or ambiguous?

4.4 How does the way we live affect our beliefs and rituals?

4.5 How can people reorder their view of the world if it becomes unsatisfactory?

QUESTION 4.1: How Does Language Affect the Meanings People Assign to Experience?

Language is one medium through which we make contact with the world that we take for granted. We tend to assume that it is only a transparent medium for the transmission of thought, a tool for communication. Anthropologist Edward Sapir challenged this view of language, suggesting that specific languages serve not only as a medium of communication, but also to define and guide our perception of experience. That is, specific languages—French, English, Navajo, Chinese, Tupi, or any of the other thousands of languages that human beings speak—somehow order the experiences of those who speak them. Benjamin Lee Whorf later elaborated on Sapir's ideas and suggested that each language constitutes a frame of reference that orders a particular people's views of the world.

The relationship between language and thought can exist at various levels. The most obvious is at the level of vocabulary. According to Sapir and Whorf, for example, vocabulary reflects the social and physical environment of a people. Whorf noticed, for example, that the Inuit have a variety of words for different kinds of snow, while we have only one, and that the Aztecs of Mexico used the same word for cold, ice, and snow. Sapir noted how the vocabulary of the Nootka of the northwest coast of North America precisely defined the variety of marine animals on which they subsisted, and the vocabulary of the Paiute, living in the desert regions of southern Utah and northern Arizona where complex directions were needed for finding water, contained detailed descriptions of features of the landscape. Our own rich vocabulary for expressing units of time is linked to our concern for the temporal ordering of activities. Sapir suggests that the vocabulary of a language not only reveals what is important to the speakers of a language but also cues the speakers to be more sensitive to the named features of their environment.

Sapir and Whorf also explored the relationship between the grammar of a language and the modes of thought characteristic of its speakers. In English, Whorf points out, there are two dominant types of sentences: the subject-predicate type, such as "The book is green," and the actor-action type, such as "Sally runs." In both cases, the subject of the sentence—the book in the first case, Sally in the second—is spoken of as if it were an enduring object, something stable through time that acts or is acted on by something else. Whorf maintains that this indicates a pervasive tendency in English to view the world as being made up of objects, so that experiences described in English lose the fluidity of passing experience. For example, we speak of time as if it were an object or thing, as if we could isolate a piece of it ("I'll study for three hours"), the same way we select food ("I'll take three hamburgers"). In English grammar, time occupies the same grammatical space as food. In this sense our grammar reflects, reinforces, and perhaps determines our general view of the world as consisting of objects or substances, with everything perceived as an attribute of some object.

Another implication of our way of speaking of time has to do with our sense of controlling it. Since, in English, time may take the role of an object, we are able to quantify it and to speak of "saving" it or "wasting" it.

The ideas of Edward Sapir and Benjamin Lee Whorf, generally referred to as the **Sapir-Whorf hypothesis**, suggest a link between language and culture,

ARM YOURSELF WITH THESE FOODS IN THE FIGHT AGAINST CANCER.

Americans use metaphors of war to explain and interpret many aspects of life, as in this poster designed to encourage people to change their eating habits to reduce the risk of cancer.

but both were very careful to avoid claiming that there is a causal link between language and thought. Not all anthropologists are convinced there is an explicit link between the grammar of a language and the culture of the people who speak that language. But there is another sense in which language serves to give meaning to different events, and it has to do with the idea of metaphor.

Borrowing Meaning with Metaphors

One major characteristic of human language is its economy. That is, the same words we use to describe one area of experience can also be used to describe another area. If this weren't so, we would need a specific vocabulary for every distinct experience we wished to describe; instead of a working vocabulary of hundreds of words, we would need a working vocabulary of millions! Fortunately we can escape that problem through the use of metaphor, taking linguistic expressions from one area of experience and applying them to another. Expressions such as "the shoulder of the road" or "the foot of the mountain" illustrate the metaphoric extension of parts of the human body to refer to features of the landscape. "Joe is a snake," "Sally is a fox," "Jeff is a dog," or "Charley is a pig" are expressions that represent metaphoric extensions from the animal world to the human world. Metaphors take language from one **domain of experience,** such as the domain of the body or the domain of animals, and apply it to another domain, such as persons or landscape features.

But when language is extended from one domain to another, meaning is also extended. In other words, metaphor involves not only *speaking* of one experience in terms of another but also *understanding* one experience in terms of another. For example, when we speak about argument, we might say that "His point was right on target," or "Your claims are indefensible," or "She attacked my argument, and I had to defend my position." Or we might say that "She shot down my argument," or "I think I won the argument." We speak of argument in terms of war, taking the language from the domain of war and applying it to the domain of conversation. But we have not only transferred words; we have also transferred meaning. We don't simply talk about argument in terms of war; we actually win and lose arguments.

What would happen if, instead of metaphors of war, we borrowed metaphors from the domain of dance to comprehend argument. We might talk about the rhythm of the interaction or the grace of the performance. In fact, this wouldn't be argument at all; instead of two protagonists in a win-or-lose situation, we would have two partners trying to coordinate their movements to arrive at a mutual accommodation.

Or think about the way our conception of illness is embedded in the language we use to describe it. We take language from the domain of war and use it to talk about health. We build our defenses against illness; we get ill because our resistance was low. We fight a cold, destroy germs, wage war on cancer, and have heart attacks. The language that AIDS researchers use is full of metaphors drawn from war. Recent research reports that the AIDS virus weakens the "immune system attack force" or the "killer cells" that are meant to "destroy virus-stricken cells." As one researcher put it, "If you want to think of it with a war analogy, it's as though the soldiers are still on maneuvers, but they no longer have their weapons: When they encounter the enemy, they lose their weapons."

EXERCISE 4.1A

Carefully examine the photograph above. Describe what thing is happening in the photograph, and see if you can draw some conclusions about the nature of baboon society from your description.

Not all societies borrow from the domain of conflict to give meaning to health. The Navajo, for example, see illness as a displacement of the person from his or her proper place in the universe. Illness is a disruption of harmony.

The human body and war, of course, are not the only domains from which Americans borrow to assign meaning to other areas of experience. Americans borrow also from the domain of economic exchange. In English, time is spoken of not only as if it were a distinct thing, but also as if it were a specific type of thing: "Time is money," "You're wasting my time," "This gadget will save you hours," "I don't have the time to give you," "That flat tire cost me an hour," "You need to budget your time," "He's living on borrowed time," "Is that worth your while?" Time in American culture is a valuable commodity, a scarce resource that we quantify, invest, and spend.

Sports represents another domain from which Americans borrow heavily for metaphors. For example, a male baseball enthusiast might describe a romantic encounter in this way: "I met a girl, I thought she'd play ball, and that I'd not only get to first base, but score; but I struck out." A follower of astrology might describe the same event this way: "I met a girl, I thought we'd be Leo and Cancer, that we'd be in conjunction, and she would be the sun to my moon, but our stars were crossed." The differences between the two descriptions of the same event involve more than a simple difference in language. Metaphors from different domains of experience assign different meanings to the same event. The baseball enthusiast, using a metaphor common to American youth, sees the experience as a contest to be won or lost, and as a way of demonstrating proficiency. The follower of astrology, on the other hand, sees the meeting as a fated, predetermined event; it involves not winning or losing but rather the discovery of preexistent compatibility.

Love is a highly abstract concept, and the language of love is full of metaphors that try to locate the concept into a domain of experience that helps us make sense of it. We try to make it concrete with metaphors of economic exchange, "I make you feel good about yourself, and you in exchange make me feel good about myself." We use metaphors drawn from the world of work; we find people "working out a relationship," or "working at it," and so on. Or we use metaphors and language drawn from electronics and communication; we "get through to each other," or talk about "not being able to communicate anymore." Psychologists who write about love make frequent use of medical metaphors; they speak of a lack of love as a "disease," or of love as an "addiction." Robert C. Solomon in *Love: Emotion, Myth, and Metaphor* (1981) provides an excellent discourse on such language of love.

Metaphors, then, are not simply verbal devices that we use to make our language colorful and economical. Rather, they are like theories, templates, lenses, or filters we can use to help us understand one domain of experience in terms of another. By using language from one domain of experience to describe another, whole domains of meaning are transferred; arguments become wars, time becomes a commodity, and romantic encounters become contests. Moreover, the metaphors we use to describe experiences may predispose us to seek certain solutions to problems associated with those things and people. A Navajo cure seeks to return the patient to a state of harmony with the social and natural universe. Does our speaking of illness in terms of war and battle encourage us to take for granted that it is some kind of war? And, if it does, how does that view determine the kinds of treatment for illness that we devise and seek? Doesn't the language that we use to describe illness predispose us to cures that destroy the agent of disease rather than return the patient to health?

The fact that Americans borrow so heavily from the domains of war, sports, and economic exchange for metaphors suggests another way to understand how language operates to influence people's views of the world. Most societies seem to have one or more domains from which they borrow extensively for metaphor. These domains become **key metaphors** that give to each culture a style or cast that makes the culture distinctive. By thinking and speaking of many domains of experience in terms of a particular domain, a certain coherence is achieved in the meanings in any culture.

Kwakiutl Metaphors of Hunger

Perhaps one of the most spectacular expressions of the elaboration of both a key metaphor and the human imagination is found among the Kwakiutl of British Columbia. Much of our knowledge of the traditional life of the Kwakiutl we owe to Franz Boas, one of the founders of American anthropology; his Kwakiutl assistant, George Hunt; and filmmaker and photographer Edward Curtis. Boas and Hunt's descriptions served as the basis for Ruth Benedict's description of the Kwakiutl in her classic work, *Patterns of Culture*, and more recently for Stanley Walens's analysis of Kwakiutl belief.

Walens suggests that the act of eating is a key metaphor for the Kwakiutl; that is, the Kwakiutl speak of many different things using the vocabulary and language associated with hunger, eating, and food. A fundamental meaning the Kwakiutl find in their experience is that the universe is a place in which some beings are eaten by other beings, and some beings must die so that other beings may eat them and live. Eating gives life in at least two ways; it provides nutrition, but it also frees souls. The Kwakiutl believe that when a person dies his or her soul leaves the body and enters the body of a salmon. But the soul cannot be freed until the physical body is destroyed; for this reason the Kwakiutl place their dead on scaffolds where the body can be devoured by ravens and other birds. Once the soul enters the body of a salmon it remains there, living in a salmon world that socially resembles the human world. However, when the salmon is caught and eaten by human beings, the soul is once again freed and enters the body of a newborn child. Thus, for the Kwakiutl the act of eating becomes a metaphor through which much of their life is understood and described.

The importance of eating for the meanings the Kwakiutl ascribe to experience is manifested in the images of mouths that visually dominate Kwakiutl art, ritual, and **myth.** Their world, says Walens, is replete with the mouths of animals killing to satisfy their hunger, and their art is filled with gaping jaws of killer whales, fangs of wolves and bears, and tearing beaks of hawks, eagles, and ravens. Dancers wear masks of cannibal birds with nine-foot-long beaks that shatter human skulls to suck out the brains. The woods are inhabited by wild women with protruding lips who wait to rip apart and devour travelers and misbehaving children. It is a world where suckling infants turn into monsters and devour their mothers.

The Kwakiutl use the eating metaphor to give meaning to a wide range of their experiences. Hunger is associated with greed, for, like unrestrained hunger, greed causes people to accumulate wealth far beyond what they need, often taking from others who are left without. Moreover, people who hoard food would, in effect, be hoarding souls, preventing the return of a soul from the spirit world. Consequently, the Kwakiutl place great emphasis on gift-giving and generosity. Hunger is also equated with immorality. The Kwakiutl have few means of maintaining social control; there are no police or courts, and violence is often the only recourse available to people who believe they have been wronged. Since the Kwakiutl believe that human desires create conflict and destruction that can quickly get out of hand, people must work together to prevent and control conflict before it threatens to destroy the group. And hunger is metaphorically associated with children, because they constantly demand to be fed and will, if allowed, devour all a family's food.

EXERCISE 4.1B

There are some interesting parallels between the metaphors of eating and hunger among the Kwakiutl and the metaphors of sexual intercourse and sexual desire in America. Kwakiutl art, myth, and stories are filled with mouths and images of eating and hunger. What are some of the images that fill American expressive culture (advertising, for example)? Vomit is a life-giving substance for the Kwakiutl; what symbolizes life-giving in America? Are there other ways Americans use sexual symbolism that are similar to the ways the Kwakiutl use hunger and food?

Metaphors of eating and being eaten abound in Kwakiutl life. In this religious ceremony, dancers portray cannibal birds with long beaks, and a totem pole includes faces with gaping mouths.

But to fully appreciate the impact of a metaphor it is necessary to understand that by ordering and describing a view of the world according to a particular domain of experience, people are drawn to try to control their lives by controlling the domains of experience they use to represent aspects of their lives. The Kwakiutl believe that the real solutions to the problems of greed, conflict, and child rearing are to actually control hunger. Eating is highly ritualized and controlled; food must be carefully handled. Food must also be generously given to others to avoid accusations of greed. In fact, wealthy persons are said to vomit forth goods, vomit having for the Kwakiutl a distinctly different meaning than it has for Americans. For the Kwakiutl, vomit is a life-giving substance. Animals that regurgitate their food—wolves that vomit food for their young and owls that regurgitate the bones of small animals they have eaten—occupy a special place in the Kwakiutl world. And the socialization techniques of the Kwakiutl are geared to teaching children to control their hunger. In sum, a single domain of experience—eating—has been elaborated by the Kwakiutl to give to their world a style and meaning unique to them.

The Metaphors of Contemporary Witchcraft and Magic

A metaphor is a theory, a system of interpretation that, once understood in the context of one domain of experience, can then be transferred to others. The metaphors may also be embedded in myth and history, as well as everyday experience. A good example of that is modern witchcraft and magic.

Anthropologist Tanya M. Luhrmann details some of these practices in her book *Persuasions of the Witch's Craft: Ritual Magic in Contemporary England* (1989). Luhrmann joined various covens and groups in England whose membership consists of middle-class urbanites who situate their magic in "new age" ideology, the "Age of Aquarius"—people who place an emphasis on natural foods, good health, and personal stability, and whose magical practices consist largely of conjuring spirits, reading the tarot, and magical healing.

Modern magic is based on the assumption that mind and thought can affect matter without the intervention of the thinker's actions. It assumes that thought and matter are one. Magicians believe, says Luhrmann, that it is a distortion to treat objects as isolated and unique. One manual says that we must see things:

> not as fixed objects, but as swirls of energy. The physical world is formed by that energy as stalagtites [sic] are formed by dripping water. If we can cause a change in the energy patterns, they in turn will cause a change in the physical world—just as, if we change the course of an underground river, new series of stalagtites will be formed in new veins of rock. (quoted in Luhrmann 1989:118)

A key metaphor embedded in modern witchcraft and magic is that of stratification, of "planes" and "levels." For the follower of white (good) witchcraft, or magic, or the tarot, the universe is divided into a complex collection of entities and beings, each of which exists on different "planes," "astral planes," or "levels," of which the everyday plane of material life is but the lowest. After death, for example, the soul does not die, but goes to exist on another plane, some remaining in contact with the material world. Other magical forces exist on other levels, but they too can be harnessed by human beings to influence events on the everyday

Adherents of tarot cards use them to foretell the future and to interpret their own experiences in life.

plane of existence. Moreover, the properly trained human mind can actually, simply by imagining it, create forms on the "astral plane" that may in turn affect things in the material world.

Becoming a magician, Luhrmann says, requires the acquisition of specialized and esoteric knowledge; consequently magicians read books, arrange and attend rituals, go to meetings, and learn the tarot, astrology, mythology, and seventeenth-century Gaelic cures.

The tarot deck consists of 78 cards that comprise an elaborate and complex system of metaphoric associations that link various domains of experience that range from an understanding of the planets and other celestial objects (sun, moon, etc.), to colors, material elements (e.g., mercury, iron, gold, etc.), emotions, personal qualities, and mythological beings. Each of the tarot cards is said to have some meaning that is determined by its association with a specific planet, an element, an emotion or human quality, and so forth. Aleister Crowley, one of the founders of modern magic and witchcraft, and a designer of the modern tarot deck, says that each card is, in a sense, a living being.

The magician uses the tarot cards to divine the future, but the cards also provide ways for people to interpret their own lives. The cards, says Luhrmann, provide people with a symbolic map with which to interpret and understand themselves as they transfer the meaning of the cards to their own lives and experiences. Thus, some may associate themselves with the Empress, calm and fecund, or they may say that someone has the temperament of a Hermes, mercurial and unpredictable. And in associating themselves with a particular card, people also associate themselves with a specific planet (e.g., Mars—dominant and aggressive), or color (e.g., red—emotional and passionate), and so forth. In a sense, one may begin to define oneself in terms of the tarot, and actually become the person that the cards delineate. The transfer of meaning creates meaning.

In examining the power of metaphor to define our realities, we must remember that there is no necessary connection between the domains from which people draw metaphors and the domains to which they apply them. There is no natural connection between commodities and time, war and health, eating and immortality, the tarot's Empress and someone's personality. These borrowings are the products of the human imagination. Many different metaphors can be applied to a specific experience, and one domain can never be the exact replica of the other. No man is really a tiger, no woman really a fox. How can there be "different levels" of reality? Metaphoric borrowings are intrinsically absurd. Yet we constantly seem to confuse one domain with another; we really do fight disease; we really win arguments. And so we need to explore by what magical means people are convinced that by controlling one domain of experience (e.g., eating), they can really control another (e.g., greed). Or that by imagining themselves in a different "level" of reality, they can actually contact the "astral plane."

QUESTION 4.2: *How Does Symbolic Action Reinforce a Particular View of the World?*

Language represents one way that our experience of the world is socially filtered. By sharing a language we also share a view of the world expressed in the vocabulary, grammar, and metaphors of the language. But language is not the only way that our social life mediates between our senses and the meanings that we assign to experience. We also participate in activities that express a particular view of the world. Especially important are symbolic actions such as ritual, myth, literature, art, games, and music. Symbolic actions carry bundles of meanings that represent public displays of a culture. They are dramatic renderings and social portrayals of the meanings shared by a specific body of people. More importantly, symbolic actions render particular views of the world in a way that makes them seem correct and proper.

This idea can be illustrated with the game of chess. Chess originated in India or China as a favorite pastime of the aristocracy. Its original meanings are unknown, but the game is often considered to be a representation of war. It is, however, one in which each side has exactly the same number and kinds of pieces, and the two sides alternate their moves. If it is a symbolic representation of war, it is a highly stylized and carefully regulated war, and unlike any that has ever been fought.

But chess is more than a game; it is a statement, a story about hierarchy and the social order. Pieces (pawns, rooks, knights, bishops, kings, and queens) are ranked in terms of importance and are given a freedom of movement corresponding to their ranking. Consequently, each game of chess is a story about social hierarchy that reinforces the validity of a social system based on rank order. Each time the game is played, the authenticity of this social system is proven true: The side with the highest ranking pieces remaining is almost always the winner. And, significantly, the game validates the importance of the generals (the two players), who control the movement of their side's pieces on the board. It is the strategist, the thinker who wins the war (game), not the soldiers. Even the king is dependent upon the general. Since in every chess game each side starts out with the same number and kinds of pieces, it must be the strategist, the head of the hierarchy, who determines the outcome of the game, and by extension, the well-being of the society. Chess reinforces the axiom that rank is power, and power is achieved by outwitting an opponent; a pawn, in itself, can never defeat a queen, any more than a peasant can threaten a king. There are winners and losers, but, regardless of which side wins, the match in a crude way represents the superiority of the aristocracy over the peasants.

As a game, chess assures the players of the rightness of hierarchical forms of social organization. However, participating in a single game of chess is not likely to convince anyone that the world portrayed in the game works as the game says it works. Instead, the meanings that characterize a culture are repeated again and again in other symbolic actions, the most important of which may be ritual.

The Kwakiutl as well as the witchcraft and Western Mystery groups described by Tanya Luhrmann provide good examples of how ritual portrays, reinforces, and provides evidence for a particular view of the world.

The Kwakiutl Cannibal Dance

The Kwakiutl view of the world, as we noted in Question 4.1, rests on metaphors of hunger and is graphically displayed in their language, myth, art, and ritual. One of the most important Kwakiutl rituals is the Cannibal Dance. The following description of the dance is necessarily a simplified one, but it includes the basic outline of the ceremony.

The Cannibal Dance is a four-day spectacle that serves as the highlight of the Kwakiutl Winter Ceremonial, a period of celebration and ritual observance in which all worldly activities cease. It is a time set aside for the spiritual world of the Kwakiutl, filled with monstrous and powerful beings and animal spirits, to intersect with the real world. The dance varies in some detail from group to group, but in all it is the focal point of a youth's initiation into the Cannibal Society, a group responsible for performing certain rituals. The initiate plays the role in the ceremony of the cannibal dancer, or *hamatsa*. Members of the Cannibal Society and others gather in a ceremonial house to call back the cannibal to the human world from his sojourn in the realm of Man Eater, one of the most important of the supernatural beings in the Kwakiutl pantheon of spirits.

At the beginning of the ceremony, the hamatsa (the initiate) is believed to be in the woods frantically searching for human flesh to devour. Some early ethnographic accounts of the dance report that he would actually eat human mummified remains. Meanwhile, members of the Cannibal Society gather around a fire in the ceremonial house to sing and recite prayers to entice the hamatsa into the house, periodically sending men out to see if he is approaching the village. Finally, the prayers and calls of the Cannibal Society attract the hamatsa who arrives, dressed in branches of the hemlock tree, by pushing aside roof boards and jumping down among the celebrants. Jumping through the roof is supposed to symbolize descent from the spirit world above to the world of the living, below. In a seeming frenzy, the hamatsa runs around the fire and then into an adjacent room, leaving behind only the sacred hemlock branches he had worn. During the four days of the ceremony the celebrants try by various means to entice him back into the house and, in effect, tame and socialize him, convincing him to forsake his craving for human flesh and accept normal food. For example, in one part of the ceremony the hamatsa flees the house and a member of the Cannibal Society is sent as the bait to attract him. The hamatsa rushes upon him, seizes his arm, and bites it. Each time he bites someone, he dashes into a secret room and vomits, an act that is repeated various times during the ceremony.

During pauses, members of the audience exchange gifts; wealthy persons are expected to give away more than others. Later the hamatsa appears naked and is given clothes, but he flees again. At another point a woman who serves as a co-initiate appears naked, carrying mummified remains; she dances backward trying to entice the hamatsa to enter the house, but she fails. Finally the group succeeds in subduing the hamatsa by bathing him in the smoke of cedar bark that has been soaked in menstrual blood. After the conclusion of the public part of the Cannibal Dance, the initiate and a few members of the Cannibal Society go to another house and eat a normal meal, the final symbol that the hamatsa has been tamed, that his craving for human flesh has been replaced with a desire for ordinary food.

Ritual can be viewed as a symbolic representation of reality that makes it seem as if the reality were absolutely true. In another sense, the ritual presents participants in the ritual with solutions to real problems, in the same way as symbolic representations suggest real solutions. For the Kwakiutl the hamatsa is the ultimate projection of the power of hunger, and his desire for human flesh is a manifestation of the forces that can destroy society. The participants in the ritual, by symbolically taming the hunger of the hamatsa, are asserting their moral responsibility to control greed and conflict. The ritual is the acting out of the successful efforts of the group to overcome forces that threaten society. Here is how Walens puts it (italics added):

> The *hamatsa*'s hunger is fearsome; but it is the same hunger felt by every human, and thus every human has the power to control it. Ultimately the *hamatsa* and the bestial ferocity he embodies can be conquered. Morally the force of controlled social action, the strength of ritual, can conquer even a Cannibal's hunger. In fact, ritual can totally alter the impetus of the Cannibal's hunger, changing it from a destructive act to an affirmation of self control, an act of creative power. *The winter ceremonials prove that no matter how terrible the power of hunger, no matter how many fearsome guises it assumes, no matter how many masks it wears, and no matter how many voices it speaks with, morality will be the ultimate victor.* So long as humans have the knowledge to use food correctly, they need never fear hunger nor its awful accompaniment, death. (Walens 1981:162)

The Cannibal Dance also contains a powerful message about socialization. Children, like the hamatsa, come from the spirit world and enter the world naked. Like the hamatsa, children have a female assistant, their mother, who must feed and socialize them; they dance and kick in the womb where they live off the flesh of their mothers. Children come into the world hungry, threatening to devour their parents' wealth. Thus, in the Kwakiutl view of things, all humans are cannibals who must be socialized and tamed. Through swaddling, ritual fasting, denial of food, and other actions, parents transform their children from cannibals into moral human beings. The Kwakiutl, through ritual enactment, have made their symbols real. Their world really is as the ritual depicts it, and their lives in part revolve around living the reality they have created.

The Ritual of Contemporary Witchcraft and Magic

> In a witches' coven in northeast London, members have gathered from as far
> away as Bath, Leicester, and Scotland to attend the meeting at the full moon....
> The sitting room has been transformed. The furniture has been removed, and a
> twelve-foot circle drawn on the carpet.... Four candlesticks stake out the cor-
> ners of the room, casting shadows from stag antlers on the wall. The antlers sit
> next to a sheaf of wheat, subtle sexual symbolism. In spring and summer there
> are flowers everywhere. The altar in the centre of the circle is a chest which
> seems ancient. On top an equally ancient box holds incense in different draw-
> ers. On it, flowers and herbs surround a carved wooden Pan; a Minoan god-
> dess figure sits on the latter itself amid a litter of ritual knives and tools.

This is the setting for one of rituals that Tanya Luhrmann attended in the
course of her fieldwork on contemporary witchcraft and magic. These rituals, she
says, were particularly important because they comprised one of the ways that
people became convinced of the validity of their beliefs. Going on to describe the
ritual in the above setting, Luhrmann writes:

> The high priestess begins by drawing the magic circle in the air above the
> chalk, which she does with piety, saying "let this be the boundary between the
> worlds of gods and that of men".... On this evening a coven member wanted
> us to "do" something for a friend's sick baby. Someone made a model of the
> baby and put it on the altar, at the Minoan goddess's feet. We held hands in a
> circle around the altar and then began to run, chanting a set phrase. When the
> circle was running at its peak the high priestess suddenly stopped. Everyone
> shut their eyes, raised their hands, and visualized the prearranged image: in
> this case it was Mary, the woman who wanted the spell, the "link" between us
> and the unknown child.,... By springtime, Mary reported, the child had recov-
> ered, and she thanked us for the help. (Luhrmann 1989:42)

Rituals like this one, like the Cannibal Dance of the Kwakiutl, or like those
enacted in thousands of mosques, churches, and synagogues across America are
special occasions that not only involve the enactment of key metaphors; they
serve also as special events set aside from everyday existence, events that draw
participants into an emotional involvement with the metaphors. Rituals really
do produce special feelings; people are carried away with the symbolism, the
music, and the social communion with others, and it is easy in this situation to
come to believe that it is not the ritual itself that produces these feelings, but the
forces or powers that the ritual is believed to summon or embrace. As Luhrmann
puts it:

> Just because you have a profound experience during prayer, it does not mean
> that God exists. But people often find the distinction hard to handle: they tend
> to accept the magical or theological ideas because the involvement—the spiri-
> tuality, the group meeting, the moving symbols, the sheer fun of the prac-
> tice—becomes so central to their lives. (Luhrmann 1989:178)

In contemporary witchcraft and magic great emphasis is placed on visual-
ization and meditation as part of the ritual. The high priest or priestess may relate
a story and ask the participants to imagine themselves in the story; it may be a
walk through a moonlit wood, or a voyage with Sir Francis Drake around the
Horn of Africa. After the ritual people report actually experiencing the salt spray
on their face, or the pitching of the sea, and they experience fellow participants
as shipmates aboard Drake's ship Golden Hind. In other words, the ritual not

only dramatically depicts a metaphor, it teaches the participants how to experience the world as if the forces, gods, and spirits were truly real. Consequently, it is not unusual, in any belief system, for people to claim when participating in ritual to have had a "mystical experience," to experience themselves as "one with the universe," or as being overwhelmed with love or light. Thus, ritual not only teaches us about the world depicted in our metaphors, it also teaches us how to feel within the universe we create.

Dorothy Meets Luke Skywalker

Contemporary witchcraft and magic draw heavily from myth and literature for their language, symbols, and metaphors. Luhrmann reports that many of the magicians she came to know were first attracted to their beliefs when they read J. R. R. Tolkien's *Lord of the Rings,* or Ursula LeGuin's *Earthsea Trilogy,* or Marion Zimmer Bradley's *Mists of Avalon.* The themes of many of these books, and of contemporary witchcraft and magic in general, are contained in American popular culture. These books and movies contain **key scenarios**—stories, or myths that, like ritual, portray certain values and beliefs. In the same sense that people act out and communicate their view of the world in ritual, and come to learn how to feel in that world, they can be said to act out the scenarios contained in their myths.

Joseph Campbell spent most of his life studying the myths of people around the world. In one of his earlier books, *The Hero with a Thousand Faces,* Campbell concludes that myths from all over the world contain stories about a hero who embodies the most valued qualities of that society. The myths have a consistent scenario—a hero, separated from home, family, or society, embarks on a journey in search of something: knowledge, a magical object, a person, or even a vision. In the course of the journey the hero encounters a mentor, someone who conveys some kind of power to the hero. When the hero meets up with strange creatures or powerful forces that make it difficult to reach a goal, helpers appear to assist and protect the hero. Eventually the hero faces death but, with the help of the mentor's power, escapes and ultimately reaches the goal.

EXERCISE 4.2

From what you remember about both *The Wizard of Oz* and *Star Wars,* how does each represent the process of coming of age? Are there key differences in the stories that are significant? Consider the following questions: What does each of the heroes, Luke and Dorothy, seek? From whom do they obtain their power? What form does the power take, and why are the differences significant? What helpers join the heroes, and what is the hero's relationship to them? How do the heroes destroy evil, and what is the reaction to their heroic deeds? Finally, what lesson does each hero learn, and in what way have their adventures transformed them?

If the scenario sounds familiar, it probably is; it has been the source for many stories, books, and films. George Lucas, for example, wrote the script for his movie *Star Wars* using Campbell's writings on mythology as a guide. The quest scenario is deeply rooted in American literature and myth. There are variations, however. Another popular American story that utilizes the quest scenario is Frank Baum's *The Wizard of Oz,* which differs from *Star Wars* in that instead of a male hero (Luke Skywalker) it has a female hero (Dorothy). Consequently, the stories convey different meanings; one is a story of growing up male, the other a story of growing up female. Regardless, reading, watching, or listening to stories such as these, and identifying with the hero, helps people learn something about growing up. Both *Star Wars* and *The Wizard of Oz* are coming-of-age tales. Both emphasize the American value of finding oneself; both define the qualities that are required for success. While one story describes how to be a male and the other how to be a female, both provide, to those who participate in them, scenarios for solving real problems.

QUESTION 4.3: How Do People Come to Believe What They Do, and How Do They Continue to Hold to Their Beliefs Even if They Seem Contradictory or Ambiguous?

In 1992, a New York newspaper sent one of its reporters, Dennis Covington, to cover a murder case in Scottsboro, Alabama. The case was unusual because a man was accused of trying to murder his wife by forcing her to stick her hand into a box full of poisonous snakes. Covington discovered that both the accused husband and his wife were members of a religious group who believe that the Bible, specifically the Book of Mark, directs true Christian believers to handle poisonous snakes and to drink poisonous things:

During a religious service at the Old Rock Holy Church in Alabama, participants handle poisonous snakes because they believe Scripture tells them to do so.

> And these signs shall follow them that believe: In my name shall they cast out devils; they shall speak with new tongues.
>
> They shall take up serpents; and if they drink any deadly thing, it shall not hurt them; they shall lay hands on the sick, and they shall recover.
>
> Mark 16:17–18

What Covington didn't know at first was that Holiness Churches exist throughout the United States. The church's origins go back to 1909, when a Tennessee farmer, George Hensley, claimed that the verses from the book of Mark appeared to him in a vision. He interpreted the vision as a message for him to build a church in which people would test their faith with poisonous snakes and poisonous drinks. During the course of the religious services, participants would be possessed by the Holy Spirit, who might speak to them through the possessed person. The practices of members of the Holiness Church are familiar to a couple of generations of introductory anthropology students through the now-classic ethnographic film *The Holy Ghost People* (1968).

As he researched the story and came to know members of the local Holiness Church, Covington, who had been raised a Christian, began to attend church services. He was taken with the ritual, particularly the music that typically accompanies church services. He observed people handling poisonous snakes, drinking poisonous drinks, and speaking in tongues. What he did not expect was that he would become a believer and a practitioner himself. But that is exactly what did happen. Dennis Covington became for a time a member of the church, handled poisonous snakes, and even daydreamed about becoming a traveling preacher.

Covington's conversion experience, while dramatic, is certainly not unfamiliar to anthropologists. The history of anthropological fieldwork is full of instances of the researcher being drawn into the beliefs of the people she or he is studying. Susan Harding reports that she began to use biblical parables to interpret her experiences while studying the beliefs and practices of the Christian Coalition of Jerry Falwell, and Tanya M. Luhrmann found herself using the concepts of contemporary witchcraft and magic to interpret her experiences while working among magicians and witches in London.

The Process of Interpretive Drift

The experiences of people such as Covington, Harding, and Luhrmann raise the question of how it is that people come to believe what they do. What causes them to put on new spectacles through which to see the world, to convert to a new way of interpreting their experience? In understanding her experiences, Luhrmann suggests that changing one's beliefs involves a process of what she calls **interpretive drift:**

> the slow, often unacknowledged shift in someone's manner of interpreting events as they become involved with a particular activity. As the newcomer begins to practice, he becomes progressively more skilled at seeing new patterns in events, seeing new sorts of events as significant, paying attention to new patterns. By the concept of interpretive drift, I mean to identify the adoption of something like a theory, or at least a significant shift in the interpretation of events. (Luhrmann 1989:312)

Magicians, Luhrmann says, entered magic familiar with the vague notion that the mind can directly affect the material world. They may begin to read books on magic, or they may attend parties where the host or hostess playfully pulls out a tarot deck or a Ouija board and begins to read fortunes or summon spirits. At this point they may not be "believers," but they may find themselves playfully interpreting events in their lives according to the beliefs of magic, and they may begin to find the interpretations intellectually and emotionally satisfying. They may attend a ritual, find "energy surging through them," and attribute that feeling to the presence of some mystical force or power.

Luhrmann herself experienced this, and her description is illuminating: she relates how:

> some months after I met my first London magicians I read a magical text on the train from Cambridge, and I felt that I was beginning to understand magical power. Indeed I imagined the force flowing through me and felt electrically vital, as if the magic current were pulsing through my body. In the midst of the phenomenological fantasy, a bicycle battery in the satchel next to me melted with a crisp, singed smell, and while no doubt coincidental it was disconcerting at the time. (Luhrmann 1989:318)

Later, while attending a ritual and again feeling a force, her watch stopped. While it was, she admits, a cheap watch, watches are said to stop in ritual. She concludes:

> With the watch and the battery, I had ready-made, non-magical, culturally laudable explanations of both events: they were coincidental, and had I not been involved in magic they would have been unsurprising. But I had been thinking about magic, trying to "think like" a magician, and these events were striking

because they made the alternative way of looking at the world seem viable. (Luhrmann 1989:318)

Interpretive drift continues when there are systematic changes in the way the believer begins to interpret experiences and events; he or she begins to identify evidence of the new belief, and soon, the beliefs come to make more sense, to seem more natural. The person begins to "believe" in their truth; once participation in a belief system begins, and once the assumptions begin to seem plausible, and even compelling, the person may seek and find additional compelling evidence for the viability of the belief. Instead of thinking that his or her beliefs have "changed," the believer begins to believe that the new beliefs are simply "true."

Luhrmann reports that magicians and witches all have stories they tell that, for them, provide evidence for the veracity of their beliefs. For example, when she met Robert he related how, 27 years earlier, he was vacationing in Brussels, when he met Françoise. As they toured the city, Françoise confided to him that she was epileptic and that the new medicine that her doctor prescribed seemed to have no effect. After he returned to England he wrote Françoise that he and friends practiced spiritual healing, and that if she would send a photograph and a lock of hair (as psychic links) and pray to the Virgin Mary, they would attempt a cure. After the first ritual, Françoise wrote that she stopped having severe seizures and was having only minor ones. Robert and his friends repeated the ritual, and in her next letter, the woman reported feeling a tremendous inflow of energy, was feeling better, and was seeking a job. Then her letters ceased.

A few months later, Robert wrote Françoise, asking if he could visit. She met Robert at the boat with her family, who expressed great pleasure in meeting the man who had "cured" their daughter. "When were you cured?" Robert asked, and Françoise told him since a car accident when she had been hurled through the windshield. They attributed this "healing" event to the power of the ritual.

There are of course various other interpretations for Françoise's cure; a doctor would say that the shock of the automobile accident resulted in the cure; a Christian might say it was the prayers to the Virgin Mary; an occultist, however, would attribute the cure to the magic rituals. Robert and Françoise found additional confirmation for their beliefs in the fact that the accident occurred at Full Moon on the pagan festival of Candlemas, exactly 13 weeks (a quarter of a year) after the first healing ritual was performed. For Robert, this event, even 27 years after it occurred, was a central memory, a central piece of evidence to him of the efficacy of magic and ritual. The magician dismisses the possibility of coincidence as an explanatory option; he or she learns that what might previously have been considered a coincidence is now considered a consequence of his or her magic.

Luhrmann reports that even the failure of ritual may be taken as evidence for its efficacy. For example, a person works a ritual for a new house; a few weeks later a packet of advertising leaflets on home maintenance arrives in the mail. This may be reported with some self-mockery as the ritual working, but not quite in the way intended. One coven performed a ritual for a woman who wanted to have a child. She stood in the magic circle along with another woman who was to attempt to visualize the event, willing the spell to work. Members of the coven jokingly report that the woman for whom the spell was cast had no child, but the other woman in the circle had a child 10 months later.

The intellectual changes that accompany the adoption of a new belief are, says Luhrmann, illuminating, and the fact that they are illuminating makes the belief and its practice seem effective. That is, the new beliefs provide a sense of discovery and confirmation, they work to help believers make sense of themselves, events in their lives, and the world around them.

Luhrmann says that the key element in becoming a believer is practice—that is, the actual involvement with the practices of a specific belief. In other words, people don't first come to believe something, and then practice the beliefs; rather they first practice, and then they come to believe. Dennis Covington did not first believe that the handling of poisonous snakes was evidence for the presence of the Holy Spirit, and then begin going to church. He first attended the services, spoke with the people, played with the ideas, and only then did he begin to find or seek evidence that converted him to the belief. His evidence was the power he felt, and the visions he had while handling snakes, a power he attributed to the presence of the Holy Spirit. The power of practice might be expressed by saying that people do not go to church because they believe in God; rather they believe in God because they go to church.

Adopting new beliefs, however, does not remove what others may see as contradictions, ambiguities, or just plain absurdities. And it doesn't remove alternative metaphors, theories, or beliefs for interpreting events. Consequently, people must have ways of protecting their beliefs, ways to defend them against skeptics. In other words, once a belief system is adopted, once it seems as though it is true, how can the believer continue to protect these beliefs, even if they might seem foolish to others?

Explaining Why the Sun Moves Around the Earth

For almost 2,000 years, Europeans believed that the earth was the center of the universe. Supposedly, there was a two-sphere cosmos consisting of a vaulted heaven on which was located the sun, planets, and stars that circled eastward across the heavens, and an earthly sphere that was at the center of the universe. This belief was reinforced by language; then, as now, people spoke of the sun rising and setting. This conception of the universe was incorporated into myth with the biblical story of Joshua stopping the sun in the heavens. The idea of an earth-centered universe fit well with a society in which humankind was afforded the central place in the universe.

In spite of the extent to which people took for granted an earth-centered universe, there were problems with understanding the system. It was difficult to explain the behavior of planets that revolved around the earth, because they sometimes seemed to reverse their course or increase or decrease in brightness. Moreover, some early scholars, such as Aristarchus, a Greek grammarian who proposed a sun-centered cosmology, were aware of alternative views. But people were generally able to explain away apparent contradictions.

The history of astronomy illustrates some of the ways that people are able to sustain what they believe, in spite of evidence to the contrary. For example, people can rationalize inconsistencies in what they believe; that is, they can find some way to explain away the inconsistency without changing their belief. The behavior of the planets, for example, was a problem for medieval astronomers; sometimes the planets could be observed reversing direction, a phenomenon

For centuries, Europeans believed in a cosmology that placed the earth at the center of the universe, with the sun, planets, and stars circling around it. The idea of a sun-centered cosmos was considered heretical.

now explained as a consequence of the differing speed of rotation of the planets around the sun. As the earth catches up to or is passed by a planet, the planet seems to reverse its motion. In the Ptolemaic system, however, the inconsistency was rationalized by proposing that planets moved in epicycles: figure-eight loops they supposedly made as they rotated around the Earth. The epicycle concept also explained why a planet could vary in brightness, since during its loops its distance to the earth would vary.

British anthropologist E. E. Evans-Pritchard applied the term **secondary elaboration** to this type of rationalizing process. He illustrated secondary elaboration in his classic account of divination among the Azande of northern Zaire. A Zande who needs to make an important decision or discover the cause of an event consults a diviner. The diviner or oracle worker feeds a poison representing the oracle to chickens and addresses questions to it. The poison used by the Azande sometimes kills the chicken and sometimes not, so the questions are put to the oracle in the form, "if such is the case, kill (or don't kill) the chicken." The procedure is done twice to check its accuracy.

Sometimes, however, the oracle is wrong. It may reply positively to a question, and subsequent events prove the oracle false. It is, of course, easy for us to say "We told you so," but the Azande can, if they wish, easily continue to believe in the power of the oracle by secondary elaboration. Instead of doubting the power of the oracle to predict, they can excuse the error by saying the oracle failed because the wrong poison was used, or because witchcraft interfered with the oracle, or because the poison was old, or ghosts were angry, or the diviner was incompetent.

Beliefs can also be sustained by **selective perception,** seeing only what we want to see. The earth-centered universe, for example, was easily confirmed by the evidence of the senses. There was certainly nothing to indicate the earth moved. In fact, the senses indicated just the opposite; if you dropped an object, it fell straight down. If the earth moved, the object should fall to the right or left of the spot it was dropped. You could see that the sun rises and sets. The Azande, for example, believe witches are people who have inside them a substance responsible for making them witches. This substance can be discovered through autopsy and is believed to be inherited from one generation to another. Someone accused of witchcraft can be convicted or acquitted if an autopsy is done on a kinsman who dies. The corpse is cut open, and an expert in the procedure sifts through the intestines in search of the witchcraft substance. If he finds it, as he sometimes does, he holds it aloft for everyone to see.

EXERCISE 4.3

One of the most persistent contradictions in Judeo-Christian thought has to do with the nature of God. The Judeo-Christian God, unlike creator figures in some other belief systems, is believed to be omnipotent; He controls everything. But, in addition, He is thought to be all-good. The problem is, how can God be all-good and all-powerful when evil, suffering, and injustice exist in the world? If evil exists, He must allow it, in which case He is not all-good. Or if He is all-good, and evil, suffering, and injustice exist, He must not be omnipotent. How might this contradiction be resolved? How can it be explained away while maintaining the idea of an all-powerful, all-good deity?

A belief can also be sustained by **suppressing evidence**—not allowing evidence that contradicts a cherished belief. In the Middle Ages, for example, the Catholic Church denounced as heresy any attempt to suggest that the earth moved around the sun, and astronomers would simply ignore evidence that suggested that the earth was not at the center of the universe. For the Nuer, a herding people of the Sudan in northern Africa, the animal world is divided into things that are human and things that are not. Occasionally, however, a phenomenon threatens the distinction; if a monstrous birth (a severely deformed infant) occurs, it obscures the Nuer distinction between human and nonhuman. The Nuer solve the problem by saying the infant is a baby hippopotamus born to a human parent, and they place it in the river. They have suppressed evidence that threatens their view of the world.

Beliefs can also be sustained by an appeal to faith or mystery. The belief in an earth-centered universe was sustained by an appeal to faith. If there were questions about it, people could be told that it was wrong to ask too many questions about the universe, that God sometimes worked in mysterious ways. The Catholic Church recognizes the concept of mystery in the anomalous features of such doctrines as the Trinity, the idea that God is one in essence but three in "person": Father, Son, and Holy Ghost; the Eucharist, the idea that the bread and wine of ritual are the body and blood of Christ; and the Incarnation, the idea that the human and divine natures of Christ are united. The church embraces these ideas, even though they are problematical in some way, by declaring that each is a mystery, a doctrine whose truth cannot be demonstrated but must be taken on faith.

Beliefs can also be sustained by appeals to authority. The authority of Scripture supported the truth of an earth-centered universe. And, if all else fails, it is possible to use violence or deceit to protect a belief that is threatened. In the seventeenth century, when Galileo proposed to support the idea that the earth revolves around the sun, he was imprisoned and tortured by Church officials until he finally recanted. He spent the rest of his life under house arrest.

People who practice contemporary witchcraft and magic often find themselves defending their beliefs and practices to skeptics and sometimes even to themselves. Some may claim that the magic and ritual really do work and that the beliefs and practices are as valid as any scientific belief or practice. They will produce testimony from people who actually witnessed spirits, or who were cured of some illness immediately following a ritual. Others may try to rationalize their beliefs by saying that magic may seem unprovable or unreasonable, but, they will say, a great deal of life seems unreasonable. Others may justify and defend their beliefs by an appeal to history; magic, the tarot, and astrology are ancient practices whose antiquity gives them authority and validity. They will recite the exploits of the great magicians of the past: John Dee, Nostradamus, Eliphas Levi, and so on.

Others may rationalize or legitimate their beliefs by focusing on their spirituality, freedom, aesthetic beauty, and so forth. Others yet may take a relativist perspective that says that it is impossible even to ask questions about the "objective" status of magic and witchcraft, claiming that all understanding is subjective, while others may assert that their beliefs are objectively false but valid as myth. These represent, Luhrmann points out, different standards of truth, standards that are collectively defined. For some, these standards are acceptable; for others they are not. But the main point is that if people choose to adopt and defend a given set of beliefs, they are able to do so.

QUESTION 4.4: How Does the Way We Live Affect Our Beliefs and Rituals?

In answering this question, Marshall Sahlins (1966:96) wrote:

> When we were pastoral nomads, the Lord was our Shepherd. We were his flock, and he made us lie down in green pastures.... When we were serfs and nobles, the Lord was our king. Sat regnant on the throne of heaven, His shepherd's crook now a jeweled scepter.... Finally we are businessmen—and the Lord is our accountant. He keeps a ledger on us all, enters our good deeds in black and debits our sins in red.

It is too easy to say, Sahlins points out, that people create gods in their own image, or, as Émile Durkheim suggested, that "God is another name for society." But clearly the way we live, the organization of our social, economic, and political lives, must influence what we believe, how we represent those beliefs, and how we act them out. We need to understand, also, how our beliefs and the manner in which we act them out serve to maintain certain patterns of social, political, and economic relations, and how these beliefs and acts serve to reproduce these relations.

To try to understand how what we believe is related to how we live, let's examine a belief that most Westerners have held at one time or another—the belief that they are or have been "in love."

It is likely that more has been written about romantic love than virtually any other subject. Love has been described as everything from the ultimate sensual experience to, as Spanish philosopher Ortega y Gasset described it, "a state of mental misery which has a restricting, impoverishing and paralyzing effect upon the development of consciousness." However, our purpose here is not to define romantic love, but to explore how the imprint of our culture is stamped on our conception of it.

First, what does it mean to say that romantic love is a belief? Don't we "feel" love? Isn't it real? Here is how one person described his experience of love (quoted in Illouz 1997:117):

> There was electricity. It was a tremendous satisfaction that I had these very strong feelings I haven't felt before. There is a sense of connection that happens, for a time, an intermingling of the soul, that you become the same person. There seems to be for me, an absence of sexuality, that you become a sort of spirit, more than a male or female, you become a pure essence.

Obviously this person "feels" something, and describes it as an almost religious experience. But whatever it is that is being felt—that is the meaning given to the emotion—is culturally patterned. That is not to say the emotions aren't "real." However, it is culture that assigns the meaning that we attribute to those emotions. People, of course, do have physiological reactions to other people, and some of these reactions are clearly pleasurable. However, the feelings in themselves must be interpreted and articulated. As Eva Illouz, in her book *Consuming the Romantic Utopia,* puts it, a "feeling" of "attraction" can be interpreted as two souls destined for each other, love at first sight, infatuation, or a hormonal disorder. The labels themselves contain meanings, such that a same-sex friendship might be interpreted as either a spiritual bond or a homosexual attraction. In other words, our culture helps us define how the sense of physiological arousal is to be interpreted. Romantic love is one of those interpretations. Put another way, as La Rochefoucauld put it, "There are many people who would never have been in love, had they never heard love spoken of."

EXERCISE 4.4

What was the most romantic moment of your life? Would the person with whom you experienced that moment be a desired marriage partner for you today? How does your romantic moment (or moments) compare to those described by Eva Illouz?

"Acting" in Love

As we discussed earlier (Question 4.1), the meaning that we give to the experience of romantic love is both articulated and restricted by the metaphors that we use to describe it. The description by Illouz of the feeling of love uses the metaphors of "electricity," of "connection," of religious "spirituality." Lovers have described it as like a "fire," as a "magnetic force." Articulating our belief about romantic love in metaphor is only a beginning. We must also "act" in love, put it into practice. Rituals of love, as the metaphors, are constructed and maintained in certain forms by our society. First and foremost, in American society, acting in love requires money. That is, people must be able to afford the commodities required to demonstrate that one is "in love," or "loves" a specific person. The commodification of romantic love or the "romanticization of commodities," as Eva Illouz puts it, follows the commodification of much of our lives, which, as anthropologist Stephen Fjellman points out, can be lived only through the purchase of specific commodities. Our lives, he says, consist of maneuvering for eligibility to purchase commodities. Americans, Fjellman says, "live in an overcommodified world, with needs that are generated in the interests of the market and that can be met only through the market." Or, as Illouz (1997:146) puts it:

> Although the market does not control the entire spectrum of romantic relationships, most romantic practices depend on consumption, directly or indirectly, and consumerist activities have thoroughly permeated our romantic imagination.

We must spend money to be "lovable," to wear the right clothes, the right perfumes, the proper hairstyles. We must spend money to prepare ourselves to be loved. As Eva Illouz points out, we must have money to define the romantic moment. Romantic moments are, in effect, much like religious rituals, times set aside to affirm or reaffirm our notion that the world is the way we think it is. In the commodification of romance, these moments have come to be dominated by the sharing of food and drink and by travel.

In order to act "in love" a person must be able to finance the rituals of love, those activities that convey the appropriate meanings to the actors, activities we define as "romantic moments." In our culture, dining in restaurants and travel are two such activities.

Eva Illouz discovered that, when asked to define "romantic moments," even children and those who have had no romantic experience mention the restaurant. Restaurants are romantic because they allow couples to step out of their daily lives and into a setting full of ritual meaning. Restaurant design suggests a special setting in which time and space are self-contained. The meal, unlike, say, eating at home or at a fast-food establishment, is separate from the schedules and constraints of the "outside" world. Food in these restaurants is described as "different," "more special," or "exotic" than daily foods. An intimate dinner at home can take on the same aura of ritual significance as the dinner in a restaurant, although only if it assumes some of the attributes of the restaurant dinner (e.g., candlelight, wine, etc.).

Travel is another commodity that is associated with romantic moments. Travel, much like the restaurant, requires leisure and separation from the world of work, effort, profit, self-interest, and money. Of course, in reality, travel is the epitome of consumer culture. It requires travel expenses, accommodation expenses, and participation in the tourist trade. Thus the quest for the romantic moment, the authentic self, for nature, for romance has been elaborated by consumer culture: Instead of being divorced from consumerism, the travel romance is a perfect example of it. In many ways, travel involves the commodification of landscapes to create ritual settings that allow us to act out the relationships we create. Capitalist society, says Illouz, has appropriated and destroyed both the natural landscape and the ability to enjoy a landscape uncontaminated by the visible hand of capital common to tourist resorts. Travel advertising, with its images of pristine landscapes, paradoxically portrays what has been destroyed and hence made more costly, while, at the same time, denying the presence of money and commodities.

Thus, capitalism has appropriated and destroyed not only the natural landscape but precisely the ability to enjoy a landscape uncontaminated by the visible hand of capital—the intensive exploitation characteristic of tourist resorts. Advertising images of romance paradoxically affirm the very economic values that have been made scarce and thereby costly by capitalism at the same time that they deny the presence of money and commodities. As Illouz (1997:100) says:

> The most romantic landscape is incidentally the most expensive, at least in terms of travel costs; it is primarily "wild," that is, far away from the industrial world, and isolated, that is, uncontaminated by capital and the presence of working-class or middle-class vacationers.

Of course when people recall romantic moments, they "misrecognize" the consumerist aspect of the experience, failing to recognize the restaurant, the gift, the vacation for what they are—the commodification of romance.

Love and Class Structure

Another characteristic of how we act in love relates to the class structure of our society. There are at least three ways that this happens. First, since money is required to create "romantic moments," the ability to act in love is restricted to some extent by a person's income. Eva Illouz concludes that while working-class people are able to date, the working classes are particularly at a disadvantage in creating romantic intensity in the daily bond of marriage because it is here that income, leisure resources, and education "play an important role." Thus dating presupposes access to leisure and money. The cultivation of romance is not cheap.

Second, class will determine the object of one's romantic love, that is, the person with whom one chooses to act in love with. This is not done in any obvious way. That is, most people when asked about their choice of a romantic partner will claim and believe that the person's income and family background play no part in the choice. That is, people experience romantic love as a spontaneous and free emotion. But they nevertheless choose partners who are compatible with their own social positions and ambitions. They may claim that they are looking for certain qualities in a partner such as "attractiveness," "intelligence," and "compatibility." But these categories are, of course, defined by class standards.

The rituals of love, such as dining out, traveling, giving gifts, or even "making love," follow certain rules and require a certain amount of competence. That is, people can be more or less skilled in defining and enacting the "romantic moment," can be more or less skilled in acting "in love." These skills represent "cultural capital," certain assets that a person has that permit them to create and dramatize these moments. In the case of love, people have more or less "romantic competence"; they possess the language skills, a grasp of the appropriate cultural symbols, and the economic and time resources to act "in love." These assets are perhaps best represented in movies, books, television shows, and advertisements.

Often when people speak of a romantic partner as someone he or she can "communicate with," they are expressing the fact that they have found someone with an appropriate amount of cultural capital. This amount of cultural capital will be determined by one's economic standing and education. Eva Illouz suggests, for example, that the enactment of the therapeutic metaphor of love popular in women's magazines requires specific knowledge of a language, concepts, and attitudes related to the length and quality of a person's education. In sum, our class standing determines both who we choose to love, and the rituals that we use to enact our love.

Love and Individualism

Philosopher Robert Solomon asks the question of what type of society makes romantic love possible. His answer is one that places an extraordinary emphasis on the concept of individuality. The society of romantic love must allow its members a high degree of mobility and flexibility in relationships and allow some degree of freedom in the selection of a marriage partner.

Romantic love celebrates individualism by putting the emotional interests of the person above the interests of the group. Individualism privatizes love and courtship. It has not always been this way. In the nineteenth century, for example, dating was a family matter. Love activities focused on picnics, church fairs, or dances. Technology and industry transformed "love space," making it more private—the movie theater, the automobile, the restaurant, the dance hall, the nightclub, the resort. The automobile redefined love relationships, making them both more private and more mobile by bringing parks, resorts and, finally, the drive-in movie into range. Movie theaters also offered liberation from observation and became an arena for intimacy. Resorts such as Coney Island celebrated (initially for the lower classes) extravagance, gaiety, and abandon.

Romantic Love and the Functioning of Society

One question asked about religion is the role it plays in the functioning of society. How does it contribute to feelings of social solidarity? How does it function to maintain social order? We can also ask these kinds of questions about love. For example, romantic love is the basis for marriage and reproduction. In fact, in most cases it is a requirement. Romantic love, since it requires commodities, ensures that people require an income; and since people generally must work to earn money, romantic love is one of those things that discipline people to find jobs. This is not quite as obvious a thing as one might think. But if our economy is to function, people must work; they can be forced to work, or they can choose to be employed. One way to ensure that people choose to work is to create commodities that are defined as desirable. And since romantic love is perhaps one of the most desirable states, and since it requires money and commodities to carry out, it also ensures a disciplined workforce.

Finally, we need to address the question of how the commodification of love has affected the experience of romantic love. Has the romantic bond been debased or trivialized? Or has something been gained by love's commodification? The requirement of money probably has reduced the spontaneity of love and restricted those without money in their attempts to "act in love." But we have gained freedom; our relationships are defined by commodities, but women, for example, are far freer to define the romantic relationship than they once were.

Furthermore, it can be argued that commodities add to the romantic experience. There is little doubt that "going out" is, for most people, a pleasurable experience. People do feel empowered when they experience romance. As Illouz (1997:150) concludes:

> Commodities function as expressive symbolic tools that increase the dramatistic and communicative qualities of romantic interchange. Far from inhibiting and repressing the self, commodities in fact serve as useful aids for its dramatization.

QUESTION 4.5: How Can People Reorder Their View of the World if It Becomes Unsatisfactory?

The meanings that people assign to their experience do not change easily. We very much take for granted that the view of the world created by the interaction of our own experiences of the world with the mediums of language, symbolic actions, and collective judgments is the right view. But beliefs do change. Often changes in the meanings that people assign to their experiences are triggered by social upheavals, in which the old way of looking at the world, for whatever reason, is no longer satisfactory. If sufficient numbers of people share this unease, they may together try to change both their view of the world and the organization of society. Anthropologist Anthony F. C. Wallace suggests the term **revitalization movements** for these attempts by people to construct a more satisfying culture.

Generally a period of social or economic upheaval or oppression leads to the development of a new or revised belief system that promises to return the society to a real or mythical previous state, or offers a new vision of the world that promises to relieve the oppression or frustration. During such social upheavals, the usual explanations for events are unsatisfactory, traditional solutions to problems no longer work, and rituals may be abandoned. Doubt engendered by social upheaval is replaced with a new certainty born of religious fervor or conversion. Two examples of revitalization movements are the Ghost Dance among Native Americans, and the Shakers, a religious group that came to this country from England and settled in upstate New York.

Wovoka and the Ghost Dance

As settlers moved west in the nineteenth century, they came into contact with hundreds of Native American groups. As more and more people migrated west, conflict over land resulted in wars between these groups and American military forces. The Indian Wars covered a period from about 1850 to 1880. During this time, the United States government negotiated and signed treaties with Native American groups guaranteeing Indian rights over areas of land, financial compensation, and food and other provisions.

But as more white settlers moved onto Native American territories, the United States government insisted on renegotiating treaties when land that had been given to native groups was desired by settlers. For example, the Sioux were given rights to the Black Hills of South Dakota; however, after gold was discovered there, the government unilaterally insisted on renegotiating the treaties and reduced the Indians' land by more than half in 1889. (In this case, however, courts later ruled that the government's act was illegal, and that the Sioux never ceded their rights.) In addition, the buffalo were virtually exterminated, sometimes in a conscious effort by the American military to destroy the economic basis of native society.

As a result of the Indian Wars, treaty negotiations, government deceit, and the influx of new settlers, native groups were restricted to reservations, made dependent on government rations, and denied traditional pursuits such as hunting and horse raiding. Government deliveries of food and provisions were often late or did not arrive at all, and illness and disease brought to the New World by European settlers, to which the indigenous population had little resistance, decimated the population. Children were taken to boarding schools away from the reserves and prohibited from speaking their native languages. Government agents, often at the insistence of Christian missionaries, banned traditional ceremonies and rituals. In brief, the social fabric of indigenous society was virtually destroyed. Those traditional things that help filter experience—language, ritual, and the ability of groups to collectively sustain particular views of the world—virtually vanished.

Revitalization movements usually receive their impetus from a prophet who claims to have received a vision or dream about a new way of viewing the world or a set of moral injunctions governing people's lives. The major prophet for the Ghost Dance was a Paiute named Wovoka. In 1889, Wovoka had a vision in which he was taken up to heaven, where he saw God and all the people who had died performing their traditional games and activities. God told him he must go back

Wovoka, the major prophet of the Ghost Dance, is shown here in a photograph taken by anthropologist James Mooney in 1891.

and tell people to live in peace with whites and with each other. He was also given instructions for a ritual dance. He was told that if this dance were performed for five days and nights, people would be reunited with their friends and relatives in the other world.

Converts to Wovoka's message spread the word from Nevada to Native American groups throughout the United States and Canada. Wovoka's message was sometimes reinterpreted as it spread from native group to native group. In some versions the world would be destroyed and only the Native Americans brought back to life; in others, Euro-Americans and Native Americans would live together in harmony. In some versions, the buffalo would return. In some cases a specific date was set for the millennium (July 4th, or the time of major traditional ceremonies, was one date). In some versions, Wovoka was said even to be the son of God. Whatever the interpretation, the Ghost Dance, as it became called, was adopted by numerous groups who were seeking a revival of a way of life disrupted by Euro-American expansion.

Among the groups that enthusiastically adopted the Ghost Dance were the Sioux. They had sent emissaries in 1889 to visit Wovoka and returned with descriptions of his vision and power. One account of the delegate's report is contained in James Mooney's work on the Ghost Dance. An anthropologist working for the Bureau of American Ethnology, Mooney traveled around the country interviewing key figures, including Wovoka, and collecting firsthand accounts of the dance from Euro-Americans and Native Americans. Here is his description of the report of the Sioux delegates:

> They were gone all winter, and their return in the spring of 1890 aroused an intense excitement among the Sioux, who had been anxiously awaiting their report. All the delegates agreed that there was a man near the base of the Sierras who said that he was the son of God, who had once been killed by the whites, and who bore on his body the scars of the crucifixion. He had now returned to punish the whites for their wickedness, especially for their injustice toward the Indians. With the coming of the next spring (1891) he would wipe the whites from the face of the earth, and would then resurrect all the dead

Indians, bring back the buffalo and other game, and restore the supremacy of the aboriginal race. (Mooney 1965:64)

Based on these messages, the Sioux began to dance in October 1890. However, for the Sioux, the Ghost Dance turned into a tragic reminder of Euro-American oppression. Frightened that the dance might turn into open rebellion, the Indian agent on one of the Sioux reservations called in the military. Some of the Sioux fled the reservation, chased by the Seventh Cavalry, General George Custer's group that had been decimated by a combined Native American army at Little Bighorn in 1876. After a promise of a safe return to the reservation, the fleeing Sioux surrendered their arms at a place called Wounded Knee and were surrounded by the Seventh Cavalry, equipped with Gatling guns. As soldiers rummaged through the Sioux shelters searching for guns, someone fired a shot and the army opened fire, killing hundreds of men, women, and children.

The Ghost Dance virtually ceased among the Sioux after the massacre at Wounded Knee, but it continued among other groups, each of which hoped for the return of their traditional culture. Today it represents one attempt of a people to build a new culture, a new system of meaning after the destruction of a previous one.

Mother Ann Lee and the Shakers

The next example of a revitalization movement comes from one of the most dramatic periods of religious change in American history, the first half of the nineteenth century. During that period, hundreds of religious movements warning of the coming end of the world led to the establishment of religious communities. This was a period of great social change as Americans began the transition from a rural-agricultural to an urban-industrial society. It was marked by considerable population movement, the spread of poverty, and the breakdown of the family as the prime maintainer of societal norms. Revitalization movements represented an attempt to reformulate society in ways that remain relevant today. Virtually all of them reacted to poverty by eliminating private property and requiring communal ownership of all things; reacted to inequality by recognizing the equality of men and women; and reacted to what they perceived as the breakdown of the larger society by requiring a separation of their communities from the larger society. While almost all of the movements eventually failed, the goals of many remain viable.

The Shakers, or the United Society of Believers in Christ's Second Appearing, as they called themselves, were one of the most interesting and most successful. The Shakers are known largely for their vows of celibacy and rejection of sexual intimacy. But that was only a portion of their ideology.

The founder of the Shakers was Ann Lee. We know little of her life other than information obtained from early nineteenth-century accounts written by her followers. These sources tell us that she was born in Manchester, England, in 1736. At eight years of age she was working 12 to 14 hours a day in the textile mills of Manchester, one of the worst urban slums in England. When she was 22, she attended a series of religious revival meetings held by a group led by Jane and James Wardley. The Wardleys had been Quakers but broke away to form the Wardley Society, developing an expressive kind of worship characterized by

Shaker men and women shared authority but lived separately. In their religious meetings, both genders participated but did not interact with each other.

emotional chanting, shouting, and shaking from which they got their name, the "Shaking Quakers."

Lee is reported to have exhibited an antipathy to sex early in her life and been reluctant to marry. But when she was 25, pressured by her family, she married a blacksmith, Abraham Standerin; in a rare decision for its time, she continued to call herself by her maiden name. Her first three children died in infancy, and the fourth was stillborn. The chronicle of her life states that she was paralyzed by grief and guilt and became convinced that sex and marriage were the root of all evil and the cause of her misery. She gained support (over the objections of her husband) from the Wardleys and declared her celibacy.

The Wardleys preached that the second coming of Christ was near, and, since God was both male and female, the manifestation of Christ's second coming would be a female. The movement embraced the public confession of sin, and Lee poured out all her transgressions and then joined the Wardleys to preach. She, her father, brother, and husband, all of whom had joined her, were arrested for causing a public nuisance. While in jail, she had a vision of Adam and Eve "committing the forbidden sexual act" and began publicly preaching against it. During one of her arrests, she claimed to have had a vision in which Jesus appeared to her and revealed that she was his chosen successor, that she was to be the Word of God, the second coming of Christ as a woman.

The Wardleys accepted her vision, and stories began to circulate about the miraculous healing power of Mother Ann Lee, as she came to be called. One woman claimed that she had a cancer of the mouth, and when Lee touched it, it disappeared. Others related how Lee was beaten for her beliefs but showed no injury. She later had another vision that told her to take her religion to America. In 1774, along with her husband, brother, niece, and four others, she journeyed to America to establish a church. Escaping New York City just ahead of the British in 1776, they journeyed to upstate New York and established a settlement just outside Albany. The turning point for the Shakers in America came in 1780. There was a religious revival of Baptists in the nearby community of New Lebanon, and Calvin Harlow and Joseph Meacham, Baptist ministers, heard about the Shakers and traveled to see Mother Ann Lee. They were so impressed with her and what she had to say that Meacham became her first important convert in America.

Mother Ann Lee died in 1784, perhaps as a result of a journey she and members of her group undertook in 1781 to bring her message to others in New England. The journey was marked by persecution and beatings. But the movement continued to spread, and at its height in the 1840s there were more than 6,000 members spread over 25 communities, from Maine to Florida and into the Ohio Valley.

The social message of the Shakers was relatively simple. Sexual relations were banned, both men and women shared authority, there were separate living arrangements for men and women, members were required to publicly confess their sins, and property was held in common. There was also a prohibition on eating pork, and most Shakers ate no meat at all, even avoiding milk, butter, and eggs. The Shakers professed pacifism and sought to maintain a separate government apart from the rest of society. Each community was organized into groups called families and had a ministry consisting of males and females, usually two of each. Their religious principles included the idea that God is a dual being, male and female, that Mother Ann Lee was the second coming of Christ as spirit, and that the millennium had commenced with the establishment of their church.

Much of what we know of the Shakers in the nineteenth century comes from a book by Charles Nordhoff, *The Communistic Societies of the United States: From Personal Observations.* Nordhoff was a widely respected journalist who traveled among Shaker settlements in 1874, recording his observations and interviewing members of the settlements. During his visit to Mount Lebanon he interviewed Frederick Evans, probably the most prominent of the Shakers of his time, who had met with President Abraham Lincoln to plead that Shakers should be exempted from military service, a request Lincoln granted. Evans described for Nordhoff the advantages of Shakerism, asserting that celibacy is healthful and that it prolongs life: "The joys of the celibate life are far greater than I can make you know. They are indescribable."

Nordhoff reports that the Shakers comprised a cross section of professions—teachers, lawyers, farmers, students, and merchants—and a cross section of religious denominations—Jews, Baptists, Methodists, and Presbyterians, but no Catholics. Since celibacy was a requirement, the Shakers could not reproduce themselves and had to recruit new members. In the early years they obviously did this with considerable success. They built their communities to be representations of heaven on earth and gave them heavenly names: City of Peace, City of Love, City of Union, Holy Mount, and so on. They became master builders whose physical structures were the envy of all and whose authentic furniture still brings astronomical prices today. Their organization of space, their posture, the way they cut their food—all exemplified simplicity and symmetry. The only time restrictions on posture and movement were suspended was during religious meetings. The same people who ordinarily walked straight, tiptoed, and never raised their voices sang, shouted, and whirled in dizzy circles.

It is difficult to speculate what led the people who joined the Shakers to accept their beliefs. Women, obviously, were attracted to the movement because of its promise of equality, and all may have been attracted to the strong group support offered in Shaker communities. In many ways the physical layout, the rituals and the rules of the Shakers seemed to be a denial of anything urban, anything suggesting economic or social exploitation. However, while the communities thrived from 1800 to 1850, they began to decline after the American Civil War as fewer and fewer people were attracted to the message. A small community of believers in Sabbathday Lake, Maine, remains to carry on the Shaker tradition.

CONCLUSIONS

We began by asking how it is that people can believe in things that cannot be proven: for example, why people are convinced of the existence of God, of unseen spirits, or of the powers of witchcraft. The answer to this question requires the examination of the role of such areas of social life as language, ritual, myth, and humor, along with other features of social life that persuade people of the correctness of their beliefs, or that convince them to change what they believe.

How does language affect the meanings we assign to our experience? The ideas of Edward Sapir and Benjamin Lee Whorf demonstrate that the vocabulary of a language may direct perception to certain features of an environment, and the grammar of a language may encourage certain ways of looking at the world. The selection of metaphors also has an impact on the meanings we assign to experience. By taking the language from one domain of experience and applying it to another, we carry the meaning of one domain to the other.

We explored the ways in which symbolic action reinforces a particular view of the world. Ritual, for example, symbolically depicts a certain view of reality in such a way that it convinces us of the truth of that reality. Examples include the Cannibal Dance of the Kwakiutl, which portrays the values of Kwakiutl society and provides members with a way to control their lives, and the rituals of contemporary English magic and witchcraft, which convince participants that mental forces can influence the material world.

We then examined the process through which people might come to believe what they do, a process that Tanya Luhrmann called "interpretive drift." People come to their beliefs by practicing them or participating in rituals that encourage them to seek and find evidence for their veracity, and then to defend their beliefs against the objections of skeptics. At some point people cease to think that they have changed their beliefs, and come to believe that the new beliefs are simply true.

Next, we examined how the way we live influences what we believe and how we act out those beliefs. Thus people come to believe that they are "in love," but how they come to believe it, how they articulate their love, and who they choose to be "in love" with are very much a function of social and economic patterns.

Finally we saw how, under certain conditions, people might be led to radically change what they believe. The experience of social upheaval may lead, as it did among the Plains Indians, to a new system of belief that promises to reorder society and, in the case of the Ghost Dance, promises to resurrect the past. In the case of the Shakers, the social change that marked the transition from an agricultural economic base to industrialization inspired an attempt to formulate a religious community that might bring the millennium and reshape the social order.

REFERENCES AND SUGGESTED READINGS

INTRODUCTION: THE CENTRAL QUESTION The epigraph comes from Barry Barnes's book, *Scientific Knowledge and Sociological Theory* (Routledge & Kegan Paul, 1974). The major work of Edward Tylor is found in his book, *Primitive Culture* (Murray, 1871), and Émile Durkheim's theories are outlined in his brilliant work, *The Elementary Forms of the Religious Life* (Collier, 1961). An excellent review of early anthropological theories of religion can be found in E. E. Evans-Pritchard's very readable work, *Theories of Primitive Religion* (Oxford University Press, 1968). An excellent review of how anthropologists have addressed the human way of knowing can be found in an article by Malcolm R. Crick, "Anthropology of Knowledge," in *Annual Review of Anthropology,* vol. 11 (1982), pp. 287–313.

HOW DOES LANGUAGE AFFECT THE MEANINGS PEOPLE ASSIGN TO EXPERIENCE? Edward Sapir's works span the period from 1910 to 1939, and many appear in a volume edited by David G. Mandelbaum entitled *Selected Writings of Edward Sapir in Language, Culture, and Personality* (University of California Press, 1949). Benjamin Lee Whorf's works are collected in a book entitled *Language, Thought, and Reality: Selected Writings of Benjamin Lee Whorf,* edited by John B. Carroll (MIT Press, 1964). A good summary of the work of Edward Sapir and Benjamin Whorf can be found in *Language, Thought and Experience,* edited by Paul Henle (The University of Michigan Press, 1958). The treatment of metaphor was taken from George Lakoff and Mark Johnson, *Metaphors We Live By* (University of Chicago Press, 1980). Robert C. Solomon discusses the metaphors of love in *Love: Emotion, Myth, and Metaphor* (Anchor Press/Doubleday, 1981). Some of Franz Boas's work on the Kwakiutl is contained in *Kwakiutl Ethnography,* edited by Helen Codere (University of Chicago Press, 1966). The description of Kwakiutl metaphors comes from Stanley Walens, *Feasting with Cannibals: An Essay on Kwakiutl Cosmology* (Princeton University Press, 1981). The discussion of contemporary witchcraft and magic is based on the work of Tanya M. Luhrmann, *Persuasions of the Witch's Craft: Ritual Magic in Contemporary England* (Harvard University Press, 1989). A discussion of the tarot can be found in *The Book of Thoth* (U.S. Games Systems, 1985) by Aleister Crowley. A review of the role of language in socialization is provided by Bambi B. Schieffelin and Elinor Ochs in "Language Socialization," found in *Annual Review of Anthropology,* vol. 15 (1986), pp. 163–191.

HOW DOES SYMBOLIC ACTION REINFORCE A PARTICULAR VIEW OF THE WORLD? Information on the Kwakiutl Cannibal Dance, along with other aspects of Kwakiutl ritual and mythology, can be found in Franz Boas, *Kwakiutl*

Ethnography, cited above, and Franz Boas and George Hunt, *Kwakiutl Texts. Memoir of the American Museum of Natural History,* vol. 5 (1905). A classic work is Ruth Benedict's *Patterns of Culture* (Houghton Mifflin Company, 1934). Interpretations of the Cannibal Dance are found also in Stanley Walens's book, *Feasting with Cannibals: An Essay on Kwakiutl Cosmology,* cited above. A social analysis of *The Wizard of Oz* can be found in David Payne, "The Wizard of Oz: Therapeutic Rhetoric in a Contemporary Media Ritual," *Quarterly Journal of Speech,* vol. 75 (1989). Joseph Campbell's *The Hero with a Thousand Faces* (Princeton University Press, 1949) is one of the classic works on mythology. The anthropological literature on ritual and symbolic action is extensive. Roy Wagner's "Ritual as Communication: Order, Meaning, and Secrecy in Melanesian Initiation Rites," in *Annual Review of Anthropology,* vol. 13 (1984), pp. 143–155, provides an excellent review of works on ritual, as does an article by John D. Kelly and Martha Kaplan, "History, Structure, and Ritual," in *Annual Review of Anthropology,* vol. 19 (1990), pp. 119–150. The discussion of contemporary witchcraft and magic is based on the work of Tanya M. Luhrmann, *Persuasions of the Witch's Craft: Ritual Magic in Contemporary England* (Harvard University Press, 1989).

HOW DO PEOPLE COME TO BELIEVE WHAT THEY DO, AND HOW DO THEY CONTINUE TO HOLD TO THEIR BELIEFS EVEN IF THEY SEEM CONTRADICTORY OR AMBIGUOUS? Dennis Covington's experiences with the Holiness Church are described in his book, *Salvation on Sand Mountain: Snake Handling and Redemption in Southern Appalachia* (Addison-Wesley, 1995). The history of snake handling and of the Holiness Church can be found in Weston La Barre's *They Shall Take Up Serpents: Psychology of the Southern Snake Handling Cult* (University of Minnesota Press, 1962) and Thomas Burton's *Serpent-Handling Believers* (University of Tennessee Press, 1993). An account of Susan Friend Harding's experiences can be found in *The Book of Jerry Falwell: Fundamentalist Language and Politics* (Princeton University Press, 2000). The discussion of contemporary witchcraft and magic is based on the work of Tanya M. Luhrmann, *Persuasions of the Witch's Craft: Ritual Magic in Contemporary England* (Harvard University Press, 1989). The analysis of medieval astronomy comes from Thomas Kuhn's *The Copernican Revolution: Planetary Astronomy in the Development of Western Thought* (Harvard University Press, 1957). The description of Azande witchcraft and divination appears in E. E. Evans-Pritchard's classic *Witchcraft, Oracles and Magic Among the Azande* (Oxford University Press, 1937). The example of the Nuer monstrous birth comes from Mary Douglas, *Purity and Danger* (Frederick A. Praeger, 1966).

HOW DOES THE WAY WE LIVE AFFECT OUR BELIEFS AND RITUALS? The quote from Marshall Sahlins comes from page 96 of his book, *Tribesmen* (Prentice-Hall, 1966). The rest of the discussion on how our society influences how and who we love comes from Eva Illouz's book, *Consuming the Romantic Utopia: Love and the Cultural Contradictions of Capitalism* (University of California Press, 1997). See also the volume edited by Victor C. de Munck, *Romantic Love and Sexual Behavior: Perspectives from the Social Sciences* (Praeger, 1998), for some excellent cultural analyses of love and sex.

*HOW CAN PEOPLE REORDER THEIR VIEW OF THE WORLD IF IT BE-
COMES UNSATISFACTORY?* Anthony F. C. Wallace provides a discussion of
revitalization movements, as well as the ritual process, in *Religion: An Anthropological View* (Random House, 1966). The material on the Ghost Dance comes
from James Mooney's *The Ghost Dance Religion and the Sioux Outbreak of
1890* (University of Chicago Press, 1965), and from Alice Kehoe's *The Ghost
Dance: Ethnohistory and Revitalization* (Holt, Rinehart and Winston, 1989).
The earliest work on the Shakers is contained in *Testimonies of the Life, Character, Revelations and Doctrines of Our Ever Blessed Mother Ann Lee,* by an
anonymous author, published in 1816 by J. Tallcott & J. Deming, and much of
what is known about Ann Lee is described by Nardi Reeder Campion in *Mother
Ann Lee: Morning Star of the Shakers* (University Press of New England, 1990).
Charles Nordhoff's *The Communistic Societies of the United States* was first
published by Harper and Brothers in 1875, and reissued by Dover Publications in
1966. An excellent summary of Shaker life and the relationship of their beliefs to
their architecture and living arrangements can be found in *Seven American
Utopias: The Architecture of Communitarian Socialism, 1790–1975* by Dolores
Hayden (MIT Press, 1981). A recent comprehensive description of the history and
life of the Shakers is contained in Stephen J. Stein's *The Shaker Experience in
America: A History of the United Societies of Believers* (Yale University Press,
1992). For a general review of other religious movements, see James W. Fernandez's article on religious change in Africa, "African Religious Movements," in *Annual Review of Anthropology,* vol. 7 (1978), pp. 195–234.

Henry Moore. *Family Group.* (1948–49), Bronze (cast 1950), 59¼ × 46½ × 29⅞". The Museum of Modern Art, New York. A. Conger Goodyear Fund. Photograph © 1997 The Museum of Modern Art, New York.

C H A P T E R   5

PATTERNS OF FAMILY RELATIONS

PROBLEM 5: WHAT DO WE NEED TO KNOW BEFORE WE CAN UN-
DERSTAND THE DYNAMICS OF FAMILY LIFE IN OTHER SOCIETIES?

If ever thou purpose to be a good wife, and to live comfortably, set down this with thyself: mine husband is my superior, my better; he hath authority and rule over me; nature hath given it to him…God hath given it to him.

W. Whately, *The Bride Bush*, London, 1617

A WOMAN WITHOUT A MAN IS LIKE A FISH WITHOUT A BICYCLE.

Automobile bumper sticker, ca. 1975

INTRODUCTION: *Soap Operas and Family Relations*

Could a foreign visitor to the United States learn anything about American family life from watching our soap operas? Consider this plot from a popular soap: Holden is having an affair with Lilly while his wife Angel is undergoing psychiatric treatment because she had been sexually molested by her father, who was shot and killed by Kalib, Holden's brother. In the meantime Darryl is having an affair with Francine while he and his wife, Carol, are arranging to have a child through a surrogate mother. Francine's sister Sabrina has run off with Antonio, an apparent drug dealer who has shot Bob, the sisters' father.

A visitor certainly might conclude from the popularity of this soap opera that Americans like to watch stories of illicit love, incest, infidelity, greed, and marital and family conflict. And while the behaviors of these soap opera characters may not really represent the daily lives of American husbands and wives, fathers and mothers, or sons and daughters, they must represent enough of reality to allow viewers to identify with the characters and their situations. In some ways, the plots and the relationships between the characters must seem plausible and reveal something about the dynamics of American lives. Our assumption in this chapter is that a person who understands and appreciates soap operas in America would have a good understanding of the dynamics of American life. But what relevance does that have for understanding family life in other societies?

Americans are not alone in their fascination with soap opera plots. Most societies have fictional dramas and real-life tales about family life that reveal the concerns of the people. Brazilians, for example, like Americans, are fanatical soap opera watchers, but the characters, situations, and plots are different from those on American television, and these differences reveal variations in family structure and dynamics. The focus in Brazilian soap operas tends to be on the **family of orientation**—father, mother, self, and siblings—rather than on the **family of procreation**—husband, wife, and their children. The theme of class mobility dominates Brazilian soaps, as do plots about women from poor, rural families marrying wealthy men from the city. Love is depicted as dangerous and often unrequited, as when a woman is hopelessly in love with a man destined to marry someone else. In Brazilian soaps, characters almost always interact with family and friends; in American soaps they interact much more frequently with strangers. In addition, the setting for Brazilian soaps is usually the home—the sphere of private life. In American soaps, the setting is often the workplace or some other location in the sphere of public life.

Soap operas reveal the reasons for domestic strife; they depict individuals with choices to make, choices that have an impact on others. They reveal character motivation and development. In whatever form they take—traditional dramas, real-life tales, or soap opera—such stories are an interesting way to learn about family life in different societies. Moreover, if you decided to learn enough about family life in another society to enable you to write a plausible soap opera for members of that society, you would probably understand a good deal about the dynamics of their family life.

What, then, would you need to know in order to write a good soap opera about families in other societies? First, you would need to know the composition of a typical family, and how the family is formed and maintained. You would need to examine how the themes of sexuality, love, and wealth (all prominent in American soap operas and familiar themes in the stories of other societies) are dealt with, and what kinds of situations or conflicts can disrupt family life in the society.

QUESTIONS

5.1   What is the composition of the typical family group?
5.2   How is the family formed and the ideal family type maintained?
5.3   What are the roles of sexuality, love, and wealth?
5.4   What threatens to disrupt the family unit?

To make this task more manageable, we will focus on family life in three societies: the Ju/wasi, the Trobriand Islanders of the South Pacific, and the traditional Chinese farm family. These societies have been selected for three reasons. First, they represent very different levels of social, cultural, and technological complexity. The Ju/wasi were gatherers and hunters, living in small, mobile groups; the Trobriand Islanders were horticulturists, living in villages of up to 400 people. The traditional Chinese represented a large, agricultural society. Second, family structure and roles vary significantly among the three, but together they depict family types and relations that are representative of many, if not most, societies around the world. Finally, the three societies have been well studied in the anthropological literature. I will discuss these societies in what anthropologists refer to as the ethnographic present; that is, although the actual descriptions may refer to situations that existed in the past, they will be described as if they still existed. In reality, the Ju/wasi, the Trobriand Islanders, and the rural Chinese are, to varying degrees, very different today than they were when they were studied by the anthropologists whose work I will mention.

QUESTION 5.1: What Is the Composition of the Typical Family Group?

To understand family composition in different societies, we need certain concepts and tools. One place to begin is by examining how most unmarried Americans would respond if asked about the composition of their families. They would likely list their mother, father, brothers, and sisters. If asked "Who else?" they would likely add grandparents, aunts, uncles, and cousins. If they were married, they would add their husbands or wives and children. Figure 5.1 shows how this family structure would be diagrammed using genealogical notations.

Certain features of the typical (although not universal) American family stand out. Americans consider themselves equally tied by kinship to both their mother and father, and to their maternal and paternal kin. In other words, Americans reckon kinship **bilaterally** through both parents. Second, Americans make no linguistic distinction between their mothers' siblings and their fathers' siblings; both are referred to as aunt or uncle. Nor do they distinguish linguistically the children of aunts and uncles; all are referred to as cousins. For most Americans the most important family grouping is the **nuclear family**—the group consisting of father, mother, and their biological or adopted children.

Families in other societies may be composed very differently. For example, while Americans give equal recognition to people's ties to their mothers or their fathers, other societies place greater emphasis on ties to one parent or the other. In some cases, only people related through either the mother or the father are considered family. Societies that emphasize persons' ties to their mother are said to have **matrilineal kinship** systems; those that emphasize persons' ties to their father are said to have **patrilineal kinship** systems. However, in few societies is an individual's relationship to one side of the family or the other totally ignored; rather, in most societies, relationships with mothers' families and fathers' families are viewed differently. For example, Americans traditionally inherit their surnames from their fathers, thus embracing the patrilineal principle, but in case of divorce, the American legal system usually gives priority to the matrilineal principle by awarding custody of the child to its mother.

The three examples of societies used in this chapter—the Ju/wasi, Trobriand Islanders, and traditional Chinese—each define the composition of the family and relations between members differently.

The Family Composition of the Ju/wasi

For most of the year, the Ju/wasi live in groups numbering 10 to 30 or 40 people, bilaterally related (through both parents), who hunt and gather in a territory associated with a particular water hole. Camp groups are often organized around a brother-and-sister pair who claim ownership of the water hole. They bring in their spouses and children to the group; in turn, the spouses might bring in their brothers, sisters, and even mothers and fathers.

A typical camp might look like the one described by Elizabeth Thomas in her classic work *The Harmless People* (see Figure 5.2). Membership in a camp is fluid. People move freely from camp to camp based on hunting alliances or because conflict develops in the group. Within the camp, however, the basic family group is the nuclear family of husband, wife, and children. Children spend most of their time with their mothers. The Ju/wasi acknowledge the fact that pregnancy results from sexual intercourse (not the case in all societies). They also believe that conception takes place at the end of the woman's menses, when the man's semen joins with the last of the menstrual blood.

One feature of Ju/wasi society that figures prominently in the dynamics of family life is the custom of **brideservice** at marriage. When a couple marries, the groom is expected to come and live in the bride's parents' camp and work for her

FIGURE 5.1   COMPOSITION AND DEVELOPMENT OF THE AMERICAN NUCLEAR
FAMILY

1. The traditional
American household
generally begins with a
husband and wife pair
moving from the
households of their
parents.

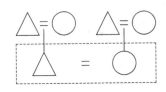

2. The arrangment is
formalized with the
birth of children,
which produces a
new nuclear family.

3. At some point the
household might be
composed of three
generations, as married
children join the
household with their
children.

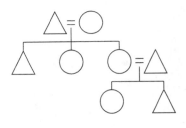

4. At a later stage, the
household might consist
of the original couple
or a single person.

KEY

Female	○
Male	△
Marriage	=
Blood Tie	⌐
Descent		

FIGURE 5.2   COMPOSITION AND DEVELOPMENT OF THE JU/WASI CAMP

1. Most Ju/wasi camps are organized around brother/sister pairs who claim ownership of a water hole.

2. Brother and sister are joined at the camp by their spouses and relatives of their spouses. The nuclear family is the main economic unit.

3. Bridegrooms join the camp of brides' parents for brideservice.

4. Camp composition changes as a result of changing social relations.

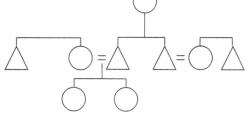

KEY
Female   ○
Male   △
Marriage =
Blood Tie ⌐
Descent |

parents for as long as 10 years. Tales of family life among the Ju/wasi are often built around the effects of this arrangement on family dynamics.

The Family Composition of the Trobriand Islanders

The people of the Trobriand Islands live in some 80 villages whose populations range from 40 to 400. Each village is surrounded by cultivated fields of yams, taro, and other crops and water holes; fruit trees; and palm groves. Each is further divided into hamlets, and each hamlet ideally consists of a **matrilineage,** or dala, as the Trobrianders call it: a group of men related to each other through the female line, along with their wives and unmarried children.

The matrilineages are ranked relative to one another, and each village has a chief who is the eldest male of the highest-ranking matrilineage. Since each person is a member of the lineage of his or her mother, neither a man's wife nor his children can be members of his own dala.

The Trobrianders' mythology and beliefs about procreation dramatically depict the matrilineal element in their lives. Their mythology contains stories of how, a long time ago, pairs of brothers and sisters emerged from the ground to begin each dala. Dala members trace their descent back to their mythological ancestors, and they base their claims to specific plots of land on the fact that it was from thence that their ancestors emerged. There is obviously an incestuous theme in Trobriand myth, since the originators of each lineage were brothers and sisters. However, Trobriand theories of procreation ostensibly deny a role to men in conception. They reinforce the matrilineal principle as well as the tie between brothers and sisters.

The Trobrianders say that when a person dies, the soul or spirit becomes young and goes to live on an island called Tuma. There the soul ages, but it regenerates itself by bathing in the sea. As the skin is sloughed off, a spirit child, or baloma, is created, which returns to the world of the living and enters the womb of a woman of the same matrilineage as itself. In effect, a Trobriand matrilineage exists in perpetuity, as souls and spirits travel back and forth between the land of the living and the island of the dead.

The baloma may enter the woman through her head, or it may be carried by water into her womb. In some areas of the Trobriand Islands, if a woman wishes to become pregnant, a pail of water is brought to her dwelling by her brother. In fact, a woman cannot conceive without the "permission" of her brother. Consequently, the act of conception among the Trobrianders is a matter of three agencies—a woman, the spirit or baloma of a deceased ancestor, and the woman's brother. While sexual intercourse is said to play no role in conception, it does play a role in the development and growth of the fetus. Trobrianders believe that the man's semen provides food and nourishment for the fetus, and that is why children physically resemble their fathers. Sexual intercourse is also said to open the womb for the child to emerge.

While Trobriand procreation beliefs may, at first glance, seem strange, in the context of their ideas about descent they make perfect sense. When a person is believed to be descended exclusively from the mother, possible relations and ties to the father are excluded not only socially but physically as well. In fact, we find in strongly patrilineal societies corresponding beliefs about conception. Earlier we examined how Carol Delaney, in her book on Turkish village society,

The Seed and the Soil, explains how villagers have what she calls a "mono-genetic" theory of procreation. "It is the males," as she puts it, "who give life; women merely give birth." Turkish villagers use an agricultural metaphor to describe procreation; men provide the seed, women are the soil. It is the seed that contains life, the soil simply nurtures it. The man is believed to plant the seed and the woman is said to be the field in which the seed is planted. In this way the male role in the patrilineal family system of the Turkish village is emphasized and the female role diminished.

The Trobrianders can rationalize and "prove" their beliefs about procreation very easily. Bronislaw Malinowski, who spent four years studying the people of the Trobriand Islands, tells of their response when he suggested to them that sexual intercourse plays a role in procreation:

> I sometimes made myself definitely and aggressively an advocate of the truer physiological doctrine of procreation. In such arguments the natives would quote, not only positive instances of women who have children without having intercourse; but would also refer to the many cases in which an unmarried woman has plenty of intercourse and no children. This argument would be repeated over and over again, with specially telling concrete examples of childless persons renowned for profligacy, or of women who lived with one white trader after another without having any baby. (Malinowski 1929:185–186)

To what extent the Trobrianders really deny a role to men in procreation is a matter of some debate. Annette Weiner, who worked with them in the early 1970s, some 50 years after the pioneering work of Malinowski, reported that they no longer denied the direct role of men in conception. However, she also reported a case where a grandmother claimed that she had used magic to make her granddaughter pregnant when the woman conceived while her husband was away.

EXERCISE 5.1

The procreation beliefs of the Trobriand Islanders prompted debate among anthropologists about whether the Trobrianders really did believe that men played little or no role in reproduction, or whether, to emphasize the matrilineal principle, they pretended not to acknowledge the male's role. In either case, we would expect to find in societies that emphasize the patrilineal principle that a woman's role in reproduction is de-emphasized. What kind of belief about reproduction can you think of that would deny the importance of the female? How does this compare with the biological roles of men and women in American society?

Regardless of the extent to which the Trobrianders recognize the role of coitus, their ideas about descent and procreation reflect important features of the composition of their families. First, the key family relationship for them is not, as it is among the Ju/wasi, between husband and wife; it is between brother and sister. Second, the father of the family is an outsider to his children, a member of another family group. His interest, ideally, is in his sister's children, since it is they who are members of his matrilineage. Third, since the matrilineal **extended**

FIGURE 5.3   COMPOSITION OF THE TROBRIAND ISLAND *DALA* AND HOUSEHOLD

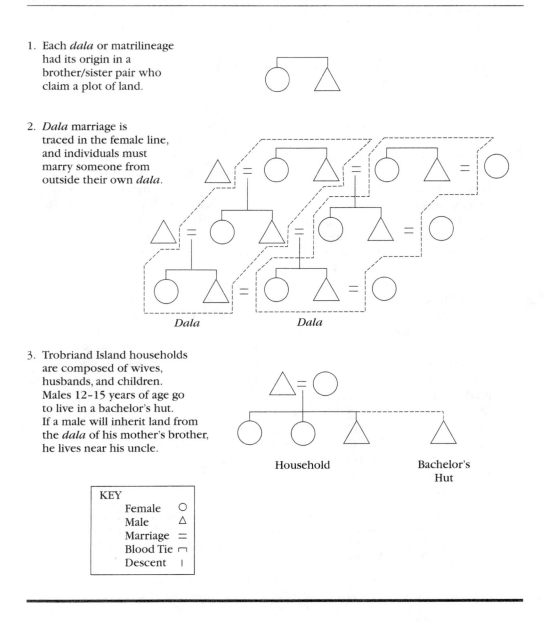

1. Each *dala* or matrilineage had its origin in a brother/sister pair who claim a plot of land.

2. *Dala* marriage is traced in the female line, and individuals must marry someone from outside their own *dala*.

Dala   *Dala*

3. Trobriand Island households are composed of wives, husbands, and children. Males 12–15 years of age go to live in a bachelor's hut. If a male will inherit land from the *dala* of his mother's brother, he lives near his uncle.

Household   Bachelor's Hut

KEY
Female   ○
Male   △
Marriage   =
Blood Tie   ⌐
Descent |

family group, the dala, is more important than the nuclear family, the Trobrianders merge certain people under the same kin term, the same way Americans refer to different kinds of kin as aunt, uncle, or cousin. In the Trobrianders' case, a person refers to all women of his or her matrilineage of the same generation by the same term; for example, a man refers to his mother, as well as his mother's sisters, by the term *ina*. A woman refers to her brother, and to all other men of her matrilineage and generation, as *iuta*. Thus, a man has many "sisters," and a woman has many "brothers."

Another consequence of matrilineal kinship is that men inherit property not from their fathers but from their mothers' brothers, and it is ideally in his maternal uncle's village that a young man goes to live. The fact that these ideal conditions are not always met creates some of the drama in Trobriand family life.

The Family Composition of the Chinese

Family life in traditional rural China centers around the patrilineal extended family household of a married couple, their married sons and daughters-in-law, and their grandchildren and unmarried daughters. To understand the traditional Chinese family, you have to understand the idea of temporal depth, for in China the **patrilineage** exists as much in time as it does in space. When Americans speak of family, they generally limit it to the living; in traditional China the family includes a long line of patrilineal ancestors. Anthropologist Francis L. K. Hsu notes that the identity of each male is defined by his relations to the dead as much as it is by his relations to the living. His social worth and destiny are but reflections of the actions of his ancestors. He thus exists, as Hsu says, "under the shadow of his ancestors." Likewise, the spirits of the dead are dependent on the contributions of the living. These contributions are ceremonially made at altars, prominently positioned in each home, from which people send gifts to their ancestors by burning paper money, paper clothes, or other paper articles.

Given the interdependence between living and dead men of the patrilineage, it is apparent why it is essential to a Chinese male to have male descendants to look after his well-being and provide for him in the afterworld. Male children and grandchildren are living proof to a man that his line will continue. For this reason, unlike the Ju/wasi or Trobriand Islanders, the Chinese express a marked preference for male children. Males are needed to maintain the patrilineal descent group, for if the only children born are daughters whose children will in turn belong to the patrilineage of their husbands, a family line will die out. A son, as the Chinese put it, is a major happiness; a daughter is but a small happiness. Here is how one woman summed up the Chinese attitude toward daughters to Margery Wolf, who did research in the Taiwanese village of Peihotien:

> Why should I want so many daughters? It is useless to raise your own daughters. I'd just have to give them away when they were grown, so when someone asked for them as infants I gave them away. Think of all the rice I saved. (quoted in Wolf 1968:40)

A more lethal implication of the relative importance of sons and daughters in China is the differential rates of infanticide and abortion of males and females. In the area in which Hsiao-Tung Fei did research, there was a ratio of 100 girls to 135 boys in the age group 0–5. The population data suggest that a larger proportion of females had been killed.

In addition to a long line of male ancestors, an ideal Chinese household should include several generations of fathers and sons sharing a common hearth or cooking stove and an ancestral altar, the symbols of the household. In the architecture of Peihotien, houses are constructed in such a way that they can easily be extended to accommodate additional sons and grandsons who bring their wives to live in the family home. In reality it is very difficult to maintain this

FIGURE 5.4   COMPOSITION AND DEVELOPMENT OF THE TRADITIONAL CHINESE
                        FAMILY

1. The traditional
   Chinese family exists
   in time as well as in
   space. Descent is
   traced patrilineally
   for generations.

2. An ideal family
   would be similar
   to that of the Lim
   household in
   Taiwan.

3. Most Chinese extended
   households eventually
   break up into separate
   nuclear family units,
   with wives of sons
   joining their husbands'
   households.

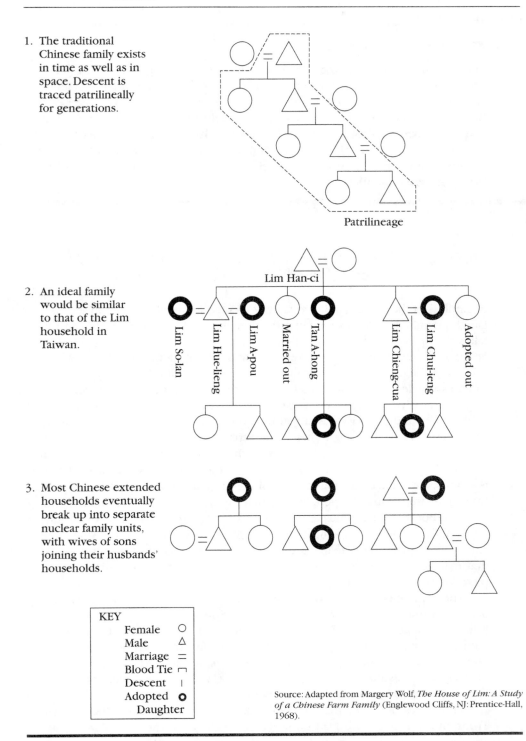

Source: Adapted from Margery Wolf, *The House of Lim: A Study
of a Chinese Farm Family* (Englewood Cliffs, NJ: Prentice-Hall,
1968).

ideal; most households in villages such as Peihotien are small, consisting of a married couple and several dependent patrilineal relatives.

RESOURCE 5.1

Kinship and Social Structure

The study of kinship organization and terminology can be highly complex, yet essential for understanding the patterns of social organization of many societies. You can find out more about this and engage in some fun interactive exercises at Brian Schwimmer's *Kinship and Social Organization: An Interactive Tutorial* at: **http://www.umanitoba.ca/faculties/arts/anthropology/kintitle.html**

There is also a wealth of information on the kinship structure of selected societies at: The Centre for Social Anthropology and Computing, **http://lucy.ukc.ac.uk/**

QUESTION 5.2: How Is the Family Formed and the Ideal Family Type Maintained?

Regardless of the size of family units or descent systems, in virtually all societies families require the socially recognized union of a male and female. Generally this takes the form of marriage, a publicly recognized joining of two people or two families. But while marriage makes or sustains families, the manner in which such an arrangement comes about varies significantly in different societies. In American society, for example, children begin learning about courtship and marriage at an early age: Five- and six-year-olds are teased about their "boyfriends" or "girlfriends," and playing house together is a popular preschool pastime. Americans begin serious courting in their early teens, and usually go through a series of relationships before choosing a partner for their first marriage, most often when they are between the ages of 18 and 30. While the choice of a marriage partner is supposedly based on feelings of love and sexual attraction, other factors also influence it. Americans, like people in virtually all societies, are prohibited by the **incest taboo** from marrying certain categories of kin, such as brothers or sisters, children or parents, or, in some cases, cousins. Ideally, also, a spouse should be chosen from an appropriate income, ethnic, gender, and racial group. The conflict that may arise when an inappropriate marriage partner is chosen is often depicted in soap opera plots.

The marriage ceremony in American society is traditionally arranged and financed by the bride's family, and after the honeymoon, the couple ideally establishes an independent residence. Their relationship based on love expressed in regular sexual intercourse is later transformed by the arrival of one or more children—a wife transformed into a mother, a husband transformed into a father. That, of course, is the ideal for most Americans, and it is the disruption of that ideal that also contributes to soap opera plots.

The cycles of events that create or sustain the family among the Ju/wasi, Trobriand Islanders, and traditional Chinese illustrate the diversity of such arrangements. The soap opera themes of these groups would be quite different.

Garlands of lilies crown these young Ju/wasi girls. In the Ju/wasi culture, most marriages are arranged by the couple's parents, and the bride-to-be frequently objects to the chosen spouse or to the prospect of marriage itself.

The Family Cycle of the Ju/wasi

Ju/wasi men and women, like Americans, begin to learn about courtship, sex, and marriage early in life. Since there is little privacy in a Ju/wasi camp and children sleep with their parents, they soon are playing at marriage and imitating the bodily movements of parents making love. Most young men and women have had sexual experiences by the time they are 15. Ju/wasi men usually marry for the first time between the ages of 18 and 25, when they are able to hunt and work for their wives' parents. Marriage is important for a man for a number of reasons. It marks him as an adult worthy of taking part in Ju/wasi public life, he gains a sex partner, and he gains a mate to provide his food. While men are obligated to share and formally distribute the meat they obtain in the hunt with everyone in the camp, women are not obligated to share what they gather outside their nuclear family group, and women gather from 60 to 80 percent of the food in a camp.

Women often marry as early as 12 to 14 years of age, generally before their first menstruation, which occurs at about 17. Girls have fewer reasons to marry than men. Single or married men are always available as sex partners, and, since the product of male labor, meat, is widely shared, a woman need not have a husband to ensure her share of the hunt. However, a girl's parents have good reasons for getting her married as soon as possible. The earlier she is married, the longer she and her husband will remain with her parents until she is of age, and the longer her husband will work for her parents. Moreover, the bride's family gains an alliance with another family and is less likely to get involved in open conflict between men over their daughter.

Marriages are almost always arranged by the couple's parents. Typically the mother or father of the male approaches the family of the girl with a proposal for marriage. If the girl's parents approve of the match, the families exchange gifts to indicate their agreement. An appropriate husband for a daughter is a man who is not too much older, is not yet married, is a good hunter, and is willing to accept responsibility. The prospective groom should also be cooperative, generous, and unaggressive.

The Ju/wasi not only avoid choosing a spouse who is a close kinsperson, they are also restricted in the choice of a marriage partner by their naming system. There are only about 30 to 40 names that can be chosen for newborns, and people with the same first name consider themselves connected, regardless of their actual kinship relation to one another. For example, if two people are named Toma, then everyone related by kinship to one Toma will be considered related in the same way to the other Toma. Consequently, if a man's name is Toma, all the brothers and sisters of everyone else named Toma would be considered his brothers and sisters, all the sons and daughters of other Tomas would be considered his sons and daughters, and so on. Therefore, a marriage partner should occupy neither an actual prohibited kinship category nor one created by the naming system. A woman, for example, could not marry a man with the same name as her father or a man whose father had the same name as her father, since she and the man would refer to themselves as brother and sister. When Richard Lee was working with the kinship system of the Ju/wasi he found that interpretations of the naming system varied, and disagreements about the kin connection between people would always be resolved by the interpretation of the older person in the relationship.

Once a suitable match is made, one more obstacle to the marriage remains. Perhaps because they have little to gain or much to lose, young women often object strenuously to the marriage or to their parents' choice of a husband. Kicking and screaming is one way women demonstrate their objections. If they protest long and hard enough, the marriage will be called off; if the protest is not sufficient to call off the arrangements, a marriage ceremony takes place. A hut set apart from the bride's family village is built for the couple by members of both families. Friends bring the couple to the hut, and the girl, head covered, is placed in the hut. Coals from the fires of both families are brought to start the fire in the couple's hut. Friends stay, joking, singing, and dancing, while bride and groom stay apart. Often, especially if the girl is young, a relative stays with them in the hut until she begins to adjust to her new status. These "honeymoons" are often the source of continuing conflict.

Working among the Ju/wasi, Marjorie Shostak (1983) forged a close relationship with a Ju/wasi woman, Nisa, who described her wedding night. Nisa said that she cried so much and objected so strongly to spending the night with her new husband, Bo, that her parents asked a female relative, Nukha, to sleep between Nisa and Bo. She soon discovered that Nukha was having sex with Bo, and after a few nights she told her parents. They took her and moved to another water hole, leaving Nukha and Bo behind.

Typically, half of all first marriages fail among the Ju/wasi, and they may enter several marriages over the course of their lives. Nisa's second marriage, to Tashay, followed the same lines as her first; on her wedding night she cried and cried and finally ran away into the bush. Relatives tried to explain the benefits of marriage and to convince her to accept Tashay. When she finally agreed, Tashay took Nisa to his parents' home to live, and Nisa's parents followed. But not until Nisa and Tashay had been living together for a long time did they have sex. Nisa remembers the aftermath of their first lovemaking as being painful, and it was a long time before she allowed it again and began to enjoy it.

The Family Cycle of the Trobriand Islanders

Courtship and sexual play begin early in the Trobriand Islands. Children play erotic games at the ages of seven and eight and begin seeking sex partners at ages 11 to 13. Trobriand adolescents are permitted to openly display their affection for each other; girls scratch, beat, thrash, or even wound their lovers, and boys accept this treatment as a sign of love, and display their wounds as proof of manliness and success in courtship. They sing about love, both successful and unrequited, and take great pains with their physical appearance. Here is what Malinowski says about adolescent courtship:

> An adolescent gets definitely attached to a given person, wishes to possess her, works purposefully toward his goal, plans to reach fulfillment of his desires by magical and other means, and finally rejoices in achievement. I have seen young people of this age grow positively miserable through ill-success in love. (Malinowski 1929:63)

Since sexual activity before marriage is common and expected among the Trobrianders, the couple often has already been living together, and the marriage simply formalizes an existing relationship. While the couple may take the initiative in arranging a marriage, parents approve or disapprove of the choice of a spouse and sometimes arrange matches. There are certain categories of people a Trobriander may not marry. All Trobrianders belong to one of four **clans,** groups whose members consider themselves descended from a common ancestor. They must observe clan **exogamy**—that is, marry out of their own clan, into another. In addition, the incest taboo applies to all close relatives, particularly brothers and sisters, who include all members of a matrilineage of the same generation. Trobriand myths tell of disastrous consequences of brother-sister incest that resulted in both parties committing suicide. Sexual relations between a father and daughter are prohibited, although Trobrianders tell stories about it and joke about the idea of a father being overwhelmed by the beauty of his daughter. From the Trobriand point of view, fathers are not related by kinship to their daughters. The best marriage for a man is to a woman from his father's clan, for then his children, who will trace their descent from their mother, will be members of his father's clan. Consequently, the close relationship a man has with members of his father's clan will continue into the next generation.

There is no formal marriage ceremony; the girl simply stays overnight in her boyfriend's house. The next morning the bride's mother brings the couple cooked yams to indicate the bride's family's approval of the marriage. If the girl's parents don't approve, they demand that their daughter return home with them. Significantly, sharing food is considered by the Trobrianders to be more intimate than having sex. Later, the wife's mother and maternal uncle bring raw yams for the couple, while the groom's father and maternal uncle begin collecting **bridewealth**—valuables such as stone ax blades, shells, and money—to give to

Among the Trobriand Islanders, lineage is traced through the mother, and individuals must marry outside their own clan. Here, a Trobriand chief on Kiriwina Island is shown with family members at the home of one of his two wives.

the wife's kin and her father. The requirement of bridewealth makes young men dependent on members of their matrilineage. This differs from the brideservice required of a Ju/wasi man, since brideservice does not obligate a man to members of his family (see Question 5.1).

During the first year of marriage, the couple lives in the hut that served as the groom's adolescent retreat, and during that year the groom's mother brings meals for them to share. At the end of the year, the groom's mother builds a stone hearth for the couple, and at that point the wife becomes responsible for the cooking.

The end of the first year of marriage marks a dramatic change in the husband-wife relationship. They no longer eat together, and the sexuality that bound them together as adolescents must be publicly submerged. After the first year of marriage it is shameful for anyone to refer to the couple's sex life together. People may tease each other with such sexual taunts as "fuck your mother" or "fuck your father" but the epithet "fuck your wife" could get a person killed. In public, a husband and wife never hold hands or display affection. Their lives become segmented into a private domain, in which affection and emotion can be displayed, and a public domain, in which the meaning of their relationship is dictated by their obligation to help ensure the continuity and honor of their respective matrilineages.

The matrilineal principle in the life of a Trobriander husband and wife requires each to have a continued involvement with others outside the nuclear family. In addition to his ties to and concerns for his wife and children, the husband is also involved in the family life of his matrilineage: his sisters and their children. The wife is continually involved with her and her children's matrilineage—particularly her brothers. This involvement is economic and centers around wealth, particularly yams, banana-leaf bundles, and skirts, all of which are controlled ultimately by women.

One reason men marry is to obtain yams. Yams are more than food in the Trobriand Islands; they are valuable symbols or objects of wealth and are used as gifts to create and sustain relationships among people. They are particularly important in marriage transactions and in the continued tie of a woman to her matrilineage. Trobriand family yam gardens belong to the wife, but they are tended first by her father and later by a "brother." Each year at harvest time the yams grown in her garden by her father or brother are ceremoniously taken to her. The amount and quality of the yams grown by a woman's brother are usually proportional to the bridewealth given to the wife's family by the groom's family when the couple was married. Early in the marriage these yams are stored in the rafters of the couple's hut, and the husband uses them as valuables to be redistributed to his kin who contributed the bridewealth. Later—often 10 to 15 years hence—if a man is recognized as important by his wife's kin, they construct a yam house for him to store the yams they bring each year. The amount and quality of the yams stored and displayed by a man are indications of the regard in which he is held by his wife's kin, and of his status in the community. The yam house is, according to Weiner, like a public bank account.

As a man seeks a wife to obtain the yams grown for him by his wife's brother, brothers seek husbands for their sisters, not only for the children nurtured by the husbands for their wives' matrilineage but for the brother-in-law's help in obtaining banana-leaf bundles. Sisters are obligated, with the help of their husbands, to prepare bundles of banana leaves to be used to finance the funerals of members of their matrilineage. Some are made by the woman, but her husband may have to purchase additional bundles. They are given away at funerals by members of the deceased's matrilineage to people who were important in the life of the deceased. The more important the person was to the deceased, the greater the number of banana-leaf bundles he or she receives. In this way, members of a matrilineage uphold their honor and status; to fail to fulfill these obligations would bring dishonor to the matrilineage.

The development of Trobriand family life, then, must be understood in the context of the movement of such goods as yams and banana-leaf bundles between husband and wife and members of the wife's matrilineage. It is the successful completion of the cycle of exchanges of yams and banana-leaf bundles that ensures the stability of a marriage and a matrilineage.

The Trobriand nuclear family promotes stable bonds between husband and wife, although divorce is both frequent and easy to obtain. The initiative is usually taken by the wife. Most divorces occur in the first year of marriage, and they are rare after the couple has been together for a few years.

While fathers are not technically members of their children's family, they are very important in the lives of the children. Once children are weaned they sleep with their fathers, and later the father is responsible for enhancing their beauty with presents of shells, necklaces, and tiny tortoise-shell earrings. These objects are evidence of a father's presence in the life of his child; in fact, Weiner says, the term for a child with unpierced ears is translated as "fatherless." So important is the tie that develops between a man and his son that when the son marries, the father may try to convince him to remain in his village rather than moving to the village of his maternal kin, as expected.

The Family Cycle of the Chinese

The key relationship in the Ju/wasi family is between husband and wife, and among the Trobriand Islanders it is between brother and sister. In China, the family centers on the relationship between father and son. Marriage in traditional China is less a matter of a man getting a wife than of bringing a child-bearer into the household. As Hsu describes it, "A marriage is made in the name of the parents taking a daughter-in-law, not in the name of the son taking a wife."

Since marriage has far less to do with relations between the husband and wife than with those between the husband's family and a daughter-in-law, marriages in traditional China are almost always arranged, often far in advance, and there is little if any courtship. When a boy is six or seven years old, his parents might hire a matchmaker to find a girl who will eventually be an appropriate bride for their son. Since they believe that the time of a person's birth influences his or her personality and fate, the parents might also enlist the services of a diviner to make the appropriate match. The matchmaker takes a red paper with the time and date of a girl's birth to a prospective groom's family. The boy's mother brings this paper (or papers, if there is a choice of brides) to a fortune-teller, who predicts the compatibility of the boy and girl. If a girl is deemed appropriate by the fortune-teller, the matchmaker tries to convince the girl's parents to accept the match. If she is successful, the bridewealth, the marriage gifts of the husband's family to the wife's parents, is then negotiated.

Another way parents can obtain a wife for their son in traditional China is to adopt an infant girl who will be reared in the household and later will marry the son. While this kind of arrangement is not as prestigious as bridewealth marriage, it has two advantages. Since the prospective bride was raised in the household of her future mother-in-law, she is more likely to be obedient, and it is not necessary to pay a brideprice for an adopted daughter-in-law. The major disadvantage is that the prospective bride and groom are raised virtually as brother and sister and often find it difficult to make the transition to husband and wife.

The adoption of a boy to serve as a husband for a daughter is a third way marriages are arranged in traditional China. This is done only when a family has no sons. The adopted boy then assumes the family name, so that his sons continue the line of his adopted father. Such marriages are not as respected as others, and a man who is adopted into his wife's family bears the stigma of having abandoned his parents and ancestors. For poor or orphaned boys, however, the prospect of heading a thriving household might outweigh such a stigma.

Compared to the Ju/wasi or Trobriand marriage ceremony, the Chinese wedding is very formal and, for the groom's family, very expensive. The date and hour of the wedding are determined by a diviner, who even decides the exact time the bride will arrive in her sedan chair. The day before the wedding, the girl's **dowry** is sent to the groom's home in a procession accompanied by a band, drummers, and ushers. The dowry consists of such goods as leather chests, tables, stools, cosmetics, housewares, clothing, and cloth, but never land or a house. On the day of the wedding, the groom is carried in a sedan chair to the house of the

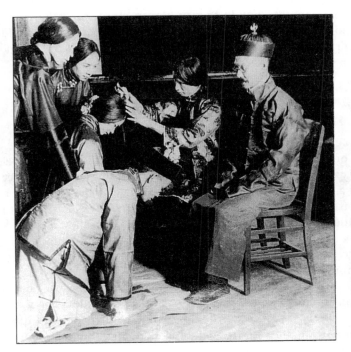

In a traditional Chinese wedding, the bride's mother places a rose in the bride's hair and then transfers it to the groom. Then the couple proceed to the household of the groom's parents, where they will make their home.

bride; when he arrives, she shows token resistance, and she and her mother weep. Then she is carried to the groom's house in a red sedan chair decorated to suggest the early birth of sons. Offerings are made at the ancestors' altar to ensure the success of the marriage. Then the couple is taken to pay respect to the boy's parents—the formal introduction of the bride to the groom's household. Feasting and dancing accompany the wedding and sometimes last for three or four days.

After the wedding, there is little time or place for romantic relations between husband and wife. Hsu reports that, after the marriage, husband and wife sleep in the same bed for only seven days, and there is no public expression of affection between them. Once the wife enters into her husband's family, she finds herself among strangers, virtually cut off from her parents and siblings. She must treat her mother-in-law with respect and acquiesce to the demands of sisters-in-law or other members of her husband's family. She occupies the lowest place at the table. She occasionally can go back to her mother and sob at her change of status, but, as the Chinese proverb puts it, "Spilled water cannot be gathered up." She does not acquire full status in her husband's family until she produces a male child. Until then, the husband must show indifference to his wife, addressing her through a third party; after the birth of a son, he can refer to her as the mother of his child. It is as if a man's wife is related to him only through his children. For the groom, marriage is simply a continued expression of his duty to his father and his ancestors. In no way is his new relationship with a wife to interfere with that duty; rather, the marriage is an expression of his filial devotion and obligation to produce male heirs.

Whereas divorce is a fairly common among the Trobrianders and among the Ju/wasi, it is virtually unheard of in traditional China. A husband can take mistresses with impunity, but, in theory, he can murder an adulterous wife. Wives have no rights of divorce. A wife may flee her husband's household, commit suicide, or become a prostitute, but a woman who wishes to leave her husband and in-laws has few other alternatives.

QUESTION 5.3: What Are the Roles of Sexuality, Love, and Wealth?

The themes of sex, love, and wealth are pervasive in American life, as well as in American soaps. Young men and women use their sexuality and appearance to influence one another and to gain potential partners and spouses. Later, as husbands and wives they attempt to manage their wealth (if they have any) to fulfill social obligations, and to maintain or rise in status. Often they seek to cement their status both as individuals and family by having children. As mothers and fathers they face the task of guiding their children and trying to ensure their success and happiness.

Although the manipulation and negotiation of sexuality, love, and wealth dominate many of the plots of American soap operas, the ideas about romantic love expressed in these plots often are not shared in other societies. Examining these ideas among the Ju/wasi, Trobriand Islanders, and Chinese, and imagining how they might be expressed in soap operas, can help us understand our own beliefs about these things.

Sex, Love, and Wealth Among the Ju/wasi

Wealth plays virtually no part in the lives of the Ju/wasi, but for women, especially, sex, love, and beauty are very important. A Ju/wasi woman's sexuality is her major means of negotiating the conditions of her relationships with others. Sexuality is important first for her own well-being. Nisa told Marjorie Shostak that if a girl grows up not learning to enjoy sex, her mind doesn't develop normally; if a grown woman doesn't have sex, her thoughts are ruined and she is always angry. Moreover, a woman's sexuality maximizes her independence. Sex attracts lovers, and a love relationship, being voluntary, recognizes the equality of the participants. By taking lovers a Ju/wasi woman proclaims her control over her social life, because she can offer her sexuality to men as a means of vitalizing them. Nisa talked candidly about sex, male impotence, and the contributions women make to men. She said:

> A woman can bring a man life, even if he is almost dead. She can give him sex and make him alive again. If she were to refuse, he would die! If there were no women around, their semen would kill men. Did you know that? Women make it possible for them to live. Women have something so good that if a man takes it and moves about inside it, he climaxes and is sustained. (quoted in Shostak 1983:288)

There is one tradeoff for Ju/wasi women who use their sexuality. Men see them as sources of male conflict and consequently as potentially dangerous.

Motherhood, unlike sexuality, is not easily bartered by Ju/wasi women. In other societies, including our own, parents are apt to stress how much they have sacrificed or suffered for their children, thus using motherhood or fatherhood as a way of creating obligations and ties. It makes little sense for a Ju/wasi woman (or man, for that matter) to make such a claim. Children owe their parents little; there is no need for bridewealth or dowries for marriage, and food and kin to care for them are plentiful. The dynamics of Ju/wasi families are built on the need of individuals to avoid permanent ties and obligations and to maintain their independence.

Sex, Love, and Wealth Among the Trobriand Islanders

Whereas the maintenance of sexuality is important throughout life among the Ju/wasi, among the Trobriand Islanders it is important for women only prior to their marriage. Armed with the magic and bodily adornments contributed by her father, but without the wealth—yams, banana-leaf bundles, and other valuables—she will later acquire, an unmarried woman uses her sexuality to negotiate her relationships with others. Once married, she ceases to emphasize her beauty and sexual attraction and instead emphasizes her fertility and motherhood. A woman's worth, once measured by her father's concern for her and her own sexuality and beauty, is determined after marriage by her ability to collect yams for her husband, produce children, and provide banana-leaf bundles for her matrilineage.

Men's sexuality is viewed very differently. Since the Trobrianders claim that men play no role in reproduction, their sexuality is never very important anyway. Their physical attractiveness, however, is important, for this is what attracts lovers and later a wife to collect the yams by which a man measures his status. Beauty is especially important for chiefs. They must maintain an aura of sexual attractiveness in order to attract more wives, whose fathers and brothers will supply the wealth they need to maintain their position of influence.

Wealth also forms different kinds of links for Trobrianders. Because the Ju/wasi have little wealth to contend for, and what there is (e.g., meat) is widely shared, the links men create with their wives' families are based not on wealth but on their labor. Among the Trobrianders, however, men who want to marry must use the wealth of members of their matrilineage as bridewealth payments to their wives' families. They are required to return this wealth to members of their family by redistributing the yams they later receive from their wives' brothers. Moreover, the yams they receive from their brothers-in-law are in some ways payment for the children their wives produce who are members of the wife's and brother-in-law's matrilineage.

Sex, Love, and Wealth Among the Chinese

The themes of sexuality, love, and wealth are played out very differently in the traditional Chinese rural family. Whereas both Ju/wasi and Trobriand adolescents have considerable freedom to utilize their sexuality to attract and influence others, quite the opposite is true in China. If a girl comes from a family that is influential and wealthy enough to make an attractive match for her, she will have little to do with boys. Virginity is both valued and necessary for a Chinese bride; for a Ju/wasi or Trobriander woman it is almost no consideration. In China, if a girl is known to have been mixed up in an affair, her only chance of marriage is to someone in a distant village.

Romantic love and sexuality are irrelevant also in the relations between traditional Chinese husbands and wives. A wife's function is to produce children. A man who can afford it takes concubines. A man who can't afford it, but does so anyway, is criticized not for his infidelity to his wife but for squandering the wealth of his ancestors and descendants.

In fact, sexuality figures very little in the life of a Chinese woman either before or after her marriage. Her sexuality is simply not negotiable; instead it is as a mother that most Chinese women establish significant relations. Her value consists in her potential to become the mother of a boy. Becoming a mother cements her relations with her husband, her father-in-law, and her mother-in-law, and it is her motherhood that secures her later life. While a son is obligated to care for his aged mother, the obligation is not so great as it is to care for a father. To compensate, a woman must establish bonds of emotion and affection with her sons. She may do this with the assistance of her husband. After a boy is six or seven, fathers become aloof and withdrawn in order to assert and reinforce their authority and control over a son. A mother can use her husband's aloofness from his son to strengthen the son's ties to her. Even if she enjoys good relations with her husband, she will try to reserve the son's affections for herself, while preserving the son's respect for his father.

The only exception to the motherhood over sexuality rule is the woman who is unable to obtain a husband or who loses one. Such a woman may become a concubine or prostitute. Margery Wolf tells the story of Tan A-Hong in the Taiwanese village of Peihotien, who was adopted by Lim Han-ci to be the wife of a son who later died. When this happens, adopted daughters are often sold to dealers who buy attractive women to train as prostitutes, to wealthy families as slaves, or to prostitutes who initiate them in their livelihood for support in their old age. Lim Han-ci arranged to have Tan A-Hong adopted into another family, but for whatever reason, the adoption didn't work out. Tan A-Hong moved to southern Taiwan and became a prostitute. She ultimately moved back to Peihotien, bringing with her an adopted daughter whom she reared in her way of life to care for her.

EXERCISE 5.3

The American family is obviously different from the Ju/wasi, Trobriand Islander, or traditional Chinese families, as you might expect. While our families are embedded in an urban-industrial society, the Ju/wasi are hunters and gatherers, the Trobriand Islanders horticulturists and fishermen, and the Chinese peasant farmers. Yet there seem to be features of family life in all three that are similar to life in the American family. Your problem is simply to list those features of family life among the Ju/wasi, Trobriand Islanders, and Chinese that resemble American families. Put another way, what features of American family life would be familiar to a Ju/wasi, a Trobriand Islander, or someone from rural China?

The attitude toward prostitutes in traditional China is not the same as it is in the United States. The Chinese do not condemn women who choose prostitution. According to Margery Wolf, prostitutes are said to be "more interesting" than other women, but people rarely make judgments about them because too many village girls "go out to work" to support family members.

QUESTION 5.4: *What Threatens to Disrupt the Family Unit?*

Threats to family formation and maintenance, are, as might be expected, major sources of soap opera drama. If soap operas are in any way accurate reflections of American life, infidelity, sickness, authority struggles, and economic hardship are the principal threats. Moreover, as our soap operas constantly remind us, any threat to an established marriage endangers the continued existence of the family unit. Ideally, the American marriage is sustained by love; if either partner says "I don't love you anymore," it is generally grounds for divorce. Diminished sexual attraction or sexual activities, or acts of sexual infidelity, are other grounds. Economic problems also threaten the stability of the American family; if a couple does not have the resources to sustain or to fulfill their obligations, strains inevitably develop.

There are also threats to the stability and maintenance of traditional Ju/wasi, Trobriand, and Chinese families, but they differ from those that threaten the American family.

Threats to the Ju/wasi Family

The major threat to family stability among the Ju/wasi is conflict between husband and wife over infidelity or the efforts of a husband to secure a second wife. Like many societies around the world, the Ju/wasi allow **polygamy.** Men are allowed to have more than one wife (**polygyny**) and apparently women are permitted to have more than one husband (**polyandry**), though this is rare. In fact, polygamy is the exception rather than the rule. A survey conducted by Lee in 1968 of 131 married Ju/wasi men found that 93 percent were living monogamously, 5 percent were living in polygynous unions, and 2 percent were living in polyandrous relationships.

One reason why polygamy is rare, even though having more than one wife is a sign of prestige, is the family difficulties it creates. According to Marjorie Shostak, a popular saying is "there is never any peace in a household with two women in it." Stories of the complications resulting from polygamous unions are an endless source of humor for those who are single or monogamous. Here is how Nisa described polygyny in her society to Shostak:

> When a man married one woman, then marries another and sets her down besides the first so there are three of them together at night, the husband changes from one wife to another. First he has sex with the older wife, then with the younger. But when he goes to the younger wife, the older one is jealous and grabs and bites him. The two women start to fight and bite each other. The older woman goes to the fire and throws burning wood at them yelling "What told you that when I, your first wife, am lying here that you should go and sleep with another woman? Don't I have a vagina? So why do you just leave it and go without having sex with me? Instead you go and have sex with that young girl!" Sometimes they fight like that all night, until dawn breaks. A co-wife is truly a terrible thing. (quoted in Shostak 1983:172)

While polygamy is rare, marital infidelity is not. At one water hole with 50 married couples, Lee recorded 16 couples in which one or another of the partners was having an affair. The Ju/wasi recognize certain benefits in taking lovers. For a woman, extramarital affairs add variety, as well as economic insurance. Here is Nisa again:

> When you are a woman, you just don't sit still and do nothing—you have lovers. You don't just sit with the man of your hut, with just one man. One man can give you very little. One man gives you only one kind of food to eat. But when you have lovers, one brings you something and another brings you something else. One comes at night with meat, another with money, another with beads. Your husband also does things and gives them to you. (quoted in Shostak 1983:271)

Men say that the emotion and passion of extramarital affairs are wonderful; "hearts are on fire and passions great," as the Ju/wasi say. When Shostak asked a young married man about his lover he said they fantasized about running away. She asked what it would be like, and he smiled and replied, "The first few months would be wonderful!" Extramarital affairs are likely to be threatening to a husband, however, and they are the most common cause of conflict and violence among the Ju/wasi. Wives are important to Ju/wasi men because as long as they have wives they are dependent on no one. Male adulthood requires acquiring and demonstrating a willingness to fight for a secure marital status.

Nisa's marital history provides an example of Ju/wasi family conflict. After the death of her second husband, Tashay, Nisa married Besa. Nisa says that even though they began fighting soon after the marriage, she became pregnant. Besa then abandoned her at a settlement where they had been working, and she miscarried. Shortly after, she met some people from Besa's village and told them to tell Besa that their marriage was over. She began a relationship with Twi, an older man, who asked her to live with him, and together they went to live in the camp of Nisa's brother. Besa returned, saying he had come to take her back with him. Nisa refused to go. Besa and Twi fought, and Besa, the younger man, pushed Twi down. Later Nisa and Twi separated because Nisa's brother Dau liked Besa and sent Twi away.

Nisa still refused to return to Besa and resumed an affair with a past lover that lasted for a time, until he died. Then she began to see another man named Bo, but Besa returned to renew his claim over her. Violence again erupted, this time between Besa and Bo; they pushed each other and called each other insulting names, such as "Big Testicles" or "Long Penis." In an almost final confrontation with Besa, Nisa publicly stripped off her apron and cried, "There! There's my vagina! Look Besa, look at me! This is what you want!" Besa, consoled by a man who accompanied him, left. Soon after, Nisa and Bo married. Besa also remarried, but later began again to approach Nisa about renewing their relationship.

The story of Nisa's relationship with Besa reveals how much a Ju/wasi man may have invested in a marriage and how he is obligated to resort to violence against his wife's lover, even if she has rejected him.

Threats to the Trobriand Island Family

Among the Trobriand Islanders it is not threats to the husband-wife relationship that are critical but threats to the matrilineage. Because the matrilineage is the major social unit, the honor of that family group relative to other groups is a central concern to all members. Lineages among the Trobriand Islanders are ranked according to the closeness of their genealogical connection to the founders of the lineage. Each lineage must be able to maintain its position vis-à-vis others through the ceremonial presentation of valuables, particularly yams and banana-leaf bundles. So important are yams in the relative ranking of matrilineages that groups try to demonstrate their wealth by giving more yams to others than they receive. Since giving may be taken as a claim of superiority, however, it can be dangerous; as the Trobrianders put it, "When you give too much, people worry."

While it may seem implausible, yams could become the focus of a Trobriand soap opera plot. For example, a man's political power, measured in yams, is a direct result of the support he receives from his wife's kin—it is her yams, grown for her by her father and brother, that create status for her husband. However, the annual yam gifts received by a husband can also be a source of conflict. If the amount or size of yams harvested does not live up to a husband's expectations, he may be insulted. On the other hand, if a woman's brother is unhappy over the bridewealth he received from the husband's family or the support given by the husband to his sister in collecting banana-leaf bundles, he may purposely communicate his unhappiness by not working hard in his sister's yam gardens. Other plots could be devised about unrequited love, attempts of fathers to convince their sons to remain in their father's villages, and even themes about incest. But a theme that would be sure to attract a Trobriand audience would be about sorcery.

The Trobrianders claim to know of spells and magic that are capable of killing. Generally only chiefs have this power, but others can seek out a chief and, for a price, convince him to use his power against their enemies. Someone who is believed to have this power is both feared and respected; Trobrianders tell of instances where they were challenged and retaliated with sorcery. Vanoi, an important Trobriand chief, told Weiner about being challenged by a Christian convert who openly mocked Vanoi's knowledge of sorcery. Vanoi offered the man a cigarette, saying that he should smoke it if he doubted the chief's knowledge of sorcery. The man did; he became ill later that night and died a week later.

A person who uses sorcery against another is dominating that person, and since each person's fate is tied to that of the matrilineage, a threat to one is considered a threat to all. That is why any death among the Trobrianders is a serious matter. Since all deaths are attributed to sorcery, every death is a sign that the power of a matrilineage is being challenged by someone from another lineage. Each funeral marks an attempt by the members of a matrilineage to reassert its power, while, at the same time, the mourners assert their innocence of sorcery. The matrilineal kin of the deceased do this by distributing banana-leaf bundles and other valuables to those who have come to publicly mourn the passing of the deceased and to assist with the funeral arrangements by decorating and carrying the corpse. In recognition of their contribution to the life of the deceased, they receive gifts. The deceased's matrilineage empties its treasury to announce its strength in the face of the threat to its integrity that is signaled by a death.

Maintaining one's identity and that of the matrilineage is a never-ending process among the Trobrianders because death threatens the network by removing someone from it. Here is how Weiner sums up the meaning of death for them:

> Because of the expanding possibilities in a person's life, each Trobriander represents her or his matrilineal identity—originally conceived through a woman and an ancestral baloma spirit—as well as the accumulation of all the other relationships that parenthood and marriage made possible. Therefore, a death demands attention to this full totality, as the members of a matrilineage seek both to repay all "others" for their past care and to hold on to them now that this death has occurred. (Weiner 1988:161)

Threats to the Chinese Family

The biggest threat to the traditional rural Chinese family is, of course, the absence of a son. The lack of a male heir endangers not only the continuance of a household but the entire patrilineage through time. A man without sons, a spirit without descendants, has no one to offer incense for him and no altar on which his spirit can find refuge and honor. The existence of a son is no guarantee of smooth family relations, however. Fathers have enormous authority and power over sons, and sons are obligated to worship, respect, obey, and care for their fathers. But often fathers become overbearing or use force to assert their authority. Margery Wolf says that Lim Han-ci in the village of Peihotien (see Question 5.3) was unusual in the frequency with which he administered physical punishment to his sons; once he beat them with a hoe handle and left bruises that lasted for weeks. However, regardless of how harshly a person may be treated (and most Chinese boys are, if anything, spoiled), breaking away from one's father is considered a violent act. Margery Wolf reports the case of the conflict between Lim Han-ci and his eldest son, Lim Hue-lieng, that illustrates both the dilemma of a father-son split and the difficulties that can arise in adopted marriages. When Lim Hue-lieng was a child, Lim Han-ci adopted Lim A-pou, then nine months old, to be reared as the eventual wife of his son. Growing up in the Lim household, Lim A-pou was a model daughter-in-law. She accepted reprimands and punishment without becoming sullen, she did not complain, and she was a hard worker. However, her relationship with her prospective husband was not a happy one. When Lim Hue-lieng was 19, he committed what in traditional China is an act of moral violence; he left home and severed his relations with his father. If a son dies before his father and so is unable to care for the father in his old age, the father ritually beats the son's coffin to punish him. Lim Hue-lieng was able to leave home only because he had become a leader in the lo mue, a secret society which is involved in crime and extortion but which also protects the downtrodden and contributes heavily to religious festivals.

Years after leaving home, much to the excitement of the villagers, Lim Hue-lieng returned to Peihotien, reconciled with his father, and went through a simple ceremony that transformed him and his foster sibling, Lim A-pou, into husband and wife. While it must have been obvious to her that Lim Hue-lieng would be less than an ideal husband, Lim A-pou did not protest, for what alternatives did she have? She could not return to the family she left as an infant, and to remain in the Lim household after refusing to marry Lim Hue-lieng was impossible. Moreover, there were advantages to marrying the eldest son; it would give her status and influence in the household. Thus, when Lim Hue-lieng took a succession of mistresses after the marriage, and even took one to live in the family house, Lim A-pou complained very little. Since she had a son by Lim

Hue-lieng, her status as the mother of the son of the eldest son in the family was secure.

Dramatic splits between fathers and sons are rare in traditional China. More frequent is conflict between brothers over the division and sharing of the family wealth at the death of a male head of the household. In most other rural, peasant societies around the world, the male head of the household designates his heirs before his death. He may in some fashion divide his property among his offspring—**partible inheritance**—or he may leave all his property to one or another descendent—**impartible inheritance.** In China the ideal is for brothers to continue to live together and share the inheritance, usually under the direction of the eldest son, thus avoiding the division of property. In fact, however, brothers rarely continue to share, and ultimately conflict between them leads to a division of household property.

EXERCISE 5.4

An international television production company has hired your firm, Creativity Enterprises, to write a pilot episode of a soap opera to be marketed in rural China. The plot of the soap you will create will revolve around the Wang family. The Wangs are a relatively well-off farming family who live in rural China. The characters in the soap opera are to include the following family members:

Wang Zhou: the 55-year-old male head of the family
Wang Lim: the wife of Wang Zhou
Wang Xiao: the eldest son of Wang Zhou
Wang Lao: the wife of Wang Xiao
Wang Jiang: the second son of Wang Zhou
Wang Jane: the wife of Wang Jiang
Wang Sally: the 20-year-old unmarried daughter of Wang Zhou
Wang Nai-Nai: the mother of Wang Zhou

Xiao and Lao have four children, two boys and two girls.
Jiang and Jane have two children, both girls.

You may, if you wish, add other characters to the story. The story line should be simple but clear, and you are free to embellish the characters in any way you want, but keep in mind that the soap must appeal to a rural Chinese audience.

Wolf documents the ultimate disintegration of the Lim household after the death of Lim Han-ci and the resulting arguments over property by the sons and their wives. When Wolf went to live in the Lim household, Lim Han-ci and his oldest son, Lim Hue-lieng, had already died. The two remaining family units consisted of the family of the second-oldest son, Lim Chieng-cua, and the family of Lim Hue-lieng's widow, Lim A-Pou. While Lim Han-ci was alive, his power and influence and his control over the family's wealth was enough to maintain the extended family. Once he died, conflict between Lim A-pou and her son on the one hand and Lim Chieng-cua on the other led to the division of family property.

The wealth that had held the extended family together served, finally, to drive it apart. After dividing the property, brothers or their families often continue to live in the same house, but they partition it into separate family units with separate stoves, as did the son and grandson of Lim Han-ci. The once extended household becomes, in effect, a family compound.

CONCLUSIONS

In this chapter we have examined the structure and dynamics of family life among three peoples—the Ju/wasi, the Trobriand Islanders, and the traditional, rural Chinese—by asking four questions. The first question had to do with the composition of the typical family group. Each society has different rules regarding whom a person regards as a family member. In some societies such as that of the Trobrianders, family membership and descent are reckoned through females (matrilineal descent), while in other societies such as that of the traditional Chinese, descent is reckoned through males (patrilineal descent). In still other societies, such as that of the Ju/wasi, family membership is reckoned through both parents (bilateral descent). In China, the family is extended in time to include many generations of living and dead ancestors. For the Ju/wasi the nuclear family is the major social unit; for the Trobrianders it is the matrilineal extended family; and for the Chinese it is the patrilineal extended family.

The next question concerned how the family is formed and the ideal family type is maintained in these societies. Among the Ju/wasi, marriages are arranged by the parents of boys and girls, often at a very young age, but if the girl protests strongly, the marriage does not take place. Among the Trobrianders, young men and women court freely and often choose their own marriage partners, but their choice must be approved by their parents. In traditional China, a marriage is almost always arranged by parents, often with the assistance of a matchmaker. Sometimes female infants or young girls are adopted into families to later marry a son. The economic responsibilities for making a marriage also vary. Among the Ju/wasi, a man is obligated to perform brideservice for the wife's family; among the Trobrianders, as well as in traditional China, a man's family is obligated to pay bridewealth to a wife's family. Key relationships also vary in the different family types. For the Ju/wasi the key relationship is between husband and wife; for the Trobrianders it is between brother and sister; for the Chinese it is between father and son.

Another question had to do with the roles played by sexuality, love, and wealth in family life. Love and sexuality figure prominently in the life of the Ju/wasi. Women especially emphasize the power of their sexuality and men's dependence on it. Wealth plays little role among the Ju/wasi. Among the Trobrianders, men and women begin sexual activities early in their lives, and they place great emphasis on being sexually attractive and on romantic love. Once they are married, however, couples deemphasize the sexual aspects of their lives, at least publicly. Instead, they work to repay the bridewealth payment made to the wife's family, and grow yams for the husband to present each year to his sister's husband. Wealth is important to maintain the social rank of the matrilineage. In traditional China, sexuality and love play little part in family life. The main obligation of a woman is to produce a son; it is her fertility, not her sexuality, that men value. Wealth is needed by a man's family to pay bridewealth to the wife's family at the time of marriage. Wealth is also required to sustain the patrilineal extended family of a man, his sons, and his sons' sons.

The forces that threaten the family unit were the topic of the final question. Marital infidelity is the greatest threat to the Ju/wasi family and divorce is frequent, especially early in a marriage. For the Trobrianders the more serious threats are to the matrilineal extended family. Since death of a family member is believed to be caused by an act of sorcery, it is a serious threat to the family unit, as is the consequent depletion of economic resources. Divorce is almost nonexistent in traditional China. The failure to produce a male heir threatens the continuity of the family, as does the death of the head of the patrilineal extended family. Disputes among brothers over the distribution of family wealth often result in the breakup of the extended family.

REFERENCES AND SUGGESTED READINGS

INTRODUCTION: SOAP OPERAS AND FAMILY RELATIONS   The epigraphs come from Lawrence Stone's *The Family, Sex and Marriage in England, 1500–1800* (Harper & Row, 1977), and from an automobile bumper sticker first observed in the mid-1970s. Susan S. Bean provides an analysis of American soap operas in "Soap Operas: Sagas of American Kinship," in *The American Dimension: Cultural Myths and Social Realities,* edited by William Arens and Susan P. Montague (Alfred Publishing, 1976). The study of Brazilian soap opera is provided by Conrad Phillip Kottak in *Prime Time Society: An Anthropological Analysis of Television and Culture* (Wadsworth Publishing, 1990).

WHAT IS THE COMPOSITION OF THE TYPICAL FAMILY GROUP?   The descriptions of the Ju/wasi are drawn largely from Richard Lee's book, *The Dobe !Kung* (Holt, Rinehart, and Winston, 1984), and Marjorie Shostak's *Nisa: The Life and Words of a Ju/wasi Woman* (Vintage Books, 1983), with additional information drawn from Elizabeth Thomas's *The Harmless People* (Alfred A. Knopf, 1959). The description of the Trobriand Islander family is taken from Annette B. Weiner's *The Trobrianders of Papua New Guinea* (Holt, Rinehart, and Winston, 1988) and from Bronislaw Malinowski's *The Sexual Life of Savages in North-Western Melanesia* (Halcyon House, 1929). The material on China comes largely from Margery Wolf, *The House of Lim* (Prentice-Hall, 1968); Francis L. K. Hsu, *Under the Ancestors' Shadow* (Anchor Books, 1967); and Hsiao-Tung Fei, *Peasant Life in China: A Field Study of Country Life in the Yangtze Valley* (Routledge & Kegan Paul, 1939). Additional information on traditional Chinese families can be found in *Village Life in China* by Arthur H. Smith (Little, Brown, 1970). The description of the procreation beliefs by Turkish villagers is described by Carol Delaney in *The Seed and the Soil: Gender and Cosmology in a Turkish Village Society* (University of California Press, 1991).

HOW IS THE FAMILY FORMED AND THE IDEAL FAMILY TYPE MAINTAINED?   The observations about the significance of brideservice and bridewealth come largely from Jane E. Collier and Michelle Rosaldo, "Politics and Gender in Simple Societies," in *Sexual Meanings: The Cultural Construction of Gender and Sexuality* (pp. 275–329), edited by Sherry B. Ortner and Harriet

Whitehead (Cambridge University Press, 1981). A good introduction to kinship and social organizations is Burton Pasternak's *Introduction to Kinship and Social Organization* (Prentice-Hall, 1976).

WHAT ARE THE ROLES OF SEXUALITY, LOVE, AND WEALTH? The extent to which women in different societies are valued for or emphasize their sexuality or their role in procreation is discussed by Collier and Rosaldo in their article cited above and by Michelle Rosaldo and Jane Monnig Atkinson in "Man the Hunter and Woman: Metaphors for the Sexes in Ilongot Magical Spells," in *The Interpretation of Symbolism,* edited by Roy Willis (John Wiley & Sons, 1975). A good general review of works on the cultural construction of sexuality can be found in an article by D. L. Davis and R. G. Whitten, "The Cross-Cultural Study of Human Sexuality," in *Annual Review of Anthropology,* vol. 16 (1987), pp. 69–98.

WHAT THREATENS TO DISRUPT THE FAMILY UNIT? A good analysis and review of factors that influence family structure can be found in "Family and Household: The Analysis of Domestic Groups," by Sylvia Junko Yanagisako, in *Annual Review of Anthropology,* vol. 8 (1979), pp. 161–205. An interesting collection of articles by anthropologists on divorce, largely in America, can be found in *Divorce and After,* edited by Paul Bohannan (Doubleday, 1970).

Morris Hirshfield. *Girl in a Mirror*. 1940. Oil on canvas, 40⅛ ×
22¼". The Museum of Modern Art, New York. Purchase. Photograph
© 1997 The Museum of Modern Art, New York.

CHAPTER 6

THE CULTURAL CONSTRUCTION
OF IDENTITY

PROBLEM 6: HOW DO PEOPLE DETERMINE WHO THEY ARE, AND
HOW DO THEY COMMUNICATE WHO THEY THINK THEY ARE TO
OTHERS?

When an individual enters the presence of others, they commonly seek to acquire information about him or to bring into play information about him already possessed. They will be interested in his general socioeconomic status, his conception of self, his attitude toward them, his competence, his trustworthiness, etc. Although some of this information seems to be sought almost as an end in itself, there are usually quite practical reasons for acquiring it. Information about the individual helps to define the situation, enabling others to know in advance what he will expect of them and what they may expect of him. Informed in these ways, the others will know how best to act in order to call forth a desired response from him.

Erving Goffman

INTRODUCTION: *The Importance of Self*

Of all the products of our culture, the one we most take for granted is our self. We are not born knowing who we are or what our places are on the social landscape; we learn to be American or Japanese, male or female, husbands or wives, Amy, Richard, Michael, Rachel, Gabriela, or Rebecca. As we become who we are, we learn how we stand in relation to others. We learn how we relate to others as sons, daughters, students, friends, or lovers. In this sense, society is a collection of **social identities** distributed over a landscape. Individuals strive to arrive at some identity/destination from which they can relate to other social identities while they seek confirmation from others that they occupy the position on the social landscape that they claim to occupy.

To appreciate the importance of the self, try to imagine a society in which every person is physically indistinguishable from every other person. How would people in such a society know how to behave toward each other? Whenever we interact with another person, the interaction must be based on some idea of who the other is: Friend? Stranger? Family member? Teacher? At the same time, the other must have some idea of who we are, a conception of the relationship that exists between us. The necessity of knowing the social identity of others is apparent when strangers meet and, directly or indirectly, seek to elicit information about one another. Each tries to place the other in some identity at some spot on the social landscape.

The opposite of a society in which all people are indistinguishable is as implausible as one in which everyone is identical. In this case, every interaction would be unique, and there would be no way to learn from one situation how to behave in another similar situation. Each person would need to have an infinite variety of behaviors with which to interact with an infinite number of types of people. We avoid this situation by categorizing people, placing them in groups so that not everyone in our social universe is unique. We group them into categories based on criteria such as gender (female or male); ethnicity (Irish, Italian, Chinese); personal characteristics (short, tall, husky, thin), and so on.

Try to imagine, also, a social landscape in which no person acknowledges any other person or communicates in any way who she or he thinks the other is.

This, too, would represent an impossible situation. People would have no way of acquiring from others confirmation that they occupy the social identities they think they occupy. In reality, our social identities are constructed in large part by others who, by their behavior toward us, confirm that we occupy the spot on the landscape we claim to occupy. Put another way, nobody is anybody except in relation to somebody.

Finally, try to imagine a social landscape in which everyone communicates to everyone else that they occupy the wrong spot on the landscape. Every person actively disagrees with every other person about who they are. This situation would be, if not impossible, at least chaotic.

To examine how people in a society determine who they are and communicate who they think they are to others, we will explore the ways different societies define the person, the ways individuals are differentiated from others, the manner in which individuals find out who they are, how they convey to others who they are, and the consequences of disagreements over identity.

QUESTIONS

6.1   How does the concept of personhood vary from society to society?
6.2   How do societies distinguish individuals from one another?
6.3   How do individuals learn who they are?
6.4   How do individuals communicate their identities to one another?
6.5   How do individuals defend their identities that are threatened?

QUESTION 6.1:   How Does the Concept of Personhood Vary from Society to Society?

Personal names in all societies are intimate markers of the person, differentiating individuals from others. Names also can reveal how people conceive of themselves and their relations to others. For Americans, they are perhaps the most enduring aspect of the self. Assigned at birth, our names remain with us throughout our lives. Some people may choose to modify them—to shorten Kathleen to Kate, or Philip to Phil. In whatever form a name takes, it represents the self. How much of the self is revealed by a name varies by culture and situation. College students meeting for the first time exchange personal names, rarely bothering with family names. Theirs is a self independent of any group or past. When American businesspeople meet they exchange first names, last names, and business titles. Businesspeople are linked to their organizations. When Moroccans from different towns meet, the names they offer to others include not only the names of their families but the names of the towns they are from. The Moroccan self is embedded in family and place of origin. Among the Gitksan of British Columbia, the names people use depend on their social position; when they enter adulthood, get married, or assume a higher rank in Gitksan society, they change their names. The Gitksan self is inseparable from one's position in society.

The differences in naming practices among different societies reveal the different ways societies conceptualize what a person is and how that person relates to the group. Most Americans believe that individuals are stable, autonomous entities who exist more or less independently of whatever situations or statuses they occupy. As Americans move from status to status or place to place—from student to husband or wife, to employee, to father or mother—they believe themselves to be the same persons nevertheless. Otherwise, each time we changed situations or statuses we would in effect become different people, and would have to change our names. In this regard, Americans are highly **individualistic.**

This does not seem to be the case in other societies where individuals are not seen as entities distinct from their social position or group. In societies such as the Gitksan, the relationship between the person and the group, or the person and his or her social position, is **holistic;** the person cannot be conceived as existing separately from society or apart from his or her status or role. The holistic view of the self is expressed in Gandhi's metaphor of individuals as drops in the ocean; the drops cannot survive without the ocean, and the ocean loses its identity without the drops.

The Egocentric and Sociocentric Self

These differences between the individualistic and holistic conceptions of the self led Richard A. Shweder and Edmund J. Bourne to distinguish two distinct ways in which the person is conceived in different societies: the egocentric and the sociocentric views of self. In the **egocentric** view, typified in many ways by the Western view adopted in American society, each person is defined as a replica of all humanity, the locus of motivations and drives, capable of acting independently from others. For Westerners, the individual is the center of awareness, a distinct whole set against other wholes. Social relations are regarded as contracts between autonomous, free-acting beings. Individuals are free to negotiate their places in society, and the dominant idea is that everyone is responsible for what and who they are. Moreover, individuals possess intrinsic qualities such as generosity, integrity, or beauty. In the egocentric view of the person, a high value is placed on individualism and self-reliance.

Robert Bellah and his coauthors also examined American ideas of the individual in *Habits of the Heart.* The American self, they say, seeks to work out its own life plot by individually pursuing happiness and satisfying its wants. Unlike individuals in some other societies, Americans seek to cut themselves off from the past, especially from their parents. Each wishes to become his or her own person, to find his or her self. Americans seem to want to give birth to themselves. Young men and women need to demonstrate that they can stand on their own two feet and be self-supporting. This belief in a self-reliant, independent self underlies the American belief in success as the outcome of free and fair competition among individuals in an open market. Most successful Americans, say Bellah and his associates, claim that they achieved success through their own hard work and seldom acknowledge the contributions made by their families, their schooling, or their position as a member of the upwardly mobile middle class. The only way they can say they deserve what they have achieved is if they have succeeded through their own efforts.

In contrast to the egocentric view of the person, say Shweder and Bourne, the **sociocentric** view of the self is context-dependent. The self exists as an en-

The cowboy image projected by John Wayne personified the idealized American self—individualistic and self-reliant.

tity only within the concrete situations or roles occupied by the person in much the same way that the Gitksans' names are linked to their position in society, and not to some autonomous, separate self. From a sociocentric view, there is no intrinsic self that can possess enduring qualities such as generosity, integrity, or beauty. Such qualities can apply only to concrete social situations. Instead of saying that a man is generous, a sociocentric perspective would be, "He gives money to his friends." Instead of saying that a woman is principled, the perspective would be, "She does not give away secrets."

Personhood in Japan and America

Some anthropologists attribute a sociocentric view of the self to the Japanese. Anthropologist Christie Kiefer explains that the Japanese are more apt to include within the boundaries of the self the social groups of which the person is a member, as opposed to the American self-concept, which does not extend beyond the physical body. Japanese children are not trained to be self-reliant, as American children are. They are taught that interdependence between the person and the family or group is more important than independence.

Robert Smith notes that the Japanese view of the self is expressed in their language. For example, Japanese language lacks anything resembling our personal pronouns. In American society, children quickly learn to use the two personal referents, I and you; Japanese boys, on the other hand, must learn six, and girls must learn five. The personal referent used in Japan depends on the relationship of the speaker to the listener. It expresses how the self is defined relative to a specific social interaction.

In addition, says Smith, Japanese language lacks vocabulary that is status-neutral. Rather, it is characterized by what the Japanese call *keigo,* or "polite speech." Keigo has the effect of establishing at the outset of a conversation the relative social standing and degree of intimacy of speaker and listener. Japanese speakers use different forms of address depending on their social position relative to the person to whom they are speaking. Since the Japanese language is status-based, people must be careful of the linguistic forms they use in conversations. When conversing with someone in a superior social position, the speaker must linguistically acknowledge his or her inferiority. Japanese advertisers have a problem with keigo because actors should not give imperative commands (e.g., "drink Coke") for fear of offending people. They solve the problem by using low-status people who are nonthreatening (e.g., clowns, coquettish women, or children) to issue the commands.

EXERCISE 6.1

People begin to learn from childhood the ways their self relates to others and their groups. That is, by the behavior of others toward them, they come to see themselves as distinct entities or as beings intimately linked to others. Schools in America are significant environments for learning about self. Try to list the ways in which American school settings, and how children act in them, convey to children their degree of individuality and responsibility for their actions. Are there ways in which individualism is submerged? Might school settings differ in the extent to which the egocentric, as opposed to the sociocentric, self is developed?

The sociocentric Japanese differ also from the egocentric Americans in their approach to social interaction. Americans believe it is desirable to assert themselves; some even undergo assertiveness training. Americans believe that it is desirable for people to stand out, to take charge. The Japanese believe that social interaction should be characterized by restraint or reserve, traits they identify as *enryo.* Americans may aggressively present themselves to others; the Japanese are more reticent. With enryo, giving opinions is avoided; this attitude is best summed up in the Japanese proverb, "The nail that sticks up shall be hammered down."

Nevertheless, the Japanese do conceive of themselves as separate entities. They are as attached to their personal names as Americans are, if not more so. Moreover, the Japanese believe in self-development. But for the Japanese the autonomy of the individual is established, not in social situations where they actively distinguish themselves from others, as Americans do, but away from society, where self-reflection and introspection are legitimate. It is through introspection that the Japanese find their true heart (kokoro) and are put in touch with their true nature—their *hara* ("belly") and *jibub* ("self").

In the remainder of this chapter, we will look at the self less from our own egocentric perspective and more from the sociocentric perspective, as something contingent and relative to the situation. Our focus will be on that part of the self that is defined by social relations and social processes and that is subject to change and redefinition.

QUESTION 6.2: *How Do Societies Distinguish Individuals from One Another?*

Differences and similarities among persons are the materials from which we construct our social landscapes that allow us to distinguish individuals from one another or assign them to one group or another. From these similarities and differences we construct our social identities. However, all societies do not use the same similarities and differences to construct a social code, nor do they use these similarities and differences in the same way. Some characteristics of persons are almost universally used to differentiate and to group them. Family membership, gender, and age, for example, are used in every society as categories of a social code. Other characteristics figure prominently only in some societies: ethnic group membership, skin color, and wealth, for example. Take the variety of personal characteristics used to construct a social landscape by students and teachers in a suburban New York high school. They include (not necessarily in this order): participation or nonparticipation in sports, performance in sports (as measured by the number of points an individual has contributed to a team), participation in extracurricular activities, dress, scholastic achievement, will to achieve, disruptive or nondisruptive behavior, willingness to cooperate with teachers and administration, gender, ethnicity (Italian, "nothing" [American], Irish, African American, Hispanic), family wealth, health, age, grade, and so on.

Perhaps the most important set of characteristics used to define the self is related to kinship and family membership. In traditional societies, kinship is the central organizing principle—the main determinant of a person's social identity. Anthropologists working with traditional societies are often "adopted" by a family. This act, while also a signal of acceptance, serves the practical purpose of assigning an outsider a social identity through which she or he can be approached by others. To have no kinship label or designation in such societies is to have no meaningful place on the social landscape.

Language spoken is another important identity marker that is sometimes viewed as essential for the maintenance of a group identity. The way a language is spoken is often important; think of how Americans use dialect to identify people as being New Englanders, New Yorkers, Texans, and the like. Language is often tied strongly to a national identity, and many countries have established institutions to oversee the "purity" of the national language. The Academie Française is charged with keeping the French language free of foreign borrowings, such as "le hot dog" or "le hamburger." In some countries conflict between groups focuses on issues of language. In Quebec, for example, efforts of one group to preserve French as the official language of the province, and thus protect what it sees as essential to group identity, have led to a movement for independence from the English-speaking remainder of Canada.

The importance of group identity can also be observed in Northern Ireland, where the fundamental marker that people use to locate others is religious affiliation. An important skill the Irish people acquire is "telling": determining whether another person is Catholic or Protestant. Adults in Northern Ireland claim that they can tell a person's religious affiliation by such cues as their area of residence, the school they go to, their given names and surnames, speech, clothing, and even facial appearance. Some have suggested that group identity, whether Protestant or Catholic, is the most important defining feature of social identity. This is reflected in the joke about a man who is stopped on a Belfast street and asked his religion. "Jewish," he replies. "Yes," says the questioner, "but are you a Catholic Jew or a Protestant Jew?"

Northern Ireland also illustrates the importance of having either a **positive identity** or a **negative identity.** Members of each group attempt to build a positive identity, to attribute to themselves characteristics they believe are desirable, and to construct a negative identity for others by attributing undesirable characteristics to them. In Northern Ireland they often do this by comparing themselves with the other religious group, Catholics to Protestants, Protestants to Catholics. Catholics build a positive identity by emphasizing their Celtic heritage, their "decency," while Protestants emphasize their past military triumphs and their loyalty to Great Britain. Protestants believe themselves to be "neater" and "cleaner" than Catholics; Catholics think of themselves as the only true Irish.

Learning to Be Male and Female

While some personal attributes of individuals are used to construct identities in almost all societies, they are not always used in the same way. Gender is a good example of an identity feature that Americans take for granted, assuming it is a biological construct. But gender is at least as much a cultural creation as it is a biological construct; that is, different standards apply to being male and being female.

American parents, for example, teach male children that it is manly to endure pain, to be strong and tough. Male children are discouraged from expressing discomfort and encouraged when they can withstand it. Female children, on the other hand, are comforted when they hurt themselves. Traditionally, American male children are encouraged to be aggressive and competitive; they learn to compete in games and play with toys that require aggressive behavior. Females are taught to be caring and helpful; they are given toys such as dolls that encourage "feminine" behavior.

Schools in America reinforce gender roles in areas such as sports participation. Douglas Foley, in his description of student life in a Texas high school notes the special role that coaches play in socializing males into their gender roles. Unlike regular teachers, they are less likely, says Foley, to be considered sissies. They occupy a special place in the culture of schools and of small communities. They are more likely to have outside interests, more likely to be known and respected in the community, and more likely to become school administrators and leaders.

Cheerleaders reinforce gender roles, says Foley, by performing at pep rallies and games. In the study, cheerleaders were objects of envy and gossip, and were considered by men to be objects to possess, dominate, and gain status through. They were objects of longing who prompted among men public bravado and private longing and frustration. Young women who could not be cheerleaders joined the pep squad that would lead cheers and decorate town and school.

These gender roles were further reinforced through the ritual of the powder-puff football game, in which the men dressed as female cheerleaders and burlesqued female behavior while young women dressed in football attire and played a game of football. As Foley (1990:51) put it:

> Males used this moment of symbolic inversion to parody females in a burlesque and ridiculous manner. Males took great liberties with the female role through this humorous form of expression. The power of these young males to appropriate and play with female symbols of sexuality was a statement about males' social and physical dominance. Conversely, the females took few liberties with their expression of the male role. They tried to play a very serious game of football. The females tried earnestly to prove they were equal. Their lack of playfulness was a poignant testimony to their subordinate status in this small town.

Anthropologist Margaret Mead pioneered the idea that gender is more a matter of culture than biology. She illustrates her point by comparing three New Guinea societies: the Arapesh, the Mundugumor, and the Tchambuli. Among the Arapesh, both male and female children are discouraged from fighting or other acts of aggression, and they are never taught to accept discomfort. Children are fed when they are hungry, and they are taught to share. The Arapesh do not believe that sex is a powerful driving force for men or for women. As a consequence, Mead says, both males and females are gentle, cooperative, and responsive to others. Unlike the Arapesh, both Mundugumor men and women are expected to be ruthless and aggressive, much like American males, says Mead. Among the Tchambuli, gender definitions are the reverse of those in American society. Women are taught to be dominant and controlling, while men were expected to be emotionally dependent. On the basis of these findings, Mead concludes that culture defines and creates gender differences in personality, values, and behavior.

The number of gender categories recognized in societies also differs. For example, many Native American societies traditionally recognized a third gender, that of *berdache* among the Cheyenne and Lakota, and the nadle among the Navajo. The berdache or nadle is a biological male who does not fill a standard male role. Such individuals are not seen as men, nor are they defined as women. They occupy a third role, one that is culturally defined, accepted, and, in some cases revered. Male children in the Navajo, Lakota, Cheyenne, and other groups thus could choose from two gender categories, rather than learning that gender roles are defined by physiology. Among the Lakota, male children learned that, if they desired, they could adopt the dress and work roles of women, and have sex with men, although the berdache role did not necessarily involve sexual behavior. The berdache or nadle did not play only women's roles, however; some were noted for their hunting skills and exploits in war. In American society, in contrast, persons who do not assume the gender roles associated with their anatomy are defined as deviant, abnormal, or nonconformist.

Anthropologist Harriet Whitehead suggests that Americans have difficulty recognizing a third gender in part because they make ethnocentric assumptions about what characteristics are most important in defining gender roles. Americans define gender largely by sexual preference—whether a person prefers to have sex with a male or female. They pay less attention to preferences in dress, behavior, and occupation. Native North Americans traditionally placed a different emphasis on these characteristics. Groups that included the socially legitimate identity of berdache or nadle defined gender primarily by choice of occupation; the gender of a sexual partner was least important.

In every society, therefore, the members have various identities. Not all, of course, are appropriate for everyone. Individuals must learn not only the characteristics of different identities but where on the social landscape they belong.

RESOURCE 6.2

Gender

The study of gender relations among different cultures has long been a major concern of anthropologists. If you would like to explore the subject further, there are some excellent Web resources. You can find an extensive list of resources on the subject of anthropology and gender at Anthro.Net at: **http://home1.gte.net/ericjw1/gender.html**

QUESTION 6.3: *How Do Individuals Learn Who They Are?*

We are not born with an identity; it is something we learn. Moreover, identities are not static phenomena. In all societies, people are constantly changing their identities as they move through the life cycle. Consequently, there must be ways in which identity changes are announced.

In a classic work published in 1908, Arnold van Gennep introduced the concept of **rites of passage.** These rituals mark a person's passage from one identity to another, as a person's progress through a house might be marked by going into different rooms. Van Gennep identifies three phases in rites of passage: First, the ritual separates the person from an existing identity; next, the person enters a transition phase; finally, the changes are incorporated into a new identity. These phases of rites of passage are not equally elaborated in specific ceremonies. The separation phase, for example, is a major part of funeral ceremonies designed to help the living let go of the deceased; transition is a major part of initiation ceremonies marking the passage of a person from, say, childhood to adulthood; and incorporation is emphasized in marriage ceremonies that, in most societies, mark the transfer of a person from one social group to another.

Anthropologists have even begun to study how American corporations use ceremony and ritual to help employees define their identities within the work organization. Some corporations use ceremonies not only to change a person's identity but to remind others in the organization of unacceptable behavior. The W. T. Grant Corporation reportedly humiliated poor-performing store managers by throwing custard pies in their faces, cutting their ties in half, and inducing them to push peanuts across the floor with their noses. W. T. Grant was later dissolved through bankruptcy.

A more successful example of the use of ritual to define identity in business was the Mary Kay Cosmetics Corporation's ceremonies to enhance employees' identification with the company. Each year, awards were presented to sales personnel, all of whom were women, in a setting that has been compared to the Miss America Pageant. Honorees, dressed in evening clothes, were seated on the stage of a large auditorium in front of a cheering audience. The ceremony celebrated the personal saga of the founder Mary Kay—how, through personal determination and optimism, she was able to adjust to her separation from her husband, support her children as a salesperson, and ultimately found her own company. The ideology of the corporation is symbolized by a bee-shaped pin with the legend "Everyone can find their wings and fly."

The Transition to Adulthood

Prominent in most societies around the world are ceremonies that mark the transition of a male from boyhood to manhood, most involving some kind of test of courage. Anthropologist David Gilmore claims that one reason so many societies incorporate tests of masculinity and tortuous initiation rituals for males is that the male identity is more problematical than the female identity. For every individual, there is in the beginning of life a subliminal identification with the mother, and men must make greater efforts to differentiate themselves from their identification with their mothers. Consequently, societies incorporate rituals that symbolically separate the boy from his mother, while at the same time incorporating him into manhood.

One example cited by Gilmore is the Maasai, a cattle-herding people of East Africa. For a Maasai male to attain the identity of "worthy man," he must own cattle, be generous to others, and be autonomous and independent, capable of defending his homestead and his honor. He must also demonstrate bravery on cattle raids against neighboring groups. The road to being a man (what the Maasai call a *moran*) begins with a boy's father looking for a sign that the boy is ready to assume the responsibilities of manhood. Tepilit Ole Saitoti tells in his autobiography how he begged his father to let him be initiated. One day Tepilit confronted a huge lioness that threatened the family's cattle, and killed it. Shortly after, his father gathered the family and said, "We are going to initiate Tepilit into manhood. He has proven before all of us that he can now save children and cattle."

The central feature of the Maasai initiation is circumcision. Circumcision is intensely painful, since the cutting, which may last up to four minutes, is done with no anesthetic. The boy, placed on view before male relatives and prospective in-laws, must remain absolutely still and silent. Tepilit Ole Saitoti describes how, shortly before his circumcision, he was told, "You must not budge; don't move a muscle or even blink. You can face only one direction until the operation is completed. The slightest movement on your part will mean you are a coward, incompetent, and unworthy to be a Maasai man."

Americans also have their rites of passage into adulthood, some of the most spectacular being those associated with high school and college fraternities. As with the Maasai, sexual identity and separation from the female identity often is a major theme in these ceremonies. To illustrate, I want to describe a study whose initial focus was an instance of fraternity gang rape. The study began in 1983 when anthropologist Peggy Reeves Sanday learned from one of her students of a gang rape at a college fraternity. Sanday's subsequent research produced a vivid portrait of how college fraternity behavior depicts the male identity in American society.

By participating in male-bonding rituals such as this food fight in a college fraternity, young American males establish new identities as members of a group.

Gang rape, or "pulling train," as it is called in fraternities, begins with the coercion of a vulnerable young woman who is seeking acceptance or may be high on alcohol or drugs and who may or may not agree to have sex with a certain man. When she passes out or is too weak or intoxicated to protest, a "train" of men proceed to have sex with her. While the incident that triggered Sanday's study occurred in a fraternity on a large, prestigious college campus, gang rape is not unique to college fraternities. It is also associated with sports teams, street gangs, and other groups of men for whom the act often serves, according to Sanday, as a male bonding ritual. Pulling train occurs with some frequency. During one six-year period in the mid-1980s, there were 75 documented cases on college campuses, and in the investigation of the event that led to Sanday's study, witnesses reported that it occurred on that campus once or twice a month. It is likely that many cases go unreported. One reason is that both perpetrators and victims often do not recognize it as rape. Most men, suggests Sanday, believe that if a woman has consented with one man, does not vigorously resist, and is not violently overpowered, the sex act does not constitute rape. Rather, they say, the woman is "asking for it." These men are unaware that any sex act in which the woman is not able to give consent constitutes a legal definition of rape. Victims may not recognize it as rape either, and may take the responsibility, saying, "I went too far" or "I let things get out of hand." Other victims are reluctant to report it because of the publicity or negative treatment they receive from authorities. Where fraternities are concerned, colleges often cloak these events in secrecy to protect the offenders, the victims, and themselves.

As Sanday and her associates interviewed fraternity members, women who were associated with them, and victims of rape, they sought to explain what it was about male identity, as represented by college fraternities, that encourages these actions. Three things seemed to stand out in her account. First, there is a heavy emphasis in fraternities on male bonding and male-bonding behavior to the extent that a college man's self-esteem and social identity are dependent on first gaining entry to a fraternity and then being accepted by the brothers. Fraternities confer status; on most college campuses where they exist, they are recognized as places "where the action is." They also provide reassurance, security, and ready-made identities. Membership in a fraternity transforms outsiders into insiders.

Second, sex constitutes a major status and identity marker. Masculinity is defined and demonstrated by sexual conquest. For example, in the fraternity in which the gang rape occurred, a major activity was "hitting" or "riffing" on women, or "working a yes out." This involves persuading a woman to have sex by talking, dancing, or drinking with her. Men who are expert riffers gain status; those who are not successful are in danger of being labeled "nerds," "wimps," or, worse, "fags." Sex in this case is a public thing. Men in the fraternities that Sanday interviewed bragged publicly about their sexual conquests and arranged for brothers to witness them. Some fraternities posted weekly newsletters listing brothers' sexual conquests.

A third element in the identity of fraternity men concerns their attitudes toward women. Many of the fraternity members interviewed by Sanday implied that women were sex objects to be abused or debased. A woman's identity among fraternity men was determined largely by her sexual interactions with them. Women who are sexually unresponsive are "frigid" or "icicles"; women who allow advances only up to a point and refuse intimacy, are "cockteasers"; and women who have sex with many men are "sluts" or "cunts." Such labels indicate that the role of girlfriend is virtually the only role with no negative connotations that a woman can play. In one fraternity, brothers marked women who attended their parties with "power dots": black, red, yellow, white, or blue stickers they attached to a girl's clothing at parties to indicate how easy the girl was to pick up.

For fraternity men, the debasement of women is interwoven with the themes of male bonding and sexual conquest. Part of the reason men bond in college, says Sanday, is to achieve domination and power they think is owed to males. One fraternity man explained how verbally harassing a girl increases male bonding. "I mean, people come back the day after a party and say, 'You should have seen me abuse this girl.' They're real proud of it in front of everyone."

EXERCISE 6.3

In her book on gang rape, Sanday also discusses the role of pornography in the definition of male and female identities in America. She suggests that pornography in America depicts women as subservient to men and that it reinforces sexist attitudes and encourages behavior toward women characteristic of men in fraternities. Do you agree or disagree, and why?

Sanday calls the use of sex and the debasement of women to demonstrate masculinity *phallocentrism,* "the deployment of the penis as a concrete symbol of masculine social power and dominance." Phallocentrism, as well as the themes of male bonding, sexual prowess, and the debasement of women, all are manifested in the act of pulling train. It is a form of bonding, it publicly legitimizes a male's heterosexuality, and it makes women an object of scorn and abuse.

Sanday is quick to emphasize that not all college men subscribe to the ideology of phallocentrism, and not all fraternity men measure their masculinity by sexual conquest and the victimization of women. In the case that initiated her study, the six men charged with gang rape were all described by girls who knew them as "among the nicest guys in the fraternity." Individually, probably none of them would have committed the act they were charged with. In the context of the fraternity, however, gang rape is the credible outcome of a process of identity formation that is manifested in fraternity life in general and in the fraternity initiation ritual in particular.

The fraternity initiation ritual on most college campuses is the culmination of a period of pledging in which initiates are required to perform various demeaning acts. Particulars may vary from fraternity to fraternity and campus to campus, but in general the ritual stigmatizes the initiates as infants, children, or girls and then proceeds to cleanse them of this negative identity prior to incorporating them into the fraternity as full-fledged brothers.

In one fraternity initiation described to Sanday, the initiates were blindfolded and stripped down to their jockstraps. Then they were told to drop their jockstraps and were ridiculed: "Look at the pin-dicks, pussies, fags. They're all a bunch of girls, it's amazing they don't have tits." As the brothers screamed at them, their testicles were rubbed with Ben-Gay. After about 10 minutes a brother spoke saying "Sorry we had to do that, but we had to cleanse you of your nerd sin." Then the pledges were put to tests of trust. In one case, a pledge was thrown to the ground and swords were placed at his crotch by one brother and at his chest by another. The pledge was then asked if he trusted the brothers not to kill him. As the pledge nodded yes, the brother brought the sword down on his chest; since it was made of wood, it shattered. In another fraternity initiates were taken blindfolded to a bathroom and told to eat some feces out of a toilet bowl and trust that they would not become sick. As they picked it out and ate it, they realized it was a banana.

The final stage of most fraternity initiations generally includes a secret ritual in which the pledges come before the brothers who are dressed in robes and hoods or other ritual paraphernalia. In one ritual reported to Sanday, a brother addressed the initiates with the following words:

> You have shown trust in the fraternity and trust in the brothers. We know we can trust you now. A bond has been formed between us. No one has experienced the hell you have except us and the brothers before us. Bonded by strength, loyalty, and trust we are one. Cleansed of weakness and filth, we are men. As men we stand tall. As men we stand for the fraternity, and [name of fraternity] stands for us. (quoted in Sanday 1990:163)

In these ceremonies, the abusers of the initiates then gain credence by accepting those they had just heaped with abuse. One initiate described to Sanday how he felt at this point:

I felt exhilarated. I kept saying, "Oh wow!" and hugging my big brother and shaking hands with everybody. I was incredibly happy. I was made to feel worthless by the fraternity as an individual, and now that it was all over, I was made to feel wonderful by the fraternity as a brother. My worth was celebrated by the same process that had previously denied it, because of the change that it had effected within me. I now saw myself as a brother, and what may feel terrible to an individual confronted by brothers feels tremendous to an individual who is a brother. (quoted in Sanday 1990:149)

Sanday concludes that fraternity initiation rituals serve to solidify a fraternity man's identity by separating him from his previous identity as a member of a family and perhaps separating him from his mother. The ritual incorporates the man into a group whose activities reinforce a male identity, defined largely by degradation of the negative identity of females and acted out in sexual conquest and abuse of females. Pulling train is both an expression of male sexuality and a display of the power of the brotherhood to control and dominate women. In other words, gang rape is but one instance of the abuse and domination that begin in the initiation and are continued later in relations with women and new pledges. Sanday says that once initiates have suffered abuse as a means of establishing their bond to the fraternity, they "resort to abusing others—new generations of pledges and party women—to uphold the original contract and renew their sense of the autonomous power of the brotherhood."

QUESTION 6.4: How Do Individuals Communicate Their Identities to One Another?

There is an episode in Jonathan Swift's *Gulliver's Travels* in which Gulliver learns of an experiment conducted by professors at the Academy of Lagado. They believe that, since words are only names for things, they can abolish words by having people carry with them everything they need to engage in discourse with others. Gulliver describes such a "conversation": Two people meet, open their packs of things, "talk" by using them for an hour, pack up their things, and go off.

In many ways our interactions with others are similar to the interaction of the inhabitants of Laputa. We, too, communicate with things by using them to make statements of our identity—who we think we are, or who we want to be. The clothes we wear, the things we possess, and the people we associate with are all used to display an identity that we think we have or that we desire. For example, if sex or gender is used as a criterion to distinguish individuals, there must be ways that sexual differences are displayed so they can be read by others. Men in some groups in New Guinea, for example, wear penis gourds, while in seventeenth-century Europe, men wore codpieces to emphasize the male anatomy. In areas of Africa, people from different villages have different hairstyles; in America, teenagers encode their schools, or gangs, or teams by the jackets they wear. People signal their connectedness to others by holding hands, by wearing rings, or by feasting and drinking together.

One of the most influential works in the history of anthropology is a book written by Marcel Mauss, modestly entitled *The Gift*. Mauss identifies what he calls the **principle of reciprocity:** the giving and receiving of gifts. His major point is that gifts, which in theory are voluntary, disinterested, and spontaneous,

Trobriand Islanders define and maintain their social identities by participating in the *kula* ring, a ritualized pattern of gift-giving involving the exchange of necklaces and armbands.

are in fact obligatory. The giving of the gift creates a tie with the person who receives it, and who, on some future occasion, is obliged to reciprocate. To Mauss, what is important is not what is given but the relationship that is maintained or established by the gift. The types of things given and received signal the identities of the participants in the exchange and the kind of relationship that exists between them. If the gifts are roughly of equal value, the relationship is one of equality. But if the gifts are unequal in value, the person who gives the more valuable gift is generally of higher status than the receiver.

EXERCISE 6.4

Suppose you were to travel to Gulliver's island of Laputa, and if you could communicate to people only with objects that you carried with you, and if you could take only five things with you to "tell" people about yourself, what would they be?

A well-known example of gift-giving in the anthropological literature is the kula ring of the Trobriand Islanders, the circulation of gifts among trading partners on different islands. The sea-going Trobrianders leave their homes on islands off the eastern coast of New Guinea and travel from island to island, visiting and trading. Noteworthy in their travels is their pattern of gift-giving. Each man has trading partners on the islands he visits, and these partnerships are signaled with gifts of red shell necklaces or white shell armbands. As a man travels and trades objects, he also gives and receives necklaces and receives armbands. A man who receives either an armband or a necklace does not keep it but passes it along to another trading partner. There is a set pattern to the exchange; necklaces travel from island to island in a clockwise direction, while armbands move counterclockwise. The time between exchanges and the distances between the islands are so great that it may take two to ten years before the necklaces and armbands make a complete circle.

The kula ring serves as a concrete representation of ties between individuals. Any change in the pattern of gift-giving reflects a change in the nature of the social ties. In addition, special gifts that are individually owned are also circulated, and the owner's status and renown grow as the goods he owns circulate along predetermined paths. A successful kula operator participates in many such exchanges and can profit from them by keeping items for as long as he can before passing them along. Of course, if he keeps them too long, others will be reluctant to exchange, so a good deal of social skill is required to kula successfully.

Another famous example of gift-giving is the potlatch ceremony of people on the northwest coast of North America. Among the Gitksan the potlatch is a feast at a funeral; someone who dies vacates a spot on the social landscape, or more specifically, leaves empty a name. The Gitksan are organized into patrilineal clans or houses. Each house has associated with it a fixed number of personal names, and each name has associated with it specific spiritual powers, honors, and objects of wealth. As a Gitksan moves through the life cycle, he is given different names associated with his higher standing in the group. The name he holds when he dies is vacated until it is claimed by or given to someone else. If the name vacated belongs to a chief or someone else of high rank, numerous people may try to claim the name and the honors and privileges associated with it. In the competition that follows, the person who contributes the most wealth to the potlatch or funeral feast is the one who gets the name. The higher ranking the name, the greater the wealth that is given away. Around 20 years ago, the cost of a name ran anywhere from $100 to $500, and some chiefs have held eight to ten names at one time. The more names held by a Gitksan, however, the greater is the burden of upholding the power and honor of each name by being generous, loyal, and upstanding. A person who disgraces his name by doing something wrong (such as having an automobile accident or being put in jail), must give a feast to "clean the name."

The potlatch feast, however, does more than allow a Gitksan to obtain a new name and identity. It also serves to symbolically reorder and validate the names, and hence the social positions, of everyone at the feast through the distribution of gifts. Members of the house of the deceased generally serve as hosts to members from the deceased's father's house. The guests are feasted for the services they perform at the funeral (they prepare the corpse and dig the grave) and as repayment for the gifts they formerly gave the deceased to help him acquire his name. Guests are seated by their hosts according to rank. Guests who think they have been given a "wrong" seat, one that assigns them to a lower rank than they think they deserve, complain to the leader of the host group, who gives them a gift of money to "wipe away" the disgrace or insult. When the guests are seated, the hosts announce the gifts they are giving to the guests, along with the name of the person from the host group who contributed the gift. Higher-ranking guests receive more gifts at a potlatch than lower-ranking guests. Consequently, the seating arrangements and the value of the gifts given to guests at the feast serve to announce or publicly notarize the social position or identity of each guest.

Exchanges that convey recognition of identities needn't be limited to material goods. The exchanges also may consist of emotion and sentiment. Hawaiians, for example, define a desired identity in part by expressions of gregariousness and hospitality. The emotional qualities of a person's relationships are one criterion by which others judge, interact with, and respond to that person. For example, if you accept an offer of hospitality in Hawaii, it is a signal that you recognize the generous nature of the offer and you wish to maintain the social link. If you reject the offer of hospitality, it is seen as a hurtful sign that you do not recognize the generous nature of the person making the offer and do not wish to maintain the relationship. Hawaiians attempt to keep social pathways open with altruistic exchanges of love (*aloha*), sincerity, feeling (with heart, *na`au*), and warmth (*pumehana*).

Gifts and Commodities

An important characteristic of traditional *kula* and potlatch goods is that they had a history; a Trobriander who received a necklace or armband could likely recite the history of the object, sometimes from its creation through all the persons who had, at one time or another, possessed it. These goods had the quality of heirlooms in our own society; the family wedding ring that had been worn by brides for three generations; the watch that was owned by a great-grandfather; the quilt that had been made by a great-aunt. The history of these kinds of objects, especially when they are given as gifts, forms a vital part of their identity, and consequently of the identity of the person who gives them. They say something special about the relationship between the giver and the receiver of the gift. The same is true to a lesser extent of gifts that are produced by the giver; they carry a special meaning apart from the object itself. A lamp made and given as a gift is often far more meaningful than a lamp purchased at a department store. However, we often must choose the gifts that we give from among thousands of mass-produced, largely impersonal goods available in department and chain stores. Herein lies a dilemma.

James Carrier, in his book *Gifts and Commodities: Exchange and Western Capitalism Since 1700,* argues that, since the sixteenth and seventeenth centuries, the production and distribution of goods have become impersonal, that the spread of industrial and commercial capitalism has meant the spread of alienated objects and relations. In previous times **commodities** were personalized in various ways. The relationship between the producer and/or the seller of goods was a personal one between relatives or friends; the buyer knew who made and sold the object purchased. Even when stores replaced home trade and markets, the buyer knew the store owner, who further personalized the goods by buying them in bulk and individually packaging and displaying them. The buyer-seller relationship was further personalized by the extension of credit from seller to buyer and by the customer loyalty expressed by the buyer to the seller. Today, the buyer knows neither the producer nor the seller; if the item is bought on credit, it is through a credit card issued by some distant bank based on the filing of an impersonal application, the transaction accomplished completely by mail. Eyes never meet.

Carrier labels goods that carry no special meaning **commodities,** to distinguish them from what he calls **possessions.** Gifts, says Carrier, must be possessions before they carry meaning in an exchange. Commodities involve a transfer of value and a countertransfer: A sells something to B, and the transaction is finished. But in a gift exchange a more or less permanent link is established between giver and receiver. Gifts are inalienable—they are bound to people after the presentation; commodities are independent of their sellers (or producers). It is easy to return, destroy, or give away a commodity; it is a dilemma to do any of those with a gift. Ralph Waldo Emerson vividly expressed the difference between gifts and commodities when he wrote:

> The only gift is a portion of thyself. Thou must bleed for me. Therefore the poet brings his poem; the shepherd, his lamb; the farmer, corn; the miner, a gem; the sailor, coral and shells; the painter, his picture; the girl, a handkerchief or her own sewing. This is right and pleasing....when a man's biography is conveyed in a gift. (quoted in Carrier 1993:56)

Or, as Emerson said again, "it is a cold, lifeless business when you go to the shops to buy me something that does not represent your life and talent" (quoted in Carrier 1993:56).

As we mentioned above, for Americans the contrast between commodities and gifts poses a special problem. Most of the items that we give as gifts are store-bought, often mass-produced, commodities. Their history is brief and undistinguished; an item of clothing assembled in some factory in Mexico or Indonesia by a young woman earning perhaps a dollar an hour; a sports item, assembled in some factory in South America, shipped to a warehouse in Chicago, and sold in a mass-produced catalogue; a radio, VCR, or CD player, assembled in Korea, distributed by a Japanese company, and sold in an American chain store. These are commodities, rather than gifts. Their meaning is contained in their worth or utility, in their materiality. The meaning of a gift is different; the perfect gift is priceless, its materiality is immaterial.

For Carrier the problem is how, in a world filled with impersonal, alienated commodities—goods without history, so to speak—we can turn these things into personal items with meaning and history, into possessions that carry something of the buyer's identity. In gift-giving, how do we turn commodities into items that say something about the relationship between the giver and receiver? How do we make commodities meaningful?

We convert commodities into possessions and gifts, says Carrier, by a process of appropriation. For example, when a person takes an impersonal space, a dorm room or a rented apartment, and decorates and modifies the space, he or she has appropriated it and given it meaning. When we buy food at the supermarket, we appropriate it by preparing or cooking it. When a person buys an automobile, one that is virtually identical to thousands of others of the same make, model, year, and color, and comes to think of it as unique, as an expression of his or her identity, that person has appropriated an object and made it a possession. Shopping itself, says Carrier, is a way of appropriating commodities; the "wise shopper" chooses what is "right" for himself or herself, or what is "right" for the recipient of a gift.

Manufacturers and sellers, of course, try to aid the process of converting a commodity into a possession by themselves stamping their products with a distinct identity. A good example is Harris Tweed, which most buyers associate with some Harris Islander weaving on a loom in his shed, creating the item as his ancestors have done for centuries, and even giving each item its own serial number. In fact, the yarn that is used is spun in textile mills and then woven on looms given to the weaver with the frames warped so that no special skill is necessary to weave the cloth. In actuality, other than the fact that they are narrower, the only difference between the looms they use, as opposed to those used in factories, is that the Harris Island weaver supplies the power with a foot treadle rather than a machine.

Endorsements from sports or movie celebrities help consumers transform a commodity into a possession, and displaying goods in catalogues in a way that helps the buyer appropriate commodities has become a fine art. For example, Carrier notes how the Smith & Hawken catalog for gardeners forges a personal link between object and producer by detailing the historical origins of the tools, and linking them to historical figures, almost always English, and most from the eighteenth or nineteenth century. The text communicates this message by using words such as "origins," "can be traced back to," "was invented by," and so on. Lands' End catalogs display pictures of employees, thereby linking commodities to the people who work at Lands' End, even though these employees are not always the actual producers of the goods.

Comfortably Yours, a medical supply distributor, sells objects to the old and infirm by telling the reader about the people who use the objects. For example, the text describes how the company owners bought a particular item for a particular person, and explain how pleased the recipient was. The company has managed to wrap its commodities directly in the cultural framework of the gift.

Gift-Giving and Christmas in America

The dilemma of converting commodities into gifts is particularly acute during the Christmas holiday season, when most gift-giving takes place in America. Christmas as we know it did not really emerge until the height of the industrial revolution. Its precursors included the traditional end-of-the-year festivities that took place in England, where gifts consisted of food or feasts given by superiors to their dependents. In the 1770s in New York City people began celebrating December 6th, the day of St. Nicholas, instead of the New Year. This was actually something of an anti-Christmas celebration; St. Nicholas was Dutch and the colonists were celebrating things Dutch to protest British rule over what had been New Amsterdam before British colonization. It wasn't until 1809 that the holiday began to spread and St. Nicholas turned into Santa Claus, giving gifts of candy to children. The appearance of Clement Moore's *A Visit from St. Nicholas* in 1823 (or *'Twas the Night Before Christmas,* as it was later known) marked the movement of the holiday to the end of the year. At this point children began to get toys rather than food. But even then Christmas was celebrated largely on New Year's Day, and in the industrial northeast.

The next major step in the evolution of Christmas was the appearance in the United States of Charles Dickens's *A Christmas Carol* in 1843; it was an immediate sensation, especially with its victory of Bob Cratchit and Tiny Tim and their

In American society, the yearly ritual of Christmas shopping provides
a means of converting impersonal commodities into personalized
gifts that show one's love for family members and close friends.

world of the home over Scrooge and the impersonal and cold world of work. In
1862 the Thomas Nast image of Santa Claus began appearing in *Harper's Weekly,* completing his construction as a fat, jolly, old man dressed in fur-trimmed
robes (inspired, Nast later admitted, by the fur-trimmed clothing of the wealthy
Astor family) and by 1865 Christmas was declared a national holiday (28 states
had already declared it a holiday). By the 1880s, writers were already beginning
to complain about the commercialization of Christmas.

Most social scientists who have written about Christmas agree that it is largely a celebration of the family, serving especially to distinguish the world of the
family from the outside world of work. Christmas serves to affirm the identity of
Americans as members of specific family groups, and the circle of kin with whom
gifts are exchanged defines the boundaries of the family. In one study conducted
in a midwestern city, some 90 percent of all gifts exchanged at Christmas were
exchanged with family members. Moreover, many of the items not exchanged
within the family hardly qualify as gifts at all. Thus, the office party where people
draw lots to discover the person for whom they will buy a gift, or the party in
which everyone gets a gift but there is no exchange, or the presentation to the
mailman or garbage collector, hardly qualify as gift-giving at all. In these situations there is little concern for reciprocity. Christmas heightens a person's sense
of family identity, expressing how warm the family is and how cold the world outside may be.

Thus, it is within the family that the Christmas gift is most important and
where the gift must contain something of the biography of the giver and the
history of the relationship—where the gift must be a possession rather than a

commodity. The question is how to resolve the problem of using commodities as family gifts; how to transform commodities to make them suitable as statements of the special role that family and family relations play in defining our identity. This problem, apparently, is not a new one. The dilemma of giving gifts that were manufactured and sold in stores apparently existed as early as the mid-nineteenth century, and department stores tried to convince buyers to purchase their gifts in stores by advertising them as "special Christmas stock." Even today, with Christmas decorations, music, and special attractions, such as the ever-present Santa Claus, retailers attempt to inject the spirit of Christmas into their stock of goods.

But there are other ways that consumers try to appropriate commodities and turn them into Christmas gifts. First, we may simply say that the nature of the gift itself is immaterial, that "it's the thought that counts." A second way is to purchase things that aren't very useful, giving frivolous or luxurious gifts, or items that are Christmas-specific, such as Christmas tree decorations, or clothing with Christmas decorations on it. Third, and very important, there is the wrapping rule: Christmas gifts must be wrapped. The wrapping itself converts the commodity into a gift. Difficult-to-wrap presents (a piano, horse, bicycle, etc.) must be decorated with a bow. The only category of things that needn't be wrapped are items made by the giver, such as breads or jams. These items need only a bow and a card.

Finally, says Carrier, there is the shopping itself, the time we spend getting the "right" gift for the "right" person. Why, he asks, do we go through all of this? It is onerous, it is stressful, and it is expensive. Yet one-third of all retail sales are made in November and December, most accounted for by Christmas shopping. One-sixth of all retail sales are related to Christmas. People complain about the materialism of Christmas and Christmas shopping, yet they shop intensely.

In the face of this bother and complaint, why do Americans, even devout Christians, spend so much effort in Christmas shopping? Why not give home-made gifts? Indeed, why give presents at all? Why not give a Christmas card instead? It is true that the giving of purchased gifts reflects a number of motives, ranging from displays of affluence to a desire to shower a loved one with lovely things. However, these more commonly recognized motives do "not explain the intensity of Christmas shopping and people's ambivalence towards it" (Carrier 1993:62).

Carrier suggests that the answer to this riddle lies in the fact that shopping in itself is a method of appropriation, of converting a commodity into a gift; we exercise a choice from among the mass of commodities presented to us. As Carrier puts it,

> Christmas shopping is an annual ritual through which we convert commodities into gifts. Performing this ritual indicates that we can celebrate and recreate personal relations with the anonymous objects available to us, just as it strengthens and reassures us as we undertake the more mundane appropriations of everyday life during the rest of the year. (Carrier 1993:63)

It also demonstrates to people, says Carrier, that they can create a world of family, a world of love, out of the impersonal commodities that flood the world "out there." Christmas is a time when Americans make a world of money into a world of family; a time of contrast between the impersonal world of commodities and the personal world of possessions and gifts.

RESOURCE 6.4 ─────────────────────────────

Totem Poles

One of the ways that family histories were represented were in totem poles. You can explore the history and significance of one Gitksan totem pole at: **http:// www.moa.ubc.ca/Virtual/Other/prelude2/start.html** This Web site, designed by a graduate student in anthropology and supported by the University of British Columbia's Museum of Anthropology, focuses on the history and meaning of a Thunderbird totem pole carved in the mid- to late-1800s.

QUESTION 6.5: *How Do Individuals Defend Their Identities That Are Threatened?*

In defining themselves and others, people sometimes disagree on their relative positions on the social map; they disagree on their respective identities. Anthony F. C. Wallace and Raymond Fogelson refer to these situations as **identity struggles**—interactions in which there is a discrepancy between the identity a person claims to possess and the identity attributed to him or her by others. Take the medicine fight among the Beaver Indians of British Columbia. The Beaver believe that a man's identity relative to others is determined by the amount of supernatural power or "medicine" he possesses. This power determines a man's success in hunting and protects him and his family from illness and misfortune. Any personal misfortune a man experiences, such as illness or failure to kill game, is interpreted by others as a loss of supernatural power and hence a loss of prestige. However, the man experiencing the misfortune does not interpret it in the same way; for him, the misfortune is caused not by a loss of his supernatural power but by someone using supernatural power against him. In other words, his view of his identity is different from what he believes is attributed to him by others. The person experiencing the misfortune will then dream the identity of the attacker and publicly accuse him. The accused may deny the charge, responding that his accuser is experiencing misfortune because he has committed some wrongful act. Thus begins the medicine fight, a series of accusations and counteraccusations that sometimes lead to violence.

Making Moka *in Papua New Guinea*

The Beaver claim or defend their social identities through spiritual means. More common is the manipulation of material goods. The Melpa, who live around the area of Mt. Hagen in the Central Highlands of Papua New Guinea, provide an example. The people of Mt. Hagen live by growing crops such as sweet potatoes and raising pigs. Pigs serve not only as a source of protein but also as signs of wealth that are required for gift exchange.

The most important identity on the Highlands social landscape is the "Big Man." Because they are leaders and among the wealthiest in terms of pig ownership, Big

Men are the most independent from others. A man who is poor and dependent on others for food and sustenance is called by a term that translates into English as "rubbish man."

Becoming a Big Man requires courage in warfare. War, in the form of highly ritualized battles with spears and arrows or raiding and murder, has long been a part of Papua New Guinea Highland society. Big Men play a pivotal role in planning war as well as establishing peace, either with their oratorical skills or with their wealth. The greatest skill required of a Big Man, however, is making *moka*. As described by anthropologist Andrew Strathern, moka is a form of ceremonial gift exchange in which a man makes an initial gift to a trading partner and then receives in return more than he gave. Ceremonial gift exchanges serve two purposes: They establish and maintain links between individuals and groups, and they establish a rank system that enables men to earn status and prestige and become Big Men. Big Men from the same clan can make moka with each other, but it is most common for a man to have partners outside his clan, and among ex-enemies or groups tied to his through marriage. Items that are included in exchanges include pigs, shells, bird plumage, salt, decorating oil, and stone axe blades. Pigs and shells used to be the most important items, but today Australian money, bicycles, cattle, and even trucks are used.

The major idea in making moka, and consequently establishing the status of Big Man, is for a man to give his trading partner more than he received at the last exchange. Thus, if A gives 100 pigs to B, and B returns a countergift of 150 pigs that A cannot repay, then B is the Big Man because he gave the last gift. A diagram of a series of moka exchanges between two trading rivals might look something like this:

First exchange: A gives x amount of goods to B.
    Result: B owes x amount of goods to A.

Second exchange: B give two times x goods to A.
    Result: A owes x amount of goods to B.

Third exchange: A gives two times x goods to B.
    Result: B owes x amount of goods to A.

Since after each exchange a man has returned the debt he owes his partner and added an increment equal to the debt, the result of the interaction is that one person always owes the other. The two participants never reach the point where things are even; the pattern of gift exchange assures that one party is always indebted to the other. The basic rule is to give more than you receive. It is strictly the incremental change in the debt that allows a man to say he made moka.

The negotiation of identity between moka partners is never an isolated affair, because a man rarely is able to make moka solely on the basis of what he possesses at a given time. For example, if a man wants or is being pressured to make moka with a rival to whom he must give six pigs or ten shell bracelets, and he doesn't have that many pigs or bracelets at that time, he must either call in outstanding moka obligations others owe him or must get what he needs from friends or kin. Thus, any given exchange may involve a host of people and groups. A map of the circulation of moka goods around Melpa society would provide a pretty good idea of how different people and groups are related to others and would indicate the social identities of each person in the exchange network. These exchanges serve for the Melpa as public statements of social identities—

the relations between people and groups—at any given time. It is as if everyone in an American town publicly announced the present state of their social relations with every other person and group in town.

At a fairly typical moka exchange, many Big Men from different groups may make moka at once. The ceremony takes place at a ceremonial ground associated with a particular clan or lineage, usually built by the Big Man of that group. Preparations for the moka exchange begin months before the actual presentation, and Big Men of donor groups negotiate the timing of the exchange. Those who are ready can push the moka through, but those who are not ready and who do not have enough to give to their trading rivals in the other group risk defaulting to their partners. Those who do not possess enough wealth to give may try to delay the timing of a moka ceremony, but may be taunted as procrastinators or as "rubbish men."

Before making moka, each man reviews his partnerships and ties to others, perhaps dropping some and adding others. Men scheduled to receive gifts at the moka exchange make initiatory gifts of shells, pigs, and legs of pork to their moka partners. Discussions about the ceremony are held at the ceremonial ground of the main group, and the men scheduled to give gifts set up stakes to indicate how many pigs they will give away to their partners. They also clear the ceremonial ground, make speeches, and review the history of the relations between the two groups. At each meeting the Big Men try to contract for more gifts, egging on their clanmates to give more pigs to their trading partners and increasing the competitive spirit. They insist that they must surpass in wealth the gifts they received from their partners the last time they received moka. The climax of these discussions is the showing of the gifts at the ceremonial grounds. Once this is done, the final transfer takes place with dancing and oratory.

When the presentation is made, the Big Men among the donors step forward and make speeches. On the final day men and women of the recipient group converge on the ceremonial grounds while the donors decorate themselves with pearl shell pendants, fine bark aprons and belts, pig grease or tree oil, and charcoal and red ochre. At the ceremony the donors run up and down the row crying, "hoo-aah, hoo-aah," and performing a war dance. Their speeches are boasts, claiming that, by the amount they have given, they have "won." Here is an excerpt of such a speech:

> My sister's sons, my cross-cousins. I am your true cross-cousin, living close to you. My sisters' sons, my cross-cousins, you say you see big pigs, big shells, well, now I have given you large pigs on the two olka stakes, given you a bicycle too, given you all the food you like to eat. Further, I have given you two steers, and so I win. I have given you all the things which are your food; I give you two steers also and so I win. (Strathern 1971:241)

Recipients who do not receive what they expect at the ceremony (and they never know exactly what they will get until the ceremony takes place) complain loudly and bitterly. Thus, the ceremony is an anxious occasion in which the honor, and consequently the social identity, of both donor and recipient is on the line. Sometimes actual fighting breaks out. If a man does not meet his commitments to his partner and does not give gifts commensurate with what he received at the last ceremony, his partner can do little but shout insults or physically attack him.

At the end of the ceremony, an orator counts the gifts while the recipient offers stylized thank-yous. The recipients of moka then gather their shells and pigs and knock over the pig stakes, except for one that is left standing as proof that the donors have made moka at their ceremonial ground.

CONCLUSIONS

The concept of the self, or personhood, varies from society to society. In the egocentric view, the person is viewed as an autonomous, discrete individual; in the sociocentric view, the self is viewed as contingent on a situation or social setting. The sociocentric view is often taken by social scientists who are interested in the social processes by which social identities are formed and maintained.

Societies distinguish individuals from one another by using criteria such as age, gender, kinship, ethnicity, and language. Differences and similarities in characteristics among individuals are used to construct social landscapes on which each person's place or identity is indicated. The characteristics that determine identity, such as gender, are treated differently in various societies.

One way that individuals learn who they are is through rites of passage or initiation ceremonies such as those practiced in college fraternities. Initiation rituals prepare individuals to accept new ways of looking at themselves and others.

People must also be able to communicate their identities to one another. One way to do this is through the process of gift exchange and the principle of reciprocity. The kula ring, or the circulation of gifts among trading partners by the Trobriand Islanders, is an example. Americans and other people in modern industrial societies have a special problem with gift-giving, needing to somehow convert an impersonal, store-bought commodity into a personal and meaningful gift. We examined how at Christmas this is a special problem, and we explored some of the ways in which Americans solve it.

Individuals must be able to defend their identities if they are threatened. An example of how this is done is making moka by the Big Men among the Melpa, who thus both claim and defend their places on the social landscape.

REFERENCES AND SUGGESTED READINGS

INTRODUCTION: THE IMPORTANCE OF SELF   The epigraph is taken from the opening passage of Erving Goffman's classic work *The Presentation of Self in Everyday Life* (Doubleday, 1959). The Gandhi reference is from Ramashray Roy, *Self and Society: A Study in Gandhian Thought* (Sage, 1985).

HOW DOES THE CONCEPT OF PERSONHOOD VARY FROM SOCIETY TO SOCIETY?   An excellent treatment of the relationship between names and identity can be found in Richard D. Alford's book, *Naming and Identity: A Cross-Cultural Study of Personal Naming Practices* (HRAF Press, 1988). The discussion of naming among the Gitksan is from John W. Adams, *The Gitksan Potlatch: Population Flux, Resource Ownership and Reciprocity* (Holt, Rinehart and Winston of Canada, 1973). The discussion of the differences between the sociocentric and egocentric self comes from an article by Richard A. Shweder and Edmund J.

Bourne, "Does the Concept of the Person Vary Cross-Culturally?" in *Cultural Conceptions of Mental Health and Therapy,* edited by A. J. Marsella and G. M. White (D. Reidel Publishing, 1984). The discussion of American individualism comes from Robert Bellah et al., *Habits of the Heart* (University of California Press, 1984). The nature of the self in Japan is discussed in Robert J. Smith, *Japanese Society: Tradition, Self and the Social Order* (Cambridge University Press, 1983), and in Christie W. Kiefer, "Psychological Anthropology," *Annual Review of Anthropology,* vol. 6 (1977), pp. 103–119.

HOW DO SOCIETIES DISTINGUISH INDIVIDUALS FROM ONE ANOTHER?
The information on identity in Northern Ireland comes from Ed Cairns, "Intergroup Conflict in Northern Ireland," in *Social Identity and Intergroup Relations,* edited by Henri Tajfel (Cambridge University Press, 1982). Margaret Mead's comparison of gender roles in New Guinea comes from her classic *Sex and Temperament in Three Primitive Societies,* first published in 1935 (Dell, 1963). An excellent account of the berdache role can be found in Walter L. Williams, *The Spirit and the Flesh: Sexual Diversity in American Indian Culture* (Beacon Press, 1986), and Harriet Whitehead, "The Bow and the Burden Strap: A New Look at Institutionalized Homosexuality in Native North America," in *Sexual Meanings: The Cultural Construction of Gender and Sexuality,* edited by Sherry B. Ortner and Harriet Whitehead (Cambridge University Press, 1981). Susan U. Philips discusses the ways language is used to convey gender identity in "Sex Differences and Language," in *Annual Review of Anthropology,* vol. 9 (1980), pp. 523-544. Douglas Foley describes gender relations in a Texas high school in *Learning Capitalist Culture: Deep in the Heart of Tejas* (University of Pennsylvania Press, 1990). For a review of anthropological studies of human sexuality, see "The Cross-Cultural Study of Human Sexuality," by D. L. Davis and R. G. Whitten, in *Annual Review of Anthropology,* vol. 16 (1987), pp. 69-98.

HOW DO INDIVIDUALS LEARN WHO THEY ARE? The classic work on rites of passage is Arnold van Gennep, *The Rites of Passage,* translated by Monica B. Vizedom and Gabrielle L. Chaffe, originally published in 1906 (University of Chicago Press, 1960). A description of how American businesses use rites of passage is in Harrison M. Trice and Janice M. Beyer, "Studying Organizational Cultures Through Rites and Ceremonies," in *Academy of Management Review,* vol. 9 (1984), pp. 653-669. David D. Gilmore's work is represented in *Manhood in the Making: Cultural Concepts of Masculinity* (Yale University Press, 1990). The account of the initiation of a Maasai man is from *The Worlds of a Maasai Warrior,* by Tepilit Ole Saitoti (Random House, 1986), an excerpt of which is reprinted in *Anthropology 90/91,* edited by Elvio Angeloni (Dushkin Publishing, 1990). Peggy Reeves Sanday's account of gang rape is in *Fraternity Gang Rape: Sex, Brotherhood, and Privilege on Campus* (New York University Press, 1990). Another account of American college life is Michael Moffatt's study *Growing Up in New Jersey* (Rutgers University Press, 1990). An interesting account of sorority initiation rites is contained in an article by Gary Schwartz and Don Merten, "Social Identity and Expressive Symbols," in *American Anthropologist,* vol. 70 (1968), pp. 1117-1131.

HOW DO INDIVIDUALS COMMUNICATE THEIR IDENTITIES TO ONE ANOTHER? The use of *Gulliver's Travels* to illustrate the importance of goods in identity work is taken from Annette Weiner, *The Trobrianders of Papua New Guinea* (Holt, Rinehart and Winston, 1988). The classic work on the importance of the gift is Marcel Mauss, *The Gift: Forms and Functions of Exchange in Archaic Societies,* translated by Ian Cunnison, published originally in 1925 (W. W. Norton, 1967). The material on the Gitksan is from John W. Adams, *The Gitksan Potlatch,* cited above. The original description of the kula ring formed the foundation of Bronislaw Malinowski's classic, *Argonauts of the Western Pacific,* originally published in 1922 (E. P. Dutton, 1961). A reinterpretation of the kula ring can be found in Annette Weiner's *The Trobrianders of Papua New Guinea,* cited above. The discussion on gifts and commodities is based on James G. Carrier's book, *Gifts and Commodities: Exchange and Western Capitalism Since 1700* (Routledge, 1995), and his article, "The Rituals of Christmas Giving," in *Unwrapping Christmas,* edited by Daniel Miller (Clarendon Press, 1993).

HOW DO INDIVIDUALS DEFEND THEIR IDENTITIES THAT ARE THREATENED? The article by Anthony F. C. Wallace and Raymond D. Fogelson, "The Identity Struggle," can be found in *Intensive Family Therapy,* edited by I. Boszormenyi-Nagy and J. L. Framo (Harper and Row, 1965). The description of the Beaver medicine fight is from Robin Ridington, "The Medicine Fight: An Instrument of Political Process Among the Beaver Indians," *American Anthropologist,* vol. 70 (1968), pp. 1152–1160.

The material on "making moka" comes from Andrew Strathern, *The Rope of Moka: Big Men and Ceremonial Exchange in Mount Hagen New Guinea* (Cambridge University Press, 1971).

"Les Constructeurs" by Fernand Léger. Bridgeman/Art Resource, New York. © COPYRIGHT ARS, NY. Musée National Fernand Léger, Biot, France.

CHAPTER 7

THE CULTURAL CONSTRUCTION OF SOCIAL HIERARCHY

PROBLEM 7: WHY ARE MODERN SOCIETIES CHARACTERIZED BY SOCIAL, POLITICAL, AND ECONOMIC INEQUALITIES?

Every social hierarchy claims to be founded on the nature of things. It thus accords itself eternity; it escapes change and the attacks of innovators. Aristotle justified slavery by the ethnic superiority of the Greeks over the barbarians; and today the man who is annoyed by feminist claims alleges that woman is *naturally* inferior.

Robert Hertz, 1909

INTRODUCTION: *The Rationale for Social Inequality*

The maldistribution of wealth, status, and privilege is a significant problem throughout the modern world. To Americans it is visible in the starving faces that stare out from our television screens in documentaries and on the evening news, interspersed with advertisements for luxuries such as automobiles, cosmetics, and household conveniences. Some people can purchase the finest amenities, while others lack the basic necessities of life, such as food, shelter, and health care. There are few, if any, modern nations in which one portion of the population does not in some way enjoy privileges that other portions do not share. In most of these cases, inequality follows from the assumption that certain people are somehow better than others. Individuals are judged by traits—gender, age, physical appearance, occupation, wealth, group membership, and so on—that seem to make them more or less worthy compared to others.

Some people believe that the hierarchical ordering of people and groups is unavoidable. In their view, scarce resources, occupational specialization, and the power of an elite group to control the behavior of others necessarily result in some form of social stratification. Others maintain that stratification is not only avoidable, but is counter to human nature. According to anthropologist Thomas Belmonte:

> Since the emergence of stratification, man's history (his changing ways of relating to nature and other men) has stood opposed to his humanity. The emergence of power-wielding elites…laid the basis for a new kind of anti-collective society whose vastly accelerated growth was founded, not on the reconciliation of antagonisms between men, but on their origination and amplification in slavery, caste, and class. (Belmonte 1989:137)

Those who support Belmonte's view note that, in societies such as those of the Ju/wasi and Inuit, there are no "poor," "rich," "inferior," or "superior" people. This is not to say that these societies are totally egalitarian; even in small-scale societies, valued statuses are not available to some members. Rather, the question is why modern societies are characterized by such extremes of poverty and wealth.

In this chapter we will examine how societies construct social hierarchies and why some groups erect social edifices that encompass social dominance and submission, high and low status, and oppressors and oppressed. We will examine why most people in stratified societies—both those at the top and those at the bottom—consider social ranks to be "in the nature of things." We will ask how people at the bottom levels of the hierarchy—those in poverty, for example—adapt to their conditions, and we will explore whether a nonstratified community can exist within a large-scale society.

QUESTIONS

7.1 How do societies rank people in social hierarchies?
7.2 Why do societies construct social hierarchies?
7.3 How do people come to accept social hierarchies as natural?
7.4 How do people living in poverty adapt to their condition?
7.5 Can a nonstratified community exist within a large society?

QUESTION 7.1:   How Do Societies Rank People in Social Hierarchies?

Social hierarchies in different societies vary along several dimensions: the criteria used to differentiate people into one level of society or another, the number of levels that exist, the kinds of privileges and rights that attach to people at different levels, and the strength of the social boundaries that separate the different levels. In American society, for example, people are stratified by income and personal possessions into **social classes** (e.g., lower class, middle class, and upper class). They are classified by cultural or family background into ethnic groups (e.g., Italian, Jewish, Hispanic, or white Anglo-Saxon Protestant), or by physical appearance or skin color into racial categories (e.g., black or white). They are also classified by gender and age, as well as by standards such as education. People in the United States may move from class to class, and they may choose to emphasize or deemphasize their ethnic group membership, but generally their racial category and gender are fixed.

EXERCISE 7.1

Below is a list of personal attributes. Your task is to rank them by number from *most* to *least* important to you in judging a person's social or personal worth. No ties allowed. If there is an attribute not included in the list that you wish to add, do so.

Rank

_____ Personal Appearance
_____ Monetary Income
_____ Gender
_____ Age
_____ Religion
_____ Ethnic or Community Origin
_____ Family Background
_____ Intelligence (as indicated by school performance)
_____ Athletic Ability
_____ Personal Possessions (clothes, car, etc.)
_____ Personality (fill in your description of type of personality) _____
        _____
        _____

In India, the population is stratified into hundreds of different **castes.** In a caste system, individuals are assigned at birth to the ranked social and occupational groups of their parents. A person's place in the social order is fixed; there is no mobility from one caste to another. Castes are separated from one another by strict rules that forbid intermarriage and other forms of interaction, such as eating together, speaking to each other, or working together.

In any stratified society, people's access to jobs, wealth, and privilege is determined largely by their position in the hierarchy. Castes in India are based on traditional roles, for example. The Brahmins, priests whose lives were devoted to worship and teaching, occupied the top of the caste hierarchy. Directly under them were the Kshattriya castes, whose members comprised the soldiers, politicians, and administrators. Next were the Vaisya castes, made up of farmers and merchants. At the bottom of the hierarchy were the Sudra castes, which were devoted to the service of other castes. The Sudra castes included "untouchable" or "unclean" persons whose occupations were believed to be polluting to others. Untouchables included washermen, tanners, shoemakers, and sweepers, people whose occupations required them to come into contact with animal or human wastes. The Indian government has outlawed discrimination against untouchables based on caste membership, but it persists nevertheless.

The Feminization of Poverty

In the United States, gender and age are significantly related to whether or not a person lives in poverty. In *Women and Children Last,* Ruth Sidel draws an analogy between the doomed ship *Titanic* and American society at the end of the 1980s. Both, she says, were gleaming symbols of wealth that placed women and children at a disadvantage. When the *Titanic* went down, women and children were indeed saved first, but only those who were traveling in first-class or second-class accommodations. Women and children in third-class and steerage were not saved. While only 8 percent of the women and 3 percent of the children in first and second class drowned the night the *Titanic* sank, 45 percent of the women and 70 percent of the children in steerage died. As with the *Titanic,* Sidel says, certain women and children in the United States are not the first to be saved; instead, they are the first to fall into poverty.

There have been dramatic changes in the role of women in the United States over the past half century. One measure is their steadily increasing participation in the work force. In 1960, only 32 percent of married women worked outside the home; in 1999, 58 percent were wage earners. Yet women in American society make up a disproportionate share of the poor. Americans are witnessing what sociologists call the feminization of poverty. According to the U.S. Bureau of the Census, in 1999, more than 11.8 percent of all Americans had incomes at or below the amount established by the federal government as the official poverty level, and this level is set well below what is required for basic subsistence. In 2000, the poverty level was $17,029 for a family of four. The number of women living in poverty in 1997 outnumbered the number of men by a ratio of 4:3.

Children pay an even greater price than women do. In a booming economy, child poverty rates fluctuated between 18 and 21 percent from 1995–2000, but only 5.7 percent of French children and 7.3 percent of British children are still considered poor. As Valdas Anelauskas (1999) points out, American children are twice as likely to be poor as Canadian children, three times as likely to be poor as British children, four times as likely to be poor as French children, and 7 to 13 times more likely to be poorer than German, Dutch, and Swedish children.

RESOURCE 7.1

Resources on Poverty and Inequality in the United States

There are many Web sites that address the issues of poverty and economic inequality in the United States. Here are a few where you can find up-to-date-statistics as well as commentary:

Poverty in the United States: 1998
http://www.census.gov/hhes/www/povty98.html

1996 State Poverty Estimates—Census Bureau
http://www.census.gov/hhes/www/saipe.html

America's Children: Key National Indicators of Well-Being, 1999 [.pdf, 114p.]
http://www.childstats.gov/ac1999/ac99.asp

Census Bureau Reports: One in Five People Had Difficulty Satisfying Basic Needs in 1995 Abstract
http://www.census.gov/Press-Release/www/1999/cb99-130.html

Child Poverty in Rich Nations—UNICEF [.pdf, 33 pages]
http://www.unicef-icdc.org/pdf/poverty.pdf

Inequality.org
http://www.inequality.org/

Institute for Research on Poverty (IRP) [.pdf]
http://www.ssc.wisc.edu/irp/

Myths about Welfare
http://www.mott.org/poverty/ending_welfare/myth_fact.htm

National Center for Children in Poverty
http://www.igpa.uiuc.edu/CFP/rsnccp.html

For information on global inequality you can start at:

Overcoming Human Poverty—UNDP Poverty Report 2000 [PowerPoint]
http://www.undp.org/povertyreport/

Institute for Research on Poverty
http://www.ssc.wisc.edu/irp/

You can find additional resources with annotations for each at:
http://faculty.plattsburgh.edu/richard.robbins/CA/CA_7.htm

In 1997, one out of every four preschoolers and one out of every five children under the age of 12 were living in poverty. Nearly 40 percent of the American poor are children under 12 years of age, and more than half of these are living in families headed by females. In other words, women and children make

In America, children make up a growing segment of those living in poverty. Here, a homeless woman is shown with her children in a Los Angeles tent city in 1987.

up the majority of America's poor. If, in addition to being a child and a female, a person is African American, Hispanic American, or Native American, the chances of being among America's poor are even greater. The greatest stigma in American society is to be a child, a female, and either African American, Hispanic American, or Native American.

There are various explanations for the unequal distribution of resources in the United States and in other countries. Americans, who are highly individualistic, tend to believe that if people live in poverty, it's probably their own fault—a rationale often referred to as "blaming the victim." In the case of children, most say poverty is their parents' fault. But since the surest predictor of a person's income is the income of his or her parents, it should be obvious that more than individual work effort and motivation are responsible for social stratification. There must be reasons why societies construct social hierarchies.

QUESTION 7.2: Why Do Societies Construct Social Hierarchies?

The construction of a social hierarchy is not a necessary feature of all human societies. Groups such as the Ju/wasi or Inuit, for example, are not totally egalitarian; instead, people go out of their way not to appear better than others. Moreover, there seems to be no universal inclination to rank people by one criterion or another; in some societies skin color makes a difference, and in others it doesn't. In some societies men are accorded far greater status than women; in others there is little if any difference in gender rank. Even the use of age as a criterion of rank varies from society to society. The only general rule that seems to hold is that as societies become more complex and populous, their propensity for social stratification increases.

Integrative and Exploitative Theories of Social Hierarchy

*as pop ↑ people spec.
↳ in tasks → div. of labour
more eff. leadership*

There are various explanations for the existence of social hierarchies. Some claim social stratification emerged with the origin of private property; others claim it was created to satisfy the organizational needs of war. We will explore two explanations here: the **integrative theory of social stratification,** based on the assumption that social hierarchy is necessary for the smooth functioning of modern society; and the **exploitative theory of social stratification,** which presumes that hierarchy exists because one group of individuals seeks to take advantage of another group for economic purposes.

Proponents of the integrative theory of social stratification assume that as societies grow and there are more people to feed, house, and clothe, more labor-efficient or technologically sophisticated means are required to produce enough food and other necessities and to erect the necessary infrastructure. Unlike the smaller societies of hunters and gatherers and horticulturists, larger-scale societies require individuals to specialize in certain tasks or occupations, as noted in Chapter 2. This results in a division of labor that requires greater coordination of tasks, more efficient management, and more complex leadership systems, all of which inevitably lead to some form of social stratification. In addition, as societies become more complex, they need to organize systems of defense against other groups who may attack them, and the development of a military organization requires the centralization of power, which again leads to the emergence of an elite group. As resources become scarce, an internal policing system may also be required to keep order and prevent crime. In any case, the integrative theory of social stratification is based on the assumption that society's need for greater integration, along with the need to assert greater controls on individual behavior, necessitates some form of centralized authority that offers its citizens security, protection, means of settling disputes, defense against other groups, and sustenance. All these are offered in exchange for the people's acceptance of, and loyalty to, state authorities and officials.

*in exchange
for loyalty
How is state
auth ?*

In the integrative theory, society is likened to a living organism whose parts must be regulated by a controlling device if they are to function efficiently for the survival of the whole. The nineteenth-century social philosopher Herbert Spencer suggested that complex societies, like complex living organisms, exhibit greater differentiation as they evolve. With greater differentiation there follows a greater degree of interrelation among parts, which in turn requires greater control by government, management, and the military. Without control, society, like a living organism, would cease to exist.

In American society, proponents of the integrative theory of hierarchy might point to the military to illustrate the necessity for stratification. Without generals or commissioned officers, they would say, privates, corporals, and sergeants could not function efficiently to do their jobs, and the military would therefore disintegrate. They might point to industry as another illustration of the need for hierarchy; if there were no executives to direct those who do the work, industry would collapse. The reason the Ju/wasi require no hierarchy, integrationists might say, is because each person or family is self-sufficient, and there is no need for the coordination or control of activities. As societies become more complex and the division of labor increases, greater control is necessary. The fact that those who assume the responsibility of control are given greater rewards is simply a way of assuring the survival of the society as a whole.

The Indian caste system, for example, is sometimes said to perform an integrative function by providing benefits to both higher-caste landowners and lower-caste workers. Landowners get workers to cultivate their land, and the lower castes are assured economic security.

Other scholars agree that in complex societies it is necessary for integration to occur, but they disagree that social hierarchy is required for integration. Proponents of the exploitative theory of social stratification claim that stratification arises when one group seeks to exploit the resources or labor of others. The exploitation might take the form of military conquest, as it did during the Spanish conquest of South America, when thousands of indigenous people were forced to labor on farms or in mines to increase the wealth of Spanish conquerors, or it might take other forms of manipulation and control. Members of India's lower castes, for example, have tried to change their status, only to bring a violent reaction from the higher castes.

Karl Marx and the Origin of Class

The most influential and controversial of the exploitative theories of social stratification is that of Karl Marx and Friedrich Engels. As witnesses to the teeming squalor of British cities during the industrial revolution, Marx and Engels concluded that landlords and factory owners (capitalists, in their terms) were able to use their control of resources to exploit the unlanded laborers in the newly emerging factories and mines of England. To understand how landlords and factory owners were able to exploit the masses, it is necessary to grasp the meaning of some key concepts in Marxist theory. The most important of these concepts is *social class.*

Social classes are an outgrowth of capitalism, not a necessary feature of modern society. According to Marx, classes arise when a group—a ruling class, landlords, bosses, and so on—gains control of the **means of production.** The means of production consist of the materials, such as land, machines, or tools, that people need to produce things. A group that controls the means of production can maintain or increase its wealth by taking advantage of the **surplus value of labor.**

The idea of the surplus value of labor works something like this: Take a product or commodity, such as bricks. Say that the labor value of bricks on the open market is $300 per 1,000 bricks; that is, people are willing to pay $300 above the cost of materials for each 1,000 bricks they purchase. If the same people both make the bricks and sell 1,000 of them for $300 plus the cost of materials, they are getting a 100 percent return on their labor. But what if the person who owns or controls the means of production for bricks hires some people to make the bricks and only pays them $30 for every 1,000 bricks they make? The value of the labor to produce the bricks is still $300 per 1,000, but the laborers are getting only one-tenth ($30) of what their labor is worth, while the person who controls the means of production is getting the surplus value of labor, or the other nine-tenths of the labor value of the bricks ($270). In other words, the capitalist, the person who controls the means of production (the brickworks, in this case), is expropriating $270 worth of labor from the worker who produced the bricks.

Karl Marx (1818–1883) believed that capitalism permitted a "ruling class" of factory owners and landlords to exploit the masses (working people) through political and social repression.

Why would a worker labor under such conditions? The reason is **political or social repression,** which occurs because the ruling class, the group that controls the means of production, also makes the rules of the society. Members of this class elect or choose representatives who pass laws that serve their interests. Such laws may require people to work for the ruling class, prohibit workers from organizing into labor unions, require them to accept whatever wages they are offered, and forbid them from protesting these laws or the working conditions they produce. Because the ruling class can enforce these rules with the threat of joblessness, jail, or even death, most people allow themselves to be exploited. Moreover, the workers readily accept their situation if the ruling class also controls the distribution of information so it can create for its own benefit an **ideology of class.**

The ideology of class is a belief that the division of society into classes is both natural and right. According to Marx and Engels, if the ruling class controls the institutions that are responsible for determining how people view the world (institutions such as the churches, schools, and newspapers) it can promote the view that their dominance of society is in the best interests of all. The church, for example, can encourage the lower class to accept its fate because it is "God's will," or it can teach poor people that their poverty is not the fault of the ruling class but reflects their own "fall from grace." The ruling class may allow only children of its own class to go to school and at the same time make education a criterion for membership in the ruling class. Or, through its control of educational institutions and mass communications media, it may convince people who don't have an education that they are unworthy of being members of the ruling class, while it makes education so expensive that only the rich can afford it. The ruling class may use the media to tell people that the whole society would perish without it, or it could promote an ideology based on the belief that if you are poor, it's your own fault. As a result of an ideology of class, members of the lower class come to believe that their position in society is as it should be and that there is nothing they can (or should) do about it.

The ideology of class thus produces a society in which a few people control the means of production through the expropriation of the surplus value of labor, maintaining their position of control through repression and the manipulation of ideology through religion, education, and the media. The only way the lower class can rectify this situation, according to Marx and Engels, is through **violent revolution.** Violent revolution is necessary because the ruling class controls the means of repression (e.g., police, militia, and military), and it won't relinquish its privileges and positions of control unless it is violently overthrown. Thus, repression and poverty brought about by the existence of social classes ultimately push the lower class (the workers), in desperation, to revolt to regain control of the means of production in order to regain the surplus value of their labor.

Two points about Marx and Engel's views are particularly relevant today; first, the position that class structure is very resistant to change seems to be corroborated by wealth and income distribution figures in the United States from 1982–1998. The information is summarized in Table 7.1.

For example, in 1983, the top 1 percent of the population held 33.8 percent of the wealth in the United States. By 1998, the top 1 percent held 38.1 percent of the wealth. In 1982, the top 5 percent of the population received 26.1 percent of the income; by 1997 the top 5 percent received 31 percent of the income. In the meantime, the net worth and income of the bottom 40 percent of the population were falling. In other words, the rich have been getting richer and the poor, poorer. Furthermore, the trends indicate that these patterns of wealth distribution will continue to accelerate.

A second major theoretical contribution of Marx and Engels lies in their ideas about the ideology of class: the notion that people in class societies come to believe that social stratification is "natural." We'll examine that idea in more detail next.

QUESTION 7.3: How Do People Come to Accept Social Hierarchies as Natural?

Cultural anthropology is about seeing beyond the facade of everyday appearances to what lies behind those appearances. Understanding how societies construct rationales to justify and legitimize social discrimination is one of the most important and, to some extent, the most difficult tasks of anthropology. Franz Boas, one of the founders of anthropology, was among the first social scientists who worked to discredit racist and sexist theories and ideologies that sought to legitimize the marginalization of people based on race, religion, gender, and ethnicity. Part of the problem is that racist and sexist theories exist not only in popular culture but in scientific ideology as well. It will be useful, then, to examine how such theories are constructed and often taken for granted, and how they are used to justify the ranking of people within the social hierarchy.

TABLE 7.1   THE SIZE DISTRIBUTION OF WEALTH AND INCOME, 1983–1998

	Percentage Share of Wealth or Income Held by:							
Year	Top 1.00%	Next 4.00%	Next 5.00%	Next 10.00%	Top 20.00%	2nd 20.00%	3rd 20.00%	Bottom 40.00%	All
A. Net Worth									
1983	33.8	22.3	12.1	13.1	81.3	12.6	5.2	0.9	100
1989	37.4	21.6	11.6	13	83.5	12.3	4.8	-0.7	100
1992	37.2	22.8	11.8	12	83.8	11.5	4.4	0.4	100
1995	38.5	21.8	11.5	12.1	83.9	11.4	4.5	0.2	100
1998	38.1	21.3	11.5	12.5	83.4	11.9	4.5	0.2	100
B. Financial Wealth									
1983	42.9	25.1	12.3	11	91.3	7.9	1.7	-0.9	100
1989	46.9	23.9	11.6	11	93.4	7.4	1.7	-2.5	100
1992	45.6	25	11.5	10.2	92.3	7.3	1.5	-1.1	100
1995	47.2	24.6	11.2	10.1	93	6.9	1.4	-1.3	100
1998	47.3	21	11.4	11.2	90.9	8.3	1.9	-1.1	100
C. Income									
1982	12.8	13.3	10.3	15.5	51.9	21.6	14.2	12.3	100
1988	16.6	13.3	10.4	15.2	55.6	20.6	13.2	10.7	100
1991	15.7	14.8	10.6	15.3	56.4	20.4	12.8	10.5	100
1994	14.4	14.5	10.4	15.9	55.1	20.6	13.6	10.7	100
1997	16.6	14.4	10.2	15	56.2	20.5	12.8	10.5	100

Source: *Recent Trends in Wealth Ownership, 1983–1998*, by Edward N. Wolff (2000).

(Reprinted with the permission of the Jerome Levy Economics Institute of Bard College.)

Constructing the Ideology of Racism

In the United States the ideology of class is based on the assumption that a person's position in the class hierarchy is determined largely by achievement or individual effort; that is, individuals who work hard and dedicate themselves to their work will succeed. Yet there is also the attempt to justify social position by a person's innate, biological makeup, largely by race, innate mental ability (intelligence), and gender. The hierarchical ordering of society thus is seen as an expression of a natural law that some people are born more fit to lead and succeed.

For centuries, European and American societies have been characterized by racial stratification. Traditionally, membership in certain racial or ethnic groups was enough to place people in particular positions in the status hierarchy that defined their social, political, and economic worth. In the United States, for example, position in the racial hierarchy often determined whether a person could vote, hold political office, pursue a particular occupation, live in a certain area, use certain public facilities, attend certain schools, or marry a particular person. Until the second half of the twentieth century, racial stratification was written into the laws of many states.

Stratification by race and ethnicity has existed for a number of reasons. It was certainly economically profitable to people who could buy black slaves or obtain workers from among groups legally or socially barred from anything but low-paying jobs. It was advantageous, also, to those who did not have to compete for jobs with people who were socially or legally barred from them. But stratified societies frequently claim that the ranking of people by race and ethnicity is natural, and a social hierarchy is not socially constructed. In the case of racial stratification, some proponents claimed that it was God's will that some persons were inferior to others; others claimed that God created different races as He created different species of animals, and the Bible says the species are to be kept apart. Others claimed that members of one race or another were intellectually or morally superior to members of other races. Generally, of course, it was the race of the person making reference to God or the Bible that was somehow superior.

Most people had little trouble constructing an ideology to justify racial stratification, especially since it was reinforced by state and religious authorities. Even the supposedly objective findings of scientists assisted in building a racist ideology. In the nineteenth century, reputable scientists devoted much time and energy to proving that the racial stratification of society was "in the nature of things." Their research findings supposedly proved that members of one race (usually whites or Europeans) were intellectually superior to members of another race (usually blacks or Asians).

Samuel George Morton was a respected scientist and physician who began in the 1820s to collect and measure skulls from all over the world. When he died in 1851, he left a collection of some 6,000 skulls. Like many in the nineteenth century, Morton believed that a person's intelligence was related to the size of his or her brain; the larger the brain, the more intelligent the person. Since the size of the brain could be determined by the size of the skull, he believed that a ranking of the races could be objectively achieved by a ranking of skull size.

Morton first measured the size or, more specifically, the cranial capacity, of skulls by filling them with mustard seed and then pouring the seed into a container to measure the skull's volume in cubic inches. Dissatisfied with the inconsistency of measurements obtained with mustard seed, he later used ⅛-inch-diameter lead shot. Morton concluded from his measurements that "white" skulls had a mean value of 92 cubic inches, "American Indian" skulls 79 cubic inches, and "black" skulls from America, Africa, and Australia 83 cubic inches. Among "white" skulls, the largest were those of Germans and English people, in the middle were those of Jews, and at bottom were those of Hindus. In other words, the social hierarchy of whites at the top, with the English and Germans at the top of the top and blacks on the bottom, was said to be supported by the evidence of brain size and intelligence.

Thus, "whites" (more specifically, northern European "whites") were not merely socially superior, they were biologically superior. Morton believed he had provided objective evidence that the distribution of status and power in nineteenth-century America accurately reflected not merely social but biological merit.

When Stephen Jay Gould, a Harvard biologist, reexamined Morton's published data in 1977, he concluded that Morton's summaries were a "patchwork of fudging and finagling" to reach conclusions that supported the socially con-

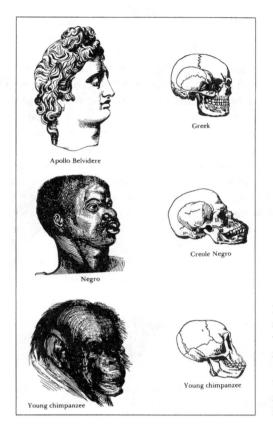

Apollo Belvidere

Greek

Negro

Creole Negro

Young chimpanzee

Young chimpanzee

Nineteenth-century scientists attempted to "prove" that whites were naturally superior to other races. In this illustration from an 1868 racist tract, the proportions of the skulls are distorted, giving the impression that blacks might even rank lower than the apes.

structed hierarchy. Gould found no evidence of conscious fraud. He concluded that Morton had simply selected or rejected certain data to ensure that the results confirmed what he and most other Americans "knew": that whites were naturally more intelligent than the people they called Indian or black.

Working with the same skulls Morton had used more than 150 years earlier, Gould discovered that the sample of 144 Native American skulls included proportionally more small-brained Inca skulls from Peru and fewer large-brained Iroquois skulls. This naturally produced a lower mean cranial capacity for indigenous Americans than would have occurred had Morton correctly adjusted for this discrepancy. Moreover, Gould discovered that Morton's failure to include the small-brained Hindu skulls with his "white" skulls had produced a higher average cranial capacity for white skulls. When Gould corrected for Morton's sample biases, he discovered that there was no difference between Euro-American and indigenous American cranial capacity. As for comparisons between "white" and "black" skulls, Gould discovered that Morton had ignored the facts that brain size is related to body size and that male skulls are larger than female skulls. Examination of Morton's black skulls indicated that the group included proportionally more female skulls and fewer male skulls. When Gould remeasured the "black" and "white" skulls, he discovered that the mean cranial capacity of black males was slightly higher than the mean for white males, while the mean for white females was slightly higher than that for black females.

Gould does not believe that Morton consciously manipulated his skull measurements to prove that whites were intellectually superior to Native Americans or blacks. Rather, he thinks Morton simply assumed that this is what his measurements would prove and set about achieving the results he expected. For example, Gould observed that when Morton used mustard seed to measure cranial capacity, he obtained even greater differences between his "white" and "black" skulls than he obtained using lead shot. Gould concludes that because mustard seeds are smaller and lighter than lead shot, Morton, probably unconsciously, packed more mustard seed into "white" skulls to obtain a greater difference in cranial capacity between "blacks" and "whites." More important, while Morton's measurements were obviously in error, as was his assumption that cranial capacity reveals intelligence, and while his conclusions were dictated by the socially constructed hierarchy of his day, they were used well into the twentieth century to support an ideology that the racial ranking of persons in society could be justified on natural rather than social grounds.

RESOURCE 7.3A

Resources on Race in Science

An excellent resource on the history of the concept of race in science is:

History of Race in Science
http://racescience.mit.edu/racesci/

Particularly valuable is the link page **http://racescience.mit.edu/racesci/links/index.shtml**, which will take you to some good examples of so-called "scientific racism."

The Social Construction of "Intelligence"

Morton's experiments represent just one example of the efforts in America and Europe to show that people somehow deserve their ranking in society, that it is not the result of chance, or family privilege, but, rather, the result of some innate, natural ability or talent. To believe otherwise would threaten a key assertion of American ideology: that all Americans enjoy an equal opportunity for success. Moreover, there are serious political and economic consequences of believing otherwise. If poverty and a low ranking in society are not the fault of the poor, then they must be the result of some failure of society. Such an admission provides a strong reason for reworking social, economic, and governmental policy (e.g., enacting laws barring racial and other forms of discrimination, programs of economic redistribution, or affirmative action). But since such changes might lead to a loss of privilege for those who benefit from present social, economic, and governmental policy, there is strong motivation to find some concept that legitimizes inherited privilege but still lays the blame for poverty or lack of success on the poor themselves.

The concept of intelligence neatly solves this problem; if people accept the idea that intelligence can explain how well people do, then the fiction that people's rank in society depends solely on their own, innate ability can be maintained. Moreover, if it can be shown that intelligence is inherited, then we can explain why it is that the children of successful people tend to be successful, and why certain groups, notably people of color and certain immigrant groups, are disproportionately poor.

Consequently, the failure of the thesis that cranial capacity, and hence brain size, revealed intelligence did not end the attempts to link intelligence to success and to race and ethnic class membership. There has been, instead, a continuing effort on the part of some members of the scientific establishment to marshal evidence to prove that intelligence is inherited, and that it differs according to racial groups. These efforts included, for example, the work of Arthur Jensen in the 1960s and '70s and, more recently, by the publication in 1994 of *The Bell Curve* by Richard J. Herrnstein and Charles Murray. Missing from most of these accounts is any acknowledgment that the concept of intelligence itself is a social construct, an idea that is invented. Consequently, we need to look closely at our concept of intelligence. How did it evolve?

To begin, anthropologist Allan Hanson notes that the concept of intelligence contains a number of questionable assumptions. First, intelligence is assumed to be a single entity. Second, it is assumed to be measurable and unequally distributed in the population. Third, the amount people have is assumed to be relatively fixed throughout life. Fourth, the amount people have is assumed to largely explain their degree of success in life. Finally, it is assumed to be largely inherited.

Each of these assumptions is critical to the intelligence construct as most people think of it, and each has been the subject of enormous scientific attention and criticism. The first assumption requires that we accept the idea that if someone is intelligent in one way, he or she will be intelligent in other ways, rather than believing that some people can be intelligent in some ways, but not others. The second assumption implies that we can somehow measure innate intelligence, as opposed to achievement, and the third presumes that we can show that whatever is measured does not vary throughout a person's life. The fourth is built on the idea that people who have more measurable intelligence are more likely to be successful, while the fifth assumption requires that we show that the children of people with high measurable intelligence also have high measurable intelligence.

In spite of the number of assumptions that lie behind the notion of intelligence and the studies that illustrate how questionable each of these assumptions really is, most Americans take the notion for granted. Yet it is a relatively unique idea, not shared by many other societies. Indigenous maritime navigators of the South Pacific, for example, learned to read wave patterns, wind direction, celestial constellations, and other signs and find their way thousands of miles from one island to another. Yet others in the same society who are unable to duplicate this feat don't view the navigators as somehow being smarter; they see them as people who can navigate. The Japanese view what we call intelligence in much the same way as we view health—except for certain (and generally temporary) circumstances, we all have enough of it.

This book is not the place to summarize the works that call the concept of intelligence into question. But we might learn something about the social construction of ideologies of class by briefly looking at the early history of the intelligence construct and reviewing how reputable scientists proceeded to develop it. Three pioneers—Francis Galton, Karl Pearson, and Charles Spearman—supplied the basic ideas and experimental proofs for the classic concept of intelligence as a fixed, "mental" entity that is differentially distributed in the population, is measurable, largely explains a person's educational and occupational success, and is inherited.

Francis Galton was one of the leading intellectual figures of the late nineteenth century, the founder of modern statistics and the founder of eugenics—the attempt to identify the most desirable human traits, specify the individuals who possess them, and, through selective reproduction, enhance the number of people possessing the desired characteristics. In his best-known work, *Hereditary Genius,* which was published in 1867, Galton sought to demonstrate that the "genius" of selected eminent men was linked to the fact that they had eminent parents, and, consequently, that their "genius" was largely inherited. In his sample of 997 eminent British men, he found that 31 percent had eminent fathers, 48 percent had eminent sons, and 41 percent had eminent brothers, far higher percentages than one would expect by chance. Galton concluded that this illustrates the power of heredity in the distribution of "genius." He was, of course, rightly criticized for ignoring the impact of environment. But he did something else that is more interesting, something that went largely unchallenged; he selected the eminent men from the British upper and upper middle classes, ignoring the "captains of industry and finance" and, of course, women; eminence was eminence only within a select range of activities and occupations. Galton, the nephew of Charles Darwin and of upper-middle-class background, was faithfully reproducing the judgments of his own status as to what constituted intelligence.

RESOURCE 7.3B

Resources on Eugenics

Eugenics as public policy emerged directly from the misapplication of Darwin's idea of natural selection. It assumed that the "weak" had to be prevented from breeding to ensure that they did not pass on their "weaknesses" to the next generation. You can find out more about eugenics and the ideology behind it at: Image Archive on the American Eugenics Movement, **http://vector.cshl.org/eugenics/**

As the authors of the site note, eugenics, which was behind much of the Nazi effort to "eliminate" those peoples viewed as undesirable such as Jews, Gypsies, Catholics, and gays, has been thoroughly discredited. Yet it continually resurfaces in other guises, and may yet be fully revived with the discovery of techniques to modify the human genome.

Much of Galton's later research was devoted to arguing that traits that he called "genius," "mediocrity," and "imbecility" were analogous in their statistical distribution within a society to certain physical characteristics. He developed a number of tests for cranial capacity and for sensory capacities—the ability to discriminate between colors or smells, for example. Galton was not the only one trying to do this; in Germany, the United States, and England, other researchers were trying to measure intelligence, largely through the evaluation of sensory and reflex activity, such as reading aloud rapidly, rapidly giving the colors of named objects, naming and classifying plants, animals, and minerals, and other tests of memory and spatial judgment. Around 1900 there was a move away from these kinds of measures, however, largely because they weren't showing any correlation with each other and, more importantly, because they showed only a low correlation with teachers' estimates of the mental capability of their students. Regardless, by 1900 the classic intelligence construct had been laid out, although its proof was somewhat wanting.

The next figure in our story is Karl Pearson, one of the most fascinating individuals of the late nineteenth and early twentieth century, whose published works included over 400 articles on mathematical physics, statistics, and biology, as well as poetry, a passion play, art history, studies of the Reformation and Medieval Germany, and political essays. In 1901, Pearson published a study in the *Proceedings of the Royal Society of London* in which he concluded that:

> The mental characteristics in man are inherited in precisely the same manner as the physical. Our mental and moral nature is quite as much as our physical nature, the outcome of hereditary factors. (Pearson 1901:155)

It is instructive to look at how Pearson reached this conclusion. He took pairs of brothers and measured specific physical characteristics, such as stature, forearm length, hair color, eye color, and cephalic index. He found, not surprisingly, that there was a high correlation among brothers for these traits, a mean correlation of .5171. Then he asked teachers, using another sample of brother-pairs, to rank them on seven "mental characteristics": intelligence, vivacity, conscientiousness, popularity, temper, self-consciousness, and shyness. Thus, under "conscientiousness" teachers were asked to rate each child as "keen" or "dull," and to choose among six subdivisions of intelligence. When the teachers' evaluations of brother-pairs were tabulated, Pearson found a strong correlation between brother ratings, a mean correlation of .5214, thereby proving the power of inheritance.

Much about this study is questionable, but of particular note is the role of teachers' judgments. Obviously, what teachers were evaluating were selected behavior patterns and personal characteristics—patterns and characteristics that they judged to be evidence of various "mental characteristics." In other words, the teachers' judgments were highly subjective and, at best, questionable. But Pearson's work marked an important development in the construction of our concept of intelligence: Whatever intelligence was, he claimed to show that it was obviously inherited at least as much as physical characteristics.

Let's move forward a couple of years to the next important stage in the formulation of the intelligence construct, Charles Spearman and "general intelligence." Spearman's research, published in the *American Journal of Psychology* in 1904, was designed to prove that there were different degrees of correspondence between an individual's performance on different types of tests. Thus, one would expect that there would be a high degree of correspondence between one's performance on geometrical tests and tests of spatial perception, and a low degree of correspondence between one's performance on, say, tests of musical ability and tests of weight discrimination.

If there were some degree of correlation between all the test results, this would indicate that there was some *general factor, g,* that would affect performance on all tests. Thus, tests that resulted in high correlation (e.g., geometrical ability and spatial perception) would be heavily saturated with *g,* while tests with little correlation would not be. For example, to use an athletic analogy, if someone hits both a baseball and a golf ball a long way, we might assume that some general factor for athletic ability could be assumed to account for both skills.

Spearman suggested that the *g* factor underlies all mental operations and if it could be ascertained, then it would approximate true intelligence. This is a major claim, for to prove the existence of *g* would result in the dismissal of the idea, widely held up to that time, that different people could be intelligent in different ways and that each person had a unique contribution to make. With *g,* people would be intellectually different in only one way, and people with lots of *g* had more to contribute than people with only a little *g.*

To experimentally prove the existence of general intelligence, Spearman isolated four kinds of intelligence that, he claimed, when correlated would show a high degree of correspondence: "present efficiency," "native capacity," "general impression produced upon other people," and "common sense." "Present efficiency" referred to the "ordinary classification according to school order" in subjects such as Greek, Latin, or mathematics. "Native capacity" was arrived at by taking the difference between a child's rank in school and his age, while "general impression produced on other people" was obtained by asking the teacher of a class who was the brightest pupil, the next brightest, and so on. "Common sense" was arrived at by asking the oldest child in a class to rank her school fellows on the basis of "sharpness and common sense out of school." As Spearman said, she seemed "to have no great difficulty in forming her judgments concerning the others, having indeed known them all her life." As a check on the reliability of judgments, he also asked the rector's wife to rank the children, although as Spearman notes regretfully, she did not know some of them. Spearman, not surprisingly, found that children who ranked high on one kind of intelligence tended to rank high on others, thereby validating the existence of *g.*

Obviously the methodology of these classic studies was seriously flawed, relying as it did on subjective judgments as to who was intelligent and who was not—judgments that were bound to be biased by such factors as the social class of teachers and students. From Galton's first major work, *Hereditary Genius,* through Spearman's work on general intelligence, members of the professional middle class were selecting as intelligent those people whose behavior patterns and appearance most conformed to their own. Moreover, little effort was made to conceal the fact; subjective judgments of members of the professional class were the major means by which intelligence was defined. Regardless, however, the intelligence construct as we know it was generally complete and considered by reputable scientists to be experimentally validated: *Intelligence is a singular trait, represented by* g, *that is inherited and is differentially distributed in the population.*

Much more was to come, of course, in the social construction of intelligence, most notably the development of the Stanford-Binet IQ test, and later the Scholastic Aptitude Test (SAT), more recently renamed the Scholastic Assessment Test. Additional and more sophisticated experiments were performed that some claimed supported the conclusions of early pioneers such as Galton, Pearson, and Spearman. But the most interesting feature is the continued part played by the social judgments of people—largely teachers, psychologists, and school administrators—in determining what did or did not constitute intelligence. As late as the 1960s, intelligence test results were still being cross-checked with teachers' judgments, and students' ranks in class, and if the test scores failed to correlate with the teachers' judgments, the tests were changed.

Yet in spite of the obvious flaws in the concept of intelligence—flaws that are acknowledged by most social scientists—it continues to serve as a means of legitimizing the social order, making it seem as if a person's place in it is "in the nature of things." Clarence J. Karier put it particularly well:

> The many varied tests, all the way from IQ to personality and scholastic achievement, periodically brought up-to-date, would serve a vital part in rationalizing the social class system. The tests also created the illusion of objectivity, which on the one side served the needs of the "professional" educators to be "scientific," and on the other side served the need of the system for a myth which would convince the lower classes that their station in life was part of the natural order of things. (Karier 1976:136)

EXERCISE 7.3

The National Space Settlement Agency (NSSA) has hired your research and consulting company, Testers, Inc., to develop a test to determine a person's sensitivity to others. The test will be used by NSSA as part of its national program for selecting candidates to participate in a program of space settlement. Since space settlers will be required to spend many months and years together in close quarters, NSSA has determined that settlers' sensitivity to others is critical for the success of its mission.

This is a pioneering effort, so you are free to approach the task in any way that you see fit. There are, however, some guidelines:

1. You must carefully *define* what constitutes sensitivity to others. This involves not only a straightforward definition, but also a list of those behavioral or personality features that would characterize a person's degree of SO.

2. You must *devise a test* that could be given to a person that would allow you to measure the behavioral or personality features that characterize sensitivity as you have defined it.

3. The test needs to be *simple* to enable it to be graded by machines (e.g., multiple-choice or true-false questions). Your test should contain no more than ten "questions."

4. The test that you devise must allow the tester to clearly *discriminate* differences among people in SO. That is, your questions must elicit a significant portion of "wrong" answers.* NSSA requires that each person tested be assigned an SO score.

5. You must suggest how to *test the test*. That is, how can you determine that it does effectively measure the degree of a person's sensitivity to others?

*Obviously if everyone gets a question right or wrong, there can be no difference between them.

RESOURCE 7.3C

Resources on Standardized Testing

Standardized testing is one of the main ways that the class structure in the United States is reproduced in each generation. You can find out more about the abuses of testing at the following Web sites:

Fair Test: The National Center for Fair and Open Testing
http://www.fairtest.org/index.htm

You can find out about the SATs at:

Frontline: The Secrets of the SAT
http://www.pbs.org/wgbh/pages/frontline/shows/sats/

You can also explore some of the reasons why certain groups perform better on standardized testing at:

The Atlantic Monthy
http://www.theatlantic.com/issues/99aug/9908stereotype.htm

Constructing Stratification by Gender

Looking back at Morton's mismeasurements and the history of the social construction of intelligence, it is easy to condemn the biases that seemed to create a scientifically supported system of stratification by race and class. Yet the biases that falsely linked race to biology and intelligence to class also led to the linkage of gender and biology—the belief that the superiority of men over women was not socially constructed but "natural." Many people believed that women's bodies defined both their social position and their function, which was to reproduce, as men's bodies dictated that they manage, control, and defend. At the beginning of the twentieth century, even the Supreme Court of the United States ruled that women should be prohibited from jobs that might endanger their reproductive function. The Court concluded that a "woman's physical structure and the performance of maternal functions place her at a disadvantage in the struggle for subsistence. Since healthy mothers are essential to vigorous offspring, the physical well-being of women becomes an object of public interest and care in order to preserve the strength and vigor of the race."

The view that the biology of females makes them lesser persons than males remains embedded in American culture, sometimes in very subtle ways. An example is the language used by professionals to describe women's bodily processes of menstruation and menopause. Anthropologist Emily Martin says that during the nineteenth century, Americans regarded the female body as if it were a factory whose job was to "labor" to produce children. Menopause was viewed negatively because it marked the end of productive usefulness, and menstruation was described as a sign of the failure of the implantation of a fertilized egg. Medical writers of the time such as Walter Heape, a Cambridge zoologist and militant antisuffragist, described how in menstruation the entire epithelium (cellular tissue) is torn away, "leaving behind a ragged wreck of tissue, torn glands, ruptured vessels, jagged edges of stroma, and masses of blood corpuscles, which it would seem hardly possible to heal satisfactorily without the aid of surgical instruments."

Martin says that the same attitudes toward female reproductive functions that existed in the nineteenth century persist today, encoded in contemporary medical and biology textbooks. Menopause is described in some texts as a breakdown of communication between the brain and the reproductive parts of the female body. In menopause, says one college textbook, the ovaries become unresponsive to hormonal stimulation and, as a result, regress. The hypothalamus, which controls hormone production, has gotten estrogen addiction from years of menstruation. Because of the withdrawal of estrogen at menopause, the hypothalamus gives inappropriate orders. Menopause is described as a breakdown of authority: Functions fail and falter; organs wither and become senile. Our language still depicts the female body as a machine that in menopause is no longer able to fulfil its proper goal; it can no longer produce babies. In this view, at menopause the female body becomes a broken-down factory.

Menstruation is likewise described even today as a breakdown in the reproductive process. When an egg is not implanted, the process is described in negative terms as a disintegration or shedding. Here is one example Martin found:

> The fall in blood progesterone and estrogen "deprives" the "highly developed endometrial lining of its hormonal support," constriction of blood vessels leads to a "diminished" supply of oxygen and nutrients, and finally "disintegration starts, the entire lining begins to slough, and the menstrual flow begins." Blood vessels in the endometrium "hemorrhage" and "the menstrual flow consists of this blood mixed with endometrial debris." The "loss" of hormonal stimulation causes "necrosis" (death of tissue). (quoted in Martin 1987:45)

Another otherwise objective text says "When fertilization fails to occur, the endometrium is shed, and a new cycle starts. This is why it used to be taught that 'menstruation is the uterus crying for lack of a baby.'"

Menstruation is depicted as a sign of an idle factory, a failed production system, a system producing "scrap" or "waste." Note the language used in the following passage from another textbook:

> If fertilization and pregnancy do not occur, the corpus luteum *degenerates* and the levels of estrogens and progesterone *decline*. As the levels of these hormones decrease and their stimulatory effects are *withdrawn,* blood vessels of the endometrium undergo *prolonged spasms* (contractions) that reduce the blood flow to the area of the endometrium supplied by the vessels. The resulting *lack* of blood causes the tissue of the affected region to *degenerate.* After some time, the vessels relax, and allow blood to flow through them again. However, capillaries in the area have become so *weakened* that blood leaks through them. This blood and the *deteriorating* endometrial tissue are discharged from the uterus as the menstrual flow. As a new ovarian cycle begins and the level of estrogen rises, the functional layer of the endometrium undergoes repair and once again begins to proliferate. (quoted in Martin 1987:47; italics added)

Martin notes that very different language is used in the same textbooks to describe male reproductive functions. For example, the textbook from which the above description of menstruation is taken describes the production of sperm as follows:

> The mechanisms which guide the *remarkable* cellular transformation from spermatid to mature sperm remain uncertain. Perhaps the most *amazing* characteristic of spermatogenesis is its *sheer magnitude:* the normal human male may manufacture several hundred million sperm per day. (quoted in Martin 1987:48; italics added)

This text, which describes menstruation as "failed production," neglects to mention that only about one of every 100 billion sperm ever makes it far enough to fertilize an egg. Moreover, other bodily processes that are similar to menstruation are not spoken of in terms of breakdown and deterioration. Seminal fluid picks up shredded cellular material as it passes through the male ducts, and the stomach lining is shed periodically. Why are these processes not also described in the same negative terms as menstruation? Martin says the reason is that both men and women have stomachs, but only women have uteruses. The stomach falls on the positive side, the uterus on the negative.

Rather than describing menstruation as failed production, Martin suggests that it might be more accurate to describe it as the successful avoidance of an egg implant. If a couple has done anything to avoid the implantation of an egg, is it still appropriate to talk of the reproductive cycle in terms of production? The following description of menstruation offered by Martin represents it not as a failure to reproduce, but as the successful avoidance of a pregnancy:

> A drop in the formerly high levels of progesterone and estrogen creates an appropriate environment for reducing the excess layers of endometrial tissue. Constriction of capillary blood vessels causes a lower level of oxygen and nutrients and paves the way for a vigorous production of menstrual fluids. As a part of the renewal of the remaining endometrium, the capillaries begin to reopen, contributing some blood and serous fluid to the volume of endometrial material already beginning to flow. (Martin 1987:52)

Emily Martin's analysis reveals that, in contemporary American society, the ideology of gender stratification remains embedded in our language and in our ideas about the bodily functions of males and females. Describing the bodily processes of women in negative terms makes women seem to be lesser human beings. Moreover, describing menstruation and menopause in negative terms leads women themselves to believe that their bodily functions are less clean and less worthy than those of men.

QUESTION 7.4: How Do People Living in Poverty Adapt to Their Condition?

The position in a social hierarchy occupied by each person is like a window through which she or he sees the world; different windows, different worlds. Furthermore, in order to survive in the impoverished conditions that exist in the lower tiers of society, people adopt specific adaptive strategies. Anthropologist Oscar Lewis coined the term **culture of poverty** to describe the lifestyle and world view of people who inhabit urban and rural slums. Some anthropologists object to that term, since it implies that poverty is somehow rooted in the subcultural values passed on from one generation to another, rather than in the social and cultural values of the larger society of which the poor are only a part. The implication is that if it weren't for the culture of poverty, the poor would have no culture at all.

Modifying that view, some anthropologists maintain that the behavior of people in poverty represents their adaptations to their socioeconomic condition—no money and no jobs. These conditions are the result of inequality, usually reinforced by racism, and further buttressed by an economic system that requires a source of cheap labor. Moreover, descriptions of poor families as broken, fatherless, or female-centered are misleading. Many of the behaviors of the poor that are viewed negatively by the dominant society are actually resilient responses to the socioeconomic conditions of those living in poverty.

But more recent views confirm that conditions of poverty and oppression that exist in United States cities do require a cultural adaptation built on trying to compensate for living at the economic and social margins of society. This poverty and marginalization of inner cities has spawned, says Phillipe Bourgois, an "inner-city street culture":

> a complex and conflictual web of beliefs, symbols, modes of interaction, values, and ideologies that have emerged in opposition to exclusion from mainstream society.... This "street culture of resistance" is not a coherent, conscious universe of political opposition but, rather, a spontaneous set of rebellious practices that in the long term have emerged as an oppositional style. (1995:8)

In fact, much has been commercialized by the mainstream United States culture through fashion, music, film, and television and adopted by middle- and upper-class youth.

Kinship as an Adaptation to Poverty

One of the classic studies of how families cope with poverty was conducted by anthropologist Carol B. Stack in the late 1960s. She worked closely with a predominantly black community she called The Flats, a section of a small, Midwestern city of some 55,000 people. Unemployment in The Flats was over 20 percent, and 63 percent of the jobs held were in low-paying service occupations such as maids, cooks, and janitors. While only 10 percent of the whites in the city lived in housing classified as deteriorating, 26 percent of blacks did. Moreover, blacks had inadequate access to health care, and their infant mortality rate was twice that of whites.

Stack's interest was in how the residents responded to their impoverished conditions. She discovered that they fostered kinship ties and created fictive kinship links to form close, interlocking, cooperative groups that would ensure economic and social support in times of need. Few people earned enough to provide them or their families with enough to eat or a place to stay on a regular basis; even welfare payments could not always guarantee food and shelter for a family. Accordingly, people in The Flats regularly "swapped" food, shelter, child care, and personal possessions. In this respect, the community resembled societies such as the Ju/wasi in which a person shares with others but expects them to reciprocate at some later time. Anthropologists call this type of sharing **generalized reciprocity,** as distinguished from **balanced reciprocity,** in which items are exchanged on the spot; a direct trade of items would be an example. **Negative reciprocity** is an attempt to get something for nothing or make a profit. The advantage of generalized reciprocity is that widespread sharing ensures that nobody lacks the basic needs for survival. People in The Flats cultivated diffuse

Anthropologists have found that people living in poverty find ways to adapt to their circumstances. For these children in a poor section of New York City, the street and sidewalk serve as a playground.

kinship and friendship relations by giving when they could, so that others would give to them when they were in need. These networks were often framed in a kinship idiom, even though no biological kin tie existed.

Another adaptation to poverty in The Flats involved child care. Given the unpredictability of employment, the sometimes young age at which women had children, and the need to respond to unpredictable living conditions and substandard housing, a child might reside with three or four different adults. Often different people performed the roles of provider, discipliner, trainer, curer, and groomer. Stack points out that those who provided child care did so because they considered it a privilege as well as a responsibility. Children were valued, but they were considered the responsibility of a wide network of kin and friends.

Male and female relations were most affected by the difficulty that men had in finding steady employment. Generally a couple in The Flats would not marry unless the man had a steady job. Men in The Flats had accepted the mainstream American model of the male provider, and being unable to find regular employment prevented their assumption of that role. Moreover, marriage removed people from the widespread sharing network, since after marriage their major obligations belonged to their husbands or wives. In addition, because a woman was cut off the welfare rolls if she married, kinship networks and welfare benefits offered a woman more security than a husband could. Nevertheless, men and women in The Flats did form intimate relationships out of which children were born. Moreover, the fathers took considerable pride in their children, as did the paternal grandparents, to whom the children often went to for help. However, the mothers often regarded the fathers as friends who had failed to fulfill their paternal obligations. Thus, the conditions of poverty drew people into kinship and friendship networks, rather than nuclear family patterns valued by the larger society.

In Search of Respect: Selling Crack in El Barrio

While people do make creative adaptations to impoverished conditions, they also attempt to resist the patterns of oppression and discrimination that are the roots of the poverty. But the resistance, itself, can lead to self-destructive behavior. Phillipe Bourgois, in his study of drug use on the Upper East Side of New York City, portrays a culture that emerges out of peoples' personal search for dignity and their rejection of racism and marginalization. But since this culture centers on drugs, it leads people into lives of violence, substance abuse, and internalized rage.

There is a tendency in the United States, with its overdeveloped value of individualism, and the willingness of people to blame the victims, to overlook the historical and economic conditions that give rise to impoverished ghettos amidst urban affluence. The question we must begin with then is how do you create an impoverished ghetto?

The Upper East Side of New York City, East Harlem, has long been home to poor minorities. After a period when it was the site of elite farms and country houses, the building of cheap transportation in the late nineteenth century turned it into the home of wave after wave of immigrant groups, creating what some called the most ethnically diverse area in the United States. In the mid-twentieth century "slum clearance" programs destroyed functioning Italian, working-class communities and replaced them with concentrated populations of poor Puerto Ricans. But what brought people, in this case from Puerto Rico, to live in East Harlem or El Barrio?

El Barrio, says Bourgois, must be seen in the historical context of a colonized island—Puerto Rico. In the late nineteenth and early twentieth century the island was taken over by American, multinational sugar growers who dispossessed thousands of rural farmers, forcing them to seek wage labor on coastal sugar plantations.

After World War II hundreds of thousands migrated to the United States, many to New York City and East Harlem. Overall some 1.5 million left the sugarcane fields, shantytowns, and highland villages for New York City. In two or three generations these migrants were transformed from semisubsistence peasants on private plots or haciendas to agricultural laborers on foreign-owned, capital-intensive agro-export plantations, to factory workers in export-platform shantytowns, to sweatshop workers in ghetto tenements, and to service-sector employees living in public, high-rise housing.

By the 1970s many of the new migrants were faring relatively well, having obtained employment in the various manufacturing jobs in and around New York City. But once again the global economy served to disrupt lives. The exodus of manufacturers from the United States to other countries in the 1970s and 1980s to take advantage of cheap labor, tax breaks, and lax environmental standards, left millions of U.S. workers without jobs. In New York City alone, from the 1960s to the early 1990s, some 800,000 manufacturing jobs were lost.

Thus, over the course of the past century, the global economy along with systematic racism and discrimination has conspired to produce high rates of unemployment, substance abuse, broken families, and deteriorated health. No group in the United States other than Native Americans fare as badly statistically as Puerto Ricans. In 1993 the median household income for Puerto Ricans was $14,000 less than whites, and over $4,000 less than other Latino groups. But perhaps the greatest irony is that, in spite of this history, most members of El Barrio see their violent actions and deteriorated lives as a result of their own actions, their own choices.

The area in East Harlem where Bourgois worked had a poverty rate of almost 40 percent and over half the population, given their incomes, should not have been able to meet subsistence requirements. That many do, says Bourgois, is a tribute to the underground economy that allows people to meet basic food and clothing needs. Underground economic activities for women include baby-sitting, working "off-the-books" as seamstresses, tending bar at social clubs, and taking in boarders. Men's jobs tend to be more visible; street-corner car repairs, working for unlicensed contractors, selling "numbers," or selling drugs. Drugs are the multibillion dollar foundation of the underground economy, with cocaine, crack, and heroin the most prevalent.

These drugs are easily accessible. Bourgois says that, within a two-block radius of the tenement in which he lived with his family while doing fieldwork, he could obtain heroin, crack, powder cocaine, hypodermic needles, methadone, Valium, angel dust, marijuana, bootleg alcohol, and tobacco. Within one hundred yards of his stoop there were three competing crack houses selling vials at two, three, and five dollars. And just a few blocks away, in what was called a "pill mill," one doctor wrote $3.9 million dollars of Medicaid prescriptions; 94 percent of these were on the NYC Department of Social Services' list of frequently abused prescription drugs.

Crack, a combination of cocaine and baking soda that can be smoked (unlike powdered cocaine) and delivers an almost instantaneous high, was by far the most in demand in El Barrio. Selling crack enabled some members of El Barrio to amass both wealth and prestige. One of the most important dealers that Bourgois came to know was Ray. Ray built his business, which required him to balance discipline and the threat of violence with respect, around his crackhouse, The Game Room. Ray formed special ties with workers, serving as godfather to children of his workers and friends in much the same way as local landlords in Puerto Rico would use godfather or *compadrazgo* ties to ensure the loyalty of their farm workers. Ray also bestowed special benefits on his employees, including bail money, lawyer fees, holiday bonuses, family gifts, and special dinners.

Some drug workers employed by Ray would earn hundreds of dollars a night running a crack house, and others earned considerable sums serving as lookouts. Yet Bourgois found that, in spite of the amount of money they earned, most workers in the crack trade were almost always penniless. He discovered that whatever they earned they would spend on gifts, expensive radios, clothes, and other consumer items—a consumption behavior that is mirrored by rapidly upward mobile persons in the legal economy.

Furthermore, says Bourgois, when you calculate the risks in crack work of getting shot, arrested or beaten up, the off-time spent in jail or when the police shut down the crack house, and the poor working conditions, employment in the crack economy is generally much worse than legal employment. For that reason most workers in the drug trade prefer legal employment. In fact, most drug workers have had legal work experience, often beginning at the age of 12 bagging or delivering groceries for tips or stocking groceries at the local *bodegas* (grocery stores) off the books. But by the time they reach the age of 21, few of the residents of El Barrio have fulfilled their dreams of finding stable, well-paying jobs. Instead they settle for low-paying, service-sector jobs—nonunion jobs in fast-food restaurants, unlicensed asbestos removers, street corner distributors of flyers, night-shift security guards for hospitals for the criminally insane, errand-runners, mail-room clerks, or photocopiers.

Many of the people involved in the crack-house economy alternate between street-level crack dealing and minimum wage jobs in the legal economy. But most, says Bourgois, either quit or are fired from these jobs because of a refusal to be exploited or because of the racist or condescending attitudes of the largely white, middle-class employers and supervisors. Often they view their return to the streets as a triumph of free-will and resistance.

Yet, says Bourgois, there is much self-reproach at not being able to hold a steady, legal job, or being seen as lazy. Often failure at legal employment or the inability to find a job (particularly during the economic recession of 1989–1991) drove some residents to more substance abuse. Furthermore, the older they got, the more difficult it was to get hired, particularly when job centers sent three or four people for the same job to allow employers to choose the person they wanted. It also became harder to explain to prospective employers the reasons for their periods of unemployment. They became what economists call "discouraged workers," those who no longer seek employment and who are no longer counted in the unemployment statistics. But this discouragement leads to a spiral of depression, increased substance abuse, evictions, and fractured social relations.

In this environment of little economic opportunity, drugs play economic, psychological, and social functions. They provide income; they provide a respite and escape from the conditions of El Barrio; and they constitute a form of symbolic resistance to the racism, discrimination, and subordination that users experience in the larger society. But, says Bourgois, this adaptation is self-destructive. Not only does drug use dissipate bodies, but, since male drug users feel powerless as their role in the household diminishes, they lash out at the women and children they can no longer control as their wage-earning fathers and grandfathers did.

Women in El Barrio face their special problems. Many, particularly those involved in the drug economy, must be able to balance the demands of the two state agencies that dominate their lives—the penal system and the welfare system. Given the Federal and State budget cuts of the past two decades, it is virtually impossible to support a family on welfare alone. Women had to supplement their welfare income with off-the-books jobs, maintain two or more social security cards, or sell drugs. Making matters worse, welfare rules required people to requalify every six months or be cut from the welfare roles. Consequently 10 to 15 percent of New York recipients were cut each year.

The dilemma of women in El Barrio is exemplified by Maria, whose boyfriend, Primo, was one of Bourgois's closest friends. Maria, who shared an apartment with her 250-pound mother, became pregnant and was overjoyed. It was, writes Bourgois, precisely her terrible living conditions that made motherhood so attractive. It offered her, he says, a romantic escape from her difficult surroundings and cemented her love for Primo, who, at the time, faced the prospect of a four-to six-year jail sentence. For young women the way to escape a troubled home is a romantic relationship with an idealized male and the embrace of motherhood.

Having a child also symbolized economic independence. Mothers are eligible for desired public housing, which for all but pregnant teenagers involves an 18-year waiting list. Once the romantic ideals disappear, as they often do when people lack the financial resources to enact them, children become a woman's main focus in life.

For children, however, life in El Barrio is especially destructive. Given the poverty, the lack of day-care support, the deteriorating schools, the prevalence of drugs, and a life centered on the streets, Bourgois witnessed the metamorphosis of cute, bright eight-year-old girls into pregnant, crack-using 13-year-old "teenagers." Or bright energetic nine-year-old boys transformed into juvenile inmates accused of "assault with a deadly weapon." For many children the crack house is the only space that is heated in the winter and air-conditioned in the summer. Children become socialized into the street culture and take it for granted.

In many ways, says Bourgois, East Harlem resembles the poverty of Third World countries, where infants and children die at a rate 10 to 100 times that of developed countries. But it is not a lack of calories and potable water that is killing them; instead it is substance abuse, racism, a withdrawal of public services, and the exodus of factory jobs to other countries. The death and destruction of inner-city children, says Bourgois, occurs in adolescence rather than infancy. In the mid-1990s in East Harlem, 18- to 24-year-olds had a greater risk of violent death than soldiers on active duty in World War II.

But while crack dominates the economic, social, and psychological life of men, women, and children in El Barrio, it is not the root of the problem. As Bourgois puts it,

> Self-destructive addiction is merely the medium for desperate people to internalize their frustration, resistance, and powerlessness. In other words, we can safely ignore the drug hysteria that periodically sweeps through the United States. Instead we should focus our ethical concerns and political energies on the contradictions posed by the persistence of inner-city poverty in the midst of extraordinary opulence. In the same vein, we need to recognize and dismantle the class- and ethnic-based apartheids that riddle the U.S. landscape. (1995:319)

The studies by Carol Stack in The Flats of a Midwestern city and by Bourgois of the Upper East Side of Manhattan provide convincing evidence that people do not passively accept their positions at the bottom of a stratified society; rather, like people in other environments and economic conditions, they adapt to their circumstances as best they can. They have the same social and economic aspirations as people higher up in the social hierarchy, who have greater income and opportunity. While Stack, like others, emphasizes this, she concludes:

> those living in poverty have little or no chance to escape from the economic situation into which they were born. Nor did they have the power to control the expansion or contraction of welfare benefits or of employment opportunities, both of which have enormous effect on their daily lives. In times of need, the only predictable resources that can be drawn upon are their own children and parents, and the fund of kin and friends obligated to them. (Stack 1974:107)

QUESTION 7.5:   *Can a Nonstratified Community Exist Within a Large Society?*

Many people who are convinced of the harmful effects of social stratification believe nevertheless that in a modern, industrial society, the system is inevitable. It may be possible for the Inuit or Ju/wasi to have a relatively egalitarian society, for example, but it is not possible in a modern, industrial state. Yet for thousands of years there have been attempts by some groups in stratified societies to create classless, egalitarian, utopian social settings. Christianity began as a utopian dream of universal equality, and the idea of a real-life utopia emerged with the idea that man, under God, has the power to create an earthly paradise. Among the earliest expressions of this idea was Christian communalism, which led to the founding of Catholic monastic orders: isolated, virtually self-sufficient communities in which the work was collective and egalitarian. In the nineteenth century, industrialists such as Robert Owen attempted to build utopian factory communities, and Karl Marx's goal was to build a national-utopian society. In the middle of the twentieth century, psychologist B. F. Skinner outlined a utopian society based on scientific technology in *Walden Two,* a controversial novel that inspired an attempt to translate his fiction into a real-life utopia at Twin Oaks in Virginia. All of these attempts to construct utopian societies are evidence of the long history of the search for an egalitarian social order.

Anthropologist Charles Erasmus examined hundreds of utopian communities in an effort to discover why most failed but some succeeded. He concluded that the main problem for these communities is trying to motivate community members to work and contribute to the common good without the promise of individual material rewards, status, or prestige. Of the successful utopian communities in this country, the most notable are those of the Hutterites, a Protestant sect that originated in Moravia in the sixteenth century. Why did the Hutterites succeed while so many others failed? Is it possible to use communities such as theirs as models for modern egalitarian communities?

The Hutterites and the Colony of Heaven

"If there will ever be a perfect culture it may not be exactly like the Hutterites—but it will be similar." These words of a member of a Hutterite colony express the feeling that the group has succeeded in building utopian communities. In fact, the Hutterite colonies are among the most successful products of the Christian communal movement, which includes the Mennonites and the more familiar Amish.

The Hutterites originated during the Protestant Reformation. In 1528 they began to establish colonies throughout what are now Germany, Austria, and Russia. Their pacifism and refusal to perform military service brought them into conflict with European governments, and in 1872, to avoid conscription, they emigrated to South Dakota and established colonies. During World War I, a confrontation over military conscription with state and federal authorities in the United States resulted in a Hutterite move to Canada. But their successful agricultural techniques were valued in the United States during the Great Depression of the 1930s, and they were convinced to return and establish new colonies here. In the early 1970s there were more than 37,000 Hutterites distributed among 360 colonies in the United States, and more than 9,000 in 246 colonies in Canada.

Cooperation is valued in Hutterite society, where community members worship, work, and eat as a group. Here, women are shown preparing a meal for the entire community.

The goal of the Hutterites is to create a "colony of heaven." Drawing their inspiration from the Old and New Testaments, the Hutterites believe in the need for communal living and the proper observance of religious practice. They reject competition, violence, and war, and believe that property is to be used and not possessed. They respect the need for government, but do not believe they should involve themselves in it or hold public office. A Hutterite colony is governed by an elected board that includes the religious leaders and the community teacher, so authority is group-centered. It is a family-based, agricultural community in which everyone is expected to contribute to the work and to share equally in the bounty. Unlike the Amish, whose beliefs they in essence share, the Hutterites accept and use modern technology; they are acknowledged to be among the most successful agriculturists in North America.

The Hutterites are not totally egalitarian. Their society is ranked by age and gender; members do not participate in the decision-making process until they are married, and women are considered intellectually and physically inferior to men. But they reject the unequal distribution of wealth and competition among members for status, prestige, or personal possessions. The Hutterites minimize competition by renouncing private adornment and ostentatious displays of wealth and by practicing collective consumption. There is little difference in dress, and adornment is usually frowned on. All the housing is plain and utilitarian. And, as in most Christian communes, they are careful to indoctrinate their children against competition. Children are taught to avoid seeking honors or placing themselves above others. They are taught never to envy others.

One way the Hutterites build commitment to the group is through frequent face-to-face interaction. Members eat together in a communal dining hall, work together, and meet frequently to discuss the affairs of the community. Almost every evening the entire community gathers for church service. While the Hutterites have no formal means of punishing those who violate group rules, they do practice a form of ostracism called *den Frieden nehmen,* "taking away the individual's peace of mind." An ostracized man is not allowed to talk to other members, including his own wife. He may also be assigned a special room in which to sleep apart, and may be required to eat alone.

In addition, the practice of "branching," or community fission, functions not only to adjust community size, reduce friction, and settle other colonies, but also to build internal commitment and reduce competition. Erasmus points out that social movements have difficulty maintaining long-range goals, especially as wealth accumulates. The Hutterites address this problem by dividing the communities, or branching, every 15 years. During a 15-year period, each community saves a portion of its earnings to purchase additional land, build houses and barns, and accumulate necessary machines and livestock to start a new colony. When the new physical facilities are complete, members of the community draw lots to determine which families will relocate. Branching provides each Hutterite community with a tangible goal. More "wealthy" colonies that delay branching are often disrupted by internal quarrels and become examples of the danger of failing to branch on schedule. Branching also has a built-in renewal factor; new communities reproduce the founding enthusiasm and ideals. If there is competition, it is between colonies, rather than individuals.

The Hutterites have resisted specialization, unlike other movements that have evolved into industries producing goods such as silverware in the Oneida community in New York and furniture and woolens in the Amana Society in Iowa. The Hutterites have also resisted hiring outside labor; instead, they exchange labor among colonies and use technology to further agricultural production.

In sum, the Hutterites, by a collective effort, have created within the larger society a community without poverty, without economic classes, with little or no crime, where each person, without the promise of material reward, contributes to the common good. There are, however, some negatives: the Hutterites are a Bible-based religious community that teaches male supremacy and severely limits individual freedoms. The question is whether these negatives outweigh the benefits of creating nonstratified communities within the larger stratified society. There is also a question of whether cooperative communities, such as the Hutterites, can serve as a model for the poor in the larger society; that is, does the establishment of closed, collective communities offer a solution to the endemic poverty of those at the bottom level of modern society, and does the success of the Hutterites suggest that it is within our means to build societies without poverty?

EXERCISE 7.5

Imagine for a moment that you have just been hired by NASA to plan the development of the first human extraterrestrial settlement. NASA wants you to use your knowledge of other societies to build an ideal community, avoiding the problems of modern society. How would you go about the task? For example, what communities or societies that you know about might you choose as models for extraterrestrial settlements? What would be the main values that you would build into your community? How would people be rewarded for the work they performed? How would you maintain order and settle conflicts? What kind of educational system would you propose? Finally, what are the most serious problems in modern society that you would want to avoid?

CONCLUSIONS

The underlying problem in this chapter is why extremes of poverty and wealth exist in modern societies. The criteria customarily used to rank people in social hierarchies include wealth or income, occupation, ethnic group membership, personal appearance, race, gender, and age. The consequences of such ranking, especially in the creation of poverty and the gap between the rich and poor, have raised some of the most challenging questions in modern societies.

There are two theories of social stratification that offer different explanations of why societies construct social hierarchies. In the integrative theory, it is assumed that stratification exists because it serves to integrate the activities of its members and to ensure its smooth functioning. In the exploitation theory, it is assumed that stratification is caused by the political dominance of one group over another for the exploitation of labor and resources.

People come to accept social hierarchies as natural because they believe that hierarchy is a biological principle. Some people are thought to be naturally more or less intelligent than others or otherwise more or less worthy. Females' biological functions, for example, have been described in terms that make women seem less worthy than men.

People at the lowest level of the social hierarchy, those who live in poverty, adapt to their conditions in various ways. Blacks in The Flats of a Midwestern city adapted by building kinship ties, and Puerto Ricans on the Upper East Side of New York City adapted by building an underground economic system centered on drugs.

A few groups have demonstrated that it is possible to build egalitarian, non-stratified communities within a larger industrial society. Perhaps the most successful in the United States have been the Hutterites, a religious group that emphasizes communal ownership of property and equal distribution of production, while rejecting competition, violence, and war.

REFERENCES AND SUGGESTED READINGS

INTRODUCTION: THE RATIONALE FOR SOCIAL INEQUALITY The epigraph comes from Robert Hertz's *Death and the Right Hand,* translated and edited by Claudia and Rodney Needham (The Free Press, 1960). The quote from Thomas Belmonte is from *The Broken Fountain* (Columbia University Press, 1989).

HOW DO SOCIETIES RANK PEOPLE IN SOCIAL HIERARCHIES? One of the classic works on social hierarchy, especially as it relates to India's caste system, is Louis Dumont's *Homo Hierarchicus: An Essay on the Caste System* (University of Chicago Press, 1970). Pierre L. van den Berghe and his associates produced a series of books on class and ethnicity in Europe, Africa, and South America. These include *Inequality in the Peruvian Andes: Class and Ethnicity in Cuzco,* with George P. Primov (University of Missouri Press, 1977); *South Africa: A Study in Conflict* (Wesleyan University Press, 1965); and *Race and Ethnicity* (Basic Books, 1970). A review of anthropological studies of social class is Raymond T. Smith's article, "Anthropology and the Concept of Social Class," in

Annual Review of Anthropology, vol. 13 (1984), pp. 467–494. Ruth Sidel's analogy of the sinking of the *Titanic* and American society is in *Women and Children Last: Social Stratification in America* (Penguin, 1986). You can find a wealth of information about inequality in the United States in Valdas Anelauskas's book, *Discovering America As It Is* (Clarity Press, 1999). An excellent review of the literature on women's status is "Anthropological Studies of Women's Status Revisited: 1977–1987" by Carol C. Mukhopadhyay and Patricia J. Higgins, in *Annual Review of Anthropology,* vol. 17 (1988), pp. 461–495.

WHY DO SOCIETIES CONSTRUCT SOCIAL HIERARCHIES? For excerpts from Herbert Spencer's organic view of society see Talcott Parsons et al., *Theories of Society,* vol. I (Free Press, 1961). Morton H. Fried explores some of the reasons for social stratification in *The Evolution of Political Society* (Random House, 1967).

HOW DO PEOPLE COME TO ACCEPT SOCIAL HIERARCHIES AS NATURAL? Stephen Jay Gould's examination of Morton's experiments on cranial capacity and intelligence are described in *The Mismeasure of Man* (W. W. Norton, 1981). An excellent anthropological examination and critique of the concept of intelligence and the role of testing in American life can be found in Allan Hanson's book, *Testing Testing* (University of California Press, 1993). An examination of the attempts to legitimize social class through testing and education can be found in Paul Henderson's article, "Class Structure and the Concept of Intelligence," and Clarence J. Karier's article, "Testing for Order and Control in the Corporate Liberal State," both in *Schooling and Capitalism: A Sociological Reader,* edited by Roger Dale, Geoff Esland, and Madeleine MacDonald (Routledge & Kegan Paul in association with The Open University Press, 1976). Karl Pearson's article, "On the Inheritance of Mental Characteristics in Man," appeared in *Proceedings of the Royal Society of London,* vol. 69 (1901), pp. 153–155, and Charles Spearman's first attempts to prove the existence of *g* appeared in his article "General Intelligence," *American Journal of Psychology,* vol. 115 (1904), pp. 201–292. The most recent and widely publicized attempt to legitimize the American class structure through the use of the concept of intelligence can be found in *The Bell Curve: Intelligence and Class Structure in American Life,* by Richard J. Herrnstein and Charles Murray (Free Press, 1994).

An evaluation of the literature on differences in IQ scores, contrasting the hereditarian and environmentalist positions, is provided by John F. Longres in *Human Behavior in the Social Environment* 3rd ed. (F. E. Peacock Publishers, 2000). Emily Martin's work on the social construction of female biology is represented by *The Woman in the Body: A Cultural Analysis of Reproduction* (Beacon Press, 1987). Robert Hertz's analysis of the symbolic use of the human body to justify hierarchy can be found in *Death and the Right Hand* (cited above). A review of the ways in which reproductive biology affects the role of women is given in "The Politics of Reproduction," by Faye Ginsburg and Rayna Rapp, in *Annual Review of Anthropology,* vol. 20 (1991), pp. 311–343.

HOW DO PEOPLE LIVING IN POVERTY ADAPT TO THEIR CONDITION? Oscar Lewis's pioneering work on the lives of people in poverty is represented by *Five Families: Mexican Case Studies in the Culture of Poverty* (Basic Books, 1959). A critique of the culture-of-poverty concept can be found in Charles A.

Valentine's work, *Culture and Poverty: Critique and Counter-Proposals* (University of Chicago Press, 1968). Carol Stack's account of The Flats appears in *All Our Kin: Strategies for Survival in a Black Community* (Harper & Row, 1974). The research on how Puerto Ricans on the Upper East Side of Manhattan adapted to their socioeconomic situation is reported in Phillipe Bourgois's book, *In Search of Respect: Selling Crack in El Barrio* (Cambridge University Press, 1995).

CAN A NONSTRATIFIED COMMUNITY EXIST WITHIN A LARGE SOCIETY? The examination of attempts to build egalitarian societies is based primarily on Charles Erasmus, *In Search of the Common Good* (Free Press, 1977). The description of the Hutterites relies on John Hostetler's study, *Hutterite Society* (Johns Hopkins University Press, 1974). For additional work, see Robert Moos and Robert Brownstein, *Environment and Utopia* (Plenum Publishing, 1977), and Kathleen Kinkade, *A Walden Two Experiment: The First Five Years of Twin Oaks Community* (William Morrow and Company, 1973).

Arise by Li Hua, 1947. Photo courtesy Ellen Johnston Laing. From her book THE WINKING OWL.

CHAPTER 8

THE CULTURAL CONSTRUCTION OF VIOLENT CONFLICT

PROBLEM 8: HOW DO SOCIETIES GIVE MEANING TO AND JUSTIFY COLLECTIVE VIOLENCE?

Rosa had her breasts cut off. Then they cut into her chest and took out her heart. The men had their arms broken, their testicles cut off, and their eyes poked out. They were killed by slitting their throats, and pulling the tongue out through the slit.

Witness to the attack (1984)

INTRODUCTION: *The Justification of Violent Conflict*

When the Spaniards invaded the New World in the sixteenth century, they met fierce resistance from the Carib. A warlike people, the Carib inhabited the northeast portion of South America around what is now Venezuela and Guyana. The neighbors of the Carib recognized their ferocity by calling them "sons of the tiger's teeth." Moreover, the Carib were cannibals. To prepare for war, a Carib chief would hold a feast at which women urged the dancing warriors to be fierce and avenge their dead. The dancing was intended to encourage the tiger spirit, Kaikusi-yuma, to take possession of the warriors, and when they went to war, it was the spirit of Kaikusi-yuma that killed, not them. A warrior could rid himself of the possession only after tasting the blood and flesh of a dead enemy.

From our perspective, the acts of the invading Spanish, like the acts of the Carib, were horrific. The Spanish invaders murdered and enslaved thousands of indigenous people, and the Carib devoured human flesh. But both the Europeans and the Carib considered their acts to be moral and proper; the Spaniards justified their killing and enslavement as the work of God, and the Carib defined their killing as the act of an animal possessing a human body. Both peoples constructed meanings for their acts that distanced them from the consequences of their violence. While we may condemn these acts, we live in a world in which governments construct systems of meaning that allow them to plan and contemplate the use of weapons that are much more deadly than the clubs, spears, crossbows, and primitive firearms of the Carib and Spaniards—weapons capable of incinerating millions of people.

Purposeful, organized, and socially sanctioned combat involving killing— what most people call war or feud—seems to be an intrinsic feature of human societies. In fact, it is difficult to find societies that do not sanction violence for one reason or another. But why is collective violence so universally sanctioned? Some suggest that human beings have an innate instinct toward aggression and that the roots of war and collective violence lie somewhere in the biological mechanisms that animals and humans have in common. Violent conflict is regarded as a part of human nature. Others reject this explanation as simplistic; collective violence, they say, is above all a cultural construction whose roots lie in the human mind, not in the genes. While there may be some innate aggressive impulse, human beings can choose whether or not they will give meaningful form to that impulse.

The fact that human beings construct systems of meaning to justify violent conflict and distance themselves from its consequences suggest that it has little to do with a natural aggressive impulse. Acts of collective violence, such as those described in the epigraph, are rationalized as purposeful, noble, or inevitable acts, not as evidence of wanton cruelty. The problem is to discover how societies construct meanings for violent conflict that mask its consequences and convince people that it is right and proper.

To evaluate this issue, the first question to be addressed is how societies create a bias in favor of collective violence. That is, what kinds of meanings are constructed to encourage people to commit violence against others? Then, if there are societies without collective violence, how do they create a bias against it? If violent conflict is not simply natural and inevitable, but is culturally constructed, it may be possible to learn from societies in which there is little, if any, violence. The question is, are there significant social, economic, or political differences between violent and peaceful societies? Next, the effects of violent conflict on societies should be examined to determine whether, as some maintain, engaging collectively in deadly quarrels may in the long run serve some useful purpose. Finally, since collective violence is sanctioned in American society, it is instructive to ask how we have created a bias toward violent conflict and constructed meanings that allow us to contemplate, plan for, and pursue the destruction of millions of people in other nations.

QUESTIONS

8.1 How do societies create a bias in favor of collective violence?
8.2 How do societies create a bias against violent conflict?
8.3 What are the economic, political, or social differences between peaceful and violent societies?
8.4 What are the effects of war on society?
8.5 How is it possible to justify the creation of weapons of mass destruction?

QUESTION 8.1:   How Do Societies Create a Bias in Favor of Collective Violence?

One way societies create a bias toward collective violence is to reward it. Among the Native Americans of the western plains, for example, raiding other groups for horses was a means by which a man gained status. Horses symbolized wealth, and in many groups a man's importance was measured by the number of horses he owned and gave to others as gifts.

Horses, Rank, and Warfare Among the Kiowa

Horses were not indigenous to North America; they were brought to the continent by Spaniards in the 1500s. Native American groups such as the Kiowa captured some horses and acquired others in trade with the Spaniards. The Kiowa also obtained horses by attacking other Native American groups with horse-raiding parties of from six to ten and occasionally as many as 30 men. The object of the raid was not only to secure as many of the enemy's horses as possible but also to demonstrate bravery. Among the Kiowa, rank was determined in two ways: by the number of horses a man possessed and by the honors accruing to him in warfare.

TABLE 8.1   KIOWA RANKING AND HONORS

Group I	Group II	Group III
1. Counting first coup 2. Charging an enemy while the party is in retreat, thus covering the retreat 3. Rescuing a comrade while the party is retreating before the enemy 4. Charging the leading man of the enemy alone before the parties have met	1. Killing an enemy 2. Counting second coup 3. Receiving a wound in hand-to-hand combat	1. Dismounting, turning horse loose, and fighting on foot 2. Counting third and fourth coup 3. Serving as raid leader 4. Success in stealing horses 5. Efficiency in war camp life

Source: Information from Bernard Mishkin, *Rank and Warfare Among the Plains Indians* (Seattle: University of Washington Press, 1940).

Kiowa society was divided into four ranks or grades. In the top rank were ongop, men who were generous, owned considerable wealth, and, most important, had distinguished themselves in war. In the second rank were ondeigupa, men who had property, especially horses, and were generous but had not yet distinguished themselves in war. The lower ranks of Kiowa society were occupied by keen or dupom, people who were poor, propertyless, or helpless. To rise in status, a young Kiowa male needed to acquire a horse. Often he would begin his climb through the ranks of Kiowa society by borrowing a horse from a kinsperson to go on a raid, hoping to repay the loan with another horse he captured. With a horse of his own, he could participate in more raids, gradually obtaining enough horses to rise to the rank of ondeigupa, or, as the Kiowa put it, "rise out of the bush of keen." Several years of raiding might bring him 20 or 30 horses, at which point people would begin speaking of him with respect.

To rise to the top rank of ongop, however, also required the accumulation of honors won in war. The Kiowa had a very elaborate system of battle honors divided into three groups of brave deeds, with group I being the most honorific (see Table 8.1). Counting first coup, for example, involved charging the enemy alone and striking one of them with a stick. The number of feathers a man wore in his headdress was a measure of his heroic exploits.

Anthropologist Bernard Mishkin estimates that approximately 10 percent of the men would rise to the top rank of Kiowa society by obtaining a significant number of horses and accumulating sufficient battle honors. In this way, the Kiowa rewarded aggressive behavior and bravery in battle.

Good Hosts Among the Yanomamo

Another way societies create a bias in favor of collective violence is to make it necessary as a way of protecting valuable resources. A classic example is the Yanomamo of Venezuela. The Yanomamo live in villages of from 40 to 250 people and practice slash-and-burn (swidden) agriculture, living primarily on the crops they grow in their gardens.

Intervillage warfare is endemic to the Yanomamo. Anthropologist Napoleon Chagnon, who has worked with the Yanomamo since 1964, reports that one village of 200 people was attacked 25 times, and 10 people were killed during a period of 15 months, representing a loss of 5 percent of the village population. Chagnon estimates that some 20 to 25 percent of all male deaths are the result of warfare.

For the Yanomamo, women and children are valuable resources. The men believe that, to protect themselves and their resources, they must be fierce, and raiding another village is one way they demonstrate their ferocity. Raids may be conducted to avenge the death of a village member at the hands of an enemy village or as the result of an act of sorcery by an enemy. Raids may also be made to capture women or children. Moreover, violence can take the form of inviting members of another village to a feast and, usually with the aid of allies from another village, killing the guests and abducting their women. Raiding by other villages also forces them to move fairly frequently, and sometimes they take refuge from their enemies in the villages of their allies. This practice is risky, however, because host villages generally expect sexual access to the wives of their guests or expect unmarried female guests to marry men of their village. These expectations often lead to open hostilities between hosts and guests.

Expressions of ferocity may be directed among village members as well. For example, men often vent anger and demonstrate their ferocity to others by beating their wives. A man who accuses another of cowardice or making excessive demands for goods or women may challenge his opponent to a chest-pounding duel in which they take turns hitting each other in the chest as hard as they can. The duel generally ends when one of the contestants is too injured to continue. Fights with clubs are another form of settling disputes between men, although they generally result in free-for-alls that can be deadly.

In this environment, where each man strives to acquire females, it is necessary to adopt an antagonistic stance toward others, encouraging the development of what the Yanomamo call waiteri (ferocity). The waiteri complex, as Chagnon calls it, is evidenced in ways other than direct conflict. The Yanomamo express it in their origin myth, which tells how the original people were created from the blood of the moon which had been shot with an arrow by beings who believed their children's souls were being devoured by the moon. The first Yanomamo born of the blood of the moon were exceptionally fierce and waged constant war on one another.

The Yanomamo also socialize male children to be aggressive and hostile. Boys are teased to strike tormentors and to bully girls. At one gathering of two villages attended by Chagnon, men were to satisfy their grievances against each other with a chest-pounding duel. Prior to the duel the men gathered all the boys between the ages of 8 and 15 and forced them to fight one another. At first, says Chagnon, the boys were reluctant and tried to run away, but their parents dragged them back and insisted that they hit each other. At the first blows the boys cried, but as the fight progressed, fear became rage, and they ended up pounding each other while they screamed and rolled in the dirt, amidst the cheers and admiration of their fathers.

Defending Honor in Kohistan

Another way societies create a bias toward collective violence is by making it part of a code of honor. Among the Kohistani in the mountains of northwest Pakistan, villagers follow a code that demands vengeance against any threat to a man's honor. When anthropologist Lincoln Keiser worked in the village of Thull in 1984, defense of honor continually led to relationships of dushmani, or blood feud. The men of Thull view each other with guarded suspicion, and relationships of friendship can easily slip into dushmani. They believe that if another person wrongs them, they must retaliate, but the act of revenge should not exceed the original wrong. However, any unwarranted behavior toward a man's daughter, wife, or unmarried sister requires deadly retaliation. Even staring at these female relatives requires death for the offender.

One of Keiser's friends related how a neighbor killed his brother Omar while he was bringing a basket of food to the neighbor's family because Omar had heard the family had nothing to eat. "But why," asked Keiser, "would a man kill his neighbor who only tried to help him?" "Who knows?" the friend said, "But I will take vengeance." Keiser says he had no doubt he would. Looking into the incident, Keiser heard gossip that Omar was killed because he really went to the house to stare at his neighbor's wife and brought the food only as a trick. Keiser himself was ultimately forced to leave Thull because of a rumor that in taking a photograph of a goatherd he was actually trying to photograph the herd owner's wife.

The people of Thull are mostly farmers and herders. As followers of Islam, a religion that emphasizes peace and harmony, they have constructed a system of meaning in which taking vengeance is considered a religious act. Central to the beliefs of the people of Thull is the idea of ghrairat—a man's personal worth, integrity, or character. Ghrairat is given to men by God and can be lost only if they fail to protect it. Women's behavior is also a matter of ghrairat because men must control their women; any act of a woman, or a person toward a woman, that threatens to bring shame is a direct attack on the man's ghrairat and must be avenged. Women must never walk outside their father's or husband's house without an escort, must never speak to an unrelated man, and must always comport themselves with modesty, hiding and minimizing their sexuality. Men who allow their women freedom are baghrairatman, "men without personal integrity."

Defending ghrairat, however, is more than simply the concern of an individual. Because of the webs of kinship, friendship, and political ties, it often involves whole groups within the community in violence against one another. Men in Thull constantly ally themselves with others in groups that may be based on kinship or may represent political factions. A man seeking vengeance for a wrong may enlist the help of others with whom he is allied. More important, an act of vengeance may be taken not only against the man who committed the wrong but also against the kinsperson or a member of his faction.

One case reported by Keiser illustrates the course of collective violence or feud. Two young men, Mamad Said and Amin, were herding their goats in the mountains. In response to a friendly shove, Mamad Said playfully swung a stick at Amin, hitting him in the face and drawing blood. Amin went to his uncle, Shah Hajji Khan, who gathered some of his friends to avenge the injury by beating Mamad Said. But they were met by friends and relatives of Mamad Said, and in the ensuing melee Shah Hajji Khan's group suffered greater injuries; his son almost lost his life from an axe blow to the head. Now, two insults needed to be avenged by Shah Hajji Khan: the original blow received by his nephew and the beating inflicted on his son by friends and relatives of Mamad Said. Some two years later, Shah Hajji Khan hatched a plot to ambush Mamad Said, who escaped by hiding in an irrigation ditch. Six months later Mamad Said died from tuberculosis, which might be expected to bring an end to the feud begun by his accidental blow to Amin's face. But Mamad Said's brother, Qui Afsal, claimed that Mamad Said had died from sickness he contracted while hiding from Shah Hajji Khan in the irrigation ditch. In revenge he allegedly killed the son of a friend of Shah Hajji Khan who had helped avenge the injury to Amin. Qui Afsal was later shot in the stomach but survived.

As a consequence of such escalation of violence, the men of Thull habitually walk around armed, design their houses for defense against the gunfire of their neighbors, and spend most of their money on rifles and arms. A prized possession is a Russian-made AK-47 assault rifle.

EXERCISE 8.1

Examples of group-sanctioned conflict are readily available in reports in newspapers. To examine the justifications for such conflict, follow a daily newspaper for a couple of days and document the instances you find of group-sanctioned violence and the reasons attributed for it.

Status, protection or acquisition of valuable resources, and the defense of honor are embodied in the meanings of collective violence, not only in small-scale societies such as those of the Kiowa, Yanomamo, or Kohistani but in large-scale nation–states as well. "Remember the Alamo" was the rallying cry for Texans in their war against Mexico in 1847, and the American desire to avenge the Japanese attack on Pearl Harbor in 1941 was a powerful factor in mobilizing the American people in the war on Japan.

In each of these examples, societies construct a bias in favor of collective violence. But this does not answer the question of why they do it. That is, people may be able to justify killing if they wish. But we know from anthropological research that violent conflict also can be given meanings that actively discourage its occurrence.

QUESTION 8.2: How Do Societies Create a Bias Against Violent Conflict?

Anthropologist Thomas Gregor suggests that, since war is so widespread in human societies, the task of the social scientist is not so much to explain war as to explain peace. Peaceful societies, he says, are difficult to find. By peaceful, he means a society that is not involved in internal collective violence and in which there is little interpersonal violence. A peaceful society has no special roles for warriors and places a positive value on nonaggressive behavior and the peaceful resolution of conflict. Societies that have been characterized as relatively peaceful include

nonviolent

the Ju/wasi, the Semai of West Malaysia, the Inuit, the Xinguano of the Amazon region in South America, and the Buid of the Philippines.

Characteristics of Peaceful Societies

Conflict over material resources is avoided in peaceful societies by a strong emphasis on sharing and cooperation. It is expected that everyone in the group has a legitimate claim to what the group possesses. Among the Ju/wasi the person whose arrow kills an animal is considered to be the owner of the game, but he is obligated to distribute it. The Ju/wasi will share arrows with the understanding that if they kill an animal with an arrow given to them by someone else, they will give the owner the game to distribute. This also works to spread out the responsibility for meat sharing and the glory (and perhaps the hostility) that accompanies meat distribution.

The Semai of West Malaysia are known for their nonaggressiveness and avoidance of physical conflict. The approximately 15,000 Semai live in small hamlets of less than 100 people each. Understanding Semai nonviolence, says anthropologist Clayton Robarchek, requires understanding the Semai notion of pehunan, a state of being in which a person is unsatisfied in regard to some need or want, such as food or sex. The Semai believe that to refuse a request and deny a person a need intensifies the danger to both the individual and the group; for that reason, the group is obligated to help. The idea of pehunan encompasses a depiction of the community as nurturant caregivers. Rather than saying that it is each person's obligation to meet his or her own needs, the Semai believe that it is the obligation of all members of the community to help and give nurturance to others. Thus, Semai values stress affiliation, mutual aid, and the belief that violence is not a viable option for settling disputes.

Another way people in peaceful societies create a bias against violence is by condemning those who boast or make claims that can be interpreted as a challenge to others. Among the Ju/wasi, for example, no one is praised for gathering food or making a kill, and people go out of their way to minimize their accomplishments. Those who make boastful claims are ridiculed. Anthropologist Richard Lee painfully learned this lesson himself when, to show his appreciation to the Ju/wasi for the help they had given him, he brought a fine ox to be slaughtered and distributed at a Christmas feast. The Ju/wasi, much to Lee's chagrin, ridiculed the ox, claiming it was thin and unappetizing. Lee later realized that they were acting toward him as they would have to one of their own. They were letting him know that he wasn't as important as the gift and the killing of the ox made him think he was.

People in peaceful societies also avoid telling others what to do and carefully control their emotions in order to maintain goodwill. The Inuit, for example, fear people who do not demonstrate their goodwill by smiling or laughing, because someone who is unhappy may be hostile. The Inuit believe that strong thoughts can kill or cause illness, and they go to great pains to satisfy other people so that resentment does not build up. Anthropologist Jean Briggs, who lived among a group of Inuit, describes them as people who emphasize kindness and concern and never, under any circumstances, demonstrate anger or resentment. So great is their fear of causing conflict that they make requests indirectly to avoid being refused or to avoid embarrassing someone by making him or her refuse a request. So great is the crime of losing one's temper that someone who does so may be ostracized from the group. Briggs herself was virtually ignored for months by her adopted family after she lost her temper with some Canadian sports fishermen who she thought were taking advantage of them.

Gregor says that villagers in the Xingu basin of the Amazon maintain harmony by purposely sanctioning village monopolies in the production of certain goods such as shell belts, stone axes, salt, cotton, fish spears, and ceramic pots. In this way, each village has something that other villages need. The villages therefore maintain good relations, since to alienate another village might deprive one's own village members of a desired good. Moreover, trade is positively valued in itself. When villagers are asked why they don't make the goods they need themselves, they reply that this might anger those who do make them. Or they may claim that they do not have the knowledge to produce the items, although when they are temporarily cut off from a supply, they seem to learn how to make or acquire them very quickly. Gregor says it is unlikely that any village could not produce the goods desired, since marriage between groups is common, and each village contains people with the skills of other villages.

Xinguanos place a strong negative value on aggression and things that symbolize aggression. Killing is wrong because it produces blood; even animal blood is considered defiling. Most game animals are considered inedible, and even fish must be well-cooked so that there is no blood. The Xinguanos also hold strong negative stereotypes of aggressive groups. They consider non-Xingu Indians to be "wild Indians" who are violent; they beat their children, rape their women, and shoot arrows at white men's planes. The wild Indian has almost the status of an animal and represents everything a Xinguano doesn't want to be. When Xingu villages have been the object of aggression by others they have defended themselves, but successful warriors take no trophies and are given no special honor. In fact, they have to take special medicine to cleanse themselves of the defilement of the blood of their victims.

The Buid of the Philippines are also known for their nonviolence. For them, says anthropologist Thomas Gibson, violence is an expression of all that is disliked. For example, they have no word for courage, and one of their most prestigious activities is the creation of poetry. The Buid believe that the outside world is filled with threatening spirits that prey upon people and that any intragroup hostility might weaken the group and expose them to these spirits.

Peaceful societies also minimize violence and conflict through ceremony. The Ju/wasi believe that everyone has what they term their "medicine" or power. In the same way that nearby Bantu tribes have witchcraft and sorcery, and Europeans have pills and syringes, the Ju/wasi have n/um, a substance they say lies in the pit of the stomach. N/um has the capacity to keep people healthy and help cure people who are sick. Most important, n/um can be transferred from someone who is acting as a healer to others through the medium of the trance dance, their most common ceremony. The idea of the dance is for a person to "heat up" his or her n/um by dancing; as the person dances, the n/um in the stomach is vaporized and travels up the spinal cord into the brain, which causes the dancer to go into a trance. The dancer then goes from person to person laying on hands and transferring power to those who are touched, thereby enabling them to ward off sickness and death. Anyone can be a healer among the Ju/wasi; in a lifetime, each person is likely to serve as a healer at one time or another.

The trance dance has meanings that go beyond the power to heal, however. Some Ju/wasi are thought to have special powers that allow them to see the ghosts of dead ancestors who hover around the fires, to see distant scenes, to see through things, and, in special cases, to change themselves into lions and stalk the veldt in search of human prey. Trance dances are most frequent when large numbers of people come together (from about once a month in small groups, up to four times a week in large camps) and during certain occasions such as the arrival of visitors to a camp, the presence of meat, or sickness. The congregation of large numbers of people, the presence of meat, and the arrival of new people are all occasions that in one way or another create the potential for interpersonal conflict. The fact that trance dances are more frequent during such times seems to indicate that they may serve to heal social conflict as well as individual maladies. By bringing people together in the ceremony, by the sharing of n/um and the ritual recognition of common threats, the trance dance unites people and serves to symbolize the relationship between group harmony and individual well-being.

In sum, peaceful societies create a bias against violence by sharing, valuing nonaggressive behavior, building relations of dependence between individuals and groups, and engaging in collective behaviors that promote harmony. They are not, of course, always successful, and even among some so-called peaceful societies, there is violence. Lee collected accounts of 22 homicides among Ju/wasi groups during a 35-year period from 1920 to 1955, for example, but found little, if any, sanctioned group violence.

QUESTION 8.3: What Are the Economic, Political, or Social Differences Between Peaceful and Violent Societies?

Thomas Hobbes, a seventeenth-century philosopher, proposed that human beings in their natural state, without government or laws, are driven by greed and the quest for gain. Without some common power to keep them in awe, Hobbes said, they live in a state of war, with every person against every other person. Here is one of the more famous passages from Leviathan, in which Hobbes describes his vision of life before civilization:

> Whatsoever therefore is consequent to a time of warre, where every man is enemy to every man; the same is consequent to a time, wherein men live without other security, than what their own strength and their own invention shall furnish them withall. In such a condition there is no place for Industry; because the fruit thereof is uncertain; and consequently no Culture of the Earth [agriculture]; no navigation, nor use of the commodities that may be imported by sea; no commodious Building; no Instruments of moving, and removing such things as require much force; no Knowledge of the face of the Earth; no account of Time; no Arts; no Letters; no Society; and which is worst of all, continual feare, and danger of violent death; And the life of man, solitary, poore, nasty, brutish, and short. (Hobbes 1881:94–96)

Hobbes saw human beings as having a natural inclination to be violent, an inclination that can only be controlled by some form of centralized authority. However, as anthropologists have discovered, societies with little formal government, such as the Ju/wasi, Inuit, Buid, and Semai, are among the most peaceful in the world (see Question 8.2). These peaceful societies also are small in scale and get their living primarily by hunting and gathering or by slash-and-burn agriculture. Most are relatively isolated and lack formal mechanisms for resolving conflict once it begins. There are no courts, no police, no jails, and no formally sanctioned threats of violence, even against wrongdoers. Since there is little that people in these societies can do once violence begins, they go to great lengths to avoid it.

Had Hobbes known the Yanomamo, however, he might have found that his vision of a stateless society, "where every man is enemy to every man," had been verified. Their social and economic life closely resembles that of the Semai, and they live in virtually the same environment and are neighbors of the peaceful Xinguano. But the Yanomamo society creates attitudes favoring collective violence in order to protect its women and children (see Question 8.1), which suggests that Hobbes may have been correct, at least in part. In this case, the lack of any centralized control or formal mechanisms for putting an end to conflict results in unrestrained violence, rather than the avoidance of conflict.

The Need to Protect Resources and Honor

In societies without any form of centralized control and a bias favoring collective violence, such as those of the Yanomamo and the Kohistani (whose code of honor demands vengeance for any threat), individuals must protect their own resources through force. Because the Yanomamo, for example, do not effectively control intravillage conflict, men of their own as well as other villages are constantly seeking to seduce one another's wives. Consequently, the men, individually or in groups, must build a reputation for fierceness in order to protect themselves and their families. Thus, failure to control conflict, along with the need for men to build a reputation for aggressiveness to protect their resources, combine to produce a society that places a positive value on violent behavior.

The conditions that give rise to violent conflict among the Yanomamo are not unlike those that promote violence in street gangs in the United States. When Lincoln Keiser worked in the 1960s with the Vice Lords, a Chicago street gang (or "club," as they preferred to call themselves), he concluded that boys joined gangs because alone they could not protect themselves from shakedowns or safeguard their interests in girls. Whereas the Yanomamo encouraged waiteri—fierceness— the Vice Lords valued heart—a willingness to follow any suggestion regardless of personal risk. Where a Yanomamo demonstrated fierceness in chest-pounding duels, axe fights, and raids against enemy villages, members of street gangs in Chicago confirmed heart in gang fights, or "gangbangs." Street gangs even formed alliances with each other against other gangs, as do Yanomamo villages with each other. The similarities in the dynamics and values of violent conflict among the Yanomamo and among street gangs in the United States illustrate how under certain conditions individuals form groups to protect themselves against other groups. To discourage attacks from others in the absence of protection from other agencies, these groups cultivate a reputation for violence.

The gang violence that Keiser observed in Chicago during the late 1960s has escalated since, and weapons more typical of Thull are now being used. Alex Kotlowitz, in *There Are No Children Here*, reports how the Vice Lords, one of

One reason for gang warfare may be a lack of other ways to protect valued resources or to settle disputes. These Ching-a-Ling gang members in the South Bronx maintain that they provide the only means of protection for people in their neighborhood.

three gang factions in Chicago in the early 1990s, were making use of an arsenal that included Uzis and grenades. The purpose was the same, although the stakes were higher. Drugs have become the major source of contention among Chicago gangs (the head of one Vice Lord faction grossed some $50,000 to $100,000 a week). When drug wars erupt over territory, the violence reflects the increased stakes and more massive firepower. A couple of years ago, four members of the Vice Lords came upon a rival gang member in the lobby of a housing project and shot him five times with an Uzi, two sawed-off shotguns, and a .25-caliber automatic handgun to establish their dominance in the neighborhood.

The social and political conditions that characterize the societies of the Vice Lords and the Yanomamo are such that, in each of them, individuals must mobilize and use force to protect or acquire desired resources. In neither case is there any effective centralized authority to guarantee the safety of resources or stop violence once it begins. There is a centralized force in Chicago—the police—but they rarely intervene in gang violence, because they are unwilling or do not have the resources to do so, or because local residents are afraid or reluctant to report violence.

The idea that violence may erupt because of a lack of centralized control to protect valued resources is evident also among the Kohistani in Thull. Good land is scarce, and ownership of land is often questioned because there is no central system of land recording or registration. Land is usually acquired by inheritance, but there is little to stop anyone from saying that some relative was wrongfully denied ownership of a particular piece of land in the past, and claiming the land on that basis. Whether such a claim is won or lost may depend on which of the claimants has the greater influence or firepower. Even Keiser was suspected of potential land-grabbing while he was conducting fieldwork. He was accused of burying papers in the woods that he would later dig up and claim were old documents giving him title to the land. Since he must have political connections, he would win. In other words, in Thull, also, an ideology that encourages collective violence may be attributable to a need to protect resources in the absence of any effective centralized authority.

Creating the Conditions for Violence

Napoleon Chagnon characterized Yanomamo warfare as a "truly primitive cultural adaptation…before it was altered or destroyed by our culture." It was, he said, the normal state of affairs before it was suppressed by colonial governments. However, there is considerable evidence that Yanomamo warfare and aggression were less a product of their "primitive" existence or nature than a consequence of Western contact.

Brian Ferguson maintains that the period of Chagnon's fieldwork (1964–1972), on which he based his best-selling ethnography, *The Fierce People,* was one of the most turbulent periods in Yanomamo history. Violence and aggression, says Ferguson, were a product of three major changes: (1) the presence of new outpost settlements of government agents, missionaries, and researchers; (2) competition for Western manufactured goods, particularly steel cutting tools, and (3) a breakdown of social relations brought about by epidemics and depletion of game and other food resources.

The Yanomamo, Ferguson points out, had been in contact with outsiders for centuries. Europeans raided the Yanomamo for slaves as early as the mid-seventeenth century and until around 1850. In the late nineteenth century the rubber boom in the Amazon, a horrendous period for indigenous groups who were forced into collecting rubber under the threat of torture and death, brought the Yanomamo into increased contact and conflict with other indigenous groups. When the Amazonian rubber boom collapsed in the 1920s from competition with Asian rubber plantations, the area in which the Yanomamo lived was relatively peaceful until the 1950s and '60s, when influenza and measles epidemics swept the area, leaving only one-quarter of the children with both parents. But more disruptive yet were the presence of new, Western outposts.

The new outposts made available manufactured items (e.g., steel knives, machetes, aluminum pots, and shotguns) desired by the Yanomamo. Steel cutting tools, for example, were ten times more efficient than the stone cutting tools used by the Yanomamo. Shotguns were effective for both hunting and raiding. The Yanomamo could obtain these items in various ways. They could relocate their villages near the outposts, they could send trading parties on long voyages to get them, or they could raid other groups for them. But the greatest advantage went to what Ferguson called "anchor villages," those that relocated near outposts. The result was a hierarchy of settlements ranging from anchor villages whose members were able to monopolize the new desired goods, and more isolated settlements whose members had fewer and lower-quality goods.

Yanomamo in anchor settlements traded Western items to distant groups for local handicrafts such as cotton hammocks, spear points, or manioc flour. But trading parties were also targets of raids of groups desiring Western goods. To protect themselves and their monopoly on Western trade goods, and discourage raiding, Yanomamo groups found it advantageous to cultivate reputations for violence and aggression. A reputation for fierceness was also an advantage in negotiating for desired goods. Thus one man told of the number of people he had killed on raids just before demanding a machete.

However, in addition to access to desired goods, proximity to Western outposts incited violence in other ways. For example, once people relocated their village near an outpost settlement, they were reluctant to move. One way that small-scale, mobile societies, such as the Yanomamo, avoid conflict, is by moving villages away from enemies when conflict is threatened. But since moving would mean giving up access to and a monopoly on Western goods, members of anchor villages were reluctant to move, and hence needed to protect themselves and the goods that they obtained from Westerners. In addition, more permanent settlements quickly depleted game resources, resources that had been used in reciprocal exchanges with other people and groups. Sharing patterns, which we noted in Question 8.2 are crucial for maintaining peaceful relations, began to break down, leading to more conflict.

Thus deaths from disease and war disrupted traditional social relations, the depletion of game weakened traditional patterns of sharing and cooperation, and access to Western technology provided new sources of conflict. Furthermore, the new technology introduced a new way of ordering society and enhanced the ability of people in anchor villages to make war.

In addition to creating situations that promoted violence and aggression, access to Western goods also explains the aggressive attitudes of Yanomamo men to women. Traditionally the Yanomamo practiced bride service; grooms were obligated to work for their bride's family for from one to four years. But families of grooms in anchor villages were able to substitute Western goods for bride service, one result being a movement of wives to villages with greater access to Western goods. This combined with the Yanomamo practice of female infanticide and polygamy, resulted in a shortage of and greater competition for females, and the more frequent raiding of other villages for women. In addition, Yanomamo wives go to live in their husband's family village, particularly where Western goods take the place of brideservice. The result is that women are removed from the protective influences of their families, and are more likely to be victims of abuse.

In sum, many of the patterns of Yanomamo warfare, violence, and aggression cannot be understood without knowledge of their history of contact with Western society and the contact conditions that increased the likelihood of violence and war. Even the power of chiefs, whose feast-giving played such an important role in Chagnon's descriptions of alliance formation and aggression, was largely a function of Western contact. Outsiders, following traditional customs, brought gifts to local leaders. But the gifts that outsiders brought were far more valuable. Thus Chagnon gave one chief a gift of 25 machetes, providing him with items that he could use to enhance his power.

Thus, as Ferguson says:

If villages were not anchored to outposts but were able to move freely, if long-established marital alliances were not disturbed by massive morality, if communal sharing of meat were still the norm, and, above all, if necessary technology were widely and equally available, my theoretical expectation is that there would be little collective violence among the Yanomami. (1992:225)

Sexism and Violent Conflict

Another difference between peaceful and violent societies that has been suggested has to do with gender roles. Among the Ju/wasi, Buid, Xinguano, and Semai, men and women are relatively equal, and there is little institutionalized violence against women. In contrast, the Yanomamo and Kohistani (and the Vice Lords) are characterized by male dominance, and they all sanction violence against women. Several reasons have been advanced to support the link between sexist values and violent conflict. A number of things are suggestive about this connection. First, it is men that make war, though women may fill certain positions in the armed forces. While there have been societies where women engage in armed combat, such instances are the exception rather than the rule. Even in a war of liberation, such as during the Sandinista rebellion in Nicaragua in the 1980s, where women took an active role, they were banned from active combat once the Sandinistas gained power. Second, there is a strong cross-cultural link between patriarchy and violent conflict. After examining information on over 1,000 societies, William Tulio Divale and Marvin Harris concluded that the intensity of collective violence is significantly higher in societies characterized by a strong male bias—patrilocal residence, patrilineal descent, polygyny, postmarital sex restrictions on females, male secret societies, and men's houses. Finally, there is evidence that societies characterized by sexual violence against women tend to be more warlike and prone to collective violence. Peggy Sanday's study of 95 societies in which there was evidence of frequency of rape supports this conclusion. The question is: Does a sexist ideology promote violent conflict, or does the incidence of violent conflict promote sexism?

Those who claim that sexism promotes violent conflict make that connection in various ways. Betty Reardon and Leslie Cagan suggest that societies that relegate women to an inferior position explicitly or implicitly sanction violence against women. Moreover, violence toward women serves as what they call a "primal" paradigm for violent warfare against other peoples. That is, once violence is allowed as a means of domination of one group such as women, it can serve as a model for dominance and violence against other groups.

For Peggy Sanday, as well as many others, both sexism and violent conflict have their roots in competition over scarce resources. She says women are generally associated with fertility and growth, while men are associated with aggression and destruction. During periods in which resources are not scarce, both males and females are valued equally. When there is an imbalance between food supply or distribution and needs, or when groups are competing for resources, males become of greater value, females become objects to be controlled, and sexual violence becomes one way that men demonstrate their dominance. Among cattle-herding people in East Africa, for example, raiding for cattle was common and sometimes led to violent conflict between groups. Violence was defined as a manly activity, leading East African societies to place great emphasis on masculinity and manliness. Manliness, however, was tested not only in battle but in male-female relations as well, for sex was a way of demonstrating strength. Among the Acoli, for example, a boy could demonstrate his strength against girls. Girls would frequently visit their boyfriends in their huts, but it took a strong boy to get a girl to lie on the bed and yield. A weak one had to keng ki ngwece, or "be content with the smell."

In sum, factors such as a lack of centralized control, competition over scarce resources, private property, and sexism may lead societies to construct an ideological bias toward violence. Examining the effects of violent conflict to see if some of them could be beneficial may provide some insights into the factors that promote violent conflict.

QUESTION 8.4:   What Are the Effects of War on Society?

Are there any beneficial effects of violent conflict? For example, biologists studying animal populations suggest that predators help the species they prey on by limiting population growth and eliminating the weak from the breeding population. Some anthropologists suggest that war may play a similar function for the human species by limiting population or by influencing the biological composition of the human species through the process of natural selection.

The Impact of War on Population

In a fascinating book entitled *The Statistics of Deadly Quarrels,* mathematician Lewis F. Richardson statistically examined the causes and effects of violent conflict between the years 1821 and 1945. During that period there were 282 wars that had battle fatalities of from 300 to 20 million people. If Richardson's estimates of the number of murders committed during that period and the number of deaths from disease caused or spread because of war are included, deaths from deadly quarrels would account for about 10 percent of all deaths that occurred between 1821 and 1945.

Anthropologist Frank Livingstone has concluded, however, that in spite of the enormity of the number of deaths inflicted by modern war, it seems to have had little appreciable effect on population growth. About 51 million people died as a result of World War II, including 9 percent of the Russian population and 5 percent of the German population. Yet this had almost no effect on their rates of population growth, for these two populations had recovered within a decade to the level at which they would have been had there been no war. In the United States the effect of World War II on population was almost negligible; only about 0.2 percent was lost.

Violent conflict in small-scale societies may have had a much greater impact on their population, as Livingstone points out. Among the Murngin of Australia, about 28 percent of male deaths were due to war, and among the Enga and the Dani of New Guinea about 25 percent of all male deaths came from violent conflict. Chagnon estimates a death rate due to fighting of 20 to 25 percent among the Yanomamo. Among the Blackfoot Indians of the American plains there was a 50 percent deficit for males in the male/female ratio in 1805 and a 33 percent deficit in 1858, when horse raiding was still common. But during the reservation period, after horse raiding was banned, the sex ratio approached 50-50. Living-stone notes, however, that it is hard to see where any of this has affected the biology of the species. The killing seems to have been more or less random. Moreover, since males were the most frequent victims, and since the incidence of polygyny (marriage to multiple wives) increases in societies that suffer losses, the number of children born should remain more or less constant.

William Tulio Divale and Marvin Harris address the problems posed by Livingstone by proposing that violent conflict does indeed regulate population growth, but it does so not by killing grown men but by encouraging the killing of infant girls. The incidence of violent conflict, they reason, is strongly associated with a strong preference for male children, along with female infanticide or the benign neglect of female infants. This is evidenced in either direct reports of female infanticide or the skewed sex ratios of children under the age of 14 in societies characterized by violent conflict. Violent societies average 128 boys to 100 girls under 14, far higher than the normal ratio of 105 boys to 100 girls.

If war or violent conflict is frequent in a society, Divale and Harris reason, the society or group that raises the largest number of fierce, aggressive warriors will be at an advantage. Consequently, the existence of violent conflict encourages a strong preference for rearing male children, supports the ideological restrictions on the rearing of female children, and, in general, creates an ideology of male supremacy. Moreover, restricting the number of childbearing females in a population is a far more effective means of population control that killing adult males. Thus, they conclude, war and violent conflict do encourage sexism, but only because they serve to promote selective population control.

The Evolution of the Nation–State

Anthropologists also suggest that violent conflict may encourage certain forms of political organization. Robert Carneiro argues, for example, that in the course of human history, violent conflict has been the primary agent that has transformed human societies from small-scale, autonomous communities into vast, complex nation–states. Carneiro reasons that war has served to promote the consolidation of isolated, politically autonomous villages into chiefdoms of united villages and into states. At first war pits village against village, resulting in chiefdom; then it pits chiefdom against chiefdom, resulting in states; and then it pits state against state. War, he says, began as the effort to oust a rival from a territory but soon evolved into an effort to subjugate and control an enemy. As the process continued, warfare became the mechanism by which the number of political units in the world began to decline. Carneiro predicts that if the number of political states continues to decline as it has in the past, by the year 2300 there should be only a single world state.

The rise of the Zulu state in Africa illustrates Carneiro's theory of how a group of largely separate political units is transformed into larger forms of state organization through violent conflict. The Zulu state took form in southeast Africa in the early nineteenth century. Prior to that time, the region was inhabited by small, sometimes warring groups. About 100,000 people lived in an area of about 80,000 square miles by practicing agriculture and cattle herding. While there were separate entities labeled tribes by Westerners, the largest political unit was the clan. Warriors from these clans raided each other for cattle, but there was no conquest for land.

Warfare increased between 1775 and 1800 as the population of southeast Africa increased. The strongest groups were those that could muster the most warriors and organize and discipline them effectively. The process of state formation whereby these separate groups combined into a larger political unit was begun by a leader of the Mtetwa tribe named Dingiswayo. He developed new ways to organize his troops and began to take control of the land of those he defeated. When he conquered an area he would appoint a person from the head family of the group he conquered to rule for him. Using new techniques of war and political control, he achieved dominance over a wide area. His reason for extending his control, according to one nineteenth-century writer, was to make peace among warring groups; Dingiswayo, it was said, "wished to do away with the incessant quarrels that occurred amongst the tribes, because no supreme head was over them to say who was right or who was wrong."

By the early 1800s, Dingiswayo had conquered and united some 30 different groups. He was aided by a young officer, named Shaka Zulu, the son of the chief of the Zulu clan. When the Zulu chief died, Dingiswayo installed Shaka as the head of the clan, and when Dingiswayo was killed by a rival, Shaka took over the army and established his Zulus as the dominant clan. By 1822 Shaka had defeated every rival and was master of all of the present South African province of Kwa-Zulu Natal.

Violence and Male Solidarity

In addition to controlling population and uniting tribal societies into large-scale states, violent conflict may also be valued as a means of promoting group solidarity. Male solidarity, for example, seems to be enhanced by collective violence. Societies in which there is frequent violence often have more men's clubs, men's sports teams, or special men's houses. But some assume that male solidarity, and the resulting domination of women, leads to increased collective violence, while others assume that increased male solidarity is itself the result of conflict. Anthropologist Ralph L. Holloway suggests that the psychological attributes that allow human beings to create sentimental bonds between members of a group are the same attributes that, when turned outward, promote violent conflict against nongroup members. That is, collective violence is simply the other side of group togetherness.

EXERCISE 8.4

There is some suggestion of a link between militarism and competitive sports; that is, societies that are prone to collective violence are more likely to value games in which men aggressively compete against other men. How does this apply to American society? Which sports in America most closely resemble or promote the values of militarism and war? Does the language of these sports reflect militaristic values? Do gender roles reflect these values?

There is evidence to support the idea that societies that engage in war place a greater emphasis on male solidarity. There are all-male clubs or organizations such as men's clubs among the Plains Indians, and men's houses among tribes in New Guinea. In Frederic Thrasher's classic study of boys' gangs in Chicago in 1927, he concluded that fighting, gang encounters, outwitting enemies, raiding, robbing, defending the hangout, and attacking enemies were the type of activity that produced male solidarity. In fact, the gang does not solidify as a group unless there is conflict.

RESOURCE 8.4

Resources on Violent Conflict

You can find some excellent resources on the Web concerning conflict and war. A wonderful source on conflict management in Africa, as well as globally, is:

African Conflict
www.synapse.net/~acdi20/welcome.htm

An excellent resource on current conflicts is:

Initiative on Conflict Resolution and Ethnicity
http://www.incore.ulst.ac.uk/cds/countries/index.html

Encyclopedia Britannica maintains a site on global conflict at:

Worlds Apart—Britannica
http://www.britannica.com/worldsapart/

QUESTION 8.5: *How Is It Possible to Justify the Creation of Weapons of Mass Destruction?*

Since the ability to mask the consequences of violent conflict may be one of the reasons for its frequency, it is useful to examine how people manage to hide for themselves the consequences of planning what now would be the ultimate form of violence—the unleashing of nuclear weapons.

When individuals participate in a social setting, they begin to adopt the culture—the system of meanings, the language, the physical environment, the institutional rules, the rituals, and the character of social interactions—of that setting. The social setting, in other words, produces in each participant a characteristic view of the world. For example, Mary Douglas and Aaron B. Wildavsky (1983) note how the strength of the boundaries members of a group construct between themselves and others, combined with the degree that each member's role in the group is proscribed, determine which dangers members of a group fear most. That is, a person's social setting will determine what he or she feels most at risk from—for example, economic collapse, or disease, or moral decay, or foreign invasion, or environmental devastation, and so on.

The Anthropology of a Nuclear Weapons Laboratory

Anthropologist Hugh Gusterson, who had been an antinuclear activist, wanted to know how nuclear weapons scientists could justify conducting research on and testing of weapons of mass destruction. That is, what could create a view of the world that would enable persons to justify for themselves that kind of work? What would they have to fear to justify creating the means to destroy everyone? To answer that question he set out to study the culture of a nuclear weapons laboratory, the Lawrence Livermore National Laboratory in Livermore, California.

Gusterson suggests that "nuclear realists" who support the manufacture and use of nuclear weapons and who question the wisdom of nuclear disarmament make four assumptions about the world. First, unlike national systems where a monopoly on the use of force guarantees stability, they claim that anarchy characterizes international relations; they see the international system existing in a state of nature. Second, they assume that states must rely on self-help to protect themselves, since no one else is going to help them. Third, nuclear realists assume that nuclear weapons are the ultimate form of self-help, since they vastly increase the cost of aggression against them. And fourth, they assume that relatively little can be done in the short term to change the anarchistic nature of the international system.

Critics of nuclear weapons and those who argue for nuclear disarmament make very different assumptions. They argue that international relations are not as anarchistic as they are made out; they claim that there are rules and norms that control aggression, many of these rules centering around the institution of trade. Marxists argue that proponents of nuclear weapons overlook the power of the military-industrial complex and the international class system, while feminists argue that the pro-nuclear perspective is dominated by male notions of power. Many critics see the nuclear arms race as "objective social madness." People who work in the area, they assume, must be in denial and must demonize the Other to justify their work. Gusterson wanted to find out, not so much who was "right," but rather how people came to hold such divergent opinions and, particularly, how nuclear weapon scientists came to their views.

When he began his research at the laboratory, Gusterson was surprised to find the variety of political and religious viewpoints of people working at Livermore. While white males did dominate, political views ran the gamut from social and political conservatives to active environmentalists, civil rights supporters, and women's rights advocates. Two-thirds of the workers were active churchgoers. How, he asked, could such a diverse population all agree on the value of nuclear weapon development, an agreement so profound that "they often asked me in puzzlement to explain why anti-nuclear activists were so afraid of nuclear weapons"?

Nuclear weapons scientists did not, says Gusterson, avoid the ethical concerns of nuclear weapons research. Most, however, accept the central axiom that nuclear research is necessary to make the world safe by developing a deterrent to the use of nuclear force. To some, working on nuclear weapons is more ethical than working on conventional weapons, because conventional weapons are more likely to be used. Nuclear weapons, the scientists assume, are simply symbolic chips in a game whose goal is to avoid using them. When asked if he would

How is it possible to justify the manufacture of weapons capable of destroying everyone on Earth? For those who work in a nuclear weapons laboratory, the manufacture of such weapons is both justified and necessary. For others, such as these nuclear weapons protestors, it is madness.

ever foresee a circumstance in which nuclear weapons would be used, one scientist said "no, even if we were under attack." The only reason you have nuclear weapons is for deterrence; once you are being attacked the whole thing has failed. Others rationalize it more baldly by saying that they are not responsible for how what they design is used; "Are automobile designers" they ask, "responsible for deaths caused by drunk drivers?"

The construction of a nuclear weapons scientist, says Gunderson, begins with the recruitment process. For people leaving the university, particularly in physics, there are few places to go aside from government-funded weapons research. Two-thirds of United States government research funding goes to military research (compared to 12.5 percent in Germany and 4.5 percent in Japan). Livermore and Los Alamos, the other major government-run nuclear weapons laboratory, themselves employ 6 percent of all physicists in the country.

When Gusterson asked people why they chose to work at Livermore, most cited the intellectual freedom they enjoyed working in a weapons laboratory. Almost all compared Livermore favorably to working in universities (which they characterized as "stodgy," "cut-throat," or "high-pressure") or in private organizations. One compared university work with being in the military! Some also cited the challenge of weapons research and the opportunity to work with state-of-the-art equipment. Livermore also paid about twice as much as a university position, although a little less than what most could have earned in industry.

Once a person was hired, secrecy played a major role in forging a person's identity as a nuclear weapons scientist. Livermore employees are investigated before being given security clearance to gain access to laboratory facilities. Personnel are divided into different security categories and given colored badges to denote their level of clearance. "Q" clearance (a green badge) is necessary for classified research, "L" clearance (a yellow badge) allows access to classified areas, but not to classified information. The labs themselves are divided into areas of lesser (e.g., cafeterias = white area) and greater security (classified research = green area; research on foreign capabilities = blue area). As Gusterson puts it, the laboratory is "an enormous grid of tabooed spaces and tabooed topics."

Without a green badge, says Gusterson, a weapons scientist is not considered a full adult in the lab. But the process in getting "Q" clearance is elaborate and may take from six months to two years. Virtually every aspect of a person's life is subject to investigation in search of clues that might make the person unfit to handle classified material. But, generally, most people pass, and, since secrecy is not that well guarded in practice, it suggests that the security clearance process functions more as a rite of passage to add mystique to the process of weapons research and to discipline the initiate.

Secrecy, says Gusterson, is one of the main ways that the diverse population of the lab is brought together. Knowing secrets, regardless of how mundane they might be, serves to mark a person as a member of a special group and lends an air of dramatic importance to one's work. Secrecy also serves to limit discussion that could change a person's view of the work that they do. As Gusterson (1995:68) puts it:

> ...the laboratories culture of secrecy does tend to produce certain effects in its scientists: it segregates laboratory scientists as a privileged but somewhat isolated elite; in inculcates a sense of group loyalty; and it thrusts on laboratory scientists an amorphous surveillance, which can become internalized.

The process of testing nuclear weapons, says Gusterson, is, in many ways, the critical step in creating the nuclear scientist. Any Livermore scientist can propose a weapons test, but reviewers (senior scientists at the Laboratory) only select about one out of twenty ideas for testing. Approval of an idea for testing, however, further reaffirms the scientist's membership in the group. Nuclear tests, says Gusterson, have elements of myth and ritual. Rarely in narratives that he collected on testing did anyone note the importance of the testing of nuclear reliability. Instead people spoke of the fulfillment of personal ambition, the struggle to master a new technology, the drama of creating something new, and the experience of community that each test created.

Thus, testing, says Gusterson, produces not only weapons, it produces also weapons designers. It is a way of producing the elite, those with special knowledge and power. The more tests one participates in, the greater the prestige and power that accrues. A successful test validates status and credentials and brings forth congratulatory support and reinforcement. The test provides what Gusterson calls a symbolic simulation of the reliability of the whole system of deterrence. As Gusterson (1995:161) puts it,

> Each time a nuclear test is successfully carried off, the scientists' faith in human control over nuclear technology is further reinforced. Seen in this light, the "reliability" the tests demonstrate has an expandable meaning, extending out from the reliability of the particular device being tested to the entire regime of nuclear deterrence.

The Language of Nuclear Destruction

Carol Cohn spent one year studying the culture of a strategic studies institute, or "think tank," for government defense analysts who plan nuclear strategy. Like Gusterson, she began her study with the question, how are people whose job it is to plan nuclear destruction able to do it? How can they think that way? One of her conclusions is that language is used to distance the planners from the consequences of the actions they are planning. The language they use obfuscates and reassembles reality in such a way that what is really being talked about—the fundamental business of war that is destroying human creations and injuring and killing human beings—is somehow hidden from view behind metaphors and euphemisms.

During her first weeks at the center, as Cohn listened to the participants (all men) talking matter-of-factly about nuclear destruction, she heard language that she labeled *technostrategic*. In this language there is reference to *clean bombs* (fusion bombs that release more energy than fission bombs, not as radiation, but as explosive power); *penetration aids* (technology that helps missiles get through enemy defenses), *collateral damage* (human deaths); and *surgical strikes* (bombing that takes out only weapons or command centers). Domestic metaphors were common in the language of technostrategic; missiles are based in *silos;* piles of nuclear weapons in a nuclear submarine are referred to as *Christmas tree farms*, and bombs and missiles are referred as *reentry vehicles* or *RVs*. Massive bombing becomes *carpet bombing* in technostrategic. Cohn says that the domestic images must be more than simply a way to distance the speakers from the grisly reality they are discussing. Calling the pattern in which a bomb falls a *footprint* seems to remove the speakers from any position of accountability for the acts they are contemplating.

Cohn's experience is similar to that of anthropologists who find themselves immersed in the reality of another culture. She discovered, for example, that the language and metaphors of those working at the institute seemed incapable of expressing certain realities. The aftermath of a nuclear attack is described in the language of technostrategic this way:

> [You have to have ways to maintain communication in a] nuclear environment, a situation bound to include EMP blackout, brute force damage to systems, a heavy jamming environment, and so on. (quoted in Cohn 1987:707)

Here is a description of the aftermath from the perspective of Hisako Matsubara, a survivor of the nuclear bombing of Hiroshima who describes it in *Cranes at Dusk:*

> Everything was black, had vanished into the black dust, was destroyed. Only the flames that were beginning to lick their way up had any color. From the dust that was like fog, figures began to loom up, black, hairless, faceless. They screamed with voices that were no longer human. Their screams drowned out the groans rising everywhere from the rubble, groans that seemed to rise from the very earth itself. (quoted in Cohn 1987:708)

There is, says Cohn, no way of describing this experience with the language of technostrategic. The speaker is a victim; the speaker in the first instance is preparing for the deployment of nuclear weapons. One of the consequences of technostrategic is that it removes the speakers from having to think about

This sketch of the effects of the U.S. bombing of Hiroshima was drawn by eyewitness Sawami Katagiri, who recalled, "I was walking among many dead people…. It was like hell…. This picture shows only a part of Hiroshima. The whole city was just like this at that time." Sawami Katagiri, from *The Unforgettable Fire*, NHK Publishing (Japan Broadcast Publishing Co., Ltd.).

themselves as victims of nuclear war. This does not mean that defense analysts convince themselves that they would not be victims, but the language removes them from the point of view of a victim and provides them with that of the planner, the initiator of nuclear war.

Cohn also discovered that she could not use ordinary language to speak to the defense analysts. If she tried, they acted as if she were ignorant or simpleminded. To communicate at all, she had to use terms such as *subholocaust engagement* and *preemptive strikes*. The word *peace* was not a legitimate part of the vocabulary; to use it was to brand oneself as a softheaded activist. The closest she could come to *peace* in the language of technostrategic was *strategic stability*.

Cohn encountered descriptions of nuclear situations that made little sense until she realized that different realities were being discussed. For example, the following passage describes a nuclear exchange in a situation in which missiles with more than one warhead are mutually banned:

> The strategic stability of regime A (a scenario) is based on the fact that both sides are deprived of any incentive ever to strike first. Since it takes roughly two warheads to destroy the enemy silo, an attacker must expend two of his missiles to destroy one of the enemy's. A first strike disarms the attacker. The aggressor ends up worse than the aggressed. (quoted in Cohn 1987:710)

By what type of reasoning, asks Cohn, can a country that dropped a thousand nuclear bombs 10 to 100 times more powerful than the one dropped on Hiroshima end up "worse off" than the country it dropped the bombs on? This would be possible only if winning depends on who has the greatest number of weapons left. In other words, nuclear war would be a kind of game in which the object is to have more weapons at the end than the enemy has.

To an anthropologist, the fact that people are limited by their culture, their language, and their point of view is, of course, no surprise. All cultures give a characteristic meaning to violent conflict, whether it be viewed as the act of an animal in possession of a human body (like the tiger spirit of the Carib), the will of God, or a kind of game to determine winners and losers. The more serious implication of Cohn's observations is that the roles of nuclear planners as scientists and academics lend weight to their claim that their perspective is "objective" and therefore has greater truth value than other perspectives. Moreover, says Cohn, if one can speak to defense analysts only in the language of technostrategic, and if the language is constructed in such a way as to be incapable of expressing different realities, then there is no way for these analysts to appreciate or understand the other realities involving the use of nuclear weapons.

CONCLUSIONS

To examine how people give meaning to and justify collective violence, our first question had to do with how societies create a bias in favor of collective violence. Violent conflict is justified in some societies as a way of achieving status or acquiring or protecting possessions, as a means of revenge, or as a necessary defense of personal honor or integrity. In peaceful societies, violence is avoided by widespread sharing of resources, building relations of dependence among groups, by devaluing or discouraging aggressive behavior, and emphasizing collective behaviors that promote intragroup and intergroup harmony.

There are economic, political, and social differences between peaceful and violent societies. One difference is the encouragement in violent societies of competition over resources, leading to a situation in which individuals are required, because of a lack of central authority, to protect their own property by violent means. The conversion of communal property to private property, which resulted in the disenfranchisement of peasant farmers, has been linked to revolution, and sexist ideologies in violent societies may promote violent behavior against other groups.

A question in examining the effects of war on society is whether there have been any beneficial effects that might explain the occurrence of violent conflict. Population does decline in war, especially in small-scale societies, but apparently not enough to exercise any control on population growth or to have any impact on the human species through biological selection. War, according to some, has served throughout human history to promote the centralization of authority and the growth of state-level political structures. While violent conflict may increase male solidarity, it also can promote greater violence against women.

We find that people can easily justify even the manufacture and testing of weapons of mass destruction. Furthermore that the language of defense analysts masks some of the realities of nuclear destruction keeps them from viewing themselves as potential victims, and turns nuclear planning into a game.

REFERENCES AND SUGGESTED READINGS

INTRODUCTION: THE JUSTIFICATION OF VIOLENT CONFLICT The opening quote is from an account of a witness to a Contra attack on a Nicaraguan village in 1984, as cited in Noam Chomsky's book, *Turning the Tide: U.S. Intervention in Central America and the Struggle for Peace* (South End Press, 1985). The account of Carib warfare is from Neil Lancelot Whitehead's article, "The Snake Warriors—Sons of the Tiger's Teeth: A Descriptive Analysis of Carib Warfare, ca. 1500-1820," in *The Anthropology of War,* edited by Jonathan Hass (Cambridge University Press, 1990). The definition of war relies on Clark McCauley's article, "Conference Overview," in The Anthropology of War. McCauley draws his definition from a book compiled from a symposium on war held in 1966, *War: The Anthropology of Armed Conflict and Aggression,* edited by Morton Fried, Marvin Harris, and Robert Murphy (The Natural History Press, 1967). Different views on the cultural or biological roots of war can be found in *Societies at Peace: Anthropological Perspectives,* edited by Signe Howell and Roy Willis (Routledge, 1989), and Carol Greenhouse, "Cultural Perspectives on War," in *The Quest for Peace: Transcending Collective Violence and War Among Societies, Cultures and States,* edited by R. Varynen (Sage Publications, 1987).

HOW DO SOCIETIES CREATE A BIAS IN FAVOR OF COLLECTIVE VIOLENCE? The account of Kiowa warfare and horse raiding is from Bernard Mishkin, *Rank and Warfare Among the Plains Indians* (Seattle: The University of Washington Press, 1940). The account of the Yanomamo is based on Napoleon Chagnon's article, "Reproductive and Somatic Conflicts of Interest in the Genesis of Violence and Warfare Among Tribesmen," in *The Anthropology of War,* cited above, and from Chagnon's book, *The Fierce People,* Third Edition (Holt, Rinehart and Winston, 1983). The feud in Kohistan is described by Lincoln Keiser in *Friend by Day, Enemy by Night: Organized Vengeance in a Kohistani Community* (Holt, Rinehart and Winston, 1991). A classic work on violent protest is Eric Hobsbaum's *Primitive Rebels: Studies in Archaic Forms of Social Movement in the 19th and 20th Centuries* (Frederick A. Praeger, 1959).

HOW DO SOCIETIES CREATE A BIAS AGAINST VIOLENT CONFLICT? Thomas Gregor discusses peaceful societies in "Uneasy Peace: Intertribal Relations in Brazil's Upper Xingu," in *The Anthropology of War,* cited above. The discussion of the Ju/wasi relies on Elizabeth Thomas's *The Harmless People* (Alfred A. Knopf, 1959) and Richard Lee's *The Dobe !Kung* (Holt, Rinehart and Winston, 1984). The description of the Semai is based on Clayton Robarchek, "Motivations and Material Causes: On the Explanation of Conflict and War," in *The Anthropology of War.* Robarchek also discusses the Hobbesian image of man as it relates to the Semai in "Hobbesian and Rousseauan Images of Man: Autonomy and Individualism in a Peaceful Society," in *Societies at Peace: Anthropological Perspectives,* edited by Signe Howell and Roy Willis (Routledge, 1989). The material on the Xinguanos comes from Thomas Gregor's article (see above). The description of the Inuit is derived from Jean Briggs, *Never in Anger* (Harvard University

Press, 1970), and an account of the Buid can be found in Thomas Gibson's "Raiding, Trading and Tribal Autonomy in Insular Southeast Asia," in *The Anthropology of War.*

WHAT ARE THE ECONOMIC, POLITICAL, OR SOCIAL DIFFERENCES BETWEEN PEACEFUL AND VIOLENT SOCIETIES? Two works cited above deal extensively with debates about the reasons for war—*War: The Anthropology of Armed Conflict and Aggression,* edited by Morton Fried, Marvin Harris, and Robert Murphy, and *The Anthropology of War,* edited by Jonathan Hass. The views of Thomas Hobbes are taken from *Leviathan,* first published in 1651 (Oxford University Press, 1881). *The Vice Lords: Warriors of the Streets* (Holt, Rinehart and Winston, 1969) contains Lincoln Keiser's account of Chicago street gangs in the 1960s. Alex Kotlowitz gives an account of the lives of two Chicago children growing up amid the violence of Chicago housing projects in *There Are No Children Here* (Anchor Books, 1991). The analysis of Yanomamo violence and the reasons for it can be found in R. Brian Ferguson's article, "A Savage Encounter: Western Contact and the Yanomami War Complex" in *War in the Tribal Zone: Expanding States and Indigenous Warfare,* edited by R. Brian Ferguson and Neil L. Whitehead (School of American Research Press: 1992). For a more detailed account see *Yanomami Warfare: A Political History* by R. Brian Ferguson (School of the Americas Research Press: 1995).

William Tulio Divale and Marvin Harris discuss the connection between male dominance and war in "Population, Warfare, and the Male Supremacist Complex," in *The American Anthropologist,* vol. 78 (1976), pp. 521–538. The feminist analysis of war is represented by Leslie Cagan, "Feminism and Militarism," in *Beyond Survival: New Directions for the Disarmament Movement,* edited by M. Albert and D. Dellinger (South End Press, 1983); Riane Eisler, *The Chalice and the Blade* (Harper and Row, 1987); and Betty Reardon, *Sexism and the War System* (Columbia University Teachers College Press, 1985). Peggy Sanday's study of rape and war was reported in "The Socio-Cultural Context of Rape: A Cross-Cultural Study," in *Journal of Social Issues,* vol. 37 (1981), pp. 5–27. A description of the Acoli appears in Dent Ocaya-Lakidi, "Manhood, Warriorhood and Sex in Eastern Africa," in *Journal of Asian and African Studies,* vol. 12 (1979), pp. 134–165.

WHAT ARE THE EFFECTS OF WAR ON SOCIETY? The figures on the number of people killed in modern war come from Lewis Richardson's classic work, *The Statistics of Deadly Quarrels* (The Boxwood Press, 1960), and Quincy Wright's extensive work, *A Study of War* (University of Chicago Press, 1965). Frank B. Livingstone discusses "The Effects of Warfare on the Biology of the Human Species," in *War: The Anthropology of Armed Conflict and Aggression,* cited above. The connection between war and female infanticide is made in Divale and Harris's article, "Population, Warfare, and the Male Supremacist Complex," cited above.

Robert Carneiro's theories about the relationship between war and the development of the state can be found in his article, "Political Expansion as an Expression of the Principle of Competitive Exclusion," in *Origins of the State,* edited by Ronald Cohn and Elman Service (Institute for the Study of Human Issues, 1978), and more recently in his article, "Chiefdom-Level Warfare as Exemplified in Fiji and Cauca Valley," in *The Anthropology of War,* cited above. The description of the rise of the Zulu state comes from Elman Service's book, *Origins of the State and Civilization* (W. W. Norton, 1975). A discussion of war and human bonding can be found in Ralph Holloway, Jr., "Human Aggression: The Need for a Species-Specific Framework," in *War: The Anthropology of Armed Conflict and Aggression,* cited above. Frederic Thrasher's study of Chicago gangs is reported in *The Gang,* originally published in 1927 (University of Chicago Press, 1963). An excellent article on the relationship between sports and war is Richard G. Sipes's "War, Sports, and Aggression: An Empirical Test of Two Rival Theories," *American Anthropologist,* vol. 74 (1973), pp. 64–86.

HOW IS IT POSSIBLE TO JUSTIFY THE CREATION OF WEAPONS OF MASS DESTRUCTION? Hugh Gusterson's research in a nuclear weapons laboratory is described in *Nuclear Rites: A Weapons Laboratory at the End of the Cold War* (University of California Press, 1995). Carol Cohn's article, "Sex and Death in the Rational World of Defense Intellectuals," appeared in *Signs,* vol. 12 (1987), pp. 687–718. For more on what Cohn calls "newspeak," see her article, "Decoding Military Newspeak," in *Ms.,* March/April 1991, p. 88. The description of the aftermath of the atomic bombing of Hiroshima comes from Hisako Matsubara, *Cranes at Dusk* (Dial Press, 1985).

View of Dutch trading port at Dejima-Nagasaki, Nagasaki School, 1720–1850, scroll. Bridgeman/Art Resource, New York. British Museum, London.

CHAPTER 9

APPLICATIONS TO PROBLEMS OF CULTURAL DIVERSITY

We are inadequately prepared to deal with cultural diversity. Experts who go abroad technically well qualified to cut down infant deaths, improve nutrition, or increase food production are unequipped to understand how the problems with which they must deal are rooted in a foreign way of life. Guidebooks tell tourists precisely what monuments and buildings to visit, but stop short of explaining lifeways they will encounter abroad. If we want to learn, we must know what questions to ask and how to interpret our observations.

John J. Honigmann

INTRODUCTION: *The Problems of Diversity*

Cultural anthropology is about cultural diversity, whether it occurs from one country to another or in a single classroom. But human beings seem ill-equipped to deal with their cultural differences. The fact that different peoples assign different meanings to events, objects, individuals, and emotions is a source of considerable conflict, miscommunication, and misunderstanding. Anthropologists seek to explain this diversity, to help people understand one another better, and, in the process, to apply their knowledge to the solution of social, economic, educational, and political problems created by diversity.

In this chapter, you will be given the opportunity to work out solutions to problems drawn from actual situations in which anthropologists were asked to apply their knowledge or experience to specific situations in various societies. Each application, in its way, is related to a problem resulting from cultural diversity—specifically, differences in the meanings that different peoples give to their experiences. The promotion of mutual respect, tolerance, and understanding for cultural differences is one of the most important contributions cultural anthropology can make in today's world.

The five problems in this chapter concern applications in health care, economic development, education, architecture, and law. For each problem you will be given a brief orientation to the application of anthropology to a general area, and then you will be given the opportunity to put yourself in the position of an anthropologist who has been asked to solve a specific problem in this area. As you read the background information on this problem, think how you might go about solving it. What kinds of questions would you need to answer, what kinds of information might you need to obtain, what practical advice would you offer? After writing down your proposed solution of the problem, compare it with the solution used by the anthropologist who actually worked on it, which is described at the end of each application.

These cases touch on just a few of the possible applications of anthropology to practical problems. Nevertheless, they clearly illustrate some of the ways experience in anthropology is used to address problems involving cultural diversity.

APPLICATION 9.1: *Anthropology in Health Care*

One example of the practical problems created by cultural diversity is in the area of health care. Disease and illness are part of a cultural text; that is, the human propensity to give meaning to such experiences as death, status, and success also gives meaning to illness and disease. Moreover, the meaning given an illness will likely suggest a cure. In a society where people believe that all illness is spread in the air, the people are not likely to be receptive to measures to stop waterborne diseases, for example. The differences in conceptions of disease understandably produce difficulties when health care practitioners try to introduce innovations from one culture into another. Anthropologists, doctors, nurses, and health care administrators with anthropological training have often been called upon to help with such problems.

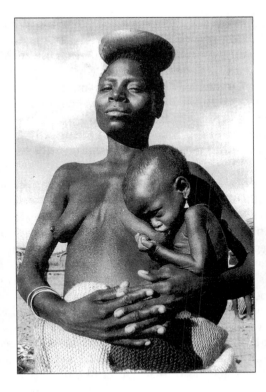

A mother in Mozambique attempts to care for her child in the customary way, with breast-feeding. Anthropologists are able to help peoples of diverse cultures deal with problems of childhood illness or malnutrition by providing their health care workers with information or products developed for their use.

Health Care Among the Swazi

THE PROBLEM Childhood diarrhea is the most serious of the waterborne parasitic infections that cause infant death in Swaziland in southeastern Africa. Suppose you have been asked by the government of Swaziland to help its health care workers acquaint the Swazi with the Western explanation for the cause of childhood diarrhea and encourage them to seek appropriate medical treatment for their children. For various reasons, the Swazi have not been receptive to the treatment that has been found to be most effective—oral rehydration therapy. This simple treatment replaces the fluids the child loses because of the diarrhea with an electrolyte solution to promote water retention that contains potassium and sodium chloride, sodium citrate, and dextrose (not unlike Gatorade). The electrolyte solution is cheap, easily administered, and effective. Other treatment for viral diarrhea is to avoid dairy products and feed the baby breast milk, clear fluids, and binding foods such as bananas, rice, cereal, and toast.

BACKGROUND OF THE PROBLEM The Swazi have their own system of cultural meanings concerning the causes of diarrhea. Generally they classify all diseases into two categories. Traditional diseases are believed to be caused by either sorcery (the deliberate use of spells and medicines) or by the withdrawal of spiritual protection by ancestors angered by some act (see Question 2.4). Nontraditional diseases, such as cholera, tuberculosis, and venereal disease, were introduced by Europeans. Traditional healers are sought when the problem is thought to be caused by sorcery or ancestral displeasure, while Western clinics and doctors are sought when the disease is thought to be European.

The Swazi also believe that diseases are frequently carried in the air. Vapors from powerful medicines mixed carelessly or deliberately may cause illness, as can traces of vapors caused by lightning or thunder. An environment can be polluted by evil spirits that have been removed from a victim and seek to enter another person. Illness may be caused by poison hidden by an enemy in a place the intended victim is likely to pass by or touch, such as the entrance to a latrine or a toilet seat. Because of fear of this kind of illness, the Swazi are reluctant to build latrines.

The Swazi classify diarrhea as a traditional disease. If home remedies fail to cure children, then their mothers usually take them to traditional healers who recognize three types of diarrhea, each with a recommended cure. Umsheko, the passing of loose, wet stools, is believed to be caused by such things as bad or insufficient food, cow's milk, powdered or spoiled milk, physical relocation of the child, or the flies that buzz around Swazi settlements. Healers use herbal medicines to treat the symptoms and recommend breast-feeding and certain foods such as sorghum and a porridge made of maize. The second type, kuhabula, is a more serious form that the Swazi believe is caused by invisible vapors to which the child may be deliberately or accidentally exposed. The child is treated with medicines and enemas to purify or drain out the bad air believed to be contributing to the illness. The third type of diarrhea is umphezulu. Babies are believed born with it because of some act of the mother; she may have passed through a place where lightning hit or where evil medicines were deliberately placed, or she did not keep her head covered during her pregnancy. A cure for this kind of diarrhea is to take the child to the place where the mother was infected and give the child an enema.

Some of these traditional curing techniques for diarrhea conflict with Western practice and belief. For example, dehydration is the most serious symptom of diarrhea, and giving the child an enema would aggravate rather than relieve the effects of the disease. Furthermore, since diarrhea is thought to be a traditional disease, mothers usually do not take their children to the Western clinics that could supply electrolyte fluids. Other beliefs and practices, such as breast-feeding the child and giving binding foods, medicinal teas, and fluids, are consistent with Western practice and belief.

Western-educated government officials at first were biased against native healers. In fact, from 1894 to 1955 when Swaziland was controlled by the British, all "witch-doctoring" was considered illegal in Swaziland, and while the government has since removed legal obstacles to the practice of traditional medicine, it is still considered "backward" by Western-educated government officials and Western health practitioners. As an anthropologist, you know that asking the Swazi to give up or change their beliefs and practices would be futile, and they do have a long tradition of treating illness. Knowing what you do about traditional Swazi beliefs and practices and understanding the medical background of the problem, what kind of recommendations would you make to help the people of Swaziland cope with childhood intestinal problems?

AN ACTUAL SOLUTION   When anthropologist Edward C. Green was hired by the government of Swaziland to solve the problem, here's how he went about it.

He recognized that the traditional healers must play a major role in any health program to prevent or cure diarrheal diseases. They are far more accessible than doctors; there is one healer per 100 people in Swaziland, but only one doctor per 10,000 people. Moreover, traditional healers are influential members of their communities whose opinions would be critical for the acceptance of new ways of treating illness.

Green also recognized that while the Swazi do not share with us the bio-medical germ theory, they have many traditional concepts of health and disease that do coincide with Western beliefs. For example, Swazis believe that unseen agents can cause some diseases. They say that these agents are spread through the air and are highly contagious; people are infected by "breathing" them into their bodies. Recent scientific experiments have revealed, in fact, that some stomach disorders are caused by airborne viruses. Green recommended building on the Swazi beliefs that recognize airborne agents as a cause of diarrhea. He also recommended building on the beliefs common to both Western and Swazi medical practices. For example, because the Swazi believe that fluids are necessary to keep up babies' strength, he proposed teaching traditional healers how to use oral rehydration therapy. If spells were believed needed to counteract the effects of sorcery or exposure to evil medicine, they could be used after rehydration.

By drawing on his training and experience as an anthropologist, Green was able to make concrete recommendations to enable health officials to translate the practices of one culture into those of another. Crossing the barrier of cultural difference thus could contribute to treating disease and thereby saving lives.

APPLICATION 9.2: Anthropology in Economic Development

One of the first areas in which anthropological research was applied was economic development in Third World countries. Government planners trained in Western countries who wanted to introduce new agricultural techniques, technology, or crops often hired anthropologists to determine whether farmers would accept these innovations, and, if not, what changes might be made to ensure their successful adoption. The anthropologists often found it necessary to point out to these economic development officials that the agricultural practices of peasant farmers that the officials considered inefficient or wasteful were, in fact, highly functional. More recently, anthropologists have been asked to direct such projects as reforestation or to help convince farmers of the need to conserve resources.

Growing Trees in Haiti

THE PROBLEM Suppose you have been asked by funding agencies in the United States to direct a reforestation program in the island Republic of Haiti. After hundreds of years of tree-cutting to clear land for farming or to harvest lumber for sale, the land has been virtually deforested. There have been other attempts to convince peasant farmers to plant trees, if only to prevent soil erosion. The U.S. Agency for International Development (AID) gave millions of dollars in aid to the government of Haiti for this purpose, but the number of jobs it created seemed to outnumber the number of seedlings planted. Those that were planted were likely to be pulled out by the peasant farmers, who might turn the reforestation projects into goat forage projects. Official threats against removing the trees and ecological messages urging conservation had little effect.

BACKGROUND OF THE PROBLEM Haiti is the poorest nation in the Western hemisphere; 60 percent of its six million people were unemployed in 1991. It occupies the western third of the large island of Hispaniola, which it shares with the Dominican Republic. Haiti is the size of Maryland; about two-thirds of its land is mountainous, and much of the rest is semiarid. The third of the land that is arable is mostly divided into tiny plots owned by peasant farmers; there are an estimated 500,000 farms in this small area.

Haitian farmers initially resisted planting trees because they felt that the land taken for reforestation would reduce the arable land, scant as it is, on which they grow their food or cash crops. They could see no benefit in growing forests for ecological reasons or in covering their cropland with government-owned trees. Because the farmers' plots average only a hectare and a half (about four acres), the traditional reforestation method of covering whole areas with seedlings would remove valuable cropland from planting. Moreover, past efforts at channeling AID money to reforestation often failed because the money was lost or misappropriated in the Haitian government bureaucracy.

Given all these problems, what steps can you, with your anthropological training, recommend to get farmers to plant and maintain trees?

AN ACTUAL SOLUTION Anthropologist Gerald F. Murray made the mistake of jokingly telling an official working on reforestation that, based on his ethnographic research with Haitian farmers, he could get more seedlings planted with a Jeep and $50,000 than they would with their multimillion-dollar program. To his surprise, two years later in 1980 they took him up on it, giving him a Jeep and $4 million to direct a four-year reforestation effort. They asked him how many seedlings he would get planted and how many farmers he would convince to participate. When his initial estimate of 2,000 farmers and one million trees was considered too small, he raised it to 6,000 farmers and three million trees. The question, of course, was how he would do it.

The first thing Murray did was to reorient the whole project from serving environmental and ecological purposes to introducing a new cash crop—trees—to the farmers. He proposed that the seedlings, rather than being owned by the government, were to be given to the farmers. They were told that when the trees matured they could cut them down and sell the lumber or the charcoal produced by burning the roots. Moreover, the trees would take up only a small amount of farmland and would not interfere with the growing of other crops. They could, however, bring in more money than the farmer's entire annual income from other crops. Murray located fast-growing, lumber-producing trees that matured quickly, in about four years. He suggested a planting pattern in which the trees would be planted along the borders of fields rather than being planted in blocs, which would allow tree-growing to be mixed with other crops. Finally, realizing that government bureaucracies might endanger the program, he set up a network in which local representatives were to take delivery of and distribute the seedlings.

The results were dramatic. By the end of the fourth year of the project, 75,000 Haitian farmers had planted 20 million trees. The project was so successful that farmers who had not signed up for the project were stealing seedlings from their neighbors and planting them on their land. There were also unexpected results; the farmers were not cutting their trees when they matured. Partly this may have been due to their pride in owning the trees, but they may have also viewed the trees as a bank account to be drawn on if their other crops failed.

Murray's account of the project is one of the most entertaining descriptions of applied anthropology you are likely to find, and I recommend that you read the original for additional information on problems and results. It is an excellent illustration of how anthropological method and theory can be used to assist economic development.

APPLICATION 9.3: *Anthropology in Education*

The manner in which people communicate with others, and the verbal and nonverbal messages they send, can differ significantly from society to society. They may unintentionally convey entirely inappropriate messages about who they think they are and who they think someone else is. Even a smile in the wrong place at the wrong time can convey entirely unintended meanings. La Ray Barna reports how a Japanese student, newly arrived in the United States, was confused by the smiles he received from American girls he didn't know. At first he assumed that the smiles constituted an invitation to a close relationship. Finally he realized that, as he put it, "They have no interest for me; it means only a kind of greeting to a foreigner. If someone smiles at a stranger in Japan, especially at a girl, she can assume he is either a sexual maniac or an impolite person."

Helaine K. Minkus, who applies anthropology in workshops she conducts for American students studying abroad and for foreign students studying in the United States, has found that the friendly, open behavior of Americans creates predictable difficulties for foreign students. They appreciate the friendliness, but are often disappointed when they discover that it is not an invitation to a close, intimate relationship. The cultural conflict is over the meaning of friendship; most Americans maintain a close core of friends, combined with a wide circle of acquaintances. They make a concerted effort to maintain close friends but devote little attention to those who form the wider circle. Even standard greeting rituals such as "How are you?" are often misinterpreted by foreign students as genuine inquiries into their state of health.

Other American customs also confuse foreign students. Our efforts to impress others with our success or proficiency make little sense to those who have been taught to be modest and self-deprecating. Most students from China or Japan expect authority figures to behave accordingly and tell them what to do; they are often surprised at the informality of American teachers. Foreign students who come from cultures where people fear appearing greedy may refuse an initial offer of refreshments, expecting to be able to accept on the second or third offer; as Minkus points out, they often leave American homes hungry after refusing the first, and only, offer of food.

Interacting with people whose cultures assign different meanings to behaviors, events, objects, and emotions can be an unsettling experience, yet intercultural interaction is a necessity in today's world. Diplomacy, business, education, recreation, and tourism are just a few of the areas in which people must overcome misunderstandings arising from cultural diversity.

One of the questions anthropologists address is how knowledge of other cultures can foster intercultural understanding and communication. The need for this knowledge and understanding is increasingly evident in American schools and colleges.

Intercultural Understanding in American Schools

THE PROBLEM Suppose you are a school administrator whose school district includes students and families from among Asian American, African American, Hispanic American, Euro-American, and Native American cultural backgrounds. Problems have been reported in relations among students and between students and teachers that you think might be due to the difficulty of communication among people of diverse cultures. You have been asked to develop a series of workshops for students, teachers, and administrators to foster better intercultural understanding and communication in the schools.

BACKGROUND OF THE PROBLEM The United States has a multicultural society that places an emphasis on maintaining cultural diversity. Because the schools must include students from a variety of cultural backgrounds, almost every American school and classroom, from the primary level to the graduate level, has its own cultural mix and, consequently, its own potential for miscommunication and misunderstanding. Differences in patterns of family interaction, languages spoken at home, attitudes toward authority, and educational standards must be accommodated. Moreover, the cultural background of the teacher often differs from that of some of the students.

Some cultural groups, such as Asian Americans, firmly link education with success. These parents strongly encourage their children to excel in school, and teachers are likely to view them as model students. Students from cultures that do not see education as essential to the good life may be disdainful of it, and teachers may view them as problem students. Other conflicts can occur in the values of teachers and parents toward education. Teachers may view education as a vehicle of change and personal improvement, while families and the community may view it as a vehicle of cultural maintenance. Parents may want their children to speak standard American English or the minority dialect or a native language. They may want their children to leave home to go to college or to remain at home and seek a job. They may want them to be obedient or to question authority.

In the light of these problems of the diverse cultures prevalent in a multicultural society such as the United States, what kinds of problems in intercultural understanding and communication should your workshop address?

AN ACTUAL SOLUTION Richard Ammann applies his anthropology in conducting cross-cultural workshops for teachers, students, and administrators in

American schools, as well as for business people working abroad. He makes five points about his workshops for educators that might apply to any cross-cultural training experience. Ammann points out that some potential cultural conflicts are common to many environments, but some are unique to the school setting.

The first two points apply generally. People need to become acquainted with the rules, values, and communication patterns of their own culture. Before they can appreciate and understand other cultures, they must be aware that they too are cultural animals. People also need to understand how the meanings they give to their experiences affect their views of other people and how they interact with them.

The next three points apply specifically to educators. Teachers and administrators need to be familiar with classroom situations that highlight cultural differences and the kinds of miscommunication and misunderstandings that can occur in these situations. They need to learn techniques and strategies to use in communicating and interacting with students from cultural backgrounds different from their own, and learn how to share them with students to help them get along with each other.

As Ammann points out, training in cross-cultural sensitivity such as he offers in his workshops is not the only solution to the problems of cultural misunderstandings that can develop in educational settings. Anthropologists and people with anthropological training are in increasing demand by schools and colleges to help solve problems in diversity among students and between them and faculties and administrators.

APPLICATION 9.4: Anthropology in Architecture

Space is a cultural construction that is often taken for granted. People in different cultures have different ideas about space. Westerners, for example, tend to view it as a void filled with objects, but in other societies there is no such thing as empty space. A space is always filled with something, even if that thing is spiritual in nature. In some societies people like to maintain some physical distance from others and are uncomfortable if someone stands closer to them than a couple of feet; in other societies people converse with faces kept inches from each other.

Edward T. Hall was a pioneer in exploring how different societies construct different ideas about space and how people and things are distributed within it. In his book *The Hidden Dimension*, he describes the different ways people think of space and movement and the difficulties that could arise when they are unaware of such differences.

Cultural differences in ideas about space have various practical consequences, not the least of which has to do with architecture. Housing styles vary considerably from culture to culture, as does the arrangement of living space. In some societies the living area is one large open space; in others, such as ours, the living area is partitioned into smaller units to protect privacy and convey ownership. In some societies the cooking area of a house is the main gathering point; in others, the preference is to have rooms reserved for social gatherings. Anthropology is applied in the architectural design of houses to make them conform to the space requirements of the people who will inhabit them.

What has been called "action anthropology" has also been applied to working with the problem of providing living space and other needs for the homeless in American society. The References section for this chapter lists a number of sources on related topics, including action anthropology on Chicago's Skid Row, public policy issues affecting the homeless, the difficulty of establishing identity for the homeless in Dade County, Florida, and working with homeless Hispanic street children in Washington, D.C.

Designing Homes Apache-Style

THE PROBLEM Suppose you have been hired as an architectural consultant to help with a government-funded project to build a new village for the Tonto Apache in central Arizona. The builders want to avoid the problems encountered by other architects who had designed and built new Native American communities based on a Euro-American design plan, only to find that the residents were so uncomfortable with their new houses that they moved back into their old ones. Your problem is to consult with the Apache about their living space needs and convey their ideas to the architects so they can be accommodated in the housing design.

BACKGROUND OF THE PROBLEM Like the traditional Apache wickiup, the existing Tonto Apache homes have a sleeping area and another large space used for all daytime activities. What Euro-Americans define as shy behavior in the Apache is more a function of their definition of appropriate social behavior (see Question 4.3). Apache like to enter a social interaction slowly, assessing it in steps and making decisions about whether to interact further. They prefer open spaces so they can view the entire social setting and still maintain enough distance that verbal interaction is unnecessary. Eating together is a major social activity for the Apache, especially if they haven't seen one another for a time. Hosts always offer food, and guests never refuse. The women cook for many people at once, and during the summer most cooking is done outdoors.

Traditionally, when Apaches died, their shelters were burned; even simple homes were torn down.

Once you are aware of such special requirements for Apache dwellings, what would you recommend to the architects about the design of new homes for them?

AN ACTUAL SOLUTION The problem you face is exactly the one faced by anthropologist George S. Esber, Jr., who made a number of recommendations to the architects. While privacy was desired for sleeping areas, there should be as few partitions as possible in the homes so people can visit yet maintain some social distance. The cooking area and the visiting space should be in full view to accommodate the roles of food preparation and visiting. Portable wood stoves that could be moved outdoors should be used, and instead of standard-size sinks, larger sinks and cupboards should be installed to meet the cooking demands in Apache homes. There wasn't too much Esber could do about the destruction of homes after a death. One suggestion was that surviving family members could stay with relatives or friends while others redecorated the home to give it a new appearance.

When Esber returned to the community after it was built, he found the Apache genuinely enthusiastic about their new homes.

APPLICATION 9.5: Anthropology in Law

All societies have some means of resolving conflict, as well as a customary legal system that maps out rules of proper and improper behavior and penalties for violation of these rules. As indigenous peoples begin to be absorbed into nation-states, or as countries become independent and develop or adopt national legal systems, however, there is often a conflict between the new legal systems or means of resolving conflicts, and customary methods of conflict resolution. In some societies of Papua New Guinea, for example, it is customary for homicide cases to be settled by a compensatory payment made by the group whose member committed the homicide to members of the victim's family or clan. How can this system of conflict resolution be reconciled with a Western judicial system that focuses on the punishment of the perpetrator, rather than on compensation to the victim?

Writing Law in Papua New Guinea

THE PROBLEM   In 1972, Papua New Guinea became an independent nation of 3.5 million people, speaking some 750 mutually unintelligible languages, and living under a combination of a Western legal system that had been imposed by Australia and almost 1,000 different customary or traditional legal systems. How could a national legal system be developed that took into account so many diverse legal principles? To solve the problem, the new government of Papua New Guinea established a Law Reform Commission to make recommendations to the parliament and hired you as an anthropologist to direct the project.

BACKGROUND OF THE PROBLEM   The problems of reconciling customary law with the legal system that had been imposed by Australia on Papua New Guinea can be illustrated by the impact of legal change on the Abelam. One Abelam man was jailed because he buried his deceased mother inside her house; custom required a corpse to be laid to rest in the house in which the person had worked and slept, covered with only a thin layer of soil. The house would be abandoned and eventually collapse around the burial. Australian officials wanted this burial practice discontinued because they felt it constituted a health hazard. Another legal problem was polygamy. While most Abelam marriages were monogamous, some men had more than one wife. One elderly man with two wives expressed concern when he discovered that he was breaking the law, but he explained that he could never choose one wife over the other because he loved both.

Homicide compensation was another problem area. As in many Melanesian societies, conflicts in Papua New Guinea were customarily resolved by payments of some sort to the aggrieved person. The payment, which was supposed to be proportionate to the act that caused the conflict, implied acceptance of responsibility by the donor and willingness to end the dispute by the recipient.

These arrangements were not recognized under state law, and the use of customary law changed as indigenous people came into contact with Western society. Some cases involved huge groups of people and claims of large compensatory payments. For example, when a man driving a truck struck and killed a man from another province, members of the clan of the victim demanded hundreds of thousands of kina (currency equivalent to the Australian dollar) in compensation from the whole of the driver's province.

As director of the Customary Law project, in what ways would you have helped legal practitioners and identified problems for the legislators who were to draft legislation to reconcile customary law with a national legal system?

AN ACTUAL SOLUTION   Richard Scaglion, an anthropologist working with the Abelam, was hired to address this problem. He began by conducting bibliographical research on studies that had been done on different groups in Papua New Guinea, most of which has been conducted by anthropologists. He discovered a lack of specific legal case studies: that is, instances of conflict with descriptions of how the conflict was resolved, along with a statement of the legal principles from which a dispute was settled. His next step was to set up a system for gathering information about customary law in Papua New Guinea. He selected and trained students from the University of Papua New Guinea to work in their home areas gathering information. Some 600 extended case studies of conflict resolution were collected, and a computer retrieval system was designed to allow lawyers, judges, and lawmakers to scan and use the material in their work. The results of his work were also disseminated in publications directed to members of the legal profession (such as the *Melanesian Law Journal*) and to other applied anthropologists working in the area of legal development in the Pacific (such as *Oceania*).

As a result of Scaglion's work, lawyers in Papua New Guinea were able to find customary precedent cases to use in arguing the cases of clients before the courts. For example, he helped one attorney who needed information about customary divorce practices in a particular area, and investigated issues related to domestic violence and women's access to justice in rural Papua New Guinea. He was able to identify problem areas for legislators and to draft legislation to resolve those problems. Because some men had reason to be concerned about the legal consequences of polygamy, a family law bill was drafted to recognize customary marriages as legal and to allow polygamous marriages under certain conditions. Domestic violence was becoming a problem because of changing patterns of residence. Traditionally, after marriage a woman went to live with her husband's family, but her own family would be nearby, and if she was abused by her husband she could return to her own family. To obtain employment in developing areas, however, families often had to move to other parts of the country, and wives could not return home easily. Lawmakers needed to be aware of these changes in problem areas.

Legislation was prepared that recognized the exchange of wealth and services as a means of resolving conflicts involving death, injuries, and property damage. It sought to regulate payments by specifying the amount of compensation to be paid in specific circumstances. Scaglion solicited opinions from other anthropologists on the draft bill to ensure that its provisions did not conflict with the customary law of the groups with which they were working. For example, Andrew Strathern noted that the draft bill might unintentionally set limits on the competitive ceremonial exchange, or moka of the Melpa (see Question 6.5). As a result of Strathern's information, a revised version of the legislation was prepared.

CONCLUSIONS

The anthropological work described in this chapter has one feature in common: It brings an anthropological perspective, one gained from intense study of other cultures, to specific problems. This perspective is useful for virtually any problem in any field—business, law, social work, public policy planning, international relations, medicine, art, theater, and so on. Every area of our life is defined, in some way, by our culture, and with that in mind we can better understand the issues and problems we face.

Most importantly, growing numbers of anthropologists are being assigned to work on some of the major problems that face us as part of a global community. Anthropologists are applying what they have learned about family organization to assist in the planning of population and family programs; they are active in devising ways to end hunger and deliver social services in remote communities all over the world. They are doing research to devise plans for conducting cattle ranching without destroying the environment, and they are involved in research to discover how our behavior and beliefs affect our health and the spread of disease. They are working with and for indigenous communities to help protect indigenous cultures and to develop strategies for sustainable development. They have risked their lives in war zones to discover the needs of peoples struck with ethnic conflict or revolution, and have worked with local governments all over the world to develop plans to alleviate urban poverty.

The anthropological perspective brings with it an appreciation of how different areas of life—the economic, social, political, ecological, and religious—interrelate with each other. In fact, anthropology is probably the most interdisciplinary of the sciences. Furthermore, as the global community becomes more and more integrated, the kinds of intercultural contact that will occur will require even greater applications of the anthropological perspective. After all, our transportation systems have already redefined our geography and our accessibility to others; we live in a world in which a person from New York is just as likely to come into contact with someone from Jakarta, Berlin, or Santiago as to meet someone from Rochester, Des Moines, or Abilene, and where San Francisco is "closer" to Chicago or Atlanta than it is to a community 100 miles away.

RESOURCE 9.1

Applied Anthropology on the Web

You can find out the other ways that anthropology can be applied at:

The Applied Anthropology Computer Network
http://www.acs.oakland.edu/~dow/anthap.html

REFERENCES AND SUGGESTED READINGS

INTRODUCTION: THE PROBLEMS OF DIVERSITY The opening quote is from John J. Honigmann, *Understanding Culture* (Harper & Row, 1963), pp. 1–2. A general review of applied anthropology can be found in an article by Erve Chambers, "Applied Anthropology in the Post-Vietnam Era: Anticipations and Ironies," in *Annual Review of Anthropology,* vol. 16 (1987), pp. 309–337.

ANTHROPOLOGY IN HEALTH CARE Edward C. Green describes his work in "Traditional Healers and Childhood Diarrheal Disease in Swaziland: The Interface of Anthropology and Health Education," in *Social Science and Medicine,* vol. 20 (1985), pp. 277–285, and in his article "Anthropology in the Context of a Water-Borne Disease Control Project," in *Practicing Development Anthropology* (Westview Press, 1986). Jeannine Coreil reports on her similar work in "Innovation Among Haitian Healers: The Adoption of Oral Rehydration Therapy," in *Human Organization,* vol. 47 (1988), pp. 48–56. For those interested in how anthropology has been used in the nursing profession, see the article by Molly C. Dougherty and Toni Tripp-Reimer, "The Interface of Nursing and Anthropology," in *Annual Review of Anthropology,* vol. 14 (1985), pp. 219–241, and the special issue of *Practicing Anthropology* on nursing, vol. 10, no. 2 (1988).

ANTHROPOLOGY IN ECONOMIC DEVELOPMENT Gerald F. Murray describes the role of anthropology in Haitian reforestation projects in "The Domestication of Wood in Haiti: A Case Study in Applied Evolution," in *Anthropological Praxis: Translating Knowledge into Action,* edited by Robert M. Wulff and Shirley J. Fiske (Westview Press, 1987). The article is reprinted in *Applying Cultural Anthropology: An Introductory Reader,* edited by Aaron Podolefsky and Peter J. Brown (Mayfield Publishing Company, 1991). The role of anthropologists working in the area of development is discussed by Allan Hoben in "Anthropologists and Development," in *Annual Review of Anthropology,* vol. 11 (1982), pp. 349–375.

ANTHROPOLOGY IN EDUCATION The experience of the Japanese student with smiling American women is reported by La Ray M. Barna in "Stumbling Blocks in Intercultural Communication," in *Intercultural Communication: A Reader,* Fourth Edition, edited by Larry A. Samovar and Richard E. Porter (Wadsworth Press, 1985). Helaine K. Minkus describes her workshops for students in "Cross-Cultural Issues for Foreign Students," in *Practicing Anthropology,* vol. 9, no. 3 (1987), and the article in which Richard Ammann reports on his work with students, teachers, and administrators appears in the same issue. Catherine Pelissier provides a review of the work done by anthropologists in education in "The Anthropology of Teaching and Learning," in *Annual Review of Anthropology,* vol. 20 (1991), pp. 75–95.

ANTHROPOLOGY IN ARCHITECTURE George S. Esber describes his work with the Apache in "Designing Apache Homes with Apache," in *Anthropological Praxis: Translating Knowledge into Action,* cited above. A number of articles on how anthropology has been applied to the problems of the homeless in American society are included in vol. 11, no. 2 (1989) of *Practicing Anthropology.* Ernest L. Schusky describes his early work in action anthropology in "An Action

Anthropologist Looks Back to Chicago's Skid Row in the 1950s"; Margaret S. Boone and Thomas Weaver provide a general introduction to the work of anthropologists involving the homeless in "Public Policy Issues Affecting the Homeless in America"; Bryan Page, Price C. Smith, and Normie Kane describe their work with the homeless in Florida in "The Papers You Carry and Who You Really Are: Homelessness and Identity in Dade County Florida"; and Helen Hopps, Sandra L. Tyler, and Beth Warner describe their activities in "Working with D.C.'s Homeless Hispanic Street Kids."

ANTHROPOLOGY IN LAW Richard Scaglion describes his work on the Customary Law Project in "Customary Law Development in Papua New Guinea," in *Anthropological Praxis: Translating Knowledge into Action.* Thomas Weaver discusses the role of anthropology in public policy in "Anthropology as a Policy Science: Part II, Development and Training," in *Human Organization,* vol. 44 (1985), pp. 197–205. A review of the literature on anthropology and public policy can be found in "Anthropology, Administration, and Public Policy," by Robert E. Hinshaw in *Annual Review of Anthropology,* vol. 9 (1980), pp. 497–522.

G L O S S A R Y

balanced reciprocity: The term suggested by Marshall D. Sahlins for a form of exchange in which items of equal or near-equal value are exchanged on the spot.

bilateral kinship: A system in which individuals trace their descent through both parents.

brideservice: The requirement that when a couple marries, the groom must work for the bride's parents for some specified period of time.

bridewealth (brideprice): The valuables that a groom or his family are expected or obligated to present to the bride's family.

caste: A system of social stratification based on assignment at birth to the ranked social or occupational groups of parents. There is no mobility from one caste to another, and intermarriage may be forbidden.

chiefdom: a segmentary social system organized into a hierarchy of more and less powerful groups.

clan: A unilineal descent group whose members claim descent from a common ancestor.

commodities: Goods that carry little personal meaning, as distinguished from possessions, which are associated somehow with the producer and/or distributor of the goods.

cultural anthropology: One of the four major subfields of anthropology, the others being physical or biological anthropology, archaeology, and linguistics.

cultural text: A way of thinking about culture as a text of significant symbols—words, gestures, drawings, natural objects—that carries meaning.

culture: The system of meanings about the nature of experience that are shared by a people and passed on from one generation to another.

culture change: The change in meanings that a people ascribe to experience and changes in their way of life.

culture of poverty: A phrase coined by Oscar Lewis to describe the lifestyle and world view of people who inhabit urban and rural slums.

division of labor: A work system characterized by division of tasks and specialization of occupations.

domain of experience: An area of human experience (e.g., business, war, science, family life) from which people borrow meaning to apply to other areas.

dowry: The goods and valuables a bride's family supplies to the groom's family or to the couple.

economic development: The term used to identify an increase in level of technology, and by some, standard of living of a population. Others view it as an ideology based on three key assumptions: (1) that economic growth and development is the solution to national as well as global problems; (2) that global economic integration will contribute to solving global ecological and social problems; and (3) that foreign assistance to undeveloped countries will make things better.

egocentric: A view of the self that defines each person as a replica of all humanity, the locus of motivations and drives, capable of acting independently from others.

ethnocentric fallacy: The mistaken notion that the beliefs and behaviors of other cultures can be judged from the perspective of one's own culture.

275

ethnocentrism: The tendency to judge the beliefs and behaviors of other cultures from the perspective of one's own culture.

ethnocide: the attempt to destroy the culture of a people.

ethnographic method: The immersion of researchers in the lives and cultures of the peoples they are trying to understand in order to comprehend the meanings these people ascribe to their existence.

ethnographic present: Use of the present tense to describe a culture, although the description may refer to situations that existed in the past.

exogamy: A rule that requires a person to marry someone outside one's own group.

exploitative theory of social stratification: A theory based on the assumption that social stratification and hierarchy exist because one group of individuals seeks to take advantage of another group for economic purposes.

extended family: A family group based on blood relations of three or more generations.

factory system: A system of production characterized by the concentration of labor and machines in specific places. It is associated with the industrial revolution.

family of orientation: The family group that consists of ego and ego's father, mother, and siblings.

family of procreation: The family group that consists of a husband, a wife, and their children.

generalized reciprocity: A form of exchange in which persons share what they have with others but expect them to reciprocate later.

genocide: the attempt to exterminate a people.

holistic: A view of the self in which the individual cannot be conceived of as existing separately from society or apart from his or her status or role.

identity struggles: A term coined by Anthony F. C. Wallace and Raymond D. Fogelson to characterize interaction in which there is a discrepancy between the identity a person claims to possess and the identity attributed to that person by others.

ideology of class: A set of beliefs characteristic of stratified societies that justifies the division of a society into groups with differential rights and privileges as being natural and right.

impartible inheritance: A form of inheritance in which family property is passed undivided to one heir.

incest taboo: A rule that prohibits sexual relations among certain categories of kin, such as brothers and sisters, parents and children, or, in some cases, cousins.

individualistic: A view of the self in which the individual is primarily responsible for his or her own actions.

industrial revolution: A period of European history, generally identified as occurring in the late eighteenth century, marked by a shift in production from agriculture to industrial goods, urbanization, and the factory system.

integrative theory of social stratification: A theory based on the assumption that social hierarchy is necessary for the smooth functioning of society.

International Monetary Fund (IMF): Formed in 1944 at the Bretton Woods conference, the IMF was formed to regulate currency transactions between countries, but now makes loans and regulates the economies of lending countries.

interpersonal theory of disease: A view of disease in which it is assumed that illness is caused by tensions or conflicts in social relations.

interpretive drift: The slow, often unacknowledged shift in someone's manner of interpreting events as he or she becomes involved with a particular activity.

irrigation agriculture: A form of cultivation in which water is used to deliver nutrients to growing plants.

key metaphors: A term coined by Sherry Ortner to identify metaphors that dominate the meanings that people in a specific culture attribute to their experience.

key scenarios: Dominant stories or myths that portray the values and beliefs of a specific society.

matrilineage: A lineage that is formed by tracing descent in the female line.

matrilineal kinship: A system of descent in which persons are related to their kin through the mother only.

means of production: The materials, such as land, machines, or tools, that people need to produce things.

metaphor: A figure of speech in which linguistic expressions are taken from one area of experience and applied to another.

myth: A story or narrative that portrays the meanings people give to their experience.

negative identity: The attribution of personal characteristics believed to be undesirable.

negative reciprocity: A form of exchange in which the object is to get something for nothing or to make a profit.

nuclear family: The family group consisting of father, mother, and their own or adopted children.

partible inheritance: A form of inheritance in which the goods or property of a family is divided among the heirs.

participant observation: The active participation of a researcher or observer in the lives of those being studied.

pathogen: An infectious agent such as a bacterium or a virus that can cause disease.

patrilineage: A lineage that is formed by tracing descent in the male line.

patrilineal kinship: A system of descent in which persons are related to their kin through the father only.

phallocentrism: A term coined by Peggy Sanday that refers to the deployment of the penis as a symbol of masculine social power and dominance.

plow agriculture: A form of cultivation in which fields must be plowed to remove weeds and grasses prior to planting.

political or social repression: The use of force by a ruling group to maintain political, economic, or social control over other groups.

polyandry: A form of marriage in which a woman is permitted to have more than one husband.

polygamy: A form of marriage in which a person is permitted to have more than one spouse.

polygyny: A form of marriage in which a man is permitted to have more than one wife.

population density: The number of people in a given geographic area.

positive identity: The attribution to people of personal characteristics believed to be desirable.

possessions (*see* **commodities**).

principle of reciprocity: The social principle that giving a gift creates social ties with the person receiving it, who eventually is obliged to reciprocate.

progress: The idea that human history is the story of a steady advance from a life dependent on the whims of nature to a life of control and domination over natural forces.

putting-out system: A means of production, common in the sixteenth and seventeenth centuries and surviving today, in which a manufacturer or merchant supplies the materials and sometimes the tools to workers, who produce the goods in their own homes.

race: emerged as a "scientific" concept as nineteenth century anthropologists, building on folk classifications of people, tried to create ways to classify people according to inherited physical characteristics. As a technical concept, it has been largely abandoned, although it remains a socially powerful means of building social hierarchies.

relativism: The attempt to understand the beliefs and behaviors of other cultures in terms of the culture in which they are found.

relativistic fallacy: The mistaken idea that it is impossible to make moral judgments about the beliefs and behaviors of members of other cultures.

revitalization movements: The term suggested by Anthony F. C. Wallace for attempts by a people to construct a more satisfying culture.

rites of passage: The term suggested by Arnold van Gennep for rituals that mark a person's passage from one identity or status to another.

ritual: A dramatic rendering or social portrayal of meanings shared by a specific body of people in a way that makes them seem correct and proper (*see* **symbolic actions**).

Sapir-Whorf hypothesis: The idea that there is an explicit link between the grammar of a language and the culture of the people who speak that language.

secondary elaboration: A term suggested by E. E. Evans-Pritchard for attempts by people to explain away inconsistencies or contradictions in their beliefs.

sedentary: A style of living characterized by permanent or semipermanent settlements.

segmentary social system: the organization of large groups into smaller units embedded in larger units; thus households combine into villages, villages into clans, and clans into tribes.

selective perception: The tendency of people to see and recognize only those things they expect to see or those that confirm their view of the world.

slash-and-burn, or swidden, agriculture: A form of civilization in which forests are cleared by burning trees and brush, and crops are planted among the ashes of the cleared ground.

social classes: A system of social stratification based on income or possession of wealth and resources. Individual social mobility is possible in a class system.

social construct: Any idea or pattern of behavior that is created and sustained by human beings in the course of social interaction.

social identities: Views that people have of their own and others' positions in society. Individuals seek confirmation from others that they occupy the positions on the social landscape that they claim to occupy.

sociocentric: A view of the self that is context-dependent; there is no intrinsic self that can possess enduring qualities.

state: A form of society characterized by a hierarchical ranking of people and centralized political control.

suppressing evidence: A tendency of people to reject or ignore evidence that challenges an accepted belief.

surplus value of labor: The term suggested by Karl Marx and Friedrich Engels for the portion of a person's labor that is retained as profit by those who control the means of production.

symbolic actions: The activities—including ritual, myth, art, dance, and music—that dramatically depict the meanings shared by a specific body of people.

totemism: the use of a symbol, generally an animal or a plant, as a physical representation for a group, generally a clan.

vector: when referring to disease, an organism, such as a mosquito, tick, flea, or snail, that can transmit disease to another animal.

violent revolution: The term suggested by Karl Marx and Friedrich Engels for the necessary response of workers to their repression by the ruling class.

World Bank: One of the institutions created at the Bretton Woods, New Hampshire, meeting in 1944 of Allied nations. The World Bank (or the Bank for Reconstruction and Development) functions as a lending institution to nations largely for projects related to economic development.

BIBLIOGRAPHY

Adams, John W. 1973. *The Gitksan Potlatch: Population Flux, Resource Ownership and Reciprocity.* Toronto: Holt, Rinehart and Winston of Canada.

Aditjondro, George. 2000. "Ninjas, Nanggalas, Monuments, and Mossad Manuals." In *Death Squad: The Anthropology of State Terror.* Edited by Jeffery A. Sluka. Philadelphia: University of Pennsylvania Press.

Alford, Richard D. 1988. *Naming and Identity: A Cross-Cultural Study of Personal Naming Practices.* New Haven: HRAF Press.

Ammann, Richard. 1987. "Cross-Cultural Training Workshops for Educators." *Practicing Anthropology* 9:8.

Anderson, Benedict R. O'G. 1991. *Imagined Communities: Reflections on the Origin & Spread of Nationalism.* New York: Verso.

Anelauskas, Valdas. 1999. *Discovering America As It Is.* Atlanta: Clarity Press.

Angeloni, Elvio. 1990. *Anthropology 90/91.* Guilford, CT: Dushkin Publishing Company.

Anonymous. 1816. *Testimonies of the Life, Character, Revelations and Doctrines of Our Ever Blessed Mother Ann Lee.* New York: J. Tallcott & J. Deming.

Arens, William. 1976. "Professional Football: An American Symbol and Ritual." In *The American Dimension: Cultural Myths and Social Realities.* Edited by William Arens and Susan P. Montague. Port Washington, NY: Alfred Publishing Company.

Barna, La Ray. 1985. "Stumbling Blocks in Intercultural Communication." In *Intercultural Communication: A Reader,* Fourth Edition. Edited by Larry A. Samovar and Richard E. Porter. Belmont, CA: Wadsworth Press.

Barnes, Barry. 1974. *Scientific Knowledge and Sociological Theory.* London: Routledge & Kegan Paul.

Bean, Susan. 1976. "Soap Operas: Sagas of American Kinship." In *The American Dimension: Cultural Myths and Social Realities.* Edited by William Arens and Susan P. Montague. Port Washington, NY: Alfred Publishing Company.

Beaud, Michel. 1983. *A History of Capitalism, 1500–1980.* New York: Monthly Review Press.

Bellah, Robert, Richard Madsen, William M. Sullivan, Ann Swidler, and Steven M. Tipton. 1984. *Habits of the Heart.* Berkeley: University of California Press.

Belmonte, Thomas. 1989. *The Broken Fountain.* New York: Columbia University Press.

Benedict, Ruth. 1934. *Patterns of Culture.* New York: Houghton Mifflin.

Boas, Franz. 1966. *Kwakiutl Ethnography.* Edited by Helen Codere. Chicago: University of Chicago Press.

Boas, Franz, and George Hunt. 1905. *Kwakiutl Texts.* Memoir of the American Museum of Natural History, vol. 5.

Bodley, John. 1985. *Anthropology and Contemporary Problems,* Second Edition. Palo Alto, CA: Mayfield Publishing Company.

Bodley, John. 1994. *Cultural Anthropology: Tribes, States, and the Global System.* Mountain View, CA: Mayfield Publishing Company.

Bodley, John. 1999. *The Victims of Progress.* Mountain View, CA: Mayfield Publishing Company.

Bohannan, Laura. 1966. "Shakespeare in the Bush." *Natural History Magazine,* August/September.

Bohannan, Paul, editor. 1970. *Divorce and After.* New York: Doubleday.

Boone, Margaret S., and Thomas Weaver. 1989. "Public Policy Issues Affecting the Homeless in America." *Practicing Anthropology* 11:2.

Bourgois, Phillipe. 1995. *In Search of Respect: Selling Crack in El Barrio.* Cambridge: Cambridge University Press.

Braudel, Fernand. 1982. *Civilization and Capitalism 15th-18th Century: Volume II, The Wheels of Commerce.* New York: Harper & Row Publishers.

Briggs, Jean. 1970. *Never in Anger.* Cambridge: Harvard University Press.

Burton, Thomas. 1993. *Serpent-Handling Believers.* Knoxville: University of Tennessee Press.

Cagan, Leslie. 1983. "Feminism and Militarism." In *Beyond Survival: New Directions for the Disarmament Movement.* Edited by M. Albert and D. Dellinger. Boston: South End Press.

Cairns, Ed. 1982. "Intergroup Conflict in Northern Ireland." In *Social Identity and Intergroup Relations.* Edited by Henri Tajfel. New York: Cambridge University Press.

Campbell, Joseph. 1949. *The Hero with a Thousand Faces.* Princeton, NJ: Princeton University Press.

Campion, Nardi Reeder. 1990. *Mother Ann Lee: Morning Star of the Shakers.* Hanover, NH: University Press of New England.

Carneiro, Robert. 1978. "Political Expansion as an Expression of the Principle of Competitive Exclusion." In *Origins of the State.* Edited by Ronald Cohn and Elman Service. Philadelphia: Institute for the Study of Human Issues.

Carneiro, Robert. 1979. "Slash-and-Burn Cultivation Among the Kuikuru and Its Implication for Cultural Development in the Amazon Basin." In *The Evolution of Horticultural Systems in Native South America: Causes and Consequences.* Anthropologica Supplement 2. Edited by J. Wilbert. Caracas, Venezuela.

Carneiro, Robert. 1990. "Chiefdom-Level Warfare as Exemplified in Fiji and Cauca Valley." In *The Anthropology of War.* Edited by Jonathan Hass. New York: Cambridge University Press.

Carrier, James G. 1993. "The Rituals of Christmas Giving." In *Unwrapping Christmas.* Edited by Daniel Miller. Oxford: Clarendon Press.

Carrier, James G. 1995. *Gifts and Commodities: Exchange and Western Capitalism Since 1700.* London: Routledge.

Carroll, John B. 1964. *Language, Thought, and Reality: Selected Writings of Benjamin Lee Whorf.* Boston: MIT Press.

Cathcart, Dolores, and Robert Cathcart. 1985. "Japanese Social Experience and Concept of Groups." In *Intercultural Communication: A Reader,* Fourth Edition. Edited by Larry A. Samovar and Richard E. Porter. Belmont, CA: Wadsworth Publishing Company.

Chagnon, Napoleon. 1983. *The Fierce People,* Third Edition. New York: Holt, Rinehart and Winston.

Chagnon, Napoleon. 1990. "Reproductive and Somatic Conflicts of Interest in the Genesis of Violence and Warfare Among Tribesmen." In *The Anthropology of War.* Edited by Jonathan Hass. New York: Cambridge University Press.

Chambers, Erve. 1987. "Applied Anthropology in the Post-Vietnam Era: Anticipations and Ironies." In *Annual Review of Anthropology,* vol. 16, pp. 309–337. Palo Alto, CA: Annual Reviews.

Chomsky, Noam. 1984. *Turning the Tide: U.S. Intervention in Central America and the Struggle for Peace.* Boston: South End Press.

Clay, Jason W. 1984. "Yahgan and Ona—The Road to Extinction." *Cultural Survival Quarterly* 8:5–8.

Cohen, Mark. 1977. *The Food Crisis in Prehistory.* New Haven, CT: Yale University Press.

Cohen, Mark. 1989. *Health and the Rise of Civilization.* New Haven, CT: Yale University Press.

Cohn, Carol. 1987. "Sex and Death in the Rational World of Defense Intellectuals." *Signs* 12:687–718.

Cohn, Carol. 1991. "Decoding Military Newspeak." *Ms.* 5.

Collier, Jane E., and Michelle Rosaldo. 1981. "Politics and Gender in Simple Societies." In *Sexual Meanings: The Cultural Construction of Gender and Sexuality*. Edited by Sherry B. Ortner and Harriet Whitehead. New York: Cambridge University Press.

Coreil, Jeannine. 1988. "Innovation Among Haitian Healers: The Adoption of Oral Rehydration Therapy." *Human Organization* 47:48–56.

Covington, Dennis. 1995. *Salvation on Sand Mountain: Snake Handling and Redemption in Southern Appalachia.* New York: Addison-Wesley.

Cowell, Daniel David. 1985/86. "Funerals, Family, and Forefathers: A View of Italian-American Funeral Practices." *Omega* 16:69–85.

Crick, Malcolm R. 1982. "Anthropology of Knowledge." In *Annual Review of Anthropology,* vol. 11, pp. 287–313. Palo Alto, CA: Annual Reviews.

Crowley, Aleister. 1985. *The Book of Thoth.* Stamford: U.S. Games Systems.

Culler, Jonathan. 1977. "In Pursuit of Signs." *Daedalus* 106:95–112.

D'Andrade, Roy. 1995. "Moral Models in Anthropology." *Current Anthropology* 36:399–408.

Davis, D. L., and R. G. Whitten. 1987. "The Cross-Cultural Study of Human Sexuality." In *Annual Review of Anthropology,* vol. 16, pp. 69–98. Palo Alto, CA: Annual Reviews.

Delany, Carol. 1991. *The Seed and the Soil: Gender and Cosmology in a Turkish Village Society.* Berkeley: University of California Press.

De Munck, Victor. 1998. *Romantic Love and Sexual Behavior: Perspectives from the Social Sciences.* Westport: Praeger.

Desai, Ashok V. 1972. "Population and Standards of Living in Akbar's Time." In the *Indian Economic and Social History Review,* vol. 9, pp. 42–62.

Devita, Philip, editor. 1990. *The Humbled Anthropologist: Tales from the Pacific.* Belmont, CA: Wadsworth Publishing Company.

Devita, Philip, editor. 1991. *The Naked Anthropologist: Tales from Around the World.* Belmont, CA: Wadsworth Publishing Company.

Devita, Philip, and James Armstrong, editors. 1992. *Distant Mirrors: America as a Foreign Culture.* Belmont, CA: Wadsworth Publishing Company.

Divale, William Tulio, and Marvin Harris. 1976. "Population, Warfare, and the Male Supremacist Complex." *American Anthropologist* 78:521–538.

Dougherty, Molly C., and Toni Tripp-Reimer. 1985. "The Interface of Nursing and Anthropology." In *Annual Review of Anthropology,* vol. 14, pp. 219–241. Palo Alto, CA: Annual Reviews.

Douglas, Mary. 1966. *Purity and Danger.* New York: Frederick A. Praeger.

Douglas, Mary, and Aaron B. Wildavsky. 1983. *Risk and Culture: An Essay on the Selection of Technical and Environmental Dangers.* Berkeley: University of California Press.

Dréze, Jean, and Amartya Sen. 1991. *Hunger and Public Action.* New York: Cambridge University Press.

Dumont, Louis. 1970. *Homo Hierarchicus: An Essay on the Caste System.* Chicago: University of Chicago Press.

Durham, William H. 1990. "Advances in Evolutionary Culture Theory." In *Annual Review of Anthropology,* vol. 19, pp. 187–210. Palo Alto, CA: Annual Reviews.

Durkheim, Émile. 1961. *The Elementary Forms of the Religious Life.* New York: Collier.

Eisler, Riane. 1987. *The Chalice and the Blade.* New York: Harper & Row.

Erasmus, Charles. 1977. *In Search of the Common Good.* Glencoe, IL: The Free Press.

Esber, George S. 1987. "Designing Apache Homes With Apache." In *Anthropological Praxis: Translating Knowledge into Action.* Edited by Robert M. Wulff and Shirley J. Fiske. Boulder, CO: Westview Press.

Evans-Pritchard, E. E. 1937. *Witchcraft, Oracles and Magic Among the Azande.* London: Oxford University Press.

Evans-Pritchard, E. E. 1940. *The Nuer: A Description of the Modes of Livelihood and Political Institutions of a Nilotic People.* Oxford: Clarendon Press.

Evans-Pritchard, E. E. 1968. *Theories of Primitive Religion.* Oxford: Oxford University Press.

Fei, Hsiao-Tung. 1939. *Peasant Life in China: A Field Study of Country Life in the Yangtze Valley.* London: Routledge & Kegan Paul Ltd.

Ferguson, R. Brian. 1992. "A Savage Encounter: Western Contact and the Yanomami War Complex." In *War in the Tribal Zone: Expanding States and Indigenous Warfare.* Edited by R. Brian Ferguson and Neil L. Whitehead. Santa Fe: School of American Research Press.

Ferguson, R. Brian. 1995. *Yanomami Warfare: A Political History.* Santa Fe: School of the Americas Research Press.

Fernandez, James W. 1978. "African Religious Movements." In *Annual Review of Anthropology,* vol. 7, pp. 195–234. Palo Alto, CA: Annual Reviews.

Foley, Douglas E. 1990. *Learning Capitalist Culture: Deep in the Heart of Tejas.* Philadelphia: University of Pennsylvania Press.

Foucault, Michel. 1979. *Discipline and Punishment: The Birth of the Prison.* New York: Vintage Press.

French, Hilary. 2000. *Vanishing Borders: Protecting the Planet in the Age of Globalization,* New York: W. W. Norton.

Fried, Morton H. 1967. *The Evolution of Political Society: An Essay in Political Anthropology.* New York: Random House.

Fried, Morton, Marvin Harris, and Robert Murphy. 1967. *War: The Anthropology of Armed Conflict and Aggression.* Garden City, NY: The Natural History Press.

Geertz, Clifford. 1972. "Deep Play: Notes on the Balinese Cockfight." *Daedalus* 101:1–37.

Geertz, Clifford. 1973. "The Impact of Culture on the Concept of Man." In *The Interpretation of Cultures.* New York: Basic Books.

Gellner, Ernest. 1983. *Nations and Nationalism.* Ithaca: Cornell University Press.

George, Susan, and Fabrizo Sabelli. 1994. *Faith and Credit: The World Bank's Secular Empire.* Boulder, CO: Westview Press.

Gibson, Thomas. 1990. "Raiding, Trading and Tribal Autonomy in Insular Southeast Asia." In *The Anthropology of War.* Edited by Jonathan Hass. New York: Cambridge University Press.

Gilmore, David D. 1990. *Manhood in the Making: Cultural Concepts of Masculinity.* New Haven, CT: Yale University Press.

Ginsburg, Faye, and Rayna Rapp. 1991. "The Politics of Reproduction." In *Annual Review of Anthropology,* vol. 20, pp. 311-343. Palo Alto, CA: Annual Reviews.

Goffman, Erving. 1959. *The Presentation of Self in Everyday Life.* New York: Doubleday.

Gould, Stephen Jay. 1981. *The Mismeasure of Man.* New York: W. W. Norton.

Green, Edward C. 1985. "Traditional Healers and Childhood Diarrheal Disease in Swaziland: The Interface of Anthropology and Health Education." *Social Science and Medicine* 20:277–285.

Green, Edward C. 1986. "Anthropology in the Context of a Water-Borne Disease Control Project." In *Practicing Development Anthropology.* Boulder, CO: Westview Press.

Green, Nancy. 1995. "Living in a State of Fear." In *Fieldwork Under Fire: Contemporary Studies of Violence and Survival.* Edited by Carolyn Nordstrom and Antonius C. G. Robben. Berkeley: University of California Press.

Greenhouse, Carol. 1987. "Cultural Perspectives on War." In *The Quest for Peace: Transcending Collective Violence and War Among Societies, Cultures and States.* Edited by R. Varynen. Beverly Hills, CA: Sage Publishing.

Gregor, Thomas. 1990. "Uneasy Peace: Intertribal Relations in Brazil's Upper Xingu." In *The Anthropology of War.* Edited by Jonathan Hass. New York: Cambridge University Press.

Gusterson, Hugh. 1995. *Nuclear Rites: A Weapons Laboratory at the End of the Cold War.* Berkeley: University of California Press.

Hall, Edgar T. 1966. *The Hidden Dimension.* Garden City, NY: Doubleday.

Hanson, Allan. 1993. *Testing Testing.* Berkeley: University of California Press.

Harding, Susan Friend. 2000. *The Book of Jerry Falwell.* Princeton, NJ: Princeton University Press.

Harris, Marvin. 1977. *Cannibals and Kings: The Origins of Culture.* New York: Vintage Books.

Harris, Marvin, and Eric Ross. 1987. *Food and Evolution: Toward a Theory of Human Food Habits.* Philadelphia: Temple University Press.

Hayden, Dolores. 1981. *Seven American Utopias: The Architecture of Communitarian Socialism, 1790-1975.* Cambridge, MA: MIT Press.

Henderson, Paul. 1976. "Class Structure and the Concept of Intelligence." In *Schooling and Capitalism: A Sociological Reader.* Edited by Roger Dale, Geoff Esland, and Madeleine MacDonald. London: Routledge & Kegan Paul in association with The Open University Press.

Henle, Paul. 1958. *Language, Thought and Experience.* Ann Arbor: University of Michigan Press.

Herrnstein, Richard J., and Charles Murray. 1994. *The Bell Curve: Intelligence and Class Structure in American Life.* New York: Free Press.

Hertz, Robert. 1960. *Death and the Right Hand.* Translated and edited by Claudia and Rodney Needham. Glencoe, IL: Free Press (originally published in 1909).

Hinshaw, Robert E. 1980. "Anthropology, Administration, and Public Policy." In *Annual Review of Anthropology,* vol. 9, pp. 497-522. Palo Alto, CA: Annual Reviews.

Hobbes, Thomas. 1881. *Leviathan.* London: Oxford University Press (originally published in 1651).

Hoben, Allan. 1982. "Anthropologists and Development." In *Annual Review of Anthropology,* vol. 11, pp. 349-375. Palo Alto, CA: Annual Reviews.

Hobsbaum, Eric. 1959. *Primitive Rebels: Studies in Archaic Forms of Social Movement in the 19th and 20th Centuries.* New York: Frederick A. Praeger.

Holloway, Ralph, Jr. 1968. "Human Aggression: The Need for a Species-Specific Framework." In *War: The Anthropology of Armed Conflict and Aggression.* Edited by Morton Fried, Marvin Harris, and Robert Murphy. Garden City, NY: The Natural History Press.

Honigmann, John J. 1963. *Understanding Culture.* New York: Harper & Row.

Honigmann, John J. 1976. *The Development of Anthropological Ideas.* Homewood, IL: Dorsey Press.

Hopps, Helen, Sandra L. Tyler, and Beth Warner. 1989. "Working with D.C.'s Homeless Hispanic Street Kids." *Practicing Anthropology* Volume 11.

Hostetler, John. 1974. *Hutterite Society.* Baltimore: Johns Hopkins University Press.

Howell, Signe, and Roy Willis, eds. 1999. *Societies at Peace: Anthropological Perspectives.* Boston: Routledge.

House, James S., Karl R. Landis, and Debra Umberson. 1988. "Social Relationships and Health." *Science* 241:540-545.

Hsu, Francis L. K. 1967. *Under the Ancestor's Shadow.* New York: Anchor Books.

Illouz, Eva. 1997. *Consuming the Romantic Utopia: Love and the Cultural Contradictions of Capitalism.* Berkeley: University of California Press

Inhorn, Marcia C., and Peter J. Brown. 1990. "The Anthropology of Infectious Disease." In *Annual Review of Anthropology,* vol. 19, pp. 89-117. Palo Alto, CA: Annual Reviews.

Johnson, Norris Brock. 1985. *Westhaven: Classroom Culture and Society in a Rural Elementary School.* Chapel Hill: University of North Carolina Press.

Karier, Clarence J. 1976. "Testing for Order and Control in the Corporate Liberal State." In *Schooling and Capitalism: A Sociological Reader.* Edited by Roger Dale, Geoff Esland, and Madeleine MacDonald. London: Routledge & Kegan Paul in association with The Open University Press.

Kearney, Michael. 1991. "A Very Bad Disease of the Arms." In *The Naked Anthropologist: Tales from Around the World.* Edited by Philip Devita. Belmont, CA: Wadsworth Publishing Company.

Keesing, Roger. 1991. "Not a Real Fish: The Ethnographer as Inside Outsider." In *The Naked Anthropologist: Tales from Around the World.* Edited by Philip Devita. Belmont, CA: Wadsworth Publishing Company.

Kehoe, Alice. 1989. *The Ghost Dance: Ethnohistory and Revitalization.* New York: Holt, Rinehart and Winston.

Keiser, Lincoln. 1969. *The Vice Lords: Warriors of the Streets.* New York: Holt, Rinehart and Winston.

Keiser, Lincoln. 1991. *Friend by Day, Enemy by Night: Organized Vengeance in a Kohistani Community.* New York: Holt, Rinehart and Winston.

Kelly, John D., and Martha Kaplan. 1990. "History, Structure, and Ritual." In *Annual Review of Anthropology,* vol. 19, pp. 119–150. Palo Alto, CA: Annual Reviews.

Kennedy, Paul. 1993. *Preparing for the Twenty-First Century.* New York: Random House.

Kets de Vries, Manfred, and Danny Miller. 1987. "Interpreting Organizational Texts." *Journal of Management Studies* 24:233–247.

Kiefer, Christie W. 1976. "The Danchi Zoku and the Evolution of the Metropolitan Mind." In *Japan: The Paradox of Progress.* Edited by Lewis Austin, with the assistance of Adrienne Suddard and Nancy Remington. New Haven, CT: Yale University Press.

Kiefer, Christie W. 1977. "Psychological Anthropology." *Annual Review of Anthropology* 6:103–119.

Kinkade, Kathleen. 1973. *A Walden Two Experiment: The First Five Years of Twin Oaks Community.* New York: William Morrow.

Korten, David C. 1995. *When Corporations Rule the World.* Hartford: Kumarian Press.

Kotlowitz, Alex. 1991. *There Are No Children Here.* New York: Anchor Books.

Kottak, Conrad Phillip. 1990. *Prime Time Society: An Anthropological Analysis of Television and Culture.* Belmont, CA: Wadsworth Publishing Company.

Kroeber, Alfred L. 1948. *Anthropology.* New York: Harcourt, Brace.

Kuhn, Thomas. 1957. *The Copernican Revolution: Planetary Astronomy in the Development of Western Thought.* Cambridge, MA: Harvard University Press.

Kuper, Leo. 1990. "The Genocidal State: An Overview." In *State Violence and Ethnicity.* Edited by Pierre L. van den Berghe. Boulder: University of Colorado Press.

La Barre, Weston. 1962. *They Shall Take Up Serpents: Psychology of the Southern Snakehandling Cult.* Minneapolis: University of Minnesota Press.

Lakoff, George, and Mark Johnson. 1980. *Metaphors We Live By.* Chicago: University of Chicago Press.

Lappè, Frances Moore, and Joseph Collins. 1977. *Food First: Beyond the Myth of Scarcity.* New York: Random House.

Leach, Edmund. 1979. "Anthropological Aspects of Language: Animal Categories and Verbal Abuse." In *Reader in Comparative Religion,* Fourth Edition. Edited by William Lessa and Evon Z. Vogt. New York: Harper & Row.

Lee, Richard. 1969. "Eating Christmas in the Kalihari." *Natural History Magazine.* December.

Lee, Richard. 1984. *The Dobe !Kung.* New York: Holt, Rinehart and Winston.

Levi-Strauss, Claude. 1974. *Tristé Tropiques.* New York: Atheneum Publishers.

Lewellen, Ted. 1993. *Political Anthropology: An Introduction,* Second Edition. Westport, CT: Bergin & Garvey.

Lewis, Oscar. 1959. *Five Families: Mexican Case Studies in the Culture of Poverty.* New York: Basic Books.

Livingstone, Frank B. 1968. "The Effects of Warfare on the Biology of the Human Species." In *War: The Anthropology of Armed Conflict and Aggression.* Edited by Morton Fried, Marvin Harris, and Robert Murphy. Garden City, NY: Natural History Press.

Longres, John F. 2000. *Human Behavior in the Social Environment,* Third Edition. Itasca, IL: F. E. Peacock Publishers.

Luhrmann, T. M. 1989. *Persuasions of the Witch's Craft: Ritual Magic in Contemporary England.* Cambridge, MA: Harvard University Press.

Malinowski, Bronislaw. 1929. *The Sexual Life of Savages in North-Western Melanesia.* New York: Halcyon House.

Malinowski, Bronislaw. 1961. *Argonauts of the Western Pacific.* New York: E. P. Dutton (originally published 1922).

Mandelbaum, David G. 1949. *Selected Writings of Edward Sapir in Language, Culture, and Personality.* Berkeley: University of California Press.

Marshall, Lorna. 1976. *The !Kung of Nyae Nyae.* Cambridge, MA: Harvard University Press.

Martin, Emily. 1987. *The Woman in the Body: A Cultural Analysis of Reproduction.* Boston: Beacon Press.

Marwick, Max. 1965. *Sorcery in Its Social Setting.* Manchester, England: University of Manchester Press.

Matsubara, Hisako. 1985. *Cranes at Dusk.* New York: Dial Press.

Mauss, Marcel. 1967. *The Gift: Forms and Functions of Exchange in Archaic Societies.* Translated by Ian Cunnison. New York: W. W. Norton (originally published in 1925).

Maybury-Lewis, David. 1997. *Indigenous Peoples, Ethnic Groups, and the State.* Boston: Allyn & Bacon.

McCauley, Clark. 1990. "Conference Overview." In *The Anthropology of War.* Edited by Jonathan Hass. New York: Cambridge University Press.

McElroy, Ann, and Patricia Townsend. 1979. *Medical Anthropology.* North Scituate, MA: Duxbury Press.

Mead, Margaret. 1963. *Sex and Temperament in Three Primitive Societies.* New York: Dell Publishing (originally published in 1935).

Minkus, Helaine K. 1987. "Cross-Cultural Issues for Foreign Students." *Practicing Anthropology* 9:9.

Mintz, Sidney W. 1985. *Sweetness and Power: The Place of Sugar in World History.* New York: Viking Press.

Mishkin, Bernard. 1940. *Rank and Warfare Among the Plains Indians.* Monograph No. 3, American Ethnological Society. Seattle: University of Washington Press.

Moffat, Michael. 1990. *Growing Up in New Jersey.* New Brunswick, NJ: Rutgers University Press.

Montague, Susan P., and William Morais. 1976. "Football Games and Rock Concerts: The Ritual Enactment of American Success Models." In *The American Dimension: Cultural Myths and Social Realities.* Edited by William Arens and Susan P. Montague. Port Washington, NY: Alfred Publishing Company.

Mooney, James. 1965. *The Ghost Dance Religion and the Sioux Outbreak of 1890.* Chicago: University of Chicago Press.

Moos, Robert, and Robert Brownstein. 1977. *Environment and Utopia.* New York: Plenum Publishing.

Morgan, Lewis Henry. 1964. *Ancient Society.* Cambridge, MA: Belknap Press (originally published in 1877).

Mukhopadhyay, Carol C., and Patricia J. Higgins. 1988. "Anthropological Studies of Women's Status Revisited: 1977–1987." In *Annual Review of Anthropology,* vol. 17, pp. 461–495. Palo Alto, CA: Annual Reviews.

Murray, Gerald F. 1987. "The Domestication of Wood in Haiti: A Case Study in Applied Evolution." In *Anthropological Praxis: Translating Knowledge into Action.* Edited by Robert M. Wulff and Shirley J. Fiske. Boulder, CO: Westview Press. (Reprinted in *Applying Cultural Anthropology: An Introductory Reader.* Edited by Aaron Podolefsky and Peter J. Brown. Mountain View, CA: Mayfield Publishing Company, 1991.)

Myers, Fred R. 1988. "Critical Trends in the Study of Hunters-Gatherers." In *Annual Review of Anthropology,* vol. 17, pp. 261–282. Palo Alto, CA: Annual Reviews.

Nagengast, Carole. 1994. "Violence, Terror, and the Crisis of the State." *Annual Review of Anthropology* 23:109–136.

Nations, James D. 1994. "The Ecology of the Zapatista Revolt." *Cultural Survival Quarterly* 18:31–33.

Neider, Charles. 1966. *The Complete Travel Books of Mark Twain.* New York: Doubleday.

Nordhoff, Charles. 1966. *The Communistic Societies of the United States: From Personal Observation.* New York: Dover Publications (originally published in 1875).

Ocaya-Lakidi, Dent. 1979. "Manhood, Warriorhood and Sex in Eastern Africa." *Journal of Asian and African Studies* 12:134–165.

Oldfield-Hayes, Rose. 1975. "Female Genital Mutilation, Fertility Control, Women's Roles, and the Patrilineage in Modern Sudan: A Functional Analysis." *American Ethnologist* 2:617–633.

Page, Bryan, Price C. Smith, and Normie Kane. 1989. "The Papers You Carry and Who You Really Are: Homelessness and Identity in Dade County Florida." *Practicing Anthropology* Volume 11.

Palgi, Phyllis, and Henry Abramovitch. 1984. "Death: A Cross-Cultural Perspective." In *Annual Review of Anthropology,* vol. 13, pp. 385–417. Palo Alto, CA: Annual Reviews.

Parsons, Talcott, Edward Shils, Kaspar D. Naegele, and Jesse R. Pitts. 1961. *Theories of Society.* Glencoe, IL: Free Press.

Pasternak, Burton. 1976. *Introduction to Kinship and Social Organization.* Englewood Cliffs, NJ: Prentice-Hall.

Payne, David. 1989. "The Wizard of Oz: Therapeutic Rhetoric in a Contemporary Media Ritual." *Quarterly Journal of Speech* 75:25–39.

Pearson, Karl. 1901. "On the Inheritance of Mental Characteristics in Man." In *Proceedings of the Royal Society of London,* vol. 69, pp. 153–155.

Pelissier, Catherine. 1991. "The Anthropology of Teaching and Learning." In *Annual Review of Anthropology,* vol. 20, pp. 75–95. Palo Alto, CA: Annual Reviews.

Philips, Susan U. 1980. "Sex Differences and Language." In *Annual Review of Anthropology,* vol. 9, pp. 523–544. Palo Alto, CA: Annual Reviews.

Read, Kenneth E. 1965. *The High Valley.* New York: Columbia University Press.

Reardon, Betty. 1985. *Sexism and the War System.* New York: Columbia University Teachers College Press.

Reed, Richard. 1997. *Forest Dwellers, Forest Protectors: Indigenous Models for International Development.* Boston: Allyn & Bacon.

Rich, Bruce. 1994. *Mortgaging the Earth: The World Bank, Environmental Impoverishment, and the Crisis of Development.* New York: Beacon Press.

Richardson, Lewis. 1960. *The Statistics of Deadly Quarrels.* Pacific Grove, CA: The Boxwood Press.

Ridington, Robin. 1968. "The Medicine Fight: An Instrument of Political Process Among the Beaver Indians." *American Anthropologist* 70:1152–1160.

Rindos, David. 1984. *The Origins of Agriculture.* New York: Academic Press.

Robarchek, Clayton. 1990. "Motivations and Material Causes: On the Explanation of Conflict and War." In *The Anthropology of War.* Edited by Jonathan Hass. New York: Cambridge University Press.

Robbins, Richard H. 1999. *Global Problems and the Culture of Capitalism.* Boston: Allyn & Bacon.

Rosaldo, Michele, and Jane Monnig Atkinson. 1975. "Man the Hunter and Woman: Metaphors for the Sexes in Ilongot Magical Spells." In *The Interpretation of Symbolism.* New York: John Wiley & Sons.

Rosaldo, Renato. 1989. *Culture and Truth: The Remaking of Social Analysis.* Boston: Beacon Press.

Roy, Ramashray. 1985. *Self and Society: A Study in Gandhian Thought.* Beverly Hills, CA: Sage Publishing.

Rubel, Arthur. 1964. "The Epidemiology of a Folk Illness: Susto in Hispanic America." *Ethnology* 3:268–283.

Rummel R. J. 1994. *Death by Government.* New Brunswick: Transaction Press.

Sahlins, Marshall. 1966. *Tribesmen.* New York: Prentice-Hall.

Saitoti, Tepilit Ole. 1986. *The Worlds of a Maasai Warrior.* New York: Random House.

Sanday, Peggy Reeves. 1981. "The Socio-Cultural Context of Rape: A Cross-Cultural Study." *Journal of Social Issues* 37:5–27.

Sanday, Peggy Reeves. 1990. *Fraternity Gang Rape: Sex, Brotherhood, and Privilege on Campus.* New York: New York University Press.

Scaglion, Richard. 1987. "Customary Law Development in Papua New Guinea." In *Anthropological Praxis: Translating Knowledge into Action.* Edited by Robert M. Wulff and Shirley J. Fiske. Boulder, CO: Westview Press.

Scaglion, Richard. 1990. "Ethnocentrism and the Abelam." In *The Humbled Anthropologist: Tales from the Pacific.* Edited by Philip Devita. Belmont, CA: Wadsworth Publishing.

Scheper-Hughes, Nancy. 1992. *Death Without Weeping: The Violence of Everyday Life in Brazil.* Berkeley: University of California Press.

Scheper-Hughes, Nancy. 1995. "The Primacy of the Ethical: Propositions for a Militant Anthropology." *Current Anthropology* 36:409–420.

Schieffelin, Bambi B., and Elinor Ochs. 1986. "Language Socialization." In *Annual Review of Anthropology,* vol. 15, pp. 163–191. Palo Alto, CA: Annual Reviews.

Schrire, Carmel. 1984. "Wild Surmises on Savage Thoughts." In *Past and Present in Hunter Gatherer Studies.* Edited by Carmel Schrire. New York: Academic Press.

Schusky, Ernest L. 1989. "An Action Anthropologist Looks Back to Chicago's Skid Row in the 1950s." *Practicing Anthropology* Volume 11.

Schwartz, Gary, and Don Merten. 1968. "Social Identity and Expressive Symbols." *American Anthropologist* 70:1117–1131.

Service, Elman R. 1975. *Origins of the State and Civilization: The Process of Cultural Evolution.* New York: W. W. Norton.

Shipton, Parker. 1990. "African Famines and Food Security." In *Annual Review of Anthropology,* vol. 19, pp. 353–394. Palo Alto, CA: Annual Reviews.

Shostak, Marjorie. 1983. *Nisa: The Life and Words of a !Kung Woman.* New York: Vintage Books.

Shweder, Richard A., and Edmund J. Bourne. 1984. "Does the Concept of the Person Vary Cross-Culturally?" In *Cultural Conceptions of Mental Health and Therapy.* Edited by A. J. Marsella and G. M. White. Boston: D. Reidel Publishing Company.

Sidel, Ruth. 1986. *Women and Children Last: Social Stratification in America.* New York: Penguin Books.

Sipes, Richard G. 1973. "War, Sports, and Aggression: An Empirical Test of Two Rival Theories." *American Anthropologist* 74:64–86.

Smith, Arthur H. 1970. *Village Life in China.* Boston: Little, Brown and Company.

Smith, Raymond T. 1984. "Anthropology and the Concept of Social Class." In *Annual Review of Anthropology,* vol. 13, pp. 467–494. Palo Alto, CA: Annual Reviews.

Smith, Robert J. 1983. *Japanese Society: Tradition, Self and the Social Order.* New York: Cambridge University Press.

Solomon, Robert C. 1981. *Love: Emotion, Myth, and Metaphor.* New York: Anchor Press/Doubleday.

Spearman, Charles. 1904. "General Intelligence." *American Journal of Psychology* 115:201–92.

Spindler, George, and Louise Spindler. 1983. "Anthropologists View American Culture." In *Annual Review of Anthropology,* vol. 12, pp. 49–78. Palo Alto, CA: Annual Reviews.

Stack, Carol. 1974. *All Our Kin: Strategies for Survival in a Black Community.* New York: Harper & Row.

Stein, Stephen J. 1992. *The Shaker Experience in America: A History of the United Societies of Believers.* New Haven, CT: Yale University Press.

Stevens, Jacqueline. 1999. *Reproducing the State.* Princeton: Princeton University Press.

Stone, Lawrence. 1977. *The Family, Sex and Marriage in England, 1500–1800.* New York: Harper & Row.

Strathern, Andrew. 1971. *The Rope of Moka: Big Men and Ceremonial Exchange in Mount Hagen, New Guinea.* London: Cambridge University Press.

Thomas, Elizabeth. 1959. *The Harmless People.* New York: Alfred A. Knopf.

Thompson, E. P. "Time, Work-Discipline and Industrial Capitalism." *Past and Present* 38:56–97.

Thrasher, Frederic. 1963. *The Gang.* Chicago: University of Chicago Press (originally published in 1927).

Trice, Harrison M., and Janice M. Beyer. 1984. "Studying Organizational Cultures Through Rites and Ceremonials." *Academy of Management Review* 9:653–669.

Turner, Victor. 1967. *The Forest of Symbols: Aspects of Ndembu Ritual.* Ithaca, NY: Cornell University Press.

Tylor, Edward. 1871. *Primitive Culture.* London: Murray Publishers Ltd.

United Nations, Human Development Report 2000. http://www.undp.org/hdro/98.htm.

Valentine, Charles A. 1968. *Culture and Poverty: Critique and Counter-Proposals.* Chicago: University of Chicago Press.

van den Berghe, Pierre L. 1965. *South Africa: A Study in Conflict.* Middletown, CT: Wesleyan University Press.

van den Berghe, Pierre L. 1970. *Race and Ethnicity.* New York: Basic Books.

van den Berghe, Pierre L., and George P. Primov. 1977. *Inequality in the Peruvian Andes: Class and Ethnicity in Cuzco.* Columbia: University of Missouri Press.

van den Berghe, Pierre. 1992. "The Modern State: Nation-Builder or Nation-Killer?" *International Journal of Group Tensions* 22:191–208.

van Gennep, Arnold. 1960. *The Rites of Passage.* Translated by Monica B. Vizedom and Gabrielle L. Chaffe. Chicago: University of Chicago Press (originally published in 1908).

Wagner, Roy. 1984. "Ritual as Communication: Order, Meaning, and Secrecy in Melanesian Initiation Rites." In *Annual Review of Anthropology,* vol. 13, pp. 143–155. Palo Alto, CA: Annual Reviews.

Walens, Stanley. 1981. *Feasting With Cannibals: An Essay on Kwakiutl Cosmology.* Princeton, NJ: Princeton University Press.

Wallace, Anthony F. C. 1966. *Religion: An Anthropological View.* New York: Random House.

Wallace, Anthony F. C., and Raymond D. Fogelson. 1965. "The Identity Struggle." In *Intensive Family Therapy.* Edited by I. Boszormenyi-Nagy and J. L. Framo. New York: Harper & Row.

Wallerstein, Immanuel. 1989. *The Modern World-System III. The Second Era of Great Expansion of the Capitalist World-Economy, 1730–1840s.* New York: Academic Press.

Weaver, Thomas. 1985. "Anthropology as a Policy Science: Part II, Development and Training." *Human Organization* 44:197–205.

Weiner, Annette B. 1976. *Women of Value, Men of Renown.* Austin: University of Texas Press.

Weiner, Annette B. 1988. *The Trobrianders of Papua New Guinea.* New York: Holt, Rinehart, and Winston.

White, Leslie. 1949. *The Science of Culture.* New York: Farrar, Straus and Giroux.

White, Leslie. 1959. *The Evolution of Culture.* New York: McGraw-Hill.

Whitehead, Harriet. 1981. "The Bow and the Burden Strap: A New Look at Institutionalized Homosexuality in Native North America." In *Sexual Meanings: The Cultural Construction of Gender and Sexuality.* Edited by Sherry B. Ortner and Harriet Whitehead. New York: Cambridge University Press.

Whitehead, Neil Lancelot. 1990. "The Snake Warriors—Sons of the Tiger's Teeth: A Descriptive Analysis of Carib Warfare, ca. 1500–1820." In *The Anthropology of War.* Edited by Jonathan Hass. New York: Cambridge University Press.

Williams, Walter L. 1986. *The Spirit and the Flesh: Sexual Diversity in American Indian Culture.* Boston: Beacon Press.

Wilmsen, Edwin N., and James R. Denbow. 1990. "Paradigmatic History of San-speaking Peoples and Current Attempts at Revision." *Current Anthropology* 31:489–512.

Wolf, Eric R. 1966. *Peasants.* Englewood Cliffs, NJ: Prentice-Hall.

Wolf, Eric R. 1969. *Peasant Wars of the Twentieth Century.* New York: Harper & Row.

Wolf, Eric R. 1982. *Europe and the People Without History.* Berkeley: University of California Press.

Wolf, Margery. 1968. *The House of Lim.* Englewood Cliffs, NJ: Prentice-Hall.

Wolff, Edward N. 2000. Recent Trends in Wealth Ownership 1983–1998 (working paper number 300). Jerome Levy Economics Institute.
http://www.levy.org/docs/wrkpap/papers/300.html

Woodburn, James. 1968. "An Introduction to Hadza Ecology." In *Man the Hunter.* Edited by Richard Lee and Irven DeVore, with the assistance of Jill Nash. Chicago: Aldine Publishing Company.

Worsley, Peter. 1982. "Non-Western Medical Systems." In *Annual Review of Anthropology,* vol. 11, pp. 315–348. Palo Alto, CA: Annual Reviews.

Wright, Quincy. 1965. A Study of War. Chicago: University of Chicago Press.

Yanagisako, Sylvia Junko. 1979. "Family and Household: The Analysis of Domestic Groups." In *Annual Review of Anthropology,* vol. 8, pp. 161–205. Palo Alto, CA: Annual Reviews.

Young, Allan. 1982. "The Anthropologies of Illness and Sickness." In *Annual Review of Anthropology,* vol. 11, pp. 257–285. Palo Alto, CA: Annual Reviews.

Zechenter Elizabeth. 1997. "In the Name of Culture: Cultural Relativism and the Abuse of the Individual." *Journal of Anthropological Research*—Universal Human Rights Versus Cultural Relativity 53: 319–348.

I N D E X